Modernism and Non-Translation

Modernism and Non-Translation

Edited by
JASON HARDING
AND
JOHN NASH

OXFORD
UNIVERSITY PRESS

OXFORD
UNIVERSITY PRESS

Great Clarendon Street, Oxford, OX2 6DP,
United Kingdom

Oxford University Press is a department of the University of Oxford.
It furthers the University's objective of excellence in research, scholarship,
and education by publishing worldwide. Oxford is a registered trade mark of
Oxford University Press in the UK and in certain other countries

First Edition published in 2019

Impression: 1

Published in the United States of America by Oxford University Press
198 Madison Avenue, New York, NY 10016, United States of America

British Library Cataloguing in Publication Data
Data available

Library of Congress Control Number: 2019941495

ISBN 978-0-19-882144-1

DOI: 10.1093/oso/9780198821441.003.0001

Printed and bound in Great Britain by
Clays Ltd, Elcograf S.p.A.

Acknowledgements

The editors would like to thank everyone who has helped to make possible the production of this book. A dozen essays that work across many languages, ancient as well as modern, requires careful preparation. We have enjoyed excellent support from the editorial team at Oxford University Press, including Jacqueline Norton, Aimee Wright and John Smallman, as well as the product manager Seemadevi Sekar and copy-editor Jan Chamier.

This volume has its origins in an interdisciplinary project which we organised at Durham University with welcome financial support from the Institute of Advanced Study. Most of the contributors to this volume participated in a workshop as part of that project and we would like to acknowledge the contributions made by colleagues who do not appear in this volume: Ann Banfield (Visiting Fellow at the IAS), Paul Batchelor, Sylvain Belluc, Ann-Marie Einhaus, Rowena Fowler, Barry McCrea, Juliette Taylor-Batty and Robert Vilain.

Thanks are also due to the Department of English Studies at Durham University for the financial assistance which allowed Fraser Riddell and Sophie Franklin to perform sterling work in helping to prepare the chapters and index for publication.

Jason Harding
John Nash

Table of Contents

Notes on Contributors

Scarlett Baron is Associate Professor in English at University College London. She is the author of '*Strandentwining Cable': Joyce, Flaubert, and Intertextuality* (Oxford University Press, 2011) and *The Birth of Intertextuality: The Riddle of Creativity* (Routledge, 2019).

Rebecca Beasley is Associate Professor in the Faculty of English and Tutorial Fellow at The Queen's College, Oxford. Her books include: *Ezra Pound and the Visual Culture of Modernism* (Cambridge University Press, 2007), *T.S. Eliot, T.E. Hulme, Ezra Pound: Theorists of Modernist Poetry* (Routledge, 2007) and *Russia in Britain: From Melodrama to Modernism*, ed. with Philip Ross Bullock (Oxford University Press, 2013).

Caitríona Ní Dhúill is Associate Professor (Reader) in German at the School of Modern Languages and Cultures, Durham University. She is author of *Sex in Imagined Spaces: Gender and Utopia from More to Bloch* (Legenda, 2010) and *Metabiography: Reflecting on Biography* (Palgrave, 2019).

Dennis Duncan is the Munby Fellow in Bibliography at the University Library, Cambridge, and a Research Fellow at Darwin College. He has co-edited *Book Parts* (Oxford University Press, 2018) and published in *PMLA* and *Modernism/Modernity*.

Nora Goldschmidt is Associate Professor in the Department of Classics and Ancient History at Durham University. She is author of *Shaggy Crowns: Ennius' Annales and Virgil's Aeneid* (Oxford University Press, 2013) and *Afterlives of the Roman Poets: Biofiction and the Reception of Latin Poetry* (Cambridge University Press, 2019). Her latest project is about modernist fragments and the cultures of classical antiquity.

Jason Harding is Professor in the Department of English Studies at Durham University. His publications include *The Criterion: Cultural Politics and Periodical Networks in Interwar Britain* (Oxford University Press, 2002). He has edited four books and is co-editor of *The Complete Prose of T. S. Eliot: The Critical Edition: Volume 4, English Lion, 1930–1933* (Johns Hopkins University Press & Faber and Faber, 2015).

Daniel Karlin is Winterstoke Professor of English at Bristol University and the author of *Proust's English* (Oxford University Press, 2005) and *The Figure of the Singer* (Oxford University Press, 2013).

Alexandra Lukes is Assistant Professor in French at Trinity College Dublin. She is the editor of the special issue 'Nonsense, Madness, and The Limits of Translation' (*Translation Studies*, 2019) and has published in *Romanic Review* and *Modernism/modernity*.

John Nash is Associate Professor (Reader) in the Department of English Studies at Durham University. He is the author of *James Joyce and the Act of Reception* (Cambridge University Press, 2006), and editor of *James Joyce in the Nineteenth Century* (Cambridge University Press, 2013) and *Joyce's Audiences* (Rodopi, 2002).

Peter Robinson is Professor of English and American Literature at the University of Reading. He is the author of three critical studies of poetry published by OUP and has been awarded the Cheltenham Prize, the John Florio Prize, and two Poetry Book Society recommendations for his poetry and translation. He edited *The Oxford Handbook of Contemporary British and Irish Poetry* (2013).

Stephen Romer is Stipendiary Lecturer in French at Brasenose College, Oxford. A specialist of Franco-British modernism, he has published numerous critical essays on its poetry and poetics. He edited and translated an anthology, *French Decadent Tales* (Oxford World Classics, 2013). His collection *Set Thy Love in Order: New & Selected Poems* was published by Carcanet in 2017.

1

An Introduction to Modernist Non-Translation

Jason Harding and John Nash

'It can't be all in one language'

(Ezra Pound, *Canto LXXXVI*)

'New worlds are born between the lines'

(George Steiner, *After Babel*)

'Je ne parle pas français'. The title of Katherine Mansfield's short story illustrates an arresting, recurrent feature of modernist literature, especially that written in English: its incorporation of untranslated words and phrases. This short, paradoxical statement raises concerns that resonate across this book: simultaneously estranging and reassuring, the phrase performs a 'double-speak' that takes away in the act of giving. It raises questions of identity and power: who speaks? what do readers understand? who can be at home in this language? And it foreshadows matters of interpretation: how does this stale phrase differ from its translations?

To be sure, writers from all places and periods have found occasion, or necessity, to write in more than one language. Such multilingualism, including macaronic writing and various uses of the vernacular, have often reflected complex social structures and reading audiences. Nonetheless, there appears to have been a notable resurfacing of the phenomenon over the later nineteenth and early twentieth centuries, in particular in writing that was formally innovative, self-consciously 'new' and may be described as modernist. There are examples that have become justly renowned, including *The Waste Land* and *Finnegans Wake*, but there are many more instances that graft untranslated words and phrases into their linguistic and cultural texture. Why did many of the most influential English-language authors of the early twentieth century incorporate fragments of languages other than English into their regular working practices, and what implications does this carry for an understanding of that work? Nor, of course, is the phenomenon restricted to English-language writers. Our question is grounded in an exploration of modernist literary form, but it brings in an array of further areas—artistic and reading practices, historical relationships between languages, nations and social communities, translation theory and philosophy of language. The question is at once unique and global.

Jason Harding and John Nash, *An Introduction to Modernist Non-Translation* In: *Modernism and Non-Translation*. Edited by: Jason Harding and John Nash, Oxford University Press (2019). © the several contributors. DOI: 10.1093/oso/9780198821441.003.0001

The topic of this book is the incorporation of those untranslated fragments from other languages within modernist writing. We use the term *non-translation* for several reasons. It is to be distinguished from multilingualism or translingualism, in which a text is composed extensively in more than one language. By contrast, we use non-translation to refer to incorporated words or brief phrases, sometimes quotations or allusions, from other languages. In these cases, the text clearly has a dominant, or primary language, but also contains certain words, terms or phrases from other languages that remain untranslated. In this respect, non-translation returns us to the range of aesthetic, creative, and interpretative choices that the act of linguistic incorporation involves. The purpose of this volume, then, is to begin to examine a question that demands collective scholarly expertise: what are the aesthetic, critical and cultural implications of non-translation for modernist literature?

Non-translation stresses the grammatical negative in order to emphasize the differences between languages. By hinting at the possibility of translation, a possibility that has been declined, as it were, the term non-translation frames reading and writing as activities between languages and marks the text as a site of confrontation, not just of tongues but of interpretative dilemmas. The more familiar term 'multilingualism' might suggest a greater continuity, as if there were a possible semantic or cultural equivalence between languages, or as if languages were used in the same way, or as if translation were not first a dislocation and a problem. But by returning to the fundamental fact of language difference, our approach to modernism reads the juxtaposition of languages as a question of non-translation. For sure, modernist poetics 'implies a certain theory of translation'.[1] This volume seeks to include the untranslated among this implicit theorizing. This is not a study in translation theory but it is worth observing that the poles which translators have long grappled with, between 'domesticating' and 'foreignizing' versions (as Schleiermacher's terms have been rendered), exclude practices of non-translation—practices which themselves present additional problems to the would-be translator.[2] Emily Apter has been an influential voice in criticizing the impetus towards 'domesticating' translation which she sees fuelling the academic and commercial imperatives of 'world literature'.[3] Apter uses the term 'untranslatability' to endorse the fundamental incommensurability of translation. In her analysis, the literary always carries within it a measure of untranslatability. Our focus on non-translation seeks to explore some of the contours of

---

[1] Rebecca Beasley, *T. S. Eliot, T. E. Hulme, Ezra Pound: Theorists of Modernist Poetry* (London: Routledge, 2007), p. 76.

[2] Schleiermacher's favoured 'foreignizing' mode of translation is developed along poststructuralist lines by Lawrence Venuti in *The Translator's Invisibility: A History of Translation* (London: Routledge, 1995).

[3] Emily Apter, *Against World Literature* (London: Verso, 2013): 'incommensurability and what has been called the Untranslatable are insufficiently built into the literary heuristic', p. 3.

that resistance to translation as it works out in specific cases and circumstances. This focus on non-translation helps us, then, to see the cultural and interpretative matters of translation as also constitutive of the modernist text and not as secondary or derivative questions that form part of a text's reception.

Scholars of individual authors have long remarked upon the uses of 'other languages' in such canonical modernist works as *The Cantos*, *The Waste Land*, and *Ulysses*. Some of these have been groundbreaking explorations of the extent to which the phenomenon has shaped the work of a specific author.[4] By and large, however, criticism has treated multilingual terms and quotations as allusions to be glossed—arguably to be explained away—or as a difficulty that can be resolved by scholarship. Recent comparative studies of modernist multilingualism suggest a recognition of the cultural factors at work in this aspect of modernist poetics.[5] The challenge of non-translation in modernist texts demands complementary skills—not only linguistic, but also literary, cultural, and historical—and it is therefore entirely appropriate that this book takes the form of a collection of essays by different specialists. By building a series of case studies across a range of writers, texts and languages—while at the same time maintaining focus on writers foundational to the historical construction of the concept of modernist literature— this volume extends the study of modernist writing in the direction of 'untranslatability', facilitating a more wide-ranging generic, linguistic, and conceptual exploration of the complex facets of modernist non-translation.

§

Modernism is closely associated with the 'revolution of the word' that arose from an urgent sense of linguistic crisis.[6] Iterations of Stéphane Mallarmé's 'Crise de vers' (1886, 1892, 1896) are foundational in this regard.[7] Mallarmé advocated dislocations and restructuring of normal French syntax, ellipsis, and absence of punctuation, in his attempts to provide a new and purified context for words in poetry—'donner un

---

[4] See Daniel Karlin, *Proust's English* (Oxford: Oxford University Press, 2005) and Emily Delgano, *Virginia Woolf and the Migrations of Language* (Cambridge: Cambridge University Press, 2011).

[5] Juliette Taylor-Batty's *Multilingualism in Modernist Fiction* (London: Palgrave Macmillan, 2013) focuses on English-language fiction, surveying the representation of multilingual encounters brought about by travel and migration, examining in detail work by Jean Rhys, James Joyce, and Samuel Beckett. Taylor-Batty argues that these instances of multilingualism were conditioned by the sociopolitical conditions of early twentieth-century Europe. Joshua L. Miller's *Accented America: The Cultural Politics of Multilingual Modernism* (Oxford: Oxford University Press, 2011) is concerned with forms of vernacular literature shaped by the specific historical contexts of American immigration.

[6] In the pages of the avant-garde little magazine *transition* (1927–38), Eugene Jolas, a bilingual poet and translator, formulated his idiosyncratic manifesto 'Revolution of the Word' in which he announced twelve declarations, including the precepts that 'the literary creator has the right to disintegrate the primal matter of words imposed on him by text-books and dictionaries' and 'he has the right to use words of his own fashioning and to disregard existing grammatical and syntactical laws'. Eugene Jolas, 'Proclamation: The Revolution of the Word', *transition* 16–17 (June 1929): 13.

[7] 'Crise de vers' was collected in Mallarmé's *Divagations* (Paris: Bibliothèque-Charpentier, 1897), pp. 235–53.

sens plus pur aux mots de la tribu' or in Eliot's paraphrase, 'To purify the dialect of the tribe'.[8] Central to Symbolist aesthetics was a deeply meditated care for the vowel and consonant sounds of words, evocative of a musical suggestiveness. Equally foundational were Filippo Marinetti's manifestos for Italian Futurism announcing in the most explosive terms an attack upon Latin grammar and syntax as part of a drive towards 'Parole in libertà'—'liberating words' in dynamic expressive denotations of pure sound. Marinetti's manifestos of 1912 and 1913 insisted on the destruction of syntax, the abolition of adjectives, adverbs, and of punctuation, the use of verbs in the infinitive, and even of mathematical and musical signs, declaring, 'The rush of steam-emotion will burst the steampipe of the sentence, the valves of punctuation, and the regular clamp of the adjective'.[9] This crisis championed by theorists and practitioners of Symbolism and Futurism was expressed in more sober terms in many fields, including in philosophy, in linguistics, and in literary criticism, in discussion of cultural change, and, of course, it was manifest in a range of social and political issues. Hugh Kenner's claim that the province of canonical modernism was 'the entire human race speaking, and in time as well as in space' may be an exaggeration but it does suggest the unusually wide preoccupation in these years with the creativity, history, and epistemology of language.[10]

In his influential essay 'The Crisis of Language', Richard Sheppard examines in detail an example of this crisis, Hofmannsthal's 'Letter of Lord Chandos' (1902), demonstrating how a tradition of Symbolist aesthetics at the beginning of the twentieth century brooded on a lack of faith in the act of communication itself, in which, according to Sheppard, language 'ceases to be a means of communication and becomes an opaque and impenetrable wall'.[11] It is often said that the linguistic experimentation of modernist literature can be understood as a response to a loss of confidence in language's ability to adequately represent experience and reality. These cultural anxieties had been gathering momentum from the mid-nineteenth century but became an unavoidable barrier confronting a generation of writers following the mass trauma of the First World War—itself the culmination of decades of flux among the European powers and their empires. Sheppard observes that, for many modernists, 'the logic of language is displaced by a greater or lesser sense of dispossession, alienation and linguistic helplessness'.[12] These are familiar

---

[8] 'Little Gidding', *The Poems of T. S. Eliot: Volume I, Collected and Uncollected Poems*, ed. Christopher Ricks and Jim McCue (Baltimore: Johns Hopkins University Press, 2015), p. 205. Mallarmé's line appears in the poem 'Le tombeau d'Edgar Poe', *Poésies*, 8th edn (Paris: Nouvelle revue française, 1914), pp. 132–3.

[9] Filippo Marinetti, 'Destruction of Syntax – Wireless Imagination – Words-in-Freedom (May 1913)' in *Modernism: An Anthology*, ed. Lawrence Rainey (Oxford: Blackwell, 2005), pp. 27–34 (p. 30).

[10] Hugh Kenner, *The Pound Era* (London: Faber and Faber, 1972), p. 95.

[11] Richard Sheppard, 'The Crisis of Language' in *Modernism*, ed. Malcolm Bradbury and James McFarlane (London: Penguin, 1976), pp. 323–36 (p. 328).

[12] Richard Sheppard, 'Modernism, Language and Experimental Poetry: On Leaping over Bannisters and Learning How to Fly', *Modern Language Review* 92.1 (Jan 1997): 98–123 (p. 98).

terms to students of modernism, whose rich critical heritage associates this shift with 'loss' and 'crisis'. Yet linguistic alienation can be inseparable from linguistic fascination, and a painful sense of dispossession could be a source of vital creative energy. There is a vast body of criticism exploring the attempts of a plethora of experimental avant-garde movements in the early part of the twentieth-century— Symbolism, Dada and Surrealism, Italian and Russian Futurism, as well as Anglo-American groups associated with Imagism and Vorticism, not to mention the coteries that formed around individual writers such as James Joyce and Gertrude Stein—to liberate and revitalize the repressed expressive potential of language. Non-translation offered a key strategy for a number of modernist authors striving to unlock new linguistic energies, harnessing the creative friction—as synthesis, neologism, even as 'non-sense'—palpable in the disjunctions between and within and across languages.

Modernism, then, betokens profound anxieties about language, both as communication and as a marker of cultural belonging. Even when, as is often the case, it lends an ironic or faltering voice to that expression, the anxieties of relationship between voice, or style, and chosen language(s) are inescapable. The concept of non-translation bears relationship to wider practices of linguistic syncretism, mimicry, and dialect, which were constitutive features of much modernism from all cultures, apparent in T. S. Eliot as in J. M. Synge and Claude McKay. Inhabiting, or sometimes imitating, speech patterns, dialect and argot played out across a diverse spectrum, from the Harlem Renaissance, to creolization in Caribbean poets like Wilson Harris, to the racial ventriloquism of Eliot and the class-bound idiolect in George Bernard Shaw's *Pygmalion*.[13] For writers such as Harris, 'creolization…resists the colonizing structures through the diversion of the colonial language' but nonetheless reconciles, according to Simon Gikandi, 'the values of European literacy with the long-repressed traditions of African orality'.[14] Non-translation is a different practice, and it helps further to render the complexity of interaction between the written and the oral, almost pressing the reader into an adopted accent as well as an interpretation. At the same time, non-translation is different to both syncretism and imitation, of course, for the latter is already a form of translation however much it parades difference. Our point here is that non-translation plays a significant generative role in the creation of canonical modernism, exemplifying aspects of the anxiety over linguistic and cultural authenticity, and subtly shifting the borders within and between languages.

In numerous ways, modernism signalled a self-conscious break from other periods in its historical relationship with issues surrounding the nature of

---

[13] On the 'racial masquerade' of Eliot, see Michael North, *The Dialect of Modernism: Race, Language and Twentieth-Century Literature* (New York: Oxford University Press, 1994), ch. 4.
[14] Simon Gikandi, *Writing in Limbo: Modernism and Caribbean Literature* (New York: Cornell University Press, 1992), p. 16.

translation. It might reasonably be said that many earlier European writers could assume among their readers a working knowledge of the languages that they used, but by the early twentieth century this was no longer the case. Even where certain modernist texts were initially available only to a small coterie of readers, the broadening of the reading public in the late nineteenth century produced multifarious, unpredictable audiences. The use of various scripts and alphabets in modernist literature suggests a shifting relationship with readers of advanced literature predicated on redrawing a less stable or at least less predictable reception for the incorporation of non-translation. At the same time, there were material and demographic factors in this period that intensified the cultural import of translation, including new archaeological discoveries of fragments of ancient texts, as well as an exponential growth of foreign language teaching designed to tackle the cultural alienation experienced by large numbers of emigrants and refugees.[15] The traces of hybrid cultural memory and of historical trauma permeate the subtle and sinuous reflections of Walter Benjamin's celebrated essay 'The Task of the Translator' (1923), an attempt to re-theorize a redemptive role for the translator amid the displacements of a post-war world that had shattered old certainties. Benjamin's exalted conception of the translator confronts Mallarmé's lament that 'the imperfection of languages consists in their plurality' as well as the very possibility of translatability itself in order to point the way towards the 'hitherto inaccessible realm of reconciliation and fulfilment of languages.'[16]

To be sure, modernist literature is full of translations and translations of a new kind. Indeed translation between languages is so pronounced in modernism that it has been suggested that it inaugurated new translation strategies in its creative or 'foreignizing' mode of composition, abandoning a rigid scholarly attachment to the grammatical and syntactical rules of the original text that had dominated translation theory and practice. Pound's famous dictum, 'Make it New' might even be construed, as Steven G. Yao claims, to mean 'Make it Foreign.'[17] Modernist literary practice helped to formulate new approaches to translation itself. Pound's commitment to translation was radical in both creative and critical terms, mounting a thoroughgoing assault on conventional translation theory.[18] Translation became a

---

[15] See, for example, Pound's 'Papyrus', discussed by Nora Goldschmidt in her essay in this volume, and Joyce's work as a teacher of English in Trieste and his encounter with the Berlitz School.

[16] Walter Benjamin, 'The Task of the Translator' in *Illuminations*, ed. Hannah Arendt, trans. Harry Zohn (London: Jonathan Cape, 1970), pp. 77, 75.

[17] Steven G. Yao, *Translation and the Languages of Modernism: Gender, Politics, Language* (New York and Basingstoke: Palgrave Macmillan, 2002), p. 6.

[18] Yao contends that 'Undoubtedly, however, the most dramatic change wrought by Pound and the modernists in the dimensions of translation as a literary mode lies in the extent to which formal knowledge of the source language no longer constituted a requirement for its practice....modernist writers repeatedly engaged in translation, and sometimes achieved remarkable results, with partial, imprecise, faulty, and sometimes even no formal understanding of the languages in which the texts they translated were originally written.' 'Translation', *Ezra Pound in Context*, ed. Ira B. Nadel (Cambridge: Cambridge University Press, 2010), p. 38.

means of cultural rediscovery for modernists—a 'dynamic procedural lens', in Yao's terms, that spurred reinvention of classical and European traditions and exploration of Hindi, Chinese, and other languages for contemporary 'ideological and artistic purposes'.[19] But modernist translation was more than a way to extend the traditional sources in European and Anglophone writing, important as that was; it was also a practice that assisted the redefinition of writers' own languages. The 'anythongue athall' of *Finnegans Wake* represents this principle writ large.[20]

Modernist preoccupations with translation not only amounted to a key aspect of its cultural politics and its poetics but also signalled a key shift in ideas about translation. The translation theorist Lawrence Venuti has argued that during the first decades of the twentieth century, 'English-language translation theory attained a new level of critical sophistication, summoned as it was to rationalize specific modernist texts'.[21] Not only did writers such as Eliot, Yeats, Pound, H.D., William Carlos Williams, and Zukofsky publish translations and, notably in the case of Joyce, influence the translation of their own works, but they helped to ensure that translation became 'a key practice in modernist poetics' and 'centrally connected to the aims of the modernist poetic project'.[22] Nevertheless, the role played by non-translation in particular—a deliberate refusal to provide translations of foreign words, phrases and quotations—is an integral feature of modernist poetics that is distinct from translation as such. As Pound declared in *The Cantos* 'It can't be all in one language', while privately defending this aesthetic practice to correspondents during the period of the poem's composition: 'All tosh about *foreign languages* making it difficult'.[23]

§

Anxieties over communication and translation are entangled with the rise and status of dominant languages and the uncertain futures of dialects and other tongues. The power of English as an emerging world language went hand in hand with worries held by some about its present constitution and future direction. The decades following 1880 saw a marked increase in the number of publications addressing standardization in the English language and, as Michael North argues, 'a change of tone as well'. In North's terms these publications and the institutionalization of standard language amounted to a 'program' with 'a moralistic tone and an almost evangelical fervor that made relatively minor infractions seem matters of cultural life or death'.[24] New institutions such as the *New English*

---

[19] Yao, *Translation and the Languages of Modernism*, p. 7.
[20] James Joyce, *Finnegans Wake* (London: Faber and Faber, 1939), p. 117, lines 15–16.
[21] Venuti, *The Translator's Invisibility*, p. 187.
[22] Venuti, *The Translator's Invisibility*, p. 187; Beasley, *T. S. Eliot, T. E. Hulme, Ezra Pound*, p. 76.
[23] *The Letters of Ezra Pound, 1907–1941*, ed. D. D. Paige (London: Faber and Faber, 1951), p. 335.
[24] North, *The Dialect of Modernism*, p. 12. This discussion draws on North, pp. 3–34 and Tony Crowley, *Standard English and the Politics of Language* (London: Palgrave Macmillan, 2003).

Dictionary (which became the *OED*) and, later, the BBC, as well as more specialist organizations such as the Society for Pure English, became testing grounds for squabbles over acceptable grammatical and vocabulary usage that nevertheless had significant symbolic social value.[25] The important point here is that the idea of 'standard' language usage was itself an invention, rather than a lost commonality that might be recaptured, as testified by the difficulty of its definition. When one of its principal proponents declares that 'we know standard English when we hear it' and that schools should 'have nothing to do with any *patois*' he is evidently losing the battle.[26]

Such apparently trivial concerns as grammatical niceties, pronunciation, and dialect variation were serious matters due to the combination of two primary reasons. One of these reasons was the association made by Leibniz, Hamann, and later Romantic philologists between language and nation, in terms of the culture or spirit of a people, 'each culture, each idiom ... reflecting the world in a particular way'.[27] National and linguistic unity become synonymous. A significant legacy of this idea was expressed in educational debates in England following the First World War by proponents of the study of English above classical education: 'English... is itself the English mind' argued the Newbolt Report on *The Teaching of English in England*. One member of the Newbolt Committee, George Sampson, put it this way: 'The one common basis of a common culture is the common tongue'.[28] Both Newbolt and Sampson insisted on the speaking and writing of 'standard English'. The opposing tendency suggests that languages share common sources, and finds expression in the idea of language families and the pioneering etymology of the later nineteenth century. Part of the fascination and perplexity of language by the turn of the twentieth century may result from these unresolved differences in linguistics: on one hand, the essential untranslatable quality of language and culture, still popularly accepted; and on the other hand, an avowedly scientific (or arguably pseudo-scientific) approach that promulgated the autonomy of language, giving rise to contemporary hankering for a universal tongue and common origins, with its implication of equivalence between languages. Both positions are potentially troubling: the former may suggest a problematic authenticity in language while the latter appears to flatten inevitable differences.

[25] Kenner discusses the *New English Dictionary* and Skeat's *Etymological Dictionary* in *The Pound Era*, pp. 94–102.

[26] George Sampson, *English for the English: A Chapter on National Education* (Cambridge: Cambridge University Press, 1970 [1921]). Sampson opined that 'there is no need to define standard English speech' (p. 63) but ironically the very word standard is question-begging. As Crowley points out, whether 'standard' is defined as an ensign or an exemplar, both senses involve 'questions of authority, commonality and evaluation' (Crowley, Standard English and the Politics of Language, p. 78).

[27] See George Steiner, *After Babel: Aspects of Language and Translation* 2nd edn (Oxford: Oxford University Press, 1992), pp. 75–82 (p. 81).

[28] [Henry Newbolt], *The Teaching of English in England* (London: His Majesty's Stationery Office, 1924), p. 20. Sampson, *English for the English*, p. 61. See North, *The Dialect of Modernism*, p. 14.

Another reason to take standardization debates seriously is linked to the rise in global emigration and immigration which often fuelled a prejudicial social conservatism. British imperial expansion—in which the English language was both a tool of conquest and a glory to be celebrated—was often cited as a potential cause of linguistic 'decay'. As Linda Dowling observes, in Victorian Britain 'the fall of Rome was identified chronologically (if mistakenly) with the "decay" of Latin'.[29] In this context of British imperial expansion, one contributor told fellow readers of the *Edinburgh Review* that, 'whilst English tends to become the language most widely used and spoken in all parts of the globe, it is used and spoken by men less familiar than ourselves with the literary authority which determines its accuracy and fitness.' He added, 'There is no surer or more fatal sign of the decay of a language than in the interpolations of barbarous terms and foreign words'.[30] The greatest paradox in these discussions was that the idea of a 'standard' language was fanciful—as chimeric as that of a standard national culture. In fact, institutions such as the Society for Pure English were riven between those who would fix grammatical rules in the interests of a fixed standard, and those who encouraged a vital, changing language comprised of important dialectal variations and a 'voracious appetite for loan-words'.[31]

§

The so-called 'linguistic turn' at the start of the twentieth century, tracing a correspondence between the structures of language and reality, and the extent to which language is constitutive of thought, is a crucial context in which to situate the conceptualization and reception of modernist non-translation. In the domain of academic philosophy in this period, logical positivism asserted that everyday speech was the disorderly mask of logical truths about the world, such that philosophical problems must be solved by reforming the underlying logic of language or at least by understanding language use with a greater precision. Bertrand Russell lavished minute attention on the verbal confusions of what was curiously called 'ordinary language', viewed as a fundamental source of human misunderstanding and error, a preoccupation passed down to his star student, Ludwig Wittgenstein. The drive to evade our supposed 'bewitchment' by language underpins Wittgenstein's magisterial PhD thesis published as the *Tractatus Logico-Philosophicus* (1921), a work of austere philosophical rigour inflected by a gnomic poetic grandeur that claimed—vainly as it turned out—to dissolve the philosophical questions posed by ethics and aesthetics as aspects of *das Unsagbare* (the Unsayable).

---

[29] Linda Dowling, *Language and Decadence in the Victorian Fin de Siècle* (Princeton: Princeton University Press, 1986), p. 85.

[30] Henry Reeve, 'The Literature and Language of the Age', *Edinburgh Review* 169 (April 1889), pp. 328–50 (pp. 348–9). Cited in Dowling, Language and Decadence in the Victorian Fin de Siècle, pp. 86–7.

[31] *Society for Pure English*, Tract no. 6 (1933), p. 29.

Wittgenstein's later philosophical investigations unravelled the positivism of his early philosophy by arguing that thoughts and ideas mediated by discontinuous 'language-games'—among which he cited 'translating from one language into another'—are dependent on the social practices in which language usage is embedded. Developing Wittgenstein's insights, W. V. O. Quine's doctrine of the special 'indeterminacy of translation' renders translation, due to the inscrutability of reference, a matter of subjective convenience rather than of the truth of intentional meanings.[32] Relativist theories of language, most notably the Sapir-Whorf hypothesis, would extend the limitations of translation to all culture-bound speech acts. Benjamin Lee Whorf contends: 'thinking itself is in a language – in English, Sanskrit, in Chinese. And every language is a vast pattern-system, different from others, in which are culturally ordained the forms and categories by which the personality not only communicates, but also analyses nature, notices or neglects types of relationship and phenomena, channels his reasoning, and builds the house of his consciousness.'[33] In *After Babel: Aspects of Language and Translation*, George Steiner interweaves consideration of 'relativist' philosophical approaches to the diversity of language use and to the instability of translation with the creative power of writers to shape literature to adaptive evolutionary purposes, observing: 'It is unlikely that man, as we know him, would have survived without the fictive, counter-factual, anti-determinist means of language, without the semantic capacity, generated and stored in the "superfluous" zones of the cortex, to conceive of, to articulate possibilities beyond the treadmill of organic decay and death.... This evasion of the "given fact", this gainsaying is inherent in the combinational structure of grammar, in the imprecision of words, in the persistently altering nature of usage and correctness. New worlds are born between the lines.'[34] The presence of non-translation in modernist writing reflects the technical linguistic probing of philosophical investigations into the complexities of language use and translation, and the resistance of words (or signs) to fixed meanings irrespective of cultural context, but without sharing their rationalist explanatory drive, revelling instead in the creative-destructive potentialities of strategic detonations of those incorporated 'non-translated' fragments in the highly specialized, rarefied, language games of modernist literature.

Also relevant in this regard is the advent of Ferdinand de Saussure's groundbreaking *Course in General Linguistics* (1916). Saussure abandoned the diachronic approach of nineteenth-century philology to the history of languages. By

---

[32] See Ludwig Wittgenstein, *Philosophical Investigations*, trans. G. E. M. Anscombe (Oxford: Blackwell, 1967), sections 22–23; W. V. O. Quine, *Word and Object* [1960], new edn (Cambridge, MA.: Massachusetts Institute of Technology Press, 2013), p. 71.

[33] *Language, Thought, and Reality: Selected Writings of Benjamin Lee Whorf*, 2nd edn, ed. John B. Carroll, Stephen C. Levinson and Penny Lee (Cambridge, MA: Massachusetts Institute of Technology Press, 2012), pp. 322–3.

[34] Steiner, *After Babel*, pp. 227, 228.

contrast, he placed a bold new emphasis on synchronic theory: language is a self-regulating system of signs, operating on the apparently arbitrary links between signifier and signified. Thus, according to this linguistics, the English word 'tree' is no more hard-wired into the fundamental nature of reality, than the French word 'arbre', the German word 'Baum' or the Chinese character 木. This arbitrariness of the sign in its relationship to conceptual meaning could be deeply unsettling for those intent on a positivistic enquiry into the universal origins and characteristics of language. Saussure's linguistics has huge implications for the practice of modernist non-translation—a deliberate sundering and reconfiguring of the arbitrary links between signifier and signified; or, since units of language acquire meaning from their place in a system, these estranging deployments of unfamiliar signs (and noises) could be understood as free-floating signifiers—and his theories have had an indelible impact on literary criticism and translation theory throughout the twentieth century.

The 'linguistic turn' in the early decades of the twentieth century had a profound effect on the development of strands of formalist literary criticism and theory that proved particularly well suited to comprehending and interpreting the dense yet nebulous techniques of avant-garde literary experimentation. Several prominent early exegetes of modernism had been trained in the Moscow and Prague Linguistic Circles, such as Roman Jakobson, or emerged from the ferment generated by Wittgenstein's Cambridge lectures, such as I. A. Richards, who graduated from a degree in philosophy (Moral Sciences) to help pioneer a new 'close reading' at the fledgling English Faculty at Cambridge, instilling in his most brilliant student, William Empson, a lifelong concern with close-textured analysis of literary texts as a specialized branch of verbal communication. These 'new' critics were painstakingly attentive to the minutiae of linguistic meanings and 'complex words' as subtle indicators of a larger crisis in humane values in the post-war world.

Indeed the ambiguities and intricacies on display in the close readings practised by Russian Formalism, Practical Criticism, and the American New Critics might be understood as attempts to establish a new centre of meaning and value in the wake of the linguistic crisis heralded by modernism. A new expertise was required to resurrect meaning from linguistic disruption and disorder. According to Roman Jakobson (who was fluent in six languages), when language is charged to the full, as it is in modernist poetry, it is not possible to translate from one language to another without significant loss. Similarly, the critical theory of I. A. Richards was preoccupied by the problems of translation as an analogue of the difficulties faced by the critic explicating the multiple implications of literary rhetoric. In *Mencius on the Mind: Experiments in Multiple Definition* (1932), Richards provided a remedial section titled 'Towards a Technique for Comparative Studies' designed to mitigate some of the insuperable challenges faced in translating the ambiguities of plural meanings (categorized as intention, tone, feeling, and sense) from a radically different language and culture.[35] In *After Babel*, George Steiner went further by controversially proposing that all language use is a form of translation, taking many of his examples from literature. For Steiner, the migration of modernist writers ('exiles and émigrés') necessarily entailed a dislocation in literary language, even within one's 'own' language, provoking a fundamental 'unhousedness' or 'extraterritoriality' articulated through the striking multilingualism of modernist texts.[36] These theorists all suggest that the creative transposition of elements from one language into another demands a highly sophisticated hermeneutics of reader response, which inevitably strives to assimilate or naturalize alien words in order to make them legible or intelligible, but which is always expressive of an unresolved 'alterity'. Many of the chapters in this collection grapple with the concept of 'untranslatability' as a core element in the aesthetic practices of modernist non-translation.

§

The essays in this volume gather a deliberately eclectic range of writers associated with European and American modernisms, from Henry James to Ezra Pound, from Rainer Maria Rilke to Antonin Artaud. This range indicates something of the reach and vitality of the matter of translation—and specifically non-translation—across a selection of poetry, fiction, and non-fictional prose. Evidently, this collection of essays does not make any claim to be exhaustive; rather, it seeks to encourage further exploration of connections across languages and among writers. Together, these essays seek to provoke and extend debate on the aesthetic, cultural, political, and conceptual dimensions of non-translation as an important yet hitherto neglected facet of modernism, thus helping to redefine our understanding of that movement. This volume addresses the work of a range of writers in order to allow their practices to speak to one another, and, in doing so, to demonstrate the rich possibilities of reading modernism through instances of non-translation.

Literature in several languages is examined in this collection, primarily the European tongues of English, French, German, and Spanish, but also Classical Greek and Latin, as well as personal or idiosyncratic linguistic expressions that do not easily conform to any language. Of course, these represent only a handful of possible languages while including the languages of major imperial powers, which find expression in a variety of forms and by a great many nations and cultures. In the chapters that follow, the primary language of the texts addressed is English; however, none of the writers discussed in detail here was born in

---

[35] I. A. Richards, *Mencius on the Mind: Experiments in Multiple Definition* (London: Kegan Paul, 1932), pp. 86–131.

[36] George Steiner, *Extraterritorial: Papers on Literature and the Language Revolution* (London: Faber and Faber, 1972), p. 10. This is also the premise of his essay 'Understanding as Translation' in *After Babel*, which emphasizes that interpretation of older texts *within* a language is still an act of translation.

England. This is no coincidence in that the near-global spread of English by the dawn of the twentieth century, and in particular its dominant status in colonies and former colonies, encouraged dissonant voices of artistic and linguistic experimentation, of resistance and of co-optation. The question of non-translation addressed in these essays is not primarily one of imperial or nationalist agendas, relevant as these issues inevitably are to Nietzsche's thought-provoking meditations on translation as conquest, but equally a matter that resonates with a freight of deeply personal aesthetic and emotional significance.

The writers examined here tend to be well-travelled men, sometimes grand literary figures such as Henry James and T. S. Eliot, occasionally marginalized voices, such as Antonin Artaud. These writers often looked askance at their national literary cultures and mother tongues as they consciously forged new linguistic territories in their works. In all cases, they explore non-translation from the dual perspectives of both 'insider' and 'outsider', unsettling that false opposition, and articulating in the process their individuality of expression and experience. In *The Scandals of Translation*, Lawrence Venuti refers to the 'asymmetries, inequities, relations of domination and dependence in every act of translating' and it would be equally true to apply these terms to acts of *not* translating.[37] Just as translation makes us aware of Schleiermacher's orientating poles of 'domesticating' and 'foreignizing' so, too, each decision *not* to translate, each inclusion of words from an *other* language, prompts writers and readers to confront specific situations and to make interpretative choices regarding the differences between and within languages.[38] Non-translation stimulates our compulsion to interpret. Venuti is concerned with the social and practical tasks of communicative translation, but his terms can also be used to refer to the literary techniques and practices of allusion, quotation, invention, neologism. The essays in this volume all interrogate the 'asymmetries, inequities, relations of domination and dependence' that are generated by literary non-translation.

The essays oscillate between the asymmetry of languages and the cultural 'domination' of one tongue over others. They do so in a manner that places varying emphases on the aesthetic and sociocultural dimensions of the texts and writers under discussion, demonstrating that non-translation—the decision, even compulsion, to incorporate another language, and the demands and opportunities this brings to readers—is at once a personal and aesthetic matter and inextricably bound up with social and political processes. In some cases, that asymmetry prompts specific personal and artistic decisions, or perhaps evasions, by stepping momentarily into a second tongue, as in Henry James's recourse to

---

[37] Lawrence Venuti, *The Scandals of Translation: Towards an Ethics of Difference* (London: Routledge, 1998), p. 4.

[38] Venuti here adapts Schleiermacher's poles of reader-focused and author-focused translation; Venuti, *Scandals of Translation*, p. 20.

French in his notebooks discussed by Daniel Karlin, or the talismanic phrases repeated in Pound and Eliot analysed by Stephen Romer. In the essays by Dennis Duncan on Mallarmé and Alexandra Lukes on Artaud, these personal choices exhibit different, potentially more disturbing or unsettling connotations. In each case, the asymmetry and inequality of languages in the eyes of contemporary readers is made explicit by non-translation, bringing out a fascinating side of the writer that might otherwise be considered marginal. Other essays in this collection—notably those by Peter Robinson and Rebecca Beasley—are concerned with the ways in which linguistic difference performs social 'inequities' and broadly political 'relations of domination'. In all chapters, the essays draw out the complex interconnectedness of aesthetic and worldly concerns as revealed at the level of the choice of language.

In his chapter, Robinson suggests that the term non-translation implies the possibility of translation. There are different ways in which this implied possibility may be approached, just as the possible translations that might be achieved are variegated and nuanced. Translation may indeed seem within the confident grasp of the reader, such as Henry James's preference for French as a means to express what he otherwise felt he could not say outright in English, signalling the possibility of moving comfortably between tongues, as if effortlessly, but it also betokens linguistic inequality, where that movement implies also a shift of register or an affect that is a part of the signature of the writer. On the other hand, if the term non-translation implies the possibility of translation then it can be interpreted as a possibility that always remains potential, a possibility that will not be realized. In this sense, there are times when the practice of non-translation seems less like a refusal to translate than a voice that cannot be silenced—witness Artaud's painful cries and Mallarmé's radically ambiguous neologism '*ptyx*'. As these examples suggest, one thread running throughout this volume is the deployment of non-translation to express deeply private concerns.

The arrangement of the collection follows a loose chronology of the major modernist texts discussed in detail. Thus essays that deal with a principal author in relation to this topic, such as Pound, are placed in proximity. At the same time, the essays have been selected and arranged to promote reflection on the interconnections between the aesthetics of modernist non-translation, the personal decisions implicated in the practice, the conceptual problems posed by non-translation, and wider matters of historical significance. These areas of interest are not easily demarcated, and so the essays have not been categorized by imposing potentially misleading sections. The intention is to allow the richness of the subject of modernist non-translation to speak in the terms carefully defined and articulated by the authors of individual chapters in a format that remains faithful to their varying emphases, interweaving the personal with the social, the literary with the theoretical, consideration of the avowedly experimental against the legacies of national traditions.

In the opening essay, Daniel Karlin reads Henry James's notebook entries and some of his letters written while an expatriate living in London. James is surely a pivotal figure in Anglophone-based non-translation, as he is in modernism, verging between the confident incorporation of European culture and an estranging evasiveness. Karlin traces James's compulsive return to familiar French terms and expressions when writing to himself (as well as to others), sprinkled over his English 'in the way that some people add salt to whatever they eat'. James's use of French has the savour of an essential ingredient in his literary persona, illustrating tactical withdrawal from American culture and, importantly, a means of reflection on his own authorial practice. In the following essay, Dennis Duncan reads Stéphane Mallarmé's 'Sonnet en *yx*'. He traces early responses to this poem that highlighted the challenge to interpretation posed by '*ptyx*': was this a nonsensical neologism or an untranslated derivation from another language? Duncan shows how the term resonated with other artists and moved 'from the category of the untranslated to the untranslatable'. It exemplifies what Duncan describes as a kind of 'word magic' that modernism conjures out of non-translation, a quasi-mysticism of unfamiliar noises that prompts readers to dwell on formal and sonic capacities as well as the conceptual contours of language.

The next chapters establish two crucial contexts for modernist non-translation by means of original case studies: namely, the renewal of classical studies, facilitated by recent discoveries of ancient texts; and the development of language learning, especially but not exclusively of modern European languages, through specialist educational schools and publications. In the first of these chapters, Nora Goldschmidt shows how a wide range of writers—including Aldington, Pound, Eliot, Cavafy, and Joyce—deployed contemporary interpretations and translations of recently discovered fragments of ancient Greek. A wealth of these new source texts were uncovered in the nineteenth and early twentieth centuries, stimulating commentaries by classical scholars which were in turn taken up by modernist writers, foregrounding the difficulties of textual and cultural transmission. Goldschmidt emphasizes the remoteness of the ancient texts and examines how modern attempts to downplay this historical difference, as in Liddell and Scott's celebrated lexicon, could perversely prove to be barriers to understanding. Goldschmidt contends that attempts to express the meaning of an alien and irrecoverable ancient past can be more estranging even than non-translation.

Rebecca Beasley's chapter also establishes a crucial context for a modernist pre-occupation with translation and non-translation: the pedagogy of language learning. She analyses Ezra Pound's involvement with the magazine *The Future* during 1918: it was here, in a journal that promoted familiarity with modern languages, that he published three early sections of *The Cantos* alongside articles on the post-war future of international relations and discussions of language teaching. In spite of obvious differences from prose contributions to *The Future*, Pound's polyglot poetry speaks to the same concern with languages and internationalism.

Beasley shows how Pound's revisions to these early *Cantos* shifted from translating or explaining the use of foreign language material and moved towards, in his phrase, 'amicable accentuation of difference'. The non-translation in Pound's *Cantos* deploys avant-garde techniques for aesthetic effects; however, these effects are best heard with a recognition that Pound has developed an exploratory dialogue both with himself and across cultures and languages traumatized by the recent world war, a poetic dialogue that was in its own way part of a post-war desire to foster healing of trauma and greater international cooperation.

The inescapable yet somewhat intractable question of the capacity or appetite of contemporary readers of poetry for non-translation is explored further in Peter Robinson's study of William Carlos Williams's collection *Al Que Quiere!* A number of modernist works have untranslated titles or epigraphs, including poems by Pound and Eliot. These examples raise an additional matter of authority: who precisely 'speaks' a title? Such works also famously suggest a level of difficulty, even perhaps cultural elitism, in their use of untranslated quotation. In his analysis, Robinson argues for the potentially democratizing effects of what others see as elitist difficulty. 'Bilingualism projects an inner dividedness onto a divisively prejudicial dominant culture,' he argues in his analysis of Williams's personal and poetic 'equivocations regarding his part-Spanish heritage'. The example of Williams's pursuit of a modernist aesthetic is a reminder that modern democracies are called on to 'recognize and embrace' the unknown within them.

The following chapter, a study of Pound and Eliot by Stephen Romer, returns to the personal and aesthetic questions of the poets' individual choices, showing how certain untranslated quotations recur in their poetry. These 'talismanic phrases' are employed in the manner of touchstones implying comparisons—between languages, between poets, between texts—that carry emotional weight in both their creative and critical work. Phrases such as the archaic Provençal '*sovegna vos*' encapsulate a personal history as well as intertextual resonances, adding layers of emotional and cross-cultural depth, amplifying a chorus of poetic voices. These matters of avant-garde formalist experiment and technique, and the interpretive dilemmas they pose, are further explored in Jason Harding's chapter on the role of non-translation in *The Waste Land*. Eliot's modernist strategies in this celebrated poem, Harding suggests, can be profitably read in the light of the contemporaneous attempts of the school of Russian Formalism to provide a critical lexicon that captures the linguistic shifts, displacements and estrangement of avant-garde Futurist poetry. Non-translation in Eliot's poetry serves a variety of purposes, often subverting a romantic tradition that openly expresses deep personal emotion, and yet when specific key occurrences are unravelled in relation to Eliot's notes to *The Waste Land* and his later comments on the poem's themes and gestation, they signal disturbing vertiginous vents of powerful and painful affect.

In the next chapter, Caitríona Ní Dhúill analyses the figure of the acrobat in Rainer Maria Rilke's *Duino Elegies*. Her comparison of several English versions and a recent Irish version, alongside the original German, focuses on Rilke's ekphrastic rendering of an image and its Latin inscription. Here is as an example that helps to reveal not only the formal choices and difficulties involved in poetic translations and non-translation but which also illuminates the notion of hermeneutics elaborated by Hans Georg Gadamer. Gadamer's notion of 'mythopoietic inversion', proposed in the context of his reading of Rilke's poem, suggests that interpretation involves a re-translation back into subjective experience. Ni Dhúill shows how Gadamer's hermeneutic manoeuvres trace the very practice of translation as symbolized by Rilke's nimble acrobat.

The rich multilingualism evident in the oeuvre of James Joyce is addressed in two essays that follow. In the first of these, Scarlett Baron sets out the wider context of Joyce's uses of several languages, putting forward a taxonomy of foreign language use in *Ulysses*. The four types which she identifies are: Latin terms associated with the Catholic mass; Italian musical terms; phrases that are deployed in a political context; and untranslated clichés that signify cultural aspiration or pretension. Drawing on examples across the range of Joyce's writing, Baron argues that all language is already translated, and that translation can never be fully achieved. In the following essay, John Nash takes up this point in his analyses of the untranslated clichés of *Ulysses*, and in the noises of Bloom's cat. Nash contends that the practice of non-translation has implications for the notion of 'world literature'. By testing two models—those of a dominant language, as described by Pascale Casanova, and that of 'minor literature', neither of which addresses plurilingual, macaronic writing—against the writings of Joyce, this chapter shows that the idea of non-translation can inform our thinking about world literature. In contradistinction from the dualism of the models of Casanova, and of Deleuze and Guattari, Joyce's non-translation opens up a plurality and hybridity within language, both foreign and familiar. Nash argues that non-translation is a condition of language, particularly visible as the political dominance of English wanes.

The final chapter in the volume by Alexandra Lukes turns to the writing produced by Antonin Artaud during and following the periods of his confinement in mental asylums in the 1940s. These writings are notable for their striking inclusion, alongside his more standard French, of clusters of syllables that appear to be meaningless, unpronounceable, and untranslatable. Lukes argues that here Artaud is challenging both himself and his readers to examine the relationship between language and the body, positing a 'pre-verbal space' prior to socially affirmed language. To translate Artaud would be to create a new person. The possibility of translation that non-translation appears to offer becomes in this reading a mark of vitality and even liberation for the identity of the writer, and is predicated on translation as 'inherently founded upon a practice of non-translation.'

This collection of essays is testimony to the richness and complexity of the practices of modernist non-translation, elucidating the distinction between quotation and non-quotation, the uses of non-translation within translation, readers' responses to interpretive problems posed by non-translation, especially in the contexts of changing practices in the acquisition of classical and modern languages, the emotional, bodily, and affective associations of writers and readers moving between and across languages. Whatever direction subsequent work in this area takes, these essays demonstrate the constitutive importance of practices of non-translation to modernist aesthetics and modern cultures.

2

'The patient, passionate little *cahier*': French in Henry James's Notebooks

Daniel Karlin

On 25 November 1881, in the Brunswick Hotel in Boston, Henry James began a journal which he kept intermittently over the next few months. Most of the entries belong to the winter of 1881/2, before he returned to London in May. The journal opens with a self-reflexive observation: 'It is so long since I have kept any notes, taken any memoranda, written down my current reflections, taken a sheet of paper, as it were, into my confidence.'[1] The focus of this essay is on that very Jamesian notion of taking a sheet of paper into one's confidence—and of doing so with the aid of an 'other' language which is familiar, so to speak, to both parties.

The first substantive confidence that James made to his American notebook consists of a long meditation on his decision to commit himself, personally and professionally, to Europe. It begins as though it is merely an example of the advantages of keeping 'a record of passing impressions':

> Here I am back in America, for instance, after six years of absence, and likely while here to see and learn a great deal that ought not to become mere waste material. Here I am, *da vero* [in truth, indeed], and here I am likely to be for the next five months.   (*N* 214)

'For instance' is misleading on two counts. Being 'back in America' is not a casual example, which occurs to James as one among many, but a central preoccupation. And it is so not because of the potential usefulness of American 'material', but for the opposite reason. Without his seeming quite to realize it, James's train of thought jumps tracks. 'Here I am, *da vero*'—the Italian idiom has something rueful about it, and signals a shift of emphasis. James no longer thinks of making the most of his advantages, but reassures himself that there was some point to his having come back to America at all:

[1]   *The Complete Notebooks of Henry James*, ed. Leon Edel and Lyall H. Powers (New York and Oxford: Oxford University Press, 1987), p. 213. Subsequent references to this edition ('*N*') are given in the main text. Translations of foreign words and phrases are either given in square brackets or in the immediately following sentence of my text, and unless otherwise indicated are my own.

Daniel Karlin, '*The patient, passionate little* cahier': *French in Henry James's Notebooks* In: *Modernism and Non-Translation*. Edited by: Jason Harding and John Nash, Oxford University Press (2019). © the several contributors. DOI: 10.1093/oso/9780198821441.003.0002

I am glad I have come—it was a wise thing to do. I needed to see again *les miens* [those belonging to me], to revive my relations with them, and my sense of the consequences that these relations entail. Such relations, such consequences, are a part of one's life, and the best life, the most complete, is the one that takes full account of such things. One can only do this by seeing one's people from time to time, by being with them, by entering into their lives. Apart from this I hold it was not necessary I should come to this country. I am 37 years old, I have made my choice, and God knows that I have now no time to waste. My choice is the old world—my choice, my need, my life. There is no need for me today to argue about this; it is an inestimable blessing to me, and a rare good fortune, that the problem was settled long ago, and that I have now nothing to do but to act on the settlement.—My impressions here are exactly what I expected they would be, and I scarcely see the place, and feel the manners, the race, the tone of things, now that I am on the spot, more vividly than I did while I was still in Europe. My work lies there—and with this vast new world, *je n'ai que faire* [I have nothing to do, it's not my concern].   (*N* 214)

It is a small but vivid sign of alienation that James should designate those who belong to him by a foreign term, *les miens*, which distances him from them even as it affirms their closeness. The French idiom usually refers to the family, but James's own translation—'one's people'—suggestively broadens the scope, as though the American people might also stand in this familial relation to him. The gesture of rejection is more direct, more brutal even, in the use of the dismissive idiom '*je n'ai que faire*' to encompass the whole of 'this vast new world'. 'My choice is the old world—my choice, my need, my life.' James goes on to recount the history of that choice, whose origin he traces to the journey he undertook in the summer of 1875, and which took him first to Paris, and then, in November 1876, to London, where he is now fully settled and assimilated: 'I came to London as a complete stranger, and today I know much too many people. *J'y suis absolument comme chez moi*' (*N* 217).

Unlike his use of *les miens* or *je n'ai que faire*, this irruption of French into James's text may seem a bit odd. It would be more natural to apply the phrase '*J'y suis absolument comme chez moi*' to a decision to live in Paris—and, indeed, James had come close to doing so, not on his own account but on that of his friend Thomas Sergeant Perry, who was living there in 1867. Part of the letter that James wrote to Perry from Cambridge was in French, and in this passage he praises Perry's decision to stay in Paris:

Je fus bien aise de te savoir de retour à Paris, que tu n'as sans doute pas quitté. Je crois que tu ne regretteras jamais d'y avoir passé une grosse partie de ton temps; car enfin, quoiqu'on en dise, c'est une des merveilles de l'univers. On y apprend à connaître les hommes et les choses, et pour peu qu'on soit parvenu à y attraper le sentiment de *chez soi*, quelque genre de vie que l'on mène plus tard, on ne sera jamais un ignorant, un ermite—enfin un provincial.[2]

[I was very pleased to know that you were back in Paris, which you have doubtless not left. I believe you will never regret spending a large portion of your time there; for after all, whatever one says of it, it is one of the wonders of the universe. One learns there to know men and things, and with the proviso that one has been able to acquire the feeling of being at home there, whatever way of life one leads later on, one will never be an ignoramus, a hermit—in sum, a provincial.]

By writing in French, and implicitly from personal experience, James signals that he, too, will never be an ignoramus, a hermit, or (horror of horrors) a 'provincial'. The key to this blessed condition is 'le sentiment de *chez soi*', the feeling of being at home—a feeling which, if you can catch hold of it, will sustain your sense of self if you are living somewhere else—even in Massachusetts. And yet his own lengthy sojourn in Paris, nearly a decade later, had only ever been, James insists in his notebook entry, a 'stopgap': 'what I wanted was London' (*N* 215). He acknowledges the importance of the year he spent in Paris, when he met Turgenev, and Zola, and Goncourt, and Daudet—and above all Flaubert, that 'powerful, serious, melancholy, manly, deeply corrupted, yet not corrupting, nature' (*N* 216). He 'learned to know Paris and French affairs much better than before' (*N* 216), and this knowledge was of abiding significance for his work. But he found that living in Paris meant, perversely, inhabiting what he called—making use, of course, of a French phrase—'the American village encamped *en plein Paris*' (*N* 216). The sense of entrapment was accompanied by a recognition that he could not, after all, catch hold of the 'sentiment de chez soi'. 'I couldn't get out of the detestable *American* Paris [...] I saw, moreover, that I should be an eternal outsider' (*N* 216–17). In London that fate has been reversed: 'I came to London a complete stranger', but now '*J'y suis absolument comme chez moi*'. The French phrase here is accurately calibrated: James does not say *Je suis chez moi ici* [I am at home here], but *J'y suis comme chez moi*. This is the idiom a French person will use: 'Faites comme chez vous', which we would render, 'Make yourself at home'. London is of course not 'home', can never be home, yet invites James, so to speak, to make himself at home. More than that: 'J'y suis *absolument* comme chez moi.' Again, it is hard to render the oddness of this in English: 'it is absolutely the case that I am as though at home'. Only in French can James say what it means to him to dwell in England. The precision, and depth, with which he uses the French phrase in the

[2] Letter of 20 September 1867, in Philip Horne, ed., *Henry James: A Life in Letters* (London: Penguin Books, 1999), p.13. With one exception, all quotations from James's letters are taken from this volume (*L*), with date and page numbers given in the main text. Translations of foreign words and phrases are given in square brackets, and unless otherwise indicated are my own.

notebook measures its comparative shallowness in the letter to Perry. This distinction between the kinds of text where James uses French is of importance to my argument.

In one sense it is not surprising to find a French sentence in a Henry James text, of whatever kind—fiction, letters, journals, notebooks. It is not news that James's writing is thickly scattered with French, which predominates among the other languages that he occasionally uses—Italian, German, and Latin coming a long way behind in frequency and importance. This chapter is based specifically on the surviving notebooks in which James recorded ideas for stories, worked out plot developments and characterization, and gave vent to his feelings about his art—feelings of excitement, hope, frustration, misery; self-exhortation and self-reproach; passages of tentative groping (for which he uses the term *tâtonner*) and of forging ahead at full speed. There are six of these notebooks, covering the years 1878 to 1911, though not with any regularity or consistency, and they occupy about 200 pages in Edel and Powers' edition of *The Complete Notebooks*. In these pages I have counted 337 French words and phrases, and this figure under-represents the phenomenon, not just because many of these words and phrases occur more than once, but because I have recorded detached French sentences, and whole grammatical clauses, as separate items in a different list. Pages of these notebooks on which French does not occur are the exception. My question is how we might 'read' the use of French in this specific textual environment. The act of taking a sheet of paper—as opposed to the reader of a novel, or a correspondent—into his confidence, defines the peculiar quality of the notebooks. The resulting text is shaped neither by the dramatic scenario of a fiction, nor by the rhetorical design of a letter.

In James's fiction the use of French always belongs to a third party, whether that third party is the narrator or a character. The following examples are all from *The Bostonians*. In chapter 8, as the heroine Verena Tarrant prepares to give one of her 'inspired' performances, her disreputable father, the fraudulent medium and mesmeric healer Dr Tarrant, is overheard saying, "'She's just arranging her ideas, and trying to get in report'".[3] "'[I]n report'", the narrator tells us, 'was apparently Tarrant's version of *en rapport*'. Here the misuse of a French phrase is a mark of the character's vulgarity and ignorance, and the narrator's knowledge. Elsewhere the occurrence of a French word sends a social signal, as in chapter 18, when Verena and the strait-laced Olive Chancellor visit the Harvard rooms of Henry Burrage, a wealthy young law student, and Verena notes 'the *bibelots* [ornaments] that emerged into the firelight'. (It is not probable, by the way, that Verena should be familiar with this word, which wasn't naturalized in English in the period; the

---

[3] All references to *The Bostonians* are to the first English edition (London: Macmillan, 1886), pp. 59–60, 153, 207, 307.

narrator has lent her the understanding of French which he withheld from her father.) In chapter 22, Olive's fatuous and deluded sister Mrs Luna comprehensively misjudges the hero, Basil Ransom, who comes from Mississippi, by aligning the 'fallen aristocracy' of the South with the French *ancien régime*: 'was not Basil Ransom an example of it? was he not like a French *gentilhomme de province* after the Revolution? or an old monarchical *émigré* from the Languedoc?' In chapter 32, the mother of the Harvard student and collector of *bibelots*, Mrs Burrage, explains her acceptance of the unpalatable fact that her son really is in earnest in his desire to marry Verena:

> "In short, my poor boy flamed up again; and now I see that he will never again care for any girl as he cares for that one. My dear Miss Chancellor, *j'en ai pris mon parti*, and perhaps you know my way of doing that sort of thing. I am not at all good at resigning myself, but I am excellent at taking up a craze.["]

The use of the French idiom, which means something like 'I'm resigned to the inevitable', or less charitably 'I'm making the best of a bad job' is wholly in character—it is just what this wealthy New York socialite would say to her Bostonian antagonist at this precise moment, it allows Mrs Burrage to remain in control even as she pretends gracefully to acknowledge defeat, and it condescends to 'my dear Miss Chancellor' whether Olive understands it or not. And in fact James was sensitive as to how much French he allowed Olive herself to use in the novel. When the book was serialized in the *Century* in 1885, the following description of Henry Burrage was given through Olive's eyes: 'Mr. Burrage was rather a handsome youth, with a laughing, clever face, a certain sumptuosity of apparel, an air of belonging to the *jeunesse dorée*—a precocious, good-natured man of the world, curious of new sensations and containing, perhaps, the making of a dilettante'. *Jeunesse dorée*—'gilded youth'—had been circulating in English since the 1830s (*OED*'s first citation is from Hazlitt's life of Napoleon), but on reflection James seems to have decided that it would not suit Olive to use it, especially so close to another ~~French~~ foreign word, *dilettante*. Accordingly, when *The Bostonians* was published in volume form in 1886, *jeunesse dorée* was replaced by 'the "fast set"', a term that carries a more disapproving and disdainful charge.

These examples show James's keen eye for detail but they are all 'composed', like the details in a painting, and it is the composition which gives them their significance. They depend, moreover, on the reader's knowledge and skill, since French phrases are rarely translated or paraphrased. The case of letters is analogous in this respect, since a letter, after all, has a reader, even if the terms we use to describe such a figure—the *addressee*, the *recipient*—mark the distinction between them and the anonymous or conceptualized 'readership' of a novel. There are of course many instances of French in James's letters which are, to borrow the linguistic term, 'unmarked', and which seem to be more or less gratuitous. I will not dwell on them here, since later on I am going to give some examples of this gratuitous usage in the notebooks; and I am not going to do more than briefly mention the use of French which springs from James's being in France, as when he gives this gossipy account of the Parisian literary scene in May 1876:

> Yes, I have seen [Alphonse] Daudet several times. He is a little fellow (very little) with a refined & picturesque head, of a Jewish type. Former private secretary of the Duc de Morny. A brilliant talker & *raconteur*. A Bohemian. An extreme imitator of Dickens—but *à froid*, without D's real exuberance. *Jack* has had immense success here—ça se vend comme du pain. *Mme* Sand en raffole. The stepfather is a portrait—Pierre Véron, editor of the *Charivari*. The book to me was dreary & disagreeable, & in spite of cleverness intrinsically weak. I prefer an inch of Gustave Droz to a mile of Daudet. Why the Flaubert circle don't like him is their own affair—I don't care. I heard M. Zola characterize his manner sometime as *merde à la vanille*. I send you by post Zola's own last.—*merde au naturel*. Simply hideous.   (2 May 1876; *L* 70–1)

You might say of James's French here that it, too, is 'in spite of cleverness intrinsically weak'. It's a sign of his immersion, but it's also a bit forced, a display or performance of his having this kind of inside track; even the brilliant joke on 'merde' feels as though it has been carefully set up. And like many displays of linguistic virtuosity it gives itself away by a slight mistake: *ça se vend comme du pain* translates as 'it's selling like bread', which is a meaningless compliment; it should be *ça se vend comme des petits pains chauds*, i.e. it's selling like hot rolls, or as the English version has it, selling like hot cakes.

In contrast to this kind of usage, there are instances of French in James's letters which are more deliberate and more rhetorically pointed. In February he writes from Cambridge—Cambridge, Massachusetts—to Charles Eliot Norton, who happens to be in Germany:

> It is not that I have any thing very new & strange to relate. In fact, when one sits down to sum up Cambridge life *plume en main*, the strange thing seems its aridity.   (4 Feb. 1872; *L* 46)

To see oneself as *plume en main* in Cambridge is already to register an incongruity; the French phrase is comically inappropriate to the impoverished American social scene, implicitly contrasted with that of Paris. The disparagement of Cambridge solicits Norton's agreement, or assumes his complicity. But the whirligig of time brought in its revenges here. Writing to his brother William from England in August 1909, James contrasts 'what is sweetest and most attaching in the dear old American, or particularly New England, scenery' with the English countryside: 'It comes back to me as with such a magnificent beckoning looseness—in relieving contrast to the consummate tightness (a part, too, oddly, of the very wealth of effect) *du pays d'ici*.[4] The little word *ici* has an extraordinary pathos here, acknowledging both exile and presence. He was writing to William who had never been tempted to become an expatriate, whose *pays d'ici* was always New England. James had last visited his homeland in 1904–5, a trip as arduous, as emotionally draining, as it was productive. I think that in 1909 he knew he would never return.

In James's letters, I would argue, the writer's sense of his correspondent is always active; in the notebooks, by contrast, there is no addressee, or rather the writer is his own recipient. The use of French is not motivated by the desire to show off, or to draw a correspondent in to one's way of thinking. Even so there is some overlap between letters and notebooks, which comes from the fact that the use of French is habitual or routine. It is not uncommon to find an entry such as the following, written in November 1894:

> Isn't there perhaps the subject of a little—a very little—tale (*de moeurs littéraires*) in the idea of a man of letters, a poet, a novelist, finding out, after years, or a considerable period, of very happy, unsuspecting, and more or less affectionate, intercourse with a 'lady-writer', a newspaper woman, as it were, that he has been systematically *débiné*, 'slated' by her in certain critical journals to which she con-tributes? He has known her long and liked her, known of her hack-work, etc., and liked it less; and has also known that the *éreintements* ['pastings'] in ques-tion have periodically appeared—but he has never connected them with her or her with them....the reviewer may be—unconsciously, disappointedly, *régulièrement* [steadily], in love with the victim.   (*N* 107–8)

The setting of this projected story is English, the 'moeurs littéraires' are those of London literary society, and there seems no reason why the vocabulary of savage reviewing should be given in French rather than English. Why 'régulièrement' should be used seems equally mysterious. Indeed, much of James's French usage has no local or particular explanation; it is governed rather by a general predis-position, whose origins lie in the social and intellectual *cachet* attached to French in the cosmopolitan *milieu* of which James was so conspicuous an *habitué*. As in other periods, mid-eighteenth century England for example, or nineteenth-century Russia, French was fashionable, a marker of cultural sophistication and freedom from the dreaded stigma of provincialism. Often you feel James uses French in the way that some people add salt to whatever they eat. Here, for example, in an entry of 12 January 1887, he is working out the plot of a short story based on a daugh-ter's attempt to prevent her father marrying again:

---

[4] *The Letters of Henry James*, ed. Percy Lubbock, 2 vols (London: Macmillan, 1920), II, p. 139.

The father may be affected by his daughter's opposition so much as to repent of his engagement. He is *ébranlé*, he is ashamed of it, he wishes to retreat. But he tells her it is there and that he can't get out of it. 'Very well,' says she—'*je m'en charge.*'   (*N* 32)

There is simply no reason for the father not to be 'shaken', or for the daughter not to say 'I will deal with it.' But though such instances may be the norm, they also help to enable more self-conscious, more motivated usage. The question of provincialism has an edge for James, and a single French word can indicate a whole movement of thought. Here he is, in April 1883, planning the novel which eventually became *The Bostonians*:

> The whole thing as local, as American, as possible, and as full of Boston: an attempt to show that I *can* write an American story. There must, indispensably, be a type of newspaper man—the man whose ideal is the energetic reporter. I should like to *bafouer* the vulgarity and hideousness of this—the impudent invasion of privacy—the extinction of all conception of privacy, etc.   (*N* 19)

Bafouer here means something like 'expose to ridicule', and James could perfectly well have said that in English; but the French term is especially apt for an intention to make fun of a phenomenon 'as local, as American' as the 'impudent invasion of privacy' by the American press. To *bafouer* this aspect of American culture is to separate oneself from it, to mark it out as alien to one's own identity.

Let me now give a more detailed idea of the pattern of usage I am discussing. Basically, James uses French in two ways: in words and phrases interpolated into English sentences, or in whole sentences or grammatical units. The dividing line is not always easy to draw, but in general it can be said that the former category is much larger than the latter. Within this category there are many words and phrases, as I have indicated, which simply represent bits of vocabulary that James happens to deploy, without specific meaning attached to the shift from English to French. The colloquial phrases in particular (*à contre cœur* [reluctantly], *à la fin* [in the end], *au courant* [in the know], *bonne grâce* [with good grace], *comme qui dirait* [as who should say], *de part et d'autre* [on one side and the other], *en l'air* [up in the air, undecided], *outre mesure* [inordinately]) are all run-of-the-mill idioms, but there is not much special about the single words either; a British person with a reasonable knowledge of French would only need to look up a few in the dictionary, and almost none would qualify as historical slang, or as forgotten terms of art. These words and phrases are mortared in, so to speak, to the brickwork of English: 'These are old engagements, which I keep very *à contre cœur*' (6 Aug. 1884; *N* 30); 'I seem to see this out of town—at Brighton, at a watering-place *quelconque*' [at one watering-place or another] (26 Oct. 1896, *N* 167). Detached complete sentences are rare, and those that occur are quite short: '*Il y a bien quelque chose à tirer de ça*' [There's certainly something to be got out of that] refers to the anecdote which gave rise to the short story 'The Real Thing' (22 Feb. 1891; *N* 56); '*Ah, que de choses à faire, que de choses à faire!*' [Ah, so many things to do, so many things to do!] is a poignant exclamation from December, 1892 (*N* 75); '*À l'oeuvre, mon bon, à l'oeuvre—roide!*' [To work, my dear fellow, to work—straight ahead!] is a self-exhortation from December 1895 (*N* 145). (I will say more later on about 'mon bon', the idiom James uses to refer to himself, or to his creative faculty.) There is no example of two French sentences in a row. Sometimes a sentence which starts in French finishes in English: reflecting in October 1899 on his perennial struggle to keep a projected tale from exceeding its word limit, James optimistically assures himself: '*Et puis, vous savez, il n'y a pas de raison pour que je n'arrive pas à me dépêtrer—*in even 3000!' [And then, you know, there's no reason why I shouldn't be able to extricate myself] (*N* 186). It also happens the other way round: 'Henry Harper evidently wants another *Daisy Miller*; and *je ne demande pas mieux*' [I ask nothing better], he notes in October 1894. If we think of grammatical clauses rather than whole sentences, another group presents itself: 'She is in mourning *pour tous les siens*' [for all those belonging to her] (9 Jan. 1894; *N* 84); '*Je me fais fort* [I undertake] to state it again in such a manner as that the Part of the Hero will appear' (26 Dec. 1893; *N* 82); '*Je crois que je tiens* [I believe I have got hold of] my element of the Coxon bequest' (29 Apr. 1894; *N* 97); 'The little story *que j'entrevois* [that I glimpse] here' (3 Nov. 1894; *N* 104).

Grammar is not always amenable, of course, and in some cases James is prepared to bend the grammatical form of a French word, usually a verb, in order to make it fit his English syntax. Here is an example from the genesis of 'The Aspern Papers': 'Certainly there is a little subject there...the plot of the Shelley fanatic—his watchings and waitings—the way he *couvers* [covets] the treasure' (12 Jan. 1887; *N* 33–4). In May 1892, he notes a situation in which a mother tries to persuade her son to marry a certain girl: 'The son *regimbers* [balks] too much—says the girl is too ugly' (*N* 69). In February 1899, he sketches the plot of a woman's revenge on the 'lover who has *lachéd* [jilted] her' (*N* 181). In all these cases English verb-forms, governed by English nouns or pronouns, override the French; if, in the first example, James had used the French pronoun 'il', he could have had the correct form of 'couver': 'il couve the treasure'; likewise for the other two, where you can imagine 'le fils regimbe too much' and 'l'amant qui l'avait lachée'. I take such instances not to be errors, but, on the contrary, signs of a familiarity so profound that it can override correctness, melding the two languages together into a kind of personal compound.

I move now from this, so to speak, promiscuous use of French to more deliberate instances. I am going to concentrate on passages in the notebooks where James reflects on his own practice as a writer; but this is not the only area in which the use of French seems more pointed, where it is attached to recurring themes and preoccupations. I will briefly mention two of these: one is to do with sex, and the other with money and social status. Like other nineteenth-century British or American writers, James faced difficulties in dealing openly with sexual relationships and behaviour, difficulties which he repeatedly contrasted with the greater freedom enjoyed by French authors. 'One can do so little with English adultery,' he remarked with mournful exasperation, while sketching out the plot of what became *The Wings of the Dove* (3 Nov. 1894; *N* 103). It is not a coincidence, therefore, that the vocabulary of sexual conduct, and especially misconduct, turns so often to French in the notebooks, where we find among others *ancienne* [former prostitute], *cocotte* [kept woman], *femme galante* [loose woman], *coureur* [womanizer], *échauffé* [warmed up, aroused], *malpropreté* [indecency], *tarée* [of a woman whose reputation has been tarnished] and *vantard* [of a man who boasts of his sexual conquests]. And since James took many ideas for his fiction from his knowledge of the French social world, you would expect him to use French in that context, as when he reflects on the snobbery which obliged a fashionable French medical man, Henri Cazalis, to publish his poetry under the pseudonym Jean Lahor: 'the *médecin de ville d'eau* [doctor of a spa town] with his great *talent de poète* [poetic gift], changing his name to a "pen-name"—at his worldly wife's behest' (22 Sept. 1895; *N* 131). Yet there are as many instances in which James uses French regardless of the national origin of the story. In February 1899 he elaborates the complex plot of 'The Story in It' from the dictum '*L'honnête femme—n'a pas de roman*' [there is no 'story' in a virtuous woman], and concludes: 'I see it as [a] *London* thing' (*N* 177–8). In February 1892 he notes: 'An *idée de comédie* [idea for a comic tale] came to me vaguely the other day on the subject of the really terrible situation of the young man, in England, who is a great *parti* [eligible match]—the really formidable assault of the mothers, and the *filles à marier*' [marriageable girls] (*N* 64).[5] *Parti* in this sense is a favourite term, but we also find *dot* [dowry], *heritage* [legacy], *homme d'affaires* [man of business], *jeune fille* [young girl], *lancée* [having got a start in society], and *toutes les convenances* [all the proprieties]. But enough of the *monde*, and the *femmes du monde*, or even the *Faubourg*, with its *grandes dames* and their dubious *liaisons*. I turn now to the use of French in James's reflections on his own writing.

We should not be surprised to find that James's artistic and critical vocabulary is suffused with French. He was a passionate admirer of French intellectual culture, which he considered more serious, more systematic, more professional than its equivalent on either side of the Atlantic. He learned his trade from French writers and critics—Balzac, Maupassant, Flaubert, Sainte-Beuve. A short story to him was a *nouvelle*, or a *conte*; we find him in February 1891 aspiring 'To make

---

[5] The magazine title of the story was originally 'Lord Beauprey', a compound of the French word 'beau', the old-fashioned term for a suitor or admirer, and 'prey' because he is the prey of the 'formidable mothers'. When James reprinted the story in volume form, he may have thought this a bit obvious, because he changed the noble victim's name to 'Lord Beaupré', which hides the pun, so to speak, under a 'pré' or meadow.

little anecdotes of this kind real *morceaux de vie*' [slices of life] (*N* 55); planning a story in May 1883, he refers to 'the *entrée en matière* [start of the business] in London' (*N* 21); in March 1884, he sees the possibility of '*un drame—un drame intime*' in John Addington Symonds's marital unhappiness, as revealed to him by Edmund Gosse (*N* 25); an episode of *The Spoils of Poynton* 'can give, surely, some little *scène de passion;* but I want also, from this point on, the whole thing closely and admirably *mouvementé* [animated]....I must be utterly crystalline and complete, and my *charpente* [framework] must be of steel' (19 Feb. 1896; *N*,158–9). That last term illustrates in itself the technical precision that James valued in French critical discourse.

Yet if James's use of French in this area were confined to designations of genre, subject matter, and style, there would be little point in singling it out. Behind the admiration for French and the desire to emulate its discipline and technique lies something more volatile and more emotive. Here he is, in November 1899, excited by

> the idea of *transposing* the small *donnée* (transposing *and* developing, *mon bon!*) noted *supra* as the 'episode of Miss B. and Lady G.' Idea of making Miss B. a *man*—an amiable London celibate....There *is* a man-situation in the 'B. and Lady G.' affair—I mean there is *the* one, the right one. Dig—dig! *creusons, fouillons!* [let us dig, let us search!]   (*N* 187)

A cluster of key words appears in this passage, all of them associated by James with the work of imagination and the craft of fiction. First the word *donnée*, one of James's most frequently used terms (16 occurrences in the notebooks). It means the basic situation or idea on which a story is based, but it conveys something more, and does so with an economy and density of connotation that English cannot match. In part this is because it literally translates the Latin *datum*, defined by the *OED* as 'something given or granted; something known or assumed as fact, and made the basis of reasoning; an assumption or premise from which inferences are drawn.'[6] Such information is 'given' in precisely the measure that it is not made up; stories are generated not by invention but by reasoning upon a premise which is objectively determined, and gives the artist an immense security, a security which was at any rate immensely important to James. Time and again his *donnée* is actually given to him by someone else: 'Edmund Gosse mentioned to me the other day a fact which struck me as a possible *donnée*' (26 Mar. 1884; *N* 25); 'I began yesterday the little story that was suggested to me some time ago by an incident related to me by George Du Maurier....I thought I saw a subject for very brief treatment in this *donnée*' (22 Feb. 1891; *N* 55); 'I recall my walk....in company with G. T. Lapsley—my stroll, in the budding May—or

---

[6] *OED* 2a (3rd, online edition). Accessed 6 May 2019 at http://www.oed.com/view/Entry/47434

June—sunshine along the Mall of St. James's Pk. There he told me—charmingly—sounded the note of the sort of thing in which I instantly saw [a] little *donnée*' (15 Feb. 1899; *N* 176). But in truth it doesn't matter whether the idea for a story comes from someone else; to put it another way, James himself is 'someone else' as far as the *donnée* of a story is concerned.

This does not mean, of course, that the elements of the *donnée* are immutable, for if they were the artist would be nothing more than a *raconteur*. In one of the examples I have cited we see James thinking about 'transposing *and* developing' his theme, and in other entries in the notebooks he plays, sometimes at great length, with variations of plot, character, tone, and narrative method. This freedom of treatment is the province of 'mon bon', the idiom which James uses to address himself. Leon Edel, taking his cue from James's secretary Theodora Bosanquet, identifies this as a contraction of 'mon bon ange', my good angel or guardian spirit;[7] but it is only 'mon bon' that we encounter in the notebooks, and my dictionary renders this phrase as 'my dear fellow, my dear chap'. The tone of most of the notebook entries, to my ear, supports this more colloquial sense, and if 'mon bon' is a familiar spirit I would lay the emphasis on the familiar rather than the spiritual. I do not deny that *mon bon* can express enthusiasm, even creative rapture. He is implicated in this entry from 1894 in an erotic economy of literary production, marked by the double meaning of *commerce*: 'It is just this story, this chaste but workable and evincible young freshness of the inevitable, that I must shut myself up with in the sacredest and divinest of all private commerces. Live with it a little, *mon bon*, and the happy child will be born' (17 Apr. 1894; *N* 90). He is the object of fervent entreaty as James plans a scene in *The Spoils of Poynton*: 'IT MUST BE AS STRAIGHT AS A PLAY—that is the only way to do. Ah, *mon bon*, make *this*, *here*, justify, crown, in its little degree, the long years and pains, the acquired mastery of scenic presentation' (13 Feb. 1896; *N* 159). But 'mon bon' can also be a more mundane, a more workmanlike figure for memory, for application, for tenacity. 'Look also a little, *mon bon*, into what may come out, further, of the little something-or-other deposited long since in your memory—your fancy—by the queer confidence made you by the late Miss B...' (15 Feb. 1899; *N* 177). And the guardian angel—to come to the last two terms in my cluster—is not engaged in an ethereal activity but in something more earthy. 'Dig—dig! *creusons, fouillons!*' The self-exhortation here is contained in the grammar of the first-person plural: 'let us dig, let us search'. The verb 'fouiller' has a range of possible meanings—to explore, to burrow, to excavate, to rummage, to ransack. Along with 'creuser' it suggests going deeper into something, extracting more than lies on the surface, a process characteristic of *fin-de-siècle* literary discourse, in which the metaphor of depth is so prevalent.[8]

[7]   See Leon Edel, 'Introduction: Colloquies with His Good Angel', *Complete Notebooks*, p. xiii.
[8]   Compare, for example, Proust's habitual use of *approfondir* [to go more deeply into something] as a term of intellectual or aesthetic analysis.

The last of my examples of James's use of French as a way of referring to his art is the French word which occurs most often in the notebooks (21 examples), which is also couched in the first-person plural, and which designates a movement of consciousness, a thinking aloud on the page. It is the word *voyons*, which literally translates as 'let's see'. It can mark moments of hesitation, but also moments at which the possibilities for development of a story are, so to speak, visibly opening out; and it can also signify a decisive moment, a determination to follow something up. The choice of the French form seems to me to have an absolute rightness about it; if you replace 'voyons' by 'let's see' in nine-tenths of the examples I have looked at, the phrasing is instantly weakened; but I confess I am at a loss to say just why this should be so. It may simply be to do with concision, with the fact that one crisp word is more expressive than two; or with the fact that *voyons* has other meanings in French, akin to 'come now', or even 'come on now', and so introduces a less comfortable note, like a barrister cross-examining a witness. But James doesn't really use it in this interrogatory way. Often it signals the beginning of a task: '*Voyons, voyons*: may I not instantly sit down to a little close, clear, full scenario of it?' he asks himself in 1895 (14 Feb. 1895; *N* 115). On other occasions a specific problem is holding him up and needs thinking through—in this example a plot-device related to the career of the young author who is the protagonist of 'The Next Thing': 'There is something that must depend, for him, on his book's selling—something that he will get or that he can do: I mean in this final case, which constitutes the denouement. *Voyons*' (4 June 1895; *N* 125). The tone here is brisk, professional, and this is typical of most of the occurrences of the word; but *voyons* can be both more excited, and more tentative. Here are two examples in which we witness a turn, a shift in the writer's consciousness of his subject, as though he were, like a character in an epistolary novel, 'writing to the moment'. In the first example, James has begun work on 'the little subject of the child' which was to become *What Maisie Knew*.

> But the thing, before I go further, requires some more ciphering out, more extraction of the subject, of the drama—if such there really *be* in it. *Voyons un peu*—what little drama *does* reside in it? —I catch it, I catch it: I seize the tail of the little latent action *qu'il recèle* [that it conceals].   (22 Dec. 1895; *N* 147–8)

James uses the verb *recèler* elsewhere, again to suggest what lies hidden in a subject, what may be dug out; here it is as though *voyons* signals the writer literally glimpsing the 'little latent action' as it disappears into its burrow, and catching hold of its tail before it can escape.

In the second example James is planning a complicated manoeuvre on the part of the female narrator of 'The Friends of the Friends'. The narrator (in the notebook scenario) selfishly thwarts a meeting between her fiancé and a woman of whom she is jealous, and then repents of doing so; she confesses to her fiancé and 'take[s] him the next day straight out to see her'. James continues:

> Is she then, as we find, dead—or only very ill—i.e., dying? The extreme brevity of my poor little form doubtless makes it indispensable that she shall be already dead. I can't devote space to what passes while she is dying, while her illness goes on. I must jump that—I must arrive (with all the little *merveilleux* [wonder] of the story still to come) at what happens *after* this event.—Or rather, on second thoughts, have I got this—this last bit—all wrong? Don't I, *mustn't I*, see it, on reflection, in another way? *Voyons, voyons.* Say the narrator....   (10 Jan. 1896; *N* 152-3)

But I, too, have to obey the extreme brevity of my poor little form. I do not have space to present the alternative scenario, or in what the *merveilleux* of the story consists; the point here is the use of *voyons* to mediate a change of mind, but also the connection between the literal meaning of the term and what the author *sees*. 'Don't I, *mustn't I*, see it, on reflection, in another way? *Voyons, voyons*.' Here the conventional idiom, like a dead metaphor, comes back to life, since a major factor in the process of composition, for James, is visualization. '*Je vois tout ça d'ici* [I see all that from here]—the items and elements multiply and live', he says as the characters in a story take shape in his mind (13 July 1891; *N* 58).

Such passages bear witness to a kind of thinking-aloud, a thinking-aloud on paper in which the writer's self is doubled—doubled, but not duplicated. The notebook is not a hall of mirrors, but a space in which the writer encounters himself as other, an *alter ego* with the freedom to speculate, to deliberate, to question—a freedom no other space in the writer's life could offer, because no other space could guarantee the same degree of privacy. What that privacy meant to James is clear from his use of the French word for notebook, *cahier*, in the following passage, with which I will conclude. It comes towards the end of one of the longest, most sustained pieces of self-reflection in the notebooks, composed in the bitter aftermath of his five-year campaign to conquer the London theatre, culminating in the disastrous first night of *Guy Domville* in January 1895. This passage has become famous in James studies because it contains his recuperative vision of what could be salvaged from the 'wasted passion and squandered time' of his theatrical venture—namely 'the divine principle of the Scenario', the 'key' that might fit 'the complicated chambers of *both* the dramatic and the narrative lock' (14 Feb. 1895; *N* 115). But what interests me more, at least for the purpose of this essay, is the way James immediately associates this principle with the kind of writing on which he is actually engaged. The Scenario demands the notebook. Or as James puts it:

> The long figuring out, the patient, passionate little *cahier*, becomes the *mot de l'énigme* [the clue to the riddle]....Let me commemorate here, in this manner, such a portentous little discovery, the discovery, probably, of a truth of real value even if I exaggerate, as I daresay I do, its *partée* [*sic*, for *portée*], its magicality.
>
> (14 Feb. 1895; *N* 116)

It is itself a clue, a *mot de l'énigme* or figure in the carpet, that James should choose these French words and phrases. I don't think he did exaggerate the 'portée', the reach, of the 'truth of real value', and he was right to commemorate it 'here, in this manner'. Its 'magicality'—to end with an English word—may be gauged by the fact that the two novels whose 'scenarios' he outlines in this same notebook entry are *The Wings of the Dove* and *The Golden Bowl*.

3

The Protean Ptyx: Nonsense, Non-Translation, and Word Magic in Mallarmé's 'Sonnet en *yx*'

Dennis Duncan

In the summer of 1868, the young Stéphane Mallarmé was living in Avignon and working as a schoolteacher. In poor health, both mentally and physically, his limited income combined unhappily with his natural profligacy to create a somewhat precarious existence for the poet and his young family. To make matters worse, Mallarmé was frustrated at his inability to write the great work he had recently envisaged, the vast, multiform masterpiece he referred to as 'Le Livre'—The Book—and which, he intended, would encapsulate the post-Christian values of the age ('L'explication orpique de la Terre'—'The Orphic explanation of the Earth'—as he would later describe it to Verlaine).[1] Missing the cosmopolitan *milieu* of Paris and resenting the Provençals as uncultured rustics, he wrote to his friend Eugène Lefébure, asking him to make enquiries as to where a good hammock might be obtained, reasoning that if one can't write poetry, one might at least relax in the shade. The letter continues:

> Enfin, comme il se pourrait toutefois que, rythmé par le hamac, et inspiré par le laurier, je fisse un sonnet, et que je n'ai que trois rimes en *ix*, concertez-vous pour m'envoyer le sens réel du mot *ptyx*, ou m'assurer qu'il n'existe dans aucune langue, ce que je préfé[re]rais de beaucoup afin de me donner le charme de le créer par la magie de la rime.[2]

> [Finally, for it could nonetheless be that, swayed by the hammock, and inspired by the laurel trees, I might write a sonnet, and since I only have three rhymes in *ix*, do your best to send me the true meaning of the word *ptyx* or to assure me that it doesn't exist in any language, which I'd much prefer, for that would give me the charm of creating it through the magic of rhyme.]

---

[1] Letter of 16 November 1885. Stéphane Mallarmé, *Oeuvres complètes*, 2 vols, ed. Bertrand Marchal, 2nd edn (Paris: Gallimard, 1998), I, p. 788. All translations, unless otherwise indicated, are my own.
[2] Letter of 3 May 1868. Mallarmé, *Oeuvres complètes*, 2nd edn, I, pp. 728–9.

Dennis Duncan, *The Protean Ptyx: Nonsense, Non-Translation, and Word Magic in Mallarmé's 'Sonnet en* yx'
In: *Modernism and Non-Translation*. Edited by: Jason Harding and John Nash, Oxford University Press (2019).
© the several contributors.
DOI: 10.1093/oso/9780198821441.003.0003

The poem that Mallarmé was working on was his 'Sonnet en *yx*' ('Ses purs ongles très haut dédiant leur onyx'), and the first half of this chapter will survey how Mallarmé's editors and explicators, from the 1890s to the present, have responded to the problematic *ptyx*. Is it indeed a term invented by the poet 'through the magic of rhyme', or is it in fact a real, albeit foreign word, whose meaning is part of Mallarmé's design for the poem? Should we read it either as an instance of nonsense or as non-translation? The second part of the chapter looks at a third way—and another type of magic—in which the protean *ptyx*, adopted firstly by Alfred Jarry and subsequently by the avant-garde Collège de 'Pataphysique, slips its moorings altogether from any discourses of the poet's intention, moving from the category of the untranslated to the untranslatable.[3] The chapter will conclude by comparing these three versions of the *ptyx* through the lens of C. K. Ogden's interwar critique of 'word magic'.

The sonnet, as it would eventually appear in Mallarmé's *Poésies* (1887) runs like this:

> Ses purs ongles très haut dédiant leur onyx,
> L'Angoisse ce minuit, soutient, lampadophore,
> Maint rêve vespéral brûle par le Phénix
> Que ne recueille pas de cinéraire amphore
>
> Sur les crédences, au salon vide: nul ptyx,
> Aboli bibelot d'inanité sonore,
> (Car le Maître est allé puiser des pleurs au Styx
> Avec ce seul objet dont le Néant s'honore.)
>
> Mais proche la croisée au nord vacante, un or
> Agonise selon peut-être le décor
> Des licornes ruant du feu contre une nixe,
>
> Elle, défunte nue en le miroir, encor
> Que, dans l'oubli fermé par le cadre, se fixe
> De scintillations sitôt le septuor.[4]

An English version, translating for sense and overlooking the constraints of rhyme and metre, might run like this:

---

[3] Regarding the apostrophe applied to certain uses of the term 'Pataphysics, see 'L'Apostrophe de Pataphysique', *Subsidia Pataphysica*, 0 (1965): 84.

[4] Mallarmé, *Oeuvres complètes*, 2nd edn, I, pp. 37–8. There are some major differences between this version and the original draft composed in the summer of 1868. On the issue of the *ptyx*, however, the two are close enough: 'nul ptyx, / Insolite vaisseau d'inanité sonore' (1868) versus 'nul ptyx, / Aboli bibelot d'inanité sonore' (1887). It may be an emptied-out trinket or a strange vessel, but the important thing is that the *ptyx* represents resonant emptiness. For the draft version, see Mallarmé, *Oeuvres complètes*, 2nd edn, I, p. 131.

Her pure nails dedicating on high their onyx,
Anguish, this midnight, holds up, like a lamp-bearer,
Many a vesperal dream burned by the Phoenix
Which is not gathered in any funerary urn

On the sideboard, in the empty drawing-room: no ptyx
Abolished trinket of sonorous emptiness,
(For the Master has gone to draw tears from the Styx
With this sole object by which Nothingness is honoured).

But near the vacant casement to the north, a glimmer
Dies away perhaps in accordance with the decor
Of unicorns hurling fire at a nymph,

She, departed naked in the mirror, while
In the oblivion bounded by the frame is fixed
So soon the scintillations of the septet.

It is not hard to see why Mallarmé might have hoped that *ptyx* was his own invention. One of his earliest commentators, Téodor de Wyzewa, hymned it as a 'mot purement euphonique et dépourvu de tout sens' ['purely euphonic word, devoid of all sense'].[5] Yet while it might be without sense, it is certainly not without function in the poem. Its role as a 'trinket of sonorous emptiness'—the 'object by which Nothingness is honoured'—seems to rest on its failure of representation, or, to put it another way, on its being a nonsense word. In its meaninglessness, Mallarmé's *ptyx* represents Nothingness in the world of referents, language purified of signification. (One reading of the poem's opening phrase—'Ses purs ongles'—takes it as a paradoxical pun about the poem itself: 'C'est pur son': 'It is pure sound'.)[6]

'Pure sound' would be overstating the meaninglessness of *ptyx* here—on a variety of planes, even nonsense words carry some interpretable sense. Performing a linguistic examination of a nonsense letter from Edward Lear to a friend ('Inky tinky pobblebockle abblesquabs? – Flosky!' etc.), Jean-Jacques Lecercle notes that the analysis proves fruitful when approaching the text from phonological, morphological, and syntactic positions. Treating Mallarmé's poem in the same way, we can see clearly that *ptyx* belongs to the same Greek morphological register as its rhymes, *onyx*, *Phénix*, and *Styx*. We may or may not, in addition, accept Michael Riffaterre's suggestion that *ptyx* implies its own mysteriousness 'since y and x are the signs of conventional abstractness and of algebraic unknowns'.[7] Meanwhile, syntactically, A. R. Chisholm has pointed out that the word's context

[5] Téodor de Wyzewa, 'M. Stéphane Mallarmé', *Le Figaro*, 8 December 1892, p. 1.
[6] See, for example, Roger Pearson, *Unfolding Mallarmé: The Development of a Poetic Art* (Oxford: Clarendon Press, 1996), p. 204.
[7] Michael Riffaterre, *The Semiotics of Poetry* (London: Indiana University Press, 1978), p. 18.

leads us to interpret it as being an equivalent to *amphore* in the previous line, i.e. On the sideboard there is no amphora, no ptyx, to hold the ashes of the Phoenix. 'Thus,' concludes Chisholm, 'we are compelled [...] to interpret *ptyx* as some sort of container.'[8] Réné Ghil takes the reading slightly further, stating that Mallarmé invented the word 'auquel il donna le sens de vase, d'urne' ['to which he gave the sense of vase, or urn'].[9] In Lecercle's assessment, however, while we can look at the morphology or syntactic context of nonsense words and pull out successful readings, 'No such thing happens [...] when we reach the level of semantics. Here the linguist's impotence is complete.'[10] We should not get beyond ourselves: *ptyx* is still a nonsense word—a placeholder rather than a lexical item—and any meaning we attribute to it will be, of necessity, indistinct.

Except that, contrary to Mallarmé's expressed preference that it should be merely a piece of *faux* Hellenism, *ptyx* really *is* an ancient Greek term. Liddell-Scott-Jones, the standard Greek lexicon, lists it—with a caveat, of which more later—as πτύξ meaning *fold*, or by extension things that are folded: writing tablets, hilly country, the folds of song (i.e. sinuous songs). We find it today in words like *triptych* for a three-panelled, folding artwork. With this in mind, since the early twentieth century, a considerable body of Mallarmé scholars have been unwilling to accept that the poet wasn't perfectly aware of *ptyx*'s meaning when he wrote the sonnet. As Paul Allen Miller puts it, we need not 'take Mallarmé's profession of ignorance at face value, [when] his capacity for exaggerated self-deprecation was legendary'.[11] Emilie Noulet is less circumspect, briskly dismissing the Lefébure letter:

> Rappelons d'abord la lettre de Mallarmé à Lefébure où il feignait de ne pas connaître la signification du mot. Pure coquetterie de celui qui, pendant ce temps, recueillait les mots d'origine grecque![12]
>
> [Let us first remember Mallarmé's letter to Lefébure where he pretended not to know the meaning of the word. Pure coquetry from someone who, during this period, was collecting words of Greek origin!]

Meanwhile, Gretchen Kromer suggests that Mallarmé might not have been familiar with the word when he drafted the poem in 1868, but after working closely with classical languages in the 1870s and 1880s, he 'did intend *ptyx* to have a

---

[8] A. R. Chisholm, 'Mallarmé: "Ses purs ongles..."', *French Studies* 6.3 (1952): 230–4 (p. 231).

[9] Réné Ghil, *Les Dates et les oeuvres: Symbolisme et poésie scientifique* (Paris: Crès, 1923), p. 222.

[10] Jean-Jacques Lecercle, *The Violence of Language* (London: Routledge, 1990), p. 3.

[11] Paul Allen Miller, 'Black and White Myths: Etymology and Dialectics in Mallarmé's "Sonnet en *yx*"', *Texas Studies in Literature and Language* 36.2 (1994): 184–211 (p. 187).

[12] Stéphane Mallarmé, *Vingt poèmes de Stéphane Mallarmé*, edited by Emilie Noulet (Paris: Minard, 1967), p. 183.

meaning in the *second* [1887] version of the sonnet'.[13] This theory, echoed by Miller, overlooks an obscure piece of evidence.[14] In a newspaper article published a few years after Mallarmé's death, the journalist Octave Uzanne recounted the poet reciting the 'Sonnet en *yx*' in his later years and explaining to a bemused listener that *ptyx* had been invented simply because he needed a rhyme for *Styx*:

> N'en trouvant point, j'ai crée un instrument de musique inédit. [...] Le ptyx est insolite, car il est inconnu; il résonne avec sonorité, puisqu'il rime avec un majestueuse opulence; il n'en demeure pas moins un vaisseau d'inanité, puisqu'il n'a jamais existé. Et l'on dit que je ne suis pas clair![15]

> [And finding none, I created a unique musical instrument. [...] The ptyx is strange because it is unknown; it resonates with sonority because it rhymes with a majestic opulence; it remains a vessel of emptiness because it never existed. And people say I'm not clear!]

Still, if one is prepared to distrust the youthful Mallarmé writing to a friend in loneliness and frustration, it is no harder to distrust the mature poet in his days as an admired and convivial *salonnier*.

What these interpretations insist is that, whether in the schoolroom or in later life, somewhere along the line *ptyx* became meaningful to Mallarmé. Thus, far from being a neologism or nonsense word, these critics argue, we should read Mallarmé's *ptyx* as an instance of non-translation, a Greek term dropped knowingly into a French text. This being the case, their argument runs, its original sense is part of Mallarmé's intention for the poem: not only *can* we translate it, but we *should* if we want to understand the sonnet fully. Surprisingly, however, there is little agreement on what the correct meaning should be.

In 1926, in the same issue of *Nouvelle revue française*, within a few pages of each other, Paul Claudel states that the *ptyx* is a bottle or carafe, while Henry Charpentier writes bluffly that it is a sea-shell.[16] Charpentier's argument is interesting both because it is explicit, not to say combative, in calling out de Wyzewa by name and rejecting the idea of *ptyx* as a nonsense word, and because Charpentier is the first to identify the term as real Greek:

> Le *ptyx* n'est pas un mot vide de sens, composé expressément et arbitrairement pour exprimer le pur néant. [...] C'est tout simplement la transcription littérale

---

[13] Gretchen Kromer, 'The Redoubtable PTYX', *Modern Language Notes* 86.4 (1971): 563–72 (p. 571), my emphasis.

[14] Miller, 'Black and White Myths', p. 187.

[15] Octave Uzanne, 'Choses et personnes qui passent: heure d'automne', *Echo de Paris* (5 October 1905), p. 1.

[16] Paul Claudel, 'La Catastrophe d'Igitur', *Nouvelle revue française* 158 (November 1926): 531–6 (p. 532); Henry Charpentier, 'De Stéphane Mallarmé', *Nouvelle revue française* 158 (November 1926): 537–45 (p. 543).

du mot grec qui signifie la coquille, la conque creuse où l'on entend le bruit éternel de la mer.[17]

[The *ptyx* is not a word devoid of sense, composed expressly and arbitrarily to express pure nothingness. [...] It is quite simply the literal transcription of the Greek word which signifies shell, the hollow conch shell in which one can hear the eternal sound of the sea.]

There are serious problems with Charpentier's claim, which we will come to in a moment, but this did not stop it becoming almost an orthodoxy among Mallarmé's editors and commentators over the next half century. Kurt Wais, for example, repeats it when he writes in pleasing compounds of the poem's 'eigenartige leerrauschende Muschelgefäß auf der Kredenz' ['peculiar empty-roaring shell-vessel on the sideboard'].[18]

Then, in 1940, Noulet provides the etymological evidence that was conspicuously absent from the earlier non-translationists. She begins by parroting Charpentier:

Le contexte aidant, on peut en déduire que 'ptyx' désigne une conque, un de ces coquillages qui, collé à l'oreille, fait entendre le bruit de la mer.[19]

[Aided by the context, one can deduce that *ptyx* designates a conch, one of those shells that, when you hold them to your ear, produces the sound of the sea.]

To support this claim, however, she cites an instance in the *Thesaurus linguae graecae* in which St Basil refers to the valves of an oyster as πτύχας. The problem with this is that the citation represents a single usage instance—not a definition—and a transferred sense at that. This is rather as if future etymologists, two thousand years hence, should cite Keats as proof that *bride* was once an English word denoting a Grecian urn. Noulet's next step is equally problematic. A bivalve oyster shell has the hinge which makes it a plausible metonymic referent for *ptyx*—this is presumably what Basil was getting at. Meanwhile, a conch shell produces the auditory illusion of the sea which one might call 'resonant emptiness'. But an oyster and a conch are two completely different shells. A conch then is patently not a *ptyx*, whether or not Mallarmé was familiar with the Greek word. Nevertheless, during the mid-century, the idea that the *ptyx* was some type of shell had plenty of heavyweight supporters, among them Mondor and Jean-Aubry's Pléiade *Oeuvres complètes* and Henri Nicolas's Larousse collection.[20]

[17] Charpentier, 'De Stéphane Mallarmé', p. 543.
[18] Kurt Wais, *Mallarmé: Ein Dichter des Jahrhundert-Endes* (Munich: Beck, 1938), p. 405.
[19] Emilie Noulet, *L'Oeuvre poétique de Stéphane Mallarmé* (Paris: Droz, 1940), p. 454.
[20] Stéphane Mallarmé, *Oeuvres complètes*, ed. Henri Mondor and G. Jean-Aubry (Paris: Gallimard, 1945), p. 1490; Henri Nicolas, *Mallarmé et le Symbolisme* (Paris: Larousse, 1965), p. 43n4.

Meanwhile, Charles Mauron reads *ptyx* more straightforwardly as *fold*, which he takes as a reference to the poem's rhyme scheme.[21] This gives rise to a satisfyingly productive reading as the sonnet—originally entitled 'Sonnet allégorique de lui-même'—does indeed fold in on itself in a number of curious ways.[22] Firstly, it switches several times between looking outwards from, and inwards onto, the empty room. The first quatrain and the first tercet appear to be looking out into the darkness, while the second quatrain and the second tercet describe objects within the room—the sideboards, the mirror—and the poem hinges like a panel painting around these changes of view. The final tercet proclaims itself as a repetition, a defunct mirror image of the seven stars—the Great Bear—in the even greater emptiness outside (and of course the seven stars, doubled by reflection in a mirror, make fourteen, potentially representing the lines of the poem). At the same time, another significant fold divides the poem into two parts. In French poetry, a rhyme is described as feminine if it ends in a silent *e*, and masculine if it doesn't. So for the first eight lines of the sonnet, the *-yx* rhymes are masculine, while the alternate lines which end in *-ore* are feminine. But for the final six lines, Mallarmé keeps the same sounds, but inverts, or mirrors, the masculine or feminine endings. Thus *-yx* becomes *-ixe* and *-ore* becomes *-or*.

For another critic, Robert Greer Cohn, thinking of the *ptyx* as a fold would allow us to read it metaphorically as the undulations of a line of handwriting.[23] Kromer, meanwhile, arriving by a different path at a similar place, hears the echo of a phrase from Aeschylus—*en ptychais biblōn* ['in the folds of books'] (*Suppliants* l. 947)—and thus sees the *ptyx* as a metonymic reference to Le Livre, Mallarmé's unwritten masterpiece.[24]

It is not the intention of this chapter to take up a position in this debate; rather, the aim of the preceding survey is to demonstrate that after a century of argument and conjecture, no consensus has been reached on whether the mysterious *ptyx* is nonsense or non-translation. Instead there have been trends, in line with the intellectual currents of their time. The first wave of commentators, beginning in the *fin-de-siècle* period were content to preserve the mysteriousness of the term, to take Mallarmé at his word when he claimed ignorance of *ptyx*'s meaning. In 1925, Pierre Martino was still urging the reader to resist the urge to explain, to *translate*, too much in Mallarmé's poetry:

il faut se garder de les trop bien expliquer. [...] Les traductions juxtalinéaires et précises de ces poèmes risquent d'être bien sottes, d'autant que le poète s'est

---

[21] Charles Mauron, *Mallarmé l'obscur* (Paris: Denoël, 1941), p. 164.

[22] Mallarmé, *Oeuvres complètes*, 2nd edn, I, p. 131.

[23] Robert Greer Cohn, *Towards the Poems of Mallarmé* (Berkeley: University of California Press, 1965), p. 142.

[24] Kromer, 'The Redoubtable PTYX', p. 572.

amusé parfois à insérer dans la trame de ses poèmes de singulières incongruités, fort bien dissimulées. [25]

[we must resist the urge to over-explain. [...] Interlinear translations and glosses run the risk of being quite asinine, especially since the poet sometimes amused himself by inserting singular, well-disguised incongruities into the weft of his poems].

Within a year, however, Charpentier would kick off an era of *ptyx*-as-non-translation such that, by the early 1950s, Chisholm could write: 'I think it is reasonably safe to say that most modern commentators [...] accept the meaning "sea-shell".'[26] Nevertheless, twenty years later Chisholm would publicly disown this position, as later readings—Cohn in the mid-1960s, Kromer in the early 1970s—are less reductive, more speculative, not to mention more grammatological.[27] It is hardly surprising that Derrida himself should have got in on the act with a 1974 essay on Mallarmé. While not expressly concerned with the 'Sonnet en *yx*', he argues that Mallarmé's writing in general,

is organized in such a way that at its strongest points, the meaning remains *undecidable*; from then on, the signifier no longer lets itself be traversed, it remains, resists, exists, and draws attention to itself.[28]

Riffaterre too sounds a distinctly 1970s note when he mocks the earlier definitional accounts as being born out of 'a nostalgia for referentiality'.[29]

Taking the two editions of the Pléiade *Oeuvres complètes* as a gauge, we can see the move away from non-translation in the latter half of the twentieth century. While Mondor and Jean-Aubry's 1945 text quotes Noulet at length, Bertrand Marchal's second edition, appearing in 1998, gives short shrift to this type of reading:

trop de commentateurs se sont échinés à trouver un référent au mot, alors que ce mot qui n'existe pas, ce mot créé par la magie de la rime, [...] est la figure même de ce sonnet nul, allégorique de lui-même.[30]

[too many commentators have slaved to find a referent for the word, whereas this word which doesn't exist, this word created by the magic of rhyme [...] is the very figure of this null sonnet, allegorical of itself.]

---

[25] Pierre Martino, *Parnasse et Symbolisme (1850–1900)* (Paris: Armand Colin, 1925), pp. 124–5.

[26] Chisholm, 'Mallarmé: "Ses purs ongles..."', pp. 231–2.

[27] A. R. Chisholm, 'Mallarmé and the Riddle of the Ptyx', *AUMLA: Journal of the Australasian Universities Language and Literature Association* 40 (1973): 246–8 (p. 246).

[28] Jacques Derrida, 'Mallarmé', trans. Christine Roulston, in *Acts of Literature*, ed. Derek Attridge (London: Routledge, 1992), pp. 110–26 (p. 114), Derrida's emphasis.

[29] Riffaterre, *The Semiotics of Poetry*, p. 18.

[30] Mallarmé, *Oeuvres complètes*, 2nd edn, I, p. 1190.

After a century of interpretation, we are back, resolutely, with de Wyzewa's opening position. What the *ptyx* resembles most of all is a mirror, reflecting back the critical values of the age: from the mid-twenties onwards, critics projected Modernism's characteristic non-translation onto the poem; for the poststructuralists of the 1970s and later, the *ptyx* as free-floating signifier, cut off from any signified, proved an irresistible interpretation.

What this type of survey makes clear, however, is how little it matters whether the term is taken as nonsense or non-translation. If we take *ptyx* as an invented word, we can still get as far as picturing it as a vessel of some sort, a carafe possibly, or maybe an urn. If we treat it as non-translation—a known word from another language—we can take our pick from a shell (conch or otherwise), a writing tablet, a piece of handwriting, an in-the-abstract fold... The surprising thing is that it doesn't exactly bring more clarity to declare that *ptyx* is a real word. If anything, looking at the list of suggested meanings, it brings less.

The 'Sonnet en *yx*', however, has given rise to another strand of influence, one fundamentally opposed to interpreting or translating the word *ptyx* to *any* degree, instead assigning a quasi-religious importance to its meaninglessness. This strand of criticism belongs in the pataphysical school, and has its origins with the avant-garde playwright and novelist Alfred Jarry.

Beginning in the early 1880s and running until his death in 1898, Mallarmé had held a weekly salon at his home in Paris. These gatherings brought together many of the major figures in late nineteenth-century culture—Yeats, Rilke, Verlaine, Debussy, and Wilde all attended—while another visitor, Arthur Symons, considered the salon to be pre-eminent among Mallarmé's achievements:

> In estimating the significance of Stéphane Mallarmé, it is necessary to take into account not only his verse and prose, but, almost more than these, the Tuesdays of the Rue de Rome.[31]

Describing the influence these Tuesday evenings had on the younger writers who attended, Symons claims:

> It was impossible to come away from Mallarmé's without some tranquillising influence from that quiet place, some impersonal ambition towards excellence, the resolve, at least, to write a sonnet, a page of prose, that should be in its own way as perfect as one could make it, worthy of Mallarmé.[32]

From the middle of the 1890s, one of these impressionable visitors was the young Alfred Jarry.

[31] Arthur Symons, *The Symbolist Movement in Literature* [1899], revised and enlarged edn (New York: E. P. Dutton, 1919), p. 183.
[32] Symons, *The Symbolist Movement...*, p. 188

Several decades later, the German historian Alfred Haas would recall an evening when he and Jarry were the last stragglers in Mallarmé's drawing room and the ageing poet described to them his theory of the structure of the sonnet:

> Un matin, vers deux heures, alors qu'il n'y avait plus là, en dehors de moi, qu'Alfred Jarry, mort aussi depuis, il nous décrivit et nous loua inlassablement, avec des images sans cesses renouvelées, la structure du Sonnet. Les quatrains étaient deux groupes de colonnes et les deux tercets les côtés du fronton qui couronne le tout.[33]

> [One morning, around two o'clock, when no-one was left except for myself and Alfred Jarry, now dead also, [Mallarmé] was describing and tirelessly praising to us, with endlessly inventive images, the structure of the Sonnet. The quatrains were two groups of columns and the two tercets the sides of the pediment which crowned the whole thing.]

When Jarry's controversial literary output achieved first notoriety then indifference, Mallarmé remained a reliably supportive figure, both idol and mentor. And when Mallarmé died in 1898, Jarry was distraught. He cycled twenty miles to attend the funeral, in borrowed, bright yellow, women's shoes, his muddy trousers still tucked into his socks.[34]

It was during this period, the summer of 1898, that Jarry was composing his prose masterpiece, the novel *Gestes et opinions du docteur Faustroll, pataphysicien* (although it remained unpublished until 1911, four years after Jarry's death). The novel's second section, entitled 'Elements of Pataphysics' includes a chapter on Faustroll's companion, the bumfaced baboon Bosse-de-Nage, and in particular on his language. Bosse-de-Nage can say only one thing—'Ha ha'—but over the course of the novel he will mean a great variety of things by this utterance. Thus, the pataphysical precept being elucidated in this chapter is, as Paul Edwards summarizes, that 'a word deprived of any meaning can therefore be used to convey any meaning'.[35] For followers of the *ptyx*, we are in familiar territory.

Perhaps it should come as little surprise, then, that in the book's third section, when Faustroll and Bosse-de-Nage set off in their skiff on a quasi-Homeric voyage around the imaginary islands of Paris, one of their stopping points should be named the Isle of Ptyx. Like the majority of the novel's chapters, 'De l'Ile de Ptyx' is explicitly dedicated to one of Jarry's artistic heroes, in this case, naturally, Mallarmé.

> The isle of Ptyx is fashioned from a single block of the stone of this name, a priceless stone found only in this island, which is entirely composed of it. It has the serene

[33] Albert Haas, 'Souvenirs de la vie littéraire à Paris'. *Les Soirées de Paris* 24 (May 1914): 251–74 (p. 258).

[34] Alastair Brotchie, *Alfred Jarry: A Pataphysical Life* (London, MA: MIT Press, 2011), p. 231.

[35] Paul Edwards, 'Faustroll: Portrait of the Author as a Pataphysician', in Alfred Jarry, *Three Early Novels*, translated and introduced by Alastair Brotchie, Paul Edwards, Alexis Lykiard, and Simon Watson Taylor (London: Atlas, 2006), pp. 119–26 (p. 122).

translucency of white sapphire and is the only precious stone not ice-cold to the touch, for its fire enters and spreads itself like wine after drinking. Other stones are as cold as the cry of trumpets; this has the precipitated heat of the surface of kettle-drums. [...] The lord of the islands came towards us in a ship [*vaisseau*]: the funnel puffed out blue halos behind his head, magnifying the smoke from his pipe and imprinting it on the sky. And as the ship pitched and tossed, his rocking-chair jerked out his welcoming gestures. From beneath his travelling-rug he drew four eggs with painted shells, which he handed over to Doctor Faustroll after first taking a drink. In the flame of the punch we were drinking, the hatching of the oval embryos broke out over the island's shore: two distant columns, the isolation of two prismatic trinities of Pan pipes, splayed out in the spurt of their cornices the quad-ridigitate handshake of the sonnet's quatrains; and our skiff rocked its hammock [*hamac*] in the newborn reflection of the triumphal arch. Dispersing the hairy curi-osity of the fauns and the rosy bloom of the nymphs aroused from their reverie by this mellifluous creation, the pale motor vessel [*vaisseau*] withdrew its blue breath toward the island's horizon, with its jerking chair waving goodbye.[36]

Ptyx, then, in Jarry's creative appropriation, is neither shell nor container. Instead it is variously an island, a stone, a metaphor for Mallarmé himself—crystalline, Parnassian—for his warmth and his uniqueness. The passage rehearses Mallarmé's architectural theory of the sonnet, expounded to Jarry in the small hours, and presents the poet in the beloved rocking-chair from which he would hold court at his soirées. (Symons, too, remembers 'above all, the rocking-chair'.)[37] Some of the language in this episode—the skiff's *hamac*; *vaisseau* as the sole, repeated term for Mallarmé's boat—is tantalizing, holding out the faint but improbable chance that Mallarmé might, at one of his salons, have read out the earlier version of the poem (in which the *ptyx* is an 'insolite vaisseau' ['strange vessel']), or even described himself under the laurel trees of Avignon, swaying in a hammock as he composed it. It is important that for Jarry, in his vignette of the Ile de Ptyx, the *ptyx* is a metaphorical blank slate: not something to be read or translated but something to be written on; not decoded but reinvented. It is a sign to which any meaning—multiple meanings, even—can be affixed, but which is, for Jarry, intim-ately concerned with his personal experience of Mallarmé. Most importantly of all, in the act of naming, the *ptyx* has been promoted to a proper noun. If, in Mallarmé, it was untranslated, in Jarry it has become untranslatable. By enshrin-ing the term in *Faustroll*, Jarry would inadvertently ensure that the *ptyx* would cease to belong solely to Mallarmé's literary and critical estate. Replicating itself,

[36] Alfred Jarry, *Exploits and Opinions of Doctor Faustroll, Pataphysician: A Neo-Scientific Novel*, trans. Simon Watson Taylor, in *Three Early Novels* (London: Atlas, 2006), pp. 117–218 (pp. 162–3); Alfred Jarry, *Gestes et opinions du docteur Faustroll, pataphysicien*, in *Oeuvres complètes*, 8 vols (Monte Carlo: Éditions du Livre, 1948), i, pp. 195–320 (p. 244).

[37] Symons, *The Symbolist Movement...*, p. 184.

becoming slightly altered at the same time, there is a strain of *ptyx* that would become intimately associated with Jarry.

Thus it came to pass that after Jarry's own death in 1907, pataphysics, his fictional science—the science of imaginary solutions; the science of exceptions—began to take on a life of its own.[38] In the 1920s and 30s, René Daumal, falling in and out with the Surrealists, saw in its paradoxes the basis of his own emerging mysticism.[39] Then, on 11 May 1948, in Adrienne Monnier's bookshop in Paris, the Collège de 'Pataphysique—the long-running avant-garde collective which has seen Marcel Duchamp, Jean Baudrillard, and Umberto Eco among its members—came into being. According to the official history of the Collège, those present at its foundation were Oktav Votka, Maurice Saillet, Mélanie le Plumet, and Jean-Hugues Sainmont.[40] It is a claim, however, which typifies the Collège's mischievous relationship with the archival record. Votka, le Plumet, and Sainmont are all pseudonyms for the same person: Emmanuel Peillet. It is easy to see how, in its semantic uncertainty, the *ptyx* should exemplify the type of epistemological slipperiness which is effectively the founding principle of pataphysics, and it is unsurprising then that another of the Collège's founder members, Dr Irénée-Louis Sandomir (another pseudonym for Peillet) should pen an etymological exegesis of the word in one of the Collège's internal publications.[41]

Sandomir's essay is an exemplary instance of the type of 'learned and inutilious research' which the Collège declares as its *raison d'être*.[42] It hinges on the caveat with which *ptyx* appears in Liddell-Scott-Jones, namely that none of the extant classical sources which use the term actually uses it in the precise form *ptyx*, which would be the nominative singular. We can find forms *ptykhos*, *ptykhi*, *ptykha*, and infer by declension rules that there must have been a form *ptyx*, but *ptyx* itself is absent from the record.

> Thus the word *ptyx* exists and doesn't exist. It cannot be found in any of the currently known literature; but it is a necessary form and one without mystery. This means that we simply can't talk about it in terms of uncertainty, but equally we can't speak of its reality. Here is something much more striking than the imaginary we imagined.[43]

---

[38] Jarry, *Doctor Faustroll*, p. 145.

[39] See, for example, René Daumal and Julien Torma, *Pataphysical Letters*, trans. Dennis Duncan and Terry Hale (London: Atlas, 2012); René Daumal, *Pataphysical Essays*, trans. Thomas Vosteen (Cambridge, MA: Wakefield, 2012).

[40] Alastair Brotchie, ed., *A True History of the College of 'Pataphysics*, trans. Paul Edwards (London: Atlas, 1995), p. 11.

[41] Irénée-Louis Sandomir, 'Exégèse du mot *ptyx*', *Opus Pataphysicum* 86 (1959): 91–5.

[42] Brotchie, *A True History of the College of 'Pataphysics*, p. 77.

[43] Irénée-Louis Sandomir, 'Exegesis of the Word *Ptyx*', trans. Dennis Duncan, *Journal of the London Institute of 'Pataphysics* 4 (2011): 13–16 (p. 13).

Ptyx then exists in an in-between space—part fact, part conjecture; a liminal zone of certainty without proof—that is the natural territory of pataphysics. In much of its organization (its rituals; its intricate hierarchy of dataries, satraps, and provediteurs) the Collège is modelled in parody of large-scale social institutions. Like Christianity, Judaism, and Islam, it has a calendar of its own, based on the birthday of Alfred Jarry (8 September 1873), with thirteen months of twenty-eight or twenty-nine days each, each month with a name taken from Jarry's works. So what we might call 1 January 2000 CE, to the Pataphysician would be 4 Décervelage [Disembraining], 127. Not only that, but just as the Christian liturgical year is organized into its calendar of saints' days, so every day of the Pataphysical year is the feast of something or other. The second day of the year—9 September (vulg.)—is the feast of the Abolition of St Ptyx the Silentiary. It is also the date of Mallarmé's death.

What we are seeing here is a third way for the *ptyx*, neither nonsense nor non-translation, but something different. Firstly, in Jarry's *Faustroll*, individuation—the proper-noun Ptyx, its own unique island—then, within the Collège, sanctification. In the pataphysical world, the *ptyx* is protected from becoming trapped in the ordinary codes of signification. And yet Derrida's comments on the proper noun *Babel* are also ideally suited to *Ptyx*:

> Now, a proper name as such remains forever untranslatable, a fact that may lead one to conclude that it does not strictly belong [...] to the language, to the system of the language, be it translated or translating.[44]

But, Derrida continues, *Babel*'s proper noun status is problematic: it both names a place and describes a state, the former deriving from the latter.[45] The pataphysical *Ptyx*, presents exactly the same duality: it *is* a name now—and thus untranslatable—but the name, and its significance, come directly from its earlier life as a common noun—its ancestral DNA which persists within it. Another dual citizenship then—between naming and meaning—for the always-in-between *ptyx*.

The pataphysical gesture of sublimating a term from common noun to saint's name offers the perfect example of what C. K. Ogden, across the Channel, was describing as 'word magic'.[46] A lengthy chapter, penned by Ogden, of the 1923

---

[44] Jacques Derrida, 'Des Tours de Babel', in *Difference in Translation*, ed. and trans. Joseph F. Graham (Ithaca, NY: Cornell University Press, 1985), pp. 165–207 (p. 171).

[45] The story as it appears in Genesis implies that the tower's name is derived from the Hebrew verb *balal*, to mix: 'Therefore is the name of it called Babel: because the Lord did there confound the language of all the earth' (Gen. 11:9). (Modern philologists would label this a folk-etymology, however; the name is thought to come from the Akkadian meaning 'Gate of God'.)

[46] Initially outlined at considerable length in C. K. Ogden and I. A. Richards, *The Meaning of Meaning: A Study of the Influence of Language upon Thought and of the Science of Symbolism* (London: Kegan Paul, 1923), and developed further in C. K. Ogden, 'The Magic of Words', *Psyche* 14 (1934): 9–88, and C. K. Ogden, 'Word Magic', *Psyche* 18 (1938): 19–95. References given here are from the abbreviated discussion in the second edition of *The Meaning of Meaning* (London: Kegan Paul, 1927).

work *The Meaning of Meaning* argues that the words of a language, and certain words in particular, acquire a connotative value—what Ogden terms an 'affective resonance'—above their straightforward meaning.[47] Vincent Sherry eloquently summarizes Ogden and Richards's position as the critique of

> a mode of verbal sensitivity that has reduced language, in effect, to a series of material vibrations. Under this critical heading, the separate counters in a linguistic construction operate like notes in a musical score. The individual words move the auditor/reader into those subcurrents of feeling that are more powerful than an idea or a meaning attached consciously [...] to the logos.[48]

Furthermore, for Ogden and Richards, this enchantment with the non-semantic quality of words—'the carapace, the verbal husk': what we might now call the signifier—has had disastrous effects for society.[49] In the wake of the First World War, the authors clearly held word magic responsible for more than just problems in philosophy: 'In some ways the twentieth century suffers more grievously than any previous age from the ravages of such verbal superstitions.'[50]

At its simplest, we might see the 'Word Magic' section of *The Meaning of Meaning* as a critique which is deeply hostile to modernist non-translation. After all, why embed a word untranslated from its original language into your poem if not to draw on the affective power of doing so—of its sound, of the connotative implications of its source culture? But poetry belongs to a different ethical order to philosophy: its commitment is not to unambiguous expression. Mallarmé's desire that the poet 'Donner un sens plus pur aux mots de la tribu' ('Le tombeau d'Edgar Poe')—'purify the dialect of the tribe' as Eliot translates it in 'Little Gidding'—implies a different mission to that of language reformers like Ogden and Richards.[51] And one need not look far in Richards's poetry criticism to find that the characteristics he admires in, say, Eliot are close to those he and Ogden excoriate in other types of writing.[52]

---

[47] Ogden and Richards, *Meaning of Meaning*, 2nd edn, p. 42.

[48] Vincent Sherry, *The Great War and the Language of Modernism* (Oxford: Oxford University Press, 2003), p. 72.

[49] Ogden and Richards, *Meaning of Meaning*, 2nd edn, p. 42.

[50] Ogden and Richards, *Meaning of Meaning*, 2nd edn, p. 29.

[51] Ogden and Richards would soon be engaged in their own project to purify the dialect of their tribe by means of Basic English, a form of English stripped down to 850 words in which all things should nevertheless remain communicable. See, for example, the good-humoured *chutzpah* of Ogden's 'Anna Livia Plurabelle' translation (C. K. Ogden, 'James Joyce's Anna Livia Plurabelle in Basic English', *transition* 21 (1932): 259–62).

[52] See, for example, 'Mr. Eliot's Poems', *New Statesman* (20 February 1926): 584–5: 'Only those unfortunate persons who are incapable of reading poetry can resist Mr. Eliot's rhythms. The poem as a whole may elude us while every fragment, as a fragment, comes victoriously home' (p. 585). Vincent Sherry also points out the self-unravelling nature of Ogden and Richards's critique which, thanks to their urbane, literate, and allusive writing style, reveals the appeal of the principle they set out to reject.

There is a strand of modernist non-translation then that draws on the word magic which exists in tongues other than its own. '*Shantih shantih shantih*': it plays on the quasi-mystical implications of unfamiliar language, importing this occult power into a literary culture which has come to reject the traditional forms of religious incantation (the Latin mass or the rote-learned psalms and services). Reading Mallarmé's *ptyx* as Charpentier and Noulet would have us, this is exactly the type of word magic at play in the 'Sonnet en *yx*', where a word from classical Greek that might have been translated instead wasn't, its foreignness deployed as an overtone, resonating above the strict semantic meaning of the poem. If, rather, we allow that Mallarmé intended to invent the word himself, it seems there is a more powerful form of word magic at play. The emphasis now falls on the form, the carapace, of the word: its sound, its appearance—an unusual, Hellenic cluster of letters. Sense is reduced to something nebulous, something that can only be guessed at by extrapolating from the words around it. But it falls to the Pataphysicians to turn the *ptyx* into word magic's limit case, isolating it from its surroundings, declaring it a one-off, making it explicitly mystical. In its canonization as a saint whose only history is as a jug, a book, a line of poetry, the magical, mystical *ptyx* has become not a conch, but a shell without a kernel.

4

'Orts, Scraps, and Fragments': Translation, Non-Translation, and the Fragments of Ancient Greece

Nora Goldschmidt

In 1916, Ezra Pound published a short poem entitled 'Papyrus':[1]

> Spring.......
> Too long......
> Gongula......

Hugh Kenner traced the poem's genealogy in *The Pound Era*.[2] Alerted to the discovery of new fragments of Sappho from his reading of Richard Aldington's 'To Atthis (After the Manuscript of Sappho, now in Berlin)', Pound based his poem on another Sappho fragment (now fragment 95 Lobel-Page) derived from the same source. The Greek original was found in 1896, not on papyrus but on a scrap of sixth- or seventh-century parchment sent to Berlin from Egypt, which had been newly published for an English audience in the 1909 issue of *The Classical Review*, supplemented by J. M. Edmonds and accompanied by a fulsome English translation.[3]

Ignoring the better-preserved bulk of the poem where the parchment fragment widens, Pound 'translated' the three words at the top of the fragment (lines 2–4), so indecipherable that even Edmonds with all his 'tushery' overlooked them in his translation:[4]

---

[1] Ezra Pound, *Lustra* (London: E. Matthews, 1916), p. 57.

[2] Hugh Kenner, *The Pound Era* (Berkeley and Los Angeles: University of California, 1973), pp. 54–66.

[3] J. M. Edmonds, 'More Fragments of Sappho', *The Classical Review* 23.5 (1909): 156–8. Wilhelm Schubart had published a transcription in 1902 along with images of the frayed parchment ('Neue Bruchstücke der Sappho und des Alkaios', *Sitzungsberichte der Königlich Preussischen Akademie der Wissenschaften* (Berlin, 1902): 195–206) and again in W. Schubart and U. von Wilamowitz-Moellendorff, eds, *Lyrische und dramatische Fragmente*, *Berliner Klassikertexte* v (Berlin: Weidmannsche Buchhandlung, 1907), pp. 10–18.

[4] The Greek text is from Edmonds's article; for his 'tushery', see Kenner, *The Pound Era*, pp. 54–5. David Campbell's *Greek Lyric* (Cambridge, MA: Harvard University Press, 1990), vol. i, p. 118, omits lines 1–3 from the Greek text altogether.

Nora Goldschmidt, *'Orts, Scraps, and Fragments': Translation, Non-Translation, and the Fragments of Ancient Greece* In: *Modernism and Non-Translation*. Edited by: Jason Harding and John Nash, Oxford University Press (2019). © the several contributors. DOI: 10.1093/oso/9780198821441.003.0004

ἦρ' ἀ[. . . . . .
δῆρα τό[. . . . .
Γογγύλα τ[. . . .

Like several other classical 'translations' produced by modernist writers, 'Papyrus' has been taken as a literal translation in the conventional mould and subjected to the game of 'Dr Syntax and Mr Pound'.[5] Wilhelm Seelbach, noting the connection a year before Kenner, complained that even the three words of Pound's translation were philologically suspect. The first word, which Pound takes as a contracted form of ἔαρ ('spring'), may not be a noun at all, while the word Pound takes as δηρός ('long', 'too long') should rightly be δᾱρός in Sappho's Lesbian Aeolic dialect.[6] Yet 'Papyrus' is notable, above all, not for what it translates, but for what it leaves out. Where Edmonds had supplemented, Pound deliberately emphasizes loss, omitting the bulk of the surviving text and pointing specifically to the material conditions of broken textual transmission: the scrappy parchment, captured in the title's term 'papyrus', and the punctuation echoing the editorial habit of underdotting to mark traces of uncertainty as well as absence.[7] This is not Sappho as she may have been in sixth-century Lesbos, it is Sappho as she survives (or fails to survive) on a tattered parchment in the twentieth century.[8]

Kenner's insights have now become fully assimilated into mainstream scholarship from the history of papyrology to the poetry of H. D.: Pound and his circle, it is now commonly acknowledged, were influenced by the discovery and dissemination of the fragmentary remains of classical texts, and specifically of Sappho.[9] For Kenner

[5] For 'Dr Syntax and Mr Pound', see Robert Graves's satire in *The Crowning Privilege* (London: Cassell, 1955), pp. 212–24. The same game barred Aldington's 'Atthis' poem from publication in Harriet Monroe's *Poetry*, after she sent it to a professor of Greek who 'wouldn't stand for it' (Kenner, *The Pound Era*, p. 55).

[6] Wilhelm Seelbach, 'Ezra Pound und Sappho fr. 95 L.-P. ', *Antike und Abendland* 16.1 (1970): 83–4, esp. 84 n.5, conceding that there are exceptions for the latter point, primarily within Homeric contexts. Pound's source was identified earlier still by Achilles Fang, 'A Note on Pound's "Papyrus"', *Modern Language Notes* 67.3 (March 1952): 188–90, and N. E. Collinge, 'Gongyla and Mr. Pound', *Notes and Queries* 203 (June 1958): 265–6.

[7] For the echo in Pound's poem of papyrological practice when 'the editor feels doubt....', see Dirk Obbink, 'Vanishing Conjecture: Lost Books and their recovery from Aristotle to Eco', in *Culture in Pieces: Essays on Ancient Texts in Honour of Peter Parsons*, ed. Dirk Obbink and Richard Rutherford (Oxford: Oxford University Press, 2011), pp. 20–49 (p. 21 n.6). The original publication in *Lustra* included three full points, indicative of ellipses, but later editions correct to several more.

[8] The move towards emphasizing textual loss and doubt in translation is not alien to translations of Sappho before Pound's intervention: H. T. Wharton's *Sappho*, which Pound knew and praised as 'the classic achievement' (To Iris Barry, ?20 July 1916, *The Letters of Ezra Pound, 1907–1941*, ed. D. D. Paige (London: Faber and Faber, 1951), p. 137), included photographs of damaged parchment scraps from earlier finds from Egypt, one of which is rendered partly in Wharton's translation like a proto-modernist poem: '...soul...altogether...I should be able...to flash back...fair face...stained over...friend', with a further note alerting readers that 'in the absence of any contexts the meaning of the separate words is uncertain' (H. T. Wharton, *Sappho: Memoir, Text and Selected Renderings with a Literal Translation* (London: John Lane, 1885), p. 180, p. 177).

[9] For mainstream classical scholarship, see, e.g., Obbink, n.7, this chapter; Felix Budelmann, ed., *The Cambridge Companion to Greek Lyric* (Cambridge: Cambridge University Press, 2009), pp. 366–7;

and others the narrative largely ends there: 'which is all of the story, like a torn papyrus. That is how the past exists, phantasmagoric weskits, stray words, random things recorded.'[10] But the impact of Greek fragments and their translation and non-translation in the cultures and idioms of modernism is richer and more complex than that partial story suggests. Recent studies have emphasized the ways in which, in other spheres, archaeological finds impacted on modernist consciousness: from Arthur Evans' digs of 'the Minotaur's labyrinth' at Knossos to Freud's compulsion for antiquity, to the art and artefacts from Asia, Africa, and the Pacific Islands displayed in London museums, Anglo-American modernism was embedded in a cultural turn whereby the global activities of archaeologists and curators were increasingly impinging on the public imagination.[11]

That cultural turn encompassed not just the material cultures of the past, but the textual cultures of antiquity, too. At the turn of the century, archaeological discoveries of lost poetry from Ancient Greece were unleashed onto popular public consciousness, while the fruits of philology and epigraphy found in citation fragments collected in scholarly editions, and fragments literally or figuratively inscribed on stone all fed an omnivorous appetite among modernist writers for the fragments of antiquity and the processes of material and cultural transmission which their survival into modernity involved. This chapter focuses on some key examples of fragmentary translation and non-translation of ancient Greek texts in modernist writing which engage with the processes of textual and cultural transmission. In some cases, the ancient languages are translated into English and in some cases they are left in the original Greek. What is crucial is the question of transmission and its failure. Virginia Woolf, who had studied Ancient Greek, famously asserted that we cannot know Greek: even with the benefits of education we can never truly have access to the past, since Greece 'ceased to exist about the year one A. D.'[12] For modernist writers, even when they translated the words, the fragment form, and the choice of fragmentary text, could become a way of dramatizing 'non-translation' in the broader sense of non-transmission, a failure

for H. D., see Eileen Gregory, *H. D. and Hellenism: Classic Lines* (Cambridge: Cambridge University Press, 1997), p. 150.

---

[10] Kenner, *The Pound Era*, p. 5.

[11] Cathy Gere, *Knossos and the Prophets of Modernism* (Chicago and London: University of Chicago Press, 2009); Richard H. Armstrong, *A Compulsion for Antiquity: Freud and the Ancient World* (Ithaca, NY: Cornell University Press, 2005); Rupert Arrowsmith, *Modernism and the Museum* (Oxford: Oxford University Press, 2011).

[12] Virginia Woolf, 'On Not Knowing Greek', in *The Common Reader, First Series* (London: Hogarth Press, 1984), pp. 23–38; 'A Vision of Greece', June 27, 1906 (MH/A21.i, Monks House Papers, University of Sussex). On Virginia Woolf and Greece, see esp. Rowena Fowler, 'Moments and Metamorphoses: Virginia Woolf's Greece', *Comparative Literature* 51.3 (Summer 1999): 217–42; Rowena Fowler, 'On Not Knowing Greek: The Classics and the Woman of Letters', *Classical Journal* 78 (1983): 337–49; and Theodore Koulouris, *Hellenism and Loss in the Work of Virginia Woolf* (London and New York: Routledge, 2010).

not just to 'carry across' between languages, but between cultures and times. Whether they translate the Greek words or not, mimicking the texts of antiquity in the material conditions in which they pertain in modernity becomes a way of finding affinities for (to borrow one of Woolf's favourite phrases) the 'orts, scraps and fragments' of modern experience.[13]

Papyrus

In 1896, on the cusp of the twentieth century, two Oxford archaeologists, Bernard Grenfell and Arthur Hunt, began to excavate the previously neglected Egyptian city of Oxyrhynchus.[14] Little was left of the architectural remains of 'the city of sharp-nosed fish', as its name translates. The buildings and houses had been quarried for their stone and the archaeological remains initially seemed to them to be 'nothing but rubbish mounds'. However it soon transpired that, because of the unique Egyptian climate, what seemed like scrap paper—and often was, including private letters, receipts, contracts, horoscopes, and other debris of everyday life—in fact, also contained lost poems from ancient Greece, including hitherto unknown fragments of Sappho and lost plays by Euripides and Sophocles. As Grenfell put it, 'the flow of papyri soon became a torrent… [and] merely turning up the soil with one's boot would frequently disclose a layer'.[15]

Adding detail to Kenner's genealogy of Pound's 'Papyrus', Eileen Gregory has described how the finds of the Egypt Exploration Fund, who financed the digs, filtered into H. D's consciousness, and through her into the consciousnesses of the young Richard Aldington, and on to Pound, via *The Classical Review* and

[13] Virginia Woolf, *Between the Acts* (London: The Hogarth Press, 1941), p. 188. The phrase appears elsewhere in Woolf's work in various permutations. Cf. Shakespeare, *Troilus and Cressida*, V.ii.161–2.

[14] See Sir Eric Turner, 'The Graeco-Roman Branch', in *Excavating in Egypt: The Egypt Exploration Society, 1882–1982*, ed. T. G. H. James (London: British Museum Publications, 1983), pp. 161–78; Alan K. Bowman et al., eds, *Oxyrhynchus: A City and its Texts* (London: Egyptian Exploration Society, 2007); Peter Parsons, *City of the Sharp-Nosed Fish: Greek Papyri Beneath the Egyptian Sand Reveal a Long-Lost World* (London: Phoenix, 2007); Hélène Cuvigny, 'The Finds of Papyri: The Archaeology of Papyrology', in *The Oxford Handbook of Papyrology*, ed. Roger S. Bagnall (Oxford: Oxford University Press, 2009), pp. 30–58; David Gange, *Dialogues with the Dead: Egyptology in British Culture and Religion, 1822–1922* (Oxford: Oxford University Press, 2013), pp. 251–6; for the media coverage, see Dominic Montserrat, 'News Reports: The Excavations and their Journalistic Coverage' in Bowman et al., eds, *Oxyrhynchus: A City and its Texts*, pp. 23–39.

[15] B. P. Grenfell, 'Oxyrhynchus and its Papyri', *Archaeological Report (Egypt Explorations Fund)* (1896–7): 1–12 (p. 7). Sophocles' satyr play, *Ichneutai* ('Trackers'), combined with the story of Grenfell and Hunt, forms the basis for Tony Harrison's 1988 play, *The Trackers of Oxyrhynchus*. The pair also discovered a papyrus early on containing the 'Sayings of Jesus' (*Logia Iesou*, later identified as deriving from the uncanonical *Gospel of Thomas*), and the Christian drive behind the digs, though it appealed less to modernist poets, was a dominant theme in the popular reception of the finds: see Montserrat, 'News Reports' in Bowman et al. *Oxyrhynchus*, pp. 28–39; and Gange, *Dialogues with the Dead*, pp. 251–6, for the excavations as 'one product of the extensive cultural involvement with the early Church' in the period (p. 251).

J. M. Edmonds.[16] H. D. had visited the British Library in 1912 for the classically trained Richard Aldington, who at the time was too young to use it, in order to transcribe Edmonds's articles in a number of classical journals, where not only Pound's Berlin parchment, but also Grenfell and Hunt's Sappho fragments had been published, restored and translated.[17] As a result, Aldington's 'To Atthis' (fragment 96, Lobel-Page) was eventually published by Pound in *Des Imagistes* (1914), but H. D. herself, though she was struck by the image of scholars 'searching to find a precious inch of palimpsest among the funereal glories of the sand-strewn Pharaohs', never dared to quote openly from the new finds.[18]

The focus on Pound and his circle in the exclusive hallows of the old British Library, however, fundamentally underestimates the wider impact of The Egypt Exploration Funds' digs at Oxyrhynchus. Far from being confined to the closed doors of modernist eclecticism, Grenfell and Hunt's finds gripped the public imagination. What surrounded Oxyrhynchus became, in effect, what Dominic Montserrat describes as the first 'media circus' around an Egyptological event.[19] The diggers began publishing their results accompanied by images and translations in *The Oxyrhynchus Papyri*, Part I of which, containing the *Logia Iesou* and a lost Sappho poem, was featured as one of the 'Books of the Week' in *The Times* within a year of its publication.[20] Digests of the published finds increasingly appeared in daily newspapers, bringing an event which, as one reviewer put it, had the potential 'to join…the hands of then and now' to the breakfast tables of Britain.[21] Along with others associated with their digs, Grenfell and Hunt delivered public lectures illustrated by magic-lantern slides and wrote vivid accounts of their discoveries published in the popular illustrated press, *The Times*, and the *Athenaeum*. One such public lecture, by James Hope Moulton, later published as *From the Rubbish-heaps of Egypt* (1916), may have left its mark on the 'old dumplan' of 'festering rubbages' at the heart of Joyce's *Finnegans Wake*.[22] But the

---

[16] Pound also published 'Ἰμέρρω' in *Lustra*, which derives, like Aldington's poem, from fragment 96 Lobel-Page. For another possible allusion in Pound to this and a fragment of Julius Afranius found at Oxyrhynchus (*P. Oxy.* 412), see Ahuvia Kahane, 'Blood for the Ghosts? Homer, Ezra Pound, and Julius Afranius', *New Literary History* 30.4 (1999): 815–36.

[17] Gregory, *H. D. and Hellenism*, p. 150.

[18] H. D., 'The Wise Sappho', in *Notes on Thought and Vision & The Wise Sappho* (San Francisco: City Lights, 1982), p. 69; Gregory, *H. D. and Hellenism*, p. 150. There is one exception: a cryptic allusion to a fragment of Sappho published in 1922 in the epigraph to 'Choros Sequence/ from *Morpheus*' (1927), 'Dream—Dark-winged'. As Gregory points out, 'H.D. does not acknowledge Sappho as she does in the other poems' (p. 150), but her epigraph seems to echo an Oxyrhynchus fragment, originally published in the *Oxyrhynchus Papyri* 1922 and later by Edgar Lobel in Σαπφοῦς μέλη: *The Fragments of the Lyrical Poems of Sappho* (Oxford: The Clarendon Press, 1925), pp. 28–9 (now 63 Lobel-Page).

[19] Montserrat, 'News Reports', p. 28.

[20] *The Times*, 29 July 1898, cited Parsons, *City of the Sharp-Nosed Fish*, p. 1.

[21] Montserrat, 'News Reports', 28.

[22] James Hope Moulton, *From the Rubbish-heaps of Egypt: Five Popular Lectures on the New Testament* (London: Charles H. Kelly, 1916); James Joyce, *Finnegans Wake* (London: Faber and Faber, 1939), p. 79, lines 28–29, 31. (Subsequent references given as *FW* followed by page and line numbers.)

Oxyrhynchus circus also influenced more popular cultural outputs, including Owen Hall's musical comedy, *A Greek Slave*, performed 349 times between 1898 and 1899, which featured Heliodorus the wizard, whom the Chorus describe—echoing a much publicized discovery by Grenfell and Hunt of ancient papyri inside the sarcophagi of mummified crocodiles—as 'a marvel of a mage/ Through reading the papyrus of a page/ From the gummy little tummy of a rummy sort of mummy/ He's the mightiest magician of the age.'[23] Norma Lorimer's Egyptological thriller, *The Wife Out of Egypt*, meanwhile, reprinted twenty times between 1913 and 1922 in the UK and America, featured an archaeologist who shows the hero-ine, Stella Adair, a 'deliciously human' papyrus letter taken straight out of the first part of *The Oxyrhynchus Papyri*.[24] It is from this cultural enthusiasm for ancient texts found by chance in the scrap-heaps of Egypt—beyond Edmonds, the *Classical Review* and the old British Library—that Pound's 'Papyrus' emerges.

Editions

While long-lost texts on papyrus scraps were embedded in the contemporary popular imagination, more abstruse sources of Greek fragments impinged on modernist consciousness, too. Though lost to modernity, works which were not copied could nevertheless be partially recovered in fragmentary form through the quotations of other writers who did survive. The collection of these citation frag-ments and testimonia into editions was one of the central scholarly activities of the nineteenth and early twentieth centuries. One set of texts that came to prom-inence through this type of collection was the fragments of the so-called 'pre-Socratic' philosophers, collected by Hermann Diels in *Die Fragmente der Vorsokratiker*, first published in 1903.[25] Diels' edition, in particular, was instru-mental in transmitting the fragments of early Greek philosophy into modernist writing and modernist practices of translation and its absence. A fragment of Anaximander, taken specifically from Diels, provided the basis of Heidegger's 1946 'Der Spruch des Anaximander', an essay that closes with a radical translation which pushes Heidegger's own German to the limits of intelligibility and attempts

---

For Moulton's lectures and the *Wake*, see Jackson I. Cope, 'From Egyptian Rubbish-Heaps to "Finnegans Wake"', *James Joyce Quarterly* 3.3 (1966): 166–70, noting further a specific analogy made by Moulton (p.6) between the finds and 'an Irishman's coat' (p. 170). Whether or not derived directly from Moulton, the material circumstances of the digs at Oxyrhynchus together with other Egyptian 'discoveries', notably 'The Papyrus of Ani' (stolen from a government storeroom in Egypt rather than discovered in its sands), run through *Finnegans Wake*.

[23]   Montserrat, 'News Reports', p. 28.
[24]   Norma Lorimer, *The Wife out of Egypt* (New York: Brentano's, 1913), cited Parsons, *City of the Sharp-nosed Fish*, p. 24.
[25]   Hermann Diels, *Die Fragmente der Vorsokratiker*, 1st edn (Berlin: Weidmannsche Buchhandlung, 1903). Diels' edition, revised by Walther Kranz, is still standard.

to let the Greek fragment 'speak for itself', moving it 'away from us into what is strange and estranging'.[26]

Diels' edition, however, and the 'strange and estranging' fragments it contained had already infiltrated the modernist canon. Two fragments of Heraclitus, specifically cited from Diels, form the epigraph to 'Burnt Norton' in T. S. Eliot's *Four Quartets*:

τοῦ λόγου δ' ἐόντος ξυνοῦ ζώουσιν οἱ πολλοί
ὡς ἰδίαν ἔχοντες φρόνησιν.

I. p. 77. Fr. 2.

ὁδὸς ἄνω κάτω μία καὶ ὠυτή.

I. p. 89. Fr. 60.
Diels: Die Fragmente der Vorsokratiker *(Herakleitos)*.

Eliot gives the Greek—without translation—but he also meticulously gives the fragment number and page number from Diels' edition, such that the edition and referencing derived from it take up almost as much space on the page as the Greek text. Translating roughly as 'although the Word (Logos) is common, the many live as though they had a private understanding' and 'the way up and the way down are one and the same', Heraclitus' words are themselves cryptic, an obscurity compounded by the untranslated Greek: as Eliot explained in a letter to Hermann Peschmann, 'the original Greek...preserves their delightful obscurity'.[27] But the prominence of Diels' edition brings to the fore not just the difficulties of translation, but the difficulties of transmission. Diels' version of Heraclitus seemed exceptionally fragmentary to contemporary readers. John Burnet complained in his English translation of the pre-Socratics (which Eliot owned and read), that Diels' presentation of Heraclitus made it seem as if 'Herekleitos wrote like Nietzsche', and preferred to use an earlier edition instead.[28] But what might seem like aphoristic incoherence of the transmitted fragments also emphasizes the loss of the whole. As they stand, particularly in Diels' arrangement, Heraclitus' words, as Eliot saw, 'have an extraordinarily poetic suggestiveness' which would 'lose in value if we had his complete works and saw the sentences in their context'.[29] Eliot's

[26] Martin Heidegger, 'The Incipient Saying of Being in the Fragment of Anaximander' in *Basic Concepts*, trans. Gary E. Aylesworth (Bloomington: Indiana University Press, 1998), pp. 81–106 (p. 82). Heidegger's essay is frequently cited in handbooks of translation, e.g. Lawrence Venuti, *The Translation Studies Reader*, 3rd edn (London and New York: Routledge, 2012), p. 110.

[27] Letter dated 12 September 1945, and Eliot's annotated copy of Diels, in *The Poems of T. S. Eliot*, 2 vols, ed. Christopher Ricks and Jim McCue (London: Faber and Faber/Baltimore: John Hopkins University Press), I, p. 906.

[28] John Burnet, *Early Greek Philosophy*, 2nd edn (London: Adam and Charles Black, 1908), p. 146 n.1. Eliot's copy of the 2nd edition (1908) is now held in the library of Magdalene College, Cambridge.

[29] Letter to Raymond Preston, 9 August 1945, cited Ricks and McCue, *The Poems of T. S. Eliot*, I, p. 906.

version of Diels' Heraclitus estranges Heraclitus' words even further from their original context: the transmitted version of the first fragment (B2 in Diels) is longer by ten words than the portion Eliot quotes. The presence of the edition itself on Eliot's page, however, brings home not only the fragmentary condition of Heraclitus' text, but the complex transmission through which it makes its way by a hair's breadth, in pieces, into modernity. In contrast to Burnet, who never gives the citing source, Diels introduces each fragment with a reference to the source from which it was taken: the first fragment Eliot quotes does not contain the words of Heraclitus 'pure', but the words of Heraclitus as cited by Sextus Empiricus in the second century AD, while the second fragment, B60, is extracted from the Christian theologian Hippolytus of Rome's *Refutation of all Heresies*. As Eliot's citation of Diels makes clear, even the untranslated Greek words on the page are not and never can be the 'original' words of Heraclitus, but the words of Heraclitus fragmented through textual transmission and garnered up by Diels. The past comes to us in pieces, through the voices of other writers. Printed in some editions as an epigraph to the whole sequence of *Four Quartets*, the Heraclitus-Diels epigraph functions as an analogue to Eliot's own poetics. While Heraclitus' sayings seem to stress unity in apparent fragmentation, his editor's task, bringing together temporally and culturally disparate fragments, enacts 'the fight to recover what has been lost/And found and lost again and again'.[30]

Inscriptions

Another scholarly enterprise that dominated the nineteenth and early twentieth centuries, and which likewise found its way into the fragmentary aesthetics of modernism in contexts of both translation and non-translation, is the transcription and decipherment of texts inscribed on stone. Like papyrus, inscriptions bring to the fore the materiality of transmission and loss in transmission. As text written on stone and mimicked in transcription, they also sit on the cusp of literary and material culture. Fragmented, damaged or lost, written on stone, or imagined as written on stone, inscriptional and pseudo-inscriptional texts, just as much as papyrus or editions of fragments, can dramatize the processes of textual and cultural transmission.

---

[30] T. S. Eliot, 'East Coker' V, in *Collected Poems, 1909–1962* (London: Faber and Faber, 1963), p. 203. For the textual history of Eliot's Heraclitus quotations, which appeared as epigraph to the whole book in the 1979 edition, see Ricks and McCue, *The Poems of T. S. Eliot*, I, p. 905.

In Alexandria, in 1917 (the year after Pound's 'Papyrus'), C. P. Cavafy published *Ἐν τῷ μηνὶ Ἀθύρ* ('In the Month of Athyr'), an English translation of which came out five years later in E. M. Forster's *Pharoahs and Pharillon*:[31]

Μὲ δυσκολία διαβάζω	στὴν πέτρα τὴν ἀρχαία.
«Κύ[ρι]ε Ἰησοῦ Χριστέ».	Ἕνα «Ψυ[χ]ὴν» διακρίνω.
«Ἐν τῷ μη[νὶ] Ἀθύρ»	«Ὁ Λεύκιο[ς] ἐ[κοιμ]ήθη».
Στὴ μνεία τῆς ἡλικίας	«Ἐβί[ωσ]εν ἐτῶν»,
τὸ Κάππα Ζῆτα δείχνει	ποῦ νέος ἐκοιμήθη.
Μὲς στα φθαρμένα βλέπω	«Αὐτό[ν]... Ἀλεξανδρέα».
Μετά ἔχει τρεῖς γραμμὲς	πολὺ ἀκρωτηριασμένες·
μὰ κάτι λέξεις βγάζω —	σὰν «δ[ά]κρυα ἡμῶν»,
	«ὀδύνην»,
κατόπιν πάλι «δάκρυα»,	καὶ «[ἡμ]ῖν τοῖς [φ]ίλοις
	πένθος».
Μὲ φαίνεται ποῦ ὁ Λεύκιος	μεγάλως θ' αγαπήθη.
Ἐν τῷ μηνὶ Ἀθύρ	ὁ Λεύκιος ἐκοιμήθη.
With difficulty I read	upon the ancient stone:
'LO[R]D JESUS CHRIST.'	I discern a 'SO[U]L'
'IN THE MON[TH] OF ATHYR'	'LEUCIUS WAS LAID TO SL[EE]P.'
Where the age is mentioned	'HE LI[VE]D TO THE AGE OF'
The Kappa Zeta shows	he was laid to sleep so young.
In the abraded part I see	'HI[M]...ALEXANDRIAN.'
There follow three lines	quite mutilated;
And then once more 'TEARS'	and 'TO [U]S HIS FRIENDS BEREAVEMENT.'
It seems to me the love	for Leucius was deep.
During the Month of Athyr	Leucius was laid to sleep.

The poem is couched as an epitaph for the fictional Leukios or Lefkios who died during the month of Athyr, the third month of the ancient Egyptian calendar, named after the goddess of tombs and physical love. Though written in modern Greek, it has a deliberate air of antiquity, and there is a sense that the damaged

---

[31] E. M. Forster, *Pharaohs and Pharillon* (London: Hogarth Press, 1923), p. 96. The English version given here, which better preserves the typography of the original, is from *C. P. Cavafy: The Collected Poems*, trans. Evangelos Sachperoglou, ed. Anthony Hirst and Peter Mackridge (Oxford: Oxford University Press, 2007), pp. 93–4. On the theme of fragmentation and loss in the poem, see also Gregory Nagy, 'Poetics of Fragmentation in the Athyr Poem of C. P. Cavafy', in *Imagination and Logos: Essays on C. P. Cavafy*, ed. Panagiotis Roilos (Cambridge, MA: Harvard University Press, 2010), pp. 265–72.

'ancient stone' (ἀρχαία... πέτρα) might have come from the early Christian period in Greco-Roman Egypt, as far in the past as some of the papyrus material found in Oxyrhynchus. Typographically, the poem is deliberately set in two separate columns to mimic the materiality of a text inscribed on stone. Cavafy, however, does not simply mimic an inscription but an ancient inscription transcribed using the tools of the epigrapher. As E. M. Forster put it, 'he would convey the obscurity, the poignancy, that sometimes arise together out of the past, entwined into a single ghost.'[32] In order to do so, Cavafy borrows the tools of classical scholars transcribing the damaged traces of the textual monuments of the past, in what Anne Carson, writing almost a century later, would call 'an aesthetic gesture toward the papyrological event rather than an accurate record of it.'[33] Ellipses and square brackets enclose imagined places where words have been lost through physical damage and filled in by editorial conjecture, a quality brought to the fore by the words Μὲ δυσκολία διαβάζω ('with difficulty I read', line 1) in the opening, and the 'very smashed' (πολὺ ἀκρωτηριασμένες) or 'quite mutilated' lines referred to in line 7. Faced with a damaged text, both speaker and reader 'approach... antiquity as an epigrapher, searching for inscriptions between the romanticized layers of textual scholarship.'[34] As with Pound's 'Papyrus', what is prominent in Cavafy's poem is the material condition of transmission from antiquity to the modern world, but rather than, like Pound, translating a mutilated ancient Greek text, Cavafy partially fabricates one.

The fictional materiality of Lefkios' damaged tomb is shared by another pseudo-inscriptional poem, written by Ezra Pound, Part VI of 'Mœurs contemporaines' first published in *The Little Review* in 1918:[35]

VI

Stele

After years of continence
   he hurled himself into a sea of six women.
Now, quenched as the brand of Meleagar,
   he lies by the poluphloisboious sea-coast.
παρὰ θῖνα πολυφλοίσβοιο θαλάσσης
Siste Viator

---

[32] Forster, *Pharaohs and Pharillon*, p. 96.

[33] Anne Carson, *If not, winter: Fragments of Sappho* (Croydon: Virago, 2002), p. xi.

[34] Gregory Jusdanis, 'Farewell to the Classical: Excavations and Modernism', *Modernism/modernity* 11.1 (January 2004): 37–53 (p. 42).

[35] The *Little Review*, where the poem was first published, did not print the Greek at all, but it did appear in the poem's next publication in *Quia Pauper Amavi* (London: The Egoist Press, 1919), p. 17 and subsequent publications. The version given here includes my corrections.

Foregrounding conventional non-translation, the poem prominently includes untranslated Greek and Latin, ending with the Greek παρὰ θῖνα πολυφλοίσβοιο θαλάσσης ('along the shore of the loud-sounding sea') followed by the Latin 'SISTE VIATOR' ('stop traveller'). As he declared in his essay on 'Early Translators of Homer', written in the same year as 'Stele', for Pound, the Greek phrase, which he found in Homer (e.g., *Iliad* 1.34) is 'untranslated and untranslatable', and part of the purpose of the Classical intertexts in this poem is to bring to the fore the untranslatability of 'the magnificent onomatopoeia... of the rush of the waves on the sea-beach and their recession' which even the transliterated neologism *poluphloisboious* in the line above cannot capture.[36] The failure to transmit is embedded in the poem in other ways, too. A stele (Greek στήλη) is a commem-orative pillar, often set up in memory of the dead, carved with text, image or both, and often inscribed with a funerary epigram, which often, as in Pound's 'SISTE VIATOR' (a typographical echo of the capitals common in Latin inscriptions) directly addresses the traveller-as-reader to take part in the commemorative pro-cess. With its title and pseudo-inscriptional Latin, Pound's poem couches itself as a material artefact: a stone pillar inscribed with an epitaph.

The mimicry of stone in text also has a direct ancient precedent, to which Pound's poem gestures. 'The brand of Meleager', on the surface, as Ruthven guides readers, refers to the figure in Greek myth, whose 'life-span was determined by the time it took for a certain fire-brand to be consumed by fire'.[37] But 'Meleager' is also prominently the name of the Alexandrian Anthologizer of epigram, whose *Garland* (now lost) provided the core of what is known as the *Greek Anthology*, a collection of epigrams spanning the classical and Byzantine periods, Book 7 of which is devoted entirely to funerary epigram: poets writing funerary inscrip-tions which sit 'between scroll and marble', giving the illusion of having been carved on stone, but mostly never intended for that purpose.[38] Though not strictly a fragment collection, the aphoristic form of the epigrams, gathered into a 'florile-gium of a long series of decades', as Pound called the collection in a letter to Harriet Monroe, enabled the poems in the *Anthology* to act as quasi-fragments that could readily assimilate into the fragments of modernist aesthetics.[39] While Cavafy was heavily influenced by the collection, popularized by J. W. Mackail's translation *Select Epigrams from the Greek Anthology*, published in 1890 (revised

---

[36] *Literary Essays of Ezra Pound*, 10th edn, ed. T. S. Eliot (London: New Directions, 1968), p. 250. Pound's essay was serialized in the *Egoist* between August 1918 and April 1919; the quotation is from part I, 'Hugues Salel'.

[37] K. K. Ruthven, *A Guide to Ezra Pound's Personae (1926)* (Berkeley and Los Angeles: University of California Press, 1969), p. 172.

[38] For a culture 'between scroll and marble' in Hellenistic poetry, see Peter Bing, *The Scroll and the Marble: Studies in Reading and Reception in Hellenistic Poetry* (Ann Arbor: University of Michigan Press, 2009).

[39] Letter dated 27 March 1931 in *The Letters of Ezra Pound, 1907–1941*, p. 312.

1906) with frequent reprints and later by W. R. Paton in a five-volume Loeb translation (1916–18), the *Anthology* was picked up by several Anglo-American writers.[40] The American poet Edgar Lee Masters used the collection (and specifically Mackail's translation) as an inspiration for his 1915 collection *Spoon River Anthology*; Virginia Woolf was given a copy of Mackail for her twentieth birthday and later reviewed Paton's translation for the *TLS*; Richard Aldington translated from it, and H. D. continually returned to it.[41]

Pound, too, was clearly influenced by the *Greek Anthology*. In 1916, two years before 'Stele', he published, in the magazine *Poetry*, his *Homage to Quintus Septimius Florentis Christianus* (Florent Chrétien) a sixteenth-century translator of *Epigrammata ex libris Graecae Anthologiae* ('Epigrams from the Greek Anthology').[42] In a visual echo of the early modern printed text, Pound's poem is headed *Ex libris Graecae* ('from the books of the Greek—': the reader must supply *Anthologiae* to complete the phrase). In a selection of six epigrams from different authors, ranging from the unknown ('*Incerti Auctoris*') to the obscure ('Nicharchus upon Phidon his doctor'), and from Ancient Greece to early Christianity, Pound presents a series of quasi-fragments taken from different parts of the *Anthology*, including one by Anyte of Tegea, which had also been translated by Richard Aldington the previous year:[43]

II

This place is the Cyprian's, for she has ever the fancy
To be looking out across the bright sea;
Therefore the sailors are cheered, and the waves
Keep small with reverence,
                    beholding her image.

Unlike Aldington's version, Pound's translation of Chrétien's translation is openly, in parts, a non-translation. In a footnote to the original manuscript which he later deleted, Pound noted: 'I am quite well aware that certain lines above have no

[40]   David Ricks, ' "A faint sweetness in the never-ending afternoon"? Reflections on Cavafy and the Greek Epigram', *Κάμπος: Cambridge Papers in Modern Greek* 15 (2007): 149–69. For the importance of Mackail's translation, with which, along with Wharton's Sappho, '[m]embers of H. D.'s generation grew up', see Gregory, *H. D. and Hellenism*, p. 161.

[41]   [Virginia Woolf,] 'The Perfect Language', *TLS*, 24 May 1917, p.247, reprinted in *The Essays of Virginia Woolf, Volume Two 1912–1918*, ed. Andrew McNeillie (New York: Harcourt Brace Jovanovich, 1987), pp. 114–19. Fragment IX, 144 appears in Richard Aldington, 'The Poems of Anyte of Tegea', *The Egoist* II.9 (September 1915): 139–40. For the figure of Meleager in H. D., whose 'anthology represented the consummate instance of preservation and reinscription', see Gregory, *H. D. and Hellenism*, p. 50 *et passim*.

[42]   Quintus Septimius Florentis Christianus, *Epigrammata ex libris Graecae Anthologiae* ('Epigrams form the Greek Anthology') (Paris: Robertus Stephanus, 1608); *Poetry: A Magazine of Verse*, 1 September 1916. Generally on Pound's interest in the *Greek Anthology*, cf. H. K. Riikonen, 'Ezra Pound and the Greek Anthology', *Quaderni di Palazzo Serra* 15 (2008): 181–94 (p. 183).

[43]   Pound also makes the obscure even more so, as the first poem, ascribed to an unknown and unknowable author ('*Incerti Auctoris*'), is in fact attributed to the well-known Simonides.

particular relation to the words or meaning of the original.'[44] Chrétien, however, was already distanced from 'the words or meaning of the original', translating into Latin a selection from a collection that was itself already a later composite incorporating earlier composites of the words of the 'original' authors, and even interpolating Chrétien's own fabricated 'Ancient Greek'.[45] Mediated through Chrétien's early modern edition, the *Greek Anthology* offered, for Pound, a quasi-fragmentary form that could emphasize the poetics not just of non-translation but also of non- or partial transmission.

Lexica: on not knowing Greek

The texts of Ancient Greece can be fragmented not only through the facts of transmission, but by the processes involved in translation itself. The philological tools we use to decipher them might seem to provide a key to access the past, a key acquired through education. But those same tools can also become a symbol of limitation, bringing to the fore the mediated nature of the classical past, and leaving it essentially unknowable, untranslatable, and inaccessible. For English-language readers since 1843, *the* philological tool through which Greek texts were accessed was, and still is, *A Greek-English Lexicon* by Henry Liddell (the future father of 'Alice in Wonderland', Alice Liddell) and Robert Scott.[46] On its publication, 'Liddell and Scott'—which took several years to compile—attained the status of cultural myth.[47] Writing in 1898, Thomas Hardy looked back on the moment of completion:

> "Well, though it seems
> Beyond our dreams,"
> Said Liddell to Scott,
> "We've really got
> To the very end,
> All inked and penned
>
> …
>
> This sultry summer day, A.D.
> Eighteen hundred and forty-three".[48]

---

[44] Ruthven, *Guide*, p. 81.

[45] *Epigrammata ex libris Graecae Anthologiae*, p. 7 recto and verso: two epigrams written in Greek by Chrétien with Latin translation by the publisher.

[46] The full title of the first edition was *A Greek-English lexicon based on the German work of Francis Passow* (Oxford: Oxford University Press, 1843).

[47] On the myth of the dictionary, see Christopher Stray, 'Liddell and Scott: Myths and Markets', in *Classical Dictionaries: Past, Present and Future* (London: Duckworth, 2010), pp. 94–118.

[48] Thomas Hardy, 'Liddell and Scott' in *The Variorum Edition of the Complete Poems of Thomas Hardy*, ed. James Gibson (London: Macmillan: 1979), pp. 844–6 (p.844).

Having struggled through *Pi* 'when the end loomed nigh', Liddell and Scott's huge tome (weighing nearly 4kg) went on to achieve an almost concrete physical presence in modernist writing. Mediating the texts of ancient Greece, the dictionary became a symbol of both access to the past and its limitations. For Virginia Woolf, whose library contained three copies, 'Liddell and Scott' epitomized the classical education she laboured to acquire.[49] She remembers how, '[l]eft alone in this great house, father shut in his study... I mounted to my room; spread my Liddell and Scott upon the table, and settled down to read Plato or make out some scene in Euripides or Sophocles for Clara Pater, or Janet Case', recording her lexicographical labours in her reading notebooks.[50] Woolf's philological studies infiltrate her texts, not only in the allusive fabric of her writing, where Greek texts play an important role, but in the concrete presence of the dictionary itself.[51] On the desk of Jacob's room sits 'a Greek dictionary', almost certainly imagined as Liddell and Scott, 'with the petals of poppies pressed to silk between the pages';[52] for Katharine Hilbery in *Night and Day*, 'her father's Greek dictionary' with its 'sacred pages of figures and symbols' becomes part of the world from which she feels alienated, a looming presence on the bookcase between whose pages she can conceal her attempts at mathematics.[53] For all of these readers, whether or not they can decipher its 'figures and symbols', Greek remains unknowable precisely because the dictionary itself in the bedrooms and libraries of Britain can provide us only with partial knowledge. As Woolf came to realize, despite—or perhaps because of—'Liddell and Scott', we are trapped in the double-bind of 'for ever making up some notion of the meaning of Greek' while ultimately alienated from its 'real meaning'.[54]

Liddell and Scott seemed to provide an imperfect key to Ancient Greece for James Joyce, too. Like Stephen Dedalus ('Ah, Dedalus, the Greeks. I must teach you. You must read them in the original'), Joyce, who knew Latin very well, had no formal education in Classical Greek: 'just think', he told a friend, 'isn't that a world I am peculiarly fitted to enter?'[55] Joyce's work, in part, represents a series of attempts or failures to enter that world. Detailed engagement with translations of

[49] Julia King and Laila Miletic-Vejzovic, *The Library of Leonard and Virginia Woolf: A Short-title Catalogue* (Washington: Washington State University Press, 2003), p. 134.

[50] Virginia Woolf, *Moments of Being*, ed. J. Schulkind (London: Pimlico, 2002), p. 150. See also: 'There was the Academy for Nessa; my *Liddell and Scott* and the Greek choruses for me' (p. 129). See Rowena Fowler, 'Virginia Woolf: Lexicographer', *English Language Notes* 39 (2002): 54–70 (p. 56), with n.6 on Liddell and Scott among Woolf's multilingual dictionaries.

[51] For Woolf and Greece, see note 12, this chapter.

[52] Virginia Woolf, *Jacob's Room* (London: Hogarth Press, 1980), p. 37. Thoby Stephen's copy, in Woolf's library, was the intermediate version of Liddell and Scott (1889): *Short-title Catalogue*, p. 134.

[53] Virginia Woolf, *Night and Day* [1919], Definitive Collected Edition (London: Hogarth Press, 1990), pp. 436, 37.

[54] Woolf, 'On Not Knowing Greek', p. 24.

[55] James Joyce, *Ulysses*, 6:16–17: page and line numbers refer to Hans Walter Gabler et al., eds (New York and London: Garland Publishing, 1984); R. J. Schork, *Greek and Hellenic Culture in Joyce* (Gainsville: University Press of Florida, 1998), p. 240.

Greek texts and snatches of famous tags, dropped in transliterated and untranslated—from Homer's wine-dark sea (*'Epi oinopa ponton'*, 6:15–16) to Xenophon's shout of the ten thousand (*'Thalatta! Thalatta!'*, 6:17)—form part of the texture of Joyce's work and of *Ulysses* in particular.[56] But another attempted point of entry came through the tools of philology. Of the two books found on Joyce's desk when he died, one was a 'Greek lexicon', very probably an edition of Liddell and Scott.[57] Joyce's lexicographical research already runs through *Finnegans Wake*. Classical Greek words, their etymologies and the neologisms derived from them are a crucial part of the 'ideoglassary he invented' (*FW* 423.9); but the medium used to decipher them, too, is absorbed into the linguistic texture of the *Wake*.[58] Drawing perhaps from a grammar, perhaps from conversation with Stuart Gilbert, the terminology of Greek philology infiltrates the *Wake*'s language, such as the technical terms for ancient Greek diacritical accents: 'properismenon' (*FW* 59.15–16) (perispomenon); 'Oxatown and baroccidents' (*FW* 288.11) (oxytone and barytone).[59] More significantly, the monumental dictionary of Liddell and Scott itself, the source of the component parts of such untranslated words as 'kalospintheochromatokereening' (*FW* 392.28), a compound of κάλος ('beautiful'), σπινθήρ ('spark'), χρῶμα ('colour') *and* κρήνη ('spring', 'fountain'), seems to reveal itself in the permutations of the book's language, from the 'liddle giddles' (*FW* 448.25) to the 'liddel oud oddity' (*FW* 207.26–7) or the rival Oxford colleges of the editors.[60] The philological labours of Liddell and Scott become subsumed into the language of Joyce's text, not only in the creation of untranslated neologisms, but in the linguistic traces of the dictionary itself.

[56] See Schork, *Greek and Hellenic Culture*; Tim Rood, *The Sea! The Sea!: The Shout of the Ten Thousand in the Modern Imagination* (London: Duckworth, 2004), pp. 162–7; B. Arkins, 'Greek and Roman Themes', in *James Joyce in Context*, ed. John McCourt (Cambridge: Cambridge University Press, 2010), pp. 239–49.

[57] 'On his desk they found two books, a Greek Lexicon and Oliver Gogarty's *I Follow Saint Patrick*', Richard Ellmann, *James Joyce*, rev. edn (New York: Oxford University Press, 1982), p. 742. It is not immediately clear from Ellmann's source, Carola Giedion-Welcker, what the 'griechisches Lexicon' was, and since Joyce's writing-table ('Tisch') was small, and since 'it seems unlikely that Joyce would have carried a huge, heavy volume like Liddell and Scott', it has been suggested that Joyce picked up a Greek-German dictionary locally in Zürich (Keri Elizabeth Ames, 'Joyce's Aesthetic of the Double Negative and His Encounters with Homer's *Odyssey*', in *Beckett, Joyce and the Art of the Negative*, ed. Colleen Jaurretche (Amsterdam and New York: Rodopi, 2005), pp. 15–48 (p. 41); but given the centrality of Liddell and Scott in the period, the much smaller and lighter abridged version ('Middle Liddell' or 'Little Liddell')—also used by Pound—could well have been Joyce's more probable choice: cf. Schork, *Greek and Hellenic Culture*, p. 260.

[58] Schork, *Greek and Hellenic Themes*, pp. 260–74; Brendan O Hehir and John Dillon, *A Classical Lexicon for Finnegans Wake* (Berkeley, CA: University of California Press, 1977); Ioanna Ioannidou and Leo Knuth 'Greek in "The Mookse and the Gripes"', *A Wake Newslitter* 8 (1971): pp. 83–8; Ioannidou and Knuth, 'Greek in "Burrus and Caseous"', *A Wake Newslitter* 10 (1973): 12–16.

[59] Schork, *Greek and Hellenic Themes*, p. 273. Schork also highlights the use of Greek terms for metrical feet.

[60] Adaline Glasheen, *Third Census of 'Finnegans Wake': An Index of Characters and their Roles* (Berkeley and Los Angeles, CA: University of California Press, 1977), p. 257; Schork, *Greek and Hellenic Culture*, p. 261.

For Ezra Pound, Liddell and Scott's dictionary is given a walk-on part in a complex meditation on the limits of lexicography, of translation, non-translation, and textual transmission in *Canto* 23:[61]

> With the sun in a golden cup
>> and going toward the low fords of ocean
>
> Ἅλιος δ' Ὑπεριονίδας δέπας ἐσκατέβαινε χρύσεον
>
> Ὄφρα δι' ὠκεανοῖο περάσας
>> ima vada noctis obscurae
>
> Seeking doubtless the sex in bread-moulds
>
> ἥλιος, ἅλιος, ἅλιος = μάταιος
>
> ("Derivation uncertain." The idiot
>
> Odysseus furrowed the sand.)
>
> alixantos, aliotrephes, eiskatebaine, down into,
>
> descended, to the end that, beyond ocean,
>
> pass through, traverse
>> ποτὶ βένθεα
>
> νυκτὸς ἐρεμνᾶς,
>
> ποτὶ ματέρα, κουριδίαν τ'ἄλοχον
>
> παῖδας τε φίλους....ἔβα δάφναισι κατάσκιον

The untranslated Greek text is from the *Geryoneis*, a poem by the seventh-/sixth-century BC poet Stesichorus on Hercules' journey to the end of the world to obtain the cattle of the monster Geryon. Stesichorus' poem exists only in fragments, and—until the second half of the twentieth century when new papyrus fragments were found—only through citation by other authors. The fragment in *Canto* 23 describing how Helios, the sun-god, used to travel across the ocean in a golden cup is quoted in Athenaeus' *Deipnosophistae* (*Scholars at Dinner*, third century AD), a notoriously unreliable source of segments of otherwise lost works.[62] Showcasing this complex of textual transmission, Pound quotes from Athenaeus, and specifically from the nineteenth-century bilingual Greek and

---

[61] On this passage, see esp. Carroll F. Terrell, *A Companion to the Cantos of Ezra Pound* (Berkeley and Los Angeles: University of California Press, 1993), vol. I, pp. 93–4; Peter Liebregts, *Ezra Pound and Neoplatonism* (Madison, NJ: Farleigh Dickinson University Press, 2004), pp. 187–9; Leah Culligan Flack, *Modernism and Homer: The Odysseys of H. D., James Joyce, Osip Mandelstam, and Ezra Pound* (Cambridge: Cambridge University Press, 2015), pp. 51–2.

[62] The Loeb translation of the passage partially quoted by Pound runs: 'Hyperion's son Aelios embarked in a gold goblet, in order to cross the ocean and come to the depths of the sacred, gloomy night, and to his mother, and the wife he married when she was a girl, and the children he loved. Meanwhile the son of Zeus strode into the sacred grove shaded with laurel trees.' (11.469e; trans. S. Douglas Olson, *Athenaeus, The Learned Banqueters*, Loeb Classical Library (Cambridge, MA: Harvard University Press, 2009), vol. V, pp. 276–7). For Athenaeus as a source of fragments, see Christopher Pelling, 'Fun with Fragments: Athenaeus and the Historians', in David Braund and John Wilkins, eds, *Athenaeus and his World* (Exeter: University of Exeter Press, 2000), pp. 171–90.

Latin edition of Johannes Schweighäuser, whose Latin is deliberately embedded into the textual archaeology of the *Canto* ('ima vada noctis obscurae').[63] In addition, the fragment of Stesichorus is itself further fragmented: echoing the typographical moves of 'Papyrus', Pound omits several words from Athenaeus' preserved text, replacing them instead with white space and ellipses (or underdotting) as if they, too, were missing. Mediated and broken, as the *Canto* implicitly brings to the fore, the texts of the past come to us in pieces and filtered through the temporally disparate voices of others.

Even the Greek we have, Pound's canto implies, is only partially knowable. He pauses its quotation to investigate the word Ἅλιος, itself a textual variant preserved only in the vulgate manuscript tradition, which Schweighäuser prints in a note found in the critical apparatus:[64]

> ἥλιος ἅλιος ἅλιος = μάταιος
> ("Derivation uncertain." The idiot
> Odysseus furrowed the sand.)

Turning to his 'Middle Liddell', *A Lexicon: Abridged from Liddell and Scott's Greek-English Lexicon*, Pound found ἅλιος (*halios*) listed as a Doric variant of ἥλιος (*hēlios*), 'the sun' (or Helios, the sun god); but there are also two further entries, according to which ἅλιος is an adjective meaning 'of, from, or belonging to the sea', or an adjective identical with μάταιος, in Liddell and Scott's entry: 'ἅλιος-α-ον = μάταιος, *fruitless, unprofitable, idle, erring*...(Deriv. uncertain.)'.[65] Liddell and Scott's dictionary becomes a literal part of Pound's text, as much a barrier to understanding the Greek as a conduit of meaning. This lexicographic process goes on as the passage progresses, as the task of construal or its failure continues to be laid bare: the Greek is transliterated ('alixantos, aliotrephes, eiskatebaine'), and the translation options openly appear on the page ('down into descended', 'pass through, traverse'), but we seem no closer to the Greek 'original'. The poem thus dramatizes the processes of textual decipherment and the limits of philology to transmit the past, from Schweighäuser's critical edition (Ἅλιος) and translation ('ima vada noctis obscurae') to the legendary dictionary of Liddell and Scott. Even when we attempt to translate it—and perhaps more so when we do—the ancient text remains firmly in the past, allowing only the remotest fragments of

---

[63] Johann Schweighäuser, *Athenaei Naucratitae Deipnosophistarum libri quindecim* (Societas Bipontinae, 1804), vol. IV, pp. 237–8.

[64] Schweighäuser, IV, p. 237, n.3; Schweighäuser prints Ἀέλιος (Aelios) in the main text. Pound studied textual criticism as a Master's student at the University of Pennsylvania: UPF 1.9 AR [Office of Alumni Records Biographical Records, 1750–2002], box 2119. (I am very grateful to William Dingee for this reference.)

[65] *A Lexicon: Abridged from Liddell and Scott's Greek-English Lexicon* (New York: Harper, 1880), p. 33; cf. Terrell, *Companion*, I, p. 94.

meaning through to modernity. In the end, non-translation might well be the least estranging medium.

Writing about the Romantic fragment in 1798, Friedrich Schlegel observed: 'Many of the works of the ancients have become fragments. Many modern works are fragments as soon as they are written.'[66] Modernism, too, produced works which are 'fragments as soon as they are written', but those fragments were often engaged with the very processes of cultural transmission and its failure by which 'many of the works of the ancients have become fragments'. Fundamentally, the modernist fragment was engaged in dialogue with the wealth of textual and material culture from Greco-Roman antiquity coming to light in the period and the activities of classicists which attempted to process it, from papyrology to philology and from epigraphy to lexicography. It is partly through that engagement that modernist writing was able to grapple with the fact that the past does not just come to us in different or dead languages: it comes to us mediated and in pieces. Capturing that fact, mimicking—translating—the materiality of damaged and partially transmitted texts, enabled writers in the period to go beyond issues of translation or non-translation narrowly conceived in order to convey the conditions of textual and cultural transmission that have brought antiquity in fragments to modernity.

---

[66] 'Viele werke der Alten sind Fragmente geworden. Viele werke der Neuern sind es gleich bei der Enstehung'. Friedrich Schlegel, *Philosophical Fragments* [1798], trans. Peter Firchow (Minneapolis: University of Minnesota Press, 1991), p. 21.

5

The Direct Method: Ezra Pound, Non-Translation, and the International Future

Rebecca Beasley

In spring 1918, Pound published three sections of his new poem, which would come to be known as *The Cantos*, in a short-lived magazine called *The Future*. The role of these cantos in the development of the poem has been familiar to Pound scholars since they were analysed in the first book to trace the evolution of Pound's poem, Ronald Bush's *The Genesis of Ezra Pound's 'Cantos'* (1976): 'The *Future Cantos* were the first to acquire the modernistic, demanding brevity that was later to become characteristic of the poem', wrote Bush, 'Pound took advantage of the journal's limited circulation to experiment with minimalizing transitions and excising discursiveness.'[1] But the relevance of the cantos' context has remained unexplored: the journal's interest in international relations and its promotion of modern teaching suggests it may have been a more appropriate venue for Pound's linguistically experimental poem than previously noticed.

It is often said that the linguistic experiments of early twentieth-century literature are best understood as a response to a loss of confidence in language's ability to represent experience that began around the middle of the nineteenth century and became critical during the Great War. Richard Sheppard has remarked that, for modernist writers, 'the logic of language is displaced by a greater or lesser sense of dispossession, alienation and linguistic helplessness', and Christopher Butler has described how, in response, their 'language becomes more and more elliptical, and turns to juxtaposition and the alogical, to the simultaneous and the collaged'.[2] One way in which the language of modernist writers becomes elliptical or collaged is through the incorporation of words and phrases from other languages, left untranslated.

---

[1] Ronald Bush, *The Genesis of Ezra Pound's 'Cantos'* (Princeton, NJ: Princeton University Press, 1976), p. 190.

[2] Richard Sheppard, 'Modernism, Language and Experimental Poetry: On Leaping over Bannisters and Learning How to Fly', *Modern Language Review* 92.1 (1997): 98–123 (p. 128); Christopher Butler, *Early Modernism: Literature, Music and Painting in Europe, 1900–1916* (Oxford: Oxford University Press, 1994), p. 10.

Rebecca Beasley, *The Direct Method: Ezra Pound, Non-Translation, and the International Future* In: *Modernism and Non-Translation*. Edited by: Jason Harding and John Nash, Oxford University Press (2019). © the several contributors. DOI: 10.1093/oso/9780198821441.003.0005

This chapter proposes that non-translation in early twentieth-century literary texts might be understood not only as the mark of an essentially private struggle between the writer and language. Rather, it will explore how literary non-translation might be considered as an instance in a broader reevaluation of translation as a social, political, and pedagogical practice in the wake of the Great War and the rise of internationalism during the 1920s. 'Is there any utilitarian basis for our present enthronement of translation?' asked H. E. Moore in 1925. 'During six years' experience as foreign correspondent in industry and finance, in England, France and Germany, I found no use for formal translation.'[3] Two years later, Sylvia Pankhurst argued that translation actually impeded the work of international congresses, delaying the business and providing 'at best only a summarized paraphrase of the speeches, which are often garbled beyond the recognition of their authors'.[4] And in 1933 Eugene Jolas declared a loss of faith in literary translation: 'The crisis of language is now going on in every part of the Occident. It seems, therefore, essential to retain the linguistic creative material intact, and to present constructive work, as much as possible, in the original.'[5]

Moore's remark was made in *Modernism in Language Teaching*, a pamphlet that promoted the use of the direct method of language teaching, that is, teaching entirely in the language to be learned, developed in the last decades of the nineteenth century and promoted with a new insistence during and following the Great War.[6] Pankhurst's occurred in *Delphos: The Future of International Language*, in which she advocated the widespread use of Giuseppe Peano's version of Latin, Interlingua, to facilitate international communication. Jolas's statement was made in the editorial that committed his journal, *transition*, to a policy of non-translation. All three are instances of the profound concern with the future of language and translation in the new international society envisaged by the Versailles Treaty, the League of Nations, and the host of societies that aimed to reform global relations on an international, rather than a national or imperial basis.

What kind of literature would be produced by 'the international mind' of the 1920s, to use the popular phrase coined by Nicholas Butler?[7] While the increased discussion and popularity of international languages like Interlingua, Esperanto, and Basic English might suggest that translation between languages was replaced by translation into a new or modified international language, writers appear to have been more interested in preserving the diversity of national languages by incorporating non-translated elements into their texts. Pound is an important

---

[3] H. E. Moore, *Modernism in Language Teaching* (Cambridge: Heffer, 1925), p. 22.

[4] E. Sylvia Pankhurst, *Delphos: The Future of International Language* (London: Kegan Paul, Trench, Trübner, 1927), p. 7.

[5] [Eugene Jolas], 'Glossary', *transition* 22 (February 1933): 177–9 (p. 177).

[6] See Eric W. Hawkins, *Modern Languages in the Curriculum*, rev. edn (Cambridge: Cambridge University Press, 1987), pp. 117–53.

[7] Nicholas Murray Butler, *The International Mind: An Argument for the Judicial Settlement of International Disputes* (New York: Scribner's, 1912).

figure to consider here: *The Cantos* is a major and influential example of the modernist use of non-translation, and studies by critics such as Douglas Mao, Marjorie Perloff, and Daniel Tiffany have analysed the way his poetry manifests language as materiality.[8] During the same period, however, Pound has emerged as the key figure in examinations of modernism and translation, in works by Yunte Huang, Daniel Katz, and Steven Yao.[9] But as Katz remarks, 'for the modernists, "translation" in its most common acceptation is but one mode of the encounter with foreign languages, an encounter which entails the forced re-encounter with the language which is meant to be one's "own".[10] For Pound translation and non-translation are not the opposites they first appear, but rather closely related forms of encounter with foreign languages, points on a continuum of foreignization.

The Future

Pound's first connection with *The Future* was probably personal rather than ideological: its first editor and publisher, Charles Granville, whose real name was Charles Hosken, was a friend of A. R. Orage, and had published a number of works by *New Age* authors. Through his publishing company, Stephen Swift, he had published Pound's *Sonnets and Ballate of Guido Cavalcanti* and *Ripostes* in 1912, before fleeing the country with the company's funds, resulting in his arrest and imprisonment from 1913 to 1915 for fraud, and also two counts of bigamy.[11] During the first year of the journal's existence, Pound contributed four articles and at least one survey of the literary scene that had little in common with each other or, at least at first sight, the journal.[12]

---

[8] Douglas Mao, *Solid Objects: Modernism and the Test of Production* (Princeton, NJ: Princeton University Press, 1998); Marjorie Perloff, *The Poetics of Indeterminacy: Rimbaud to Cage* (Princeton, NJ: Princeton University Press, 1981); Daniel Tiffany, *Radio Corpse: Imagism and the Cryptaesthetic of Ezra Pound* (Cambridge, MA: Harvard University Press, 1998).

[9] Yunte Huang, *Transpacific Displacement: Ethnography, Translation, and Intertextual Travel in Twentieth Century American Literature* (Berkeley and Los Angeles: University of California Press, 2002); Daniel Katz, *American Modernism's Expatriate Scene: The Labour of Translation* (Edinburgh: Edinburgh University Press, 2007); Steven G. Yao, *Translation and the Languages of Modernism: Gender, Politics, Language* (Basingstoke: Palgrave, 2002).

[10] Katz, *American Modernism's Expatriate Scene*, p. 2.

[11] 'An Author's Bigamy and Fraud', *The Times*, 5 July 1913, p. 5; 'A Wife's Suit for Divorce: Hosken v. Hosken', *The Times*, 8 May 1919, p. 4.

[12] Ezra Pound, 'Sword-Dance and Spear-Dance: Texts of the Poems used with Michio Itow's Dances', *The Future* 1.2 (December 1916): 54–5; [Ezra Pound], 'In the World of Letters', *The Future* 1.2 (December 1916): 55–6; Ezra Pound, 'The Rev. G. Crabbe, LL.B.', *The Future* 1.4 (February 1917): 110–11; Ezra Pound, 'Art and Life: Beddoes (and Chronology)', *The Future* 1.11 (September 1917): 318–20; Ezra Pound, 'Art and Life: Landor (1775–1864)', *The Future* 2.1 (November 1917): 10–12. On the attribution of 'In the World of Letters', see Donald Gallup, *Ezra Pound: A Bibliography* (Charlottesville: University Press of Virginia, 1983), p. 242. It seems likely that Pound also wrote the 'In the World of Letters' column in the fourth issue.

In January 1918, Granville relinquished his editorial role and was replaced by the London-based Danish critic Axel Gerfalk. Perhaps as part of Gerfalk's drive to 'secure the assistance of men of mark in the field of Art and Politics, Commerce and Science', Pound began a more sustained engagement with *The Future* at this time and, following the publication of the three cantos in February, March, and April, he took over the regular 'Books Reviewed' column, previously unsigned, but presumably written by Granville.[13] Over the course of 1917, the concerns of the magazine had come more precisely into focus, and Pound's suitability as a contributor was more apparent. Without wishing to overestimate the significance of Pound's contributions to *The Future* for either the poet or the journal, I want to suggest that Pound's engagement with *The Future* shows how non-translation in modernist works might be read not just as the product of an individual poet's choice of style, but also as part of the wartime and post-war debate about international relations, and the role that languages and literature should play in them.

In his editorial statement of *The Future*'s aims in August 1917, Granville writes that the journal's aim is 'free discussion of matters of vital importance to the community and to humanity in general, matters that affect the well-being of the present generation as the trustees and guardians of those to come'. This entailed 'the diagnosis of the ills of our present social life' and 'the discovery of remedies', undertaken with 'honest, open minds': 'prejudices must be regarded as prejudices and discarded; truth, so far as the human mind is able to grasp it, must be naked to our view'. The focus of its national social critique was religion ('all mankind are brothers and sisters in a spiritual family'), law ('It is [...] the highest duty of the Government of a modern State to provide a code of law that shall envisage the good of the whole community, avoiding legislation for the good of one class at the expense of another'), and justice ('make justice free'). But *The Future* also, Granville wrote, 'had much to say on the need of developments in international relations'.[14] His successor, Gerfalk, agreed: 'A Brotherhood of Nations may seem Utopia to us now; yet a brotherhood of individuals is surely a possibility to be considered', he wrote in his first editorial. 'It has been formed in many instances and in many lands, ever stretching across frontiers that seemed a barrier to fraternity; and what has succeeded on the smaller scale may certainly be realised one day on a larger.'[15] Both editors discussed the war situation, one-off articles addressed topics such as the American Presidential election, German industry, Dano-English relations, and the Serbian war effort, a series on 'Russian and English Relations in the Future' was contributed by Gustav Taube, Gerfalk introduced a series on 'Foreigners of Mark', and the many articles on education frequently drew attention to a changing international context. In October 1917

---

[13] [Axel Gerfalk], 'Important Notice', *The Future* 2.2 (January 1918): 29.

[14] [Charles Granville], 'Notes', *The Future* 1.10 (August 1917): 273–6 (pp. 273, 274, 275, 276).

[15] [Axel Gerfalk], 'The Moving Spirit', *The Future* 2.3 (February 1918): 46–7 (p. 47).

Minnie Capstick, Principal of Heath Lodge girls' school in Hemel Hempstead, argued for post-war international education councils, which would develop curricula that taught history, geography, and literature from an international, rather than national or imperial, perspective. This, Capstick wrote, would equip 'the ordinary man' to play his part in an increasingly democratic world: 'It is the duty of all countries to unite so to educate the rising generation that it will view questions not from a personal, but from an impersonal standpoint; so that when viewing questions of trade and territory, politics and religion, their minds will readily embrace all sides, all claims for tolerance.'[16]

But the most prominent and practical campaign on behalf of international understanding waged by *The Future* was its promotion of the study of modern languages and literature. In his August 1917 editorial, Granville argues for the necessity of understanding 'the psychology of the peoples with whom we shall constantly be in contact' after the war, in political and commercial negotiations, which requires knowledge of their language and literature. 'We argue that, the psychology of a people being expressed in its language and literature, it is our duty to acquire a knowledge of modern languages,' he writes. In 1905, Granville had briefly been the Principal of the Rapid Language College in Marylebone, which advertised itself as 'the only institution in London specialising in Modern Languages', and *The Future* had promoted the learning of modern languages since its second issue.[17] There it had announced that it would devote space to the learning of foreign languages in future issues, and recommended two recent textbooks, *Rosenthal's Common Sense Method of Practical Linguistry: The Spanish Language* and Nevill Forbes's *Word-for-Word Russian Story-Book*. The next issue gave notice of a monthly 'modern language competition', in which prizes would be offered for the best translations of a set passage of French, Spanish, German or Russian.[18] The competitions were popular, and (along with a prize essay competition, usually on an internationalist theme) came to occupy four pages of the journal, often eliciting correspondence too. In January 1918, for example, Sydney Alers Hankey wrote in to complain that the English of the prize translations was insufficiently idiomatic, 'reproducing as they do with deplorable literalness the foreign constructions, to the detriment not only of purity of expression but also of intelligibility. Surely the first test of excellence of any translation should be that it be rendered not only into intelligible language, but language that would be used by the natives of the country'.[19]

---

[16] Minnie Capstick, 'Affairs of Moment: Education for the Future', *The Future* 1.12 (October 1917): 343–4 (p. 344).

[17] [Charles Granville], 'Notes', pp. 273–4; 'The Rapid Language College [Classified Advertising]', *The Times*, 15 August 1905, p. 2; 'The Police Courts', *The Times*, 17 February 1913, p. 3.

[18] [Charles Granville], 'Reviews of Books: Modern Languages', *The Future* 1.2 (December 1916): 64; [Charles Granville], 'Important Announcement: Competitions', *The Future* 1.3 (January 1917): 79. Russian translations were not, in fact, ever offered.

[19] S. Alers Hankey, Letter to the editor, *The Future*, 2.2 (January 1918): 43–4 (p. 43).

While *The Future*'s translation competitions might suggest that the journal's attitude to foreign languages was quite the reverse of that suggested by the non-translation practices explored in this collection, in fact they demonstrate their close relation in debates of the period. For *The Future* was not interested in translation itself as a practice, still less as an art. It was only as a means to promote the learning of modern languages that it appeared in the journal: *The Future*'s ideal was familiarity with modern languages, which would, of course, render translation unnecessary. In fact, the high profile of the translation competitions is somewhat misleading, because translation was not a tool advocated by the methods of language learning with which the journal aligned itself: the journal consistently promoted the 'direct method' of language learning by immersion rather than through grammar and translation exercises. In his *Common-Sense Method of Practical Linguistry* series (made available to *The Future*'s readers at a special price from January 1918), Richard Rosenthal wrote that learning a language 'is not to be attained by the study and translation of the classic works of literature. It is vain to attempt it by any school system':

> Instead of teaching phrases whose constructions are the same as those of our own native tongue, we ought on the contrary, to commence with idiomatic sentences, whose formations are utterly foreign to our mode of speaking, thereby dis-accustomising our minds from thinking in English, and become familiarized with the foreign ways of expression and thought.
>
> For this, after all, is the great difficulty; this is the 'punctum saliens' of the whole problem. We must learn
>
> TO THINK IN THE FOREIGN LANGUAGE ITSELF.
>
> We must no longer think about our French or about our German, Spanish or Italian, but in the language itself.[20]

The other book Granville had praised in the second issue, Forbes's *Russian Story-Book* also took this approach, teaching by phrase rather than individual words and grammar. The stories were prefaced with guidance only on the Cyrillic alphabet, its transcription and pronunciation: minimal notes followed, restricting their comments on grammar to that which emerged from the readings.[21] *The Future*'s correspondents, too, advocated the direct method. In August 1917, Marion Williams set out her plan for teaching French in infant schools:

> Until the children are ten years of age it need not be taken as a separate subject:
> a poem, preferably narrative, a song, a game or play, names, numbers, words

---

[20] Richard S. Rosenthal, *Rosenthal's Common-Sense Method of Practical Linguistry: The Spanish Language* (New York: International College of Languages, 1917), pp. 35 and 24.
[21] Nevill Forbes, *Word-for-Word Russian Story-Book* (Oxford: Basil Blackwell, 1916).

alike in both languages, could all be taught as part of the corresponding time-table subject. *Asseyez-vous, Taisez-vous. Bon jour, S'il vous plait*, etc., should be used so frequently that the children will recognise them as readily as the English equivalent. In five years the children will have acquired a fairly decent vocabulary, and will be able to tackle a simple French reading book.[22]

Even the translation competitions drew on the theory behind direct method teaching, eschewing 'extracts from the Classics for rendering into English' and 'Browningesque puzzles in the particular language', in favour of practical and everyday examples: 'six lines from a newspaper'.[23]

The journal's and its readers' views on modern languages and their method of tuition were expressed in detail during the longest-running debate in *The Future*, initiated in January 1918 by one of the 'prize essays'. A. E. Styler's winning essay on the subject, 'Which Language Should be Adopted for International Intercourse and Why?' argued for English, on the grounds of its relative grammatical simplicity, that it was already widely spoken, and that the structures for further dissemination were already in place: 'a language spreads not by express propaganda but by the military, political, commercial, literary, and other activities of the people who speak it', he wrote.[24] Styler's argument was directed less against other modern languages than invented languages, such as Esperanto; Granville noted that, though 'English, Esperanto, French, Ido, Spanish and Latin all found supporters among our competitors', Esperanto had 'received most support'.[25] He also remarked that the case Styler made against the adoption of an artificial language was 'by no means conclusive, and in any case we must not be supposed to agree wholly with his conclusions', perhaps because, since August, the British Esperanto Association had advertised on *The Future*'s back page. Prizes for translations of a passage into Esperanto had been offered since the previous September.

Esperanto was popular with *The Future*'s readers, who admired its rationality, its practicality, and its neutrality: like a number of correspondents, Styler's chief interlocutor, G. Rhys Griffiths, argued that the direction of world politics suggested there was not time to wait for one language to 'naturally' achieve international dominance, and 'a time would soon arrive when international questions will not be allowed to be threshed out through the intermediary of interpreters, or be decided upon by garbled reports appearing in the international press, but a first-hand and reliable interchange of ideas will be insisted upon'.[26] But *The Future*'s editors, both Granville and Gerfalk, were more interested in modern

---

[22] Marion Williams, Letter to the editor, *The Future* 1.8 (August 1917): 303–4.

[23] 'Important Announcement: Competitions', *The Future* 1.3 (January 1917): 79.

[24] A. E. Styler, 'Our Prize Essay: Which Language Should be Adopted for International Intercourse, and Why?', *The Future* 2.2 (January 1918): 37.

[25] [Charles Granville], 'Competitions: Our Awards', *The Future* 2.2 (January 1918): 38.

[26] G. Rhys Griffiths, Letter to the editor, *The Future* 2.3 (February 1918): 76. See also Mabel S. Rutter, Letter to the editor, *The Future* 1.11 (September 1917): 334.

languages: for Granville, Esperanto was 'a short cut in commerce especially', 'of utilitarian value', but 'should never preclude the study of languages', and for Gerfalk the use of an artificial language relinquished the opportunity to pay an individual or a nation the compliment of having learned their language. Both saw foreign language learning as 'the only way' to international understanding, because both located national identity in language and literature.[27] Styler viewed language in the same way, and in a long 'Reply to my Critics' three months into the debate, set out an argument that connected what he called 'international consciousness', the direct method and non-translation:

> Let us consider translation from a higher point of view. My advice, oft repeated to language students and long tried and tested by experience, is this paradox: 'Do not translate, and you will become a good translator.' This means that it is fatal to try to master a language by the practice of translation. An occasional translation does no harm, but the valuable habit to acquire is *direct reading*. Never leave a foreign passage until you can read it and enjoy its beauties *without* translation. [...]. Good translations are rare. I have a quaint old edition of Nepos, whose concise Latin is infinitely clearer than the 18th century French rending in which words are multiplied in vain. The same may be observed of English translations of Cervantes or Dante. What is the reason? Merely that translation is a process of rebuilding: and words are stones of varying size and form and colour. The old Latin words are Titanic blocks, disposed in strange patterns; the old Latin and Greek thoughts are hewn out with less detail than modern ones. The modern translator over-amplifies, 'reads in' every imaginable detail, minutely elaborates away the grave conciseness of the original, which only they can feel who read the ancient tongue *direct*.

Language, in any case, is not a pure construction, Styler argues: 'Languages enrich one another by their mutual borrowing and lending. English glows with exotic flowers. Consider how many beautiful passages of the English Bible are Hebraisms, literally translated; and what is some of Kipling's most striking work? Urdu word for word.'[28]

Pound and 'international literature'

It was in this context, then, that Pound contributed his poetry and essays to *The Future*. Though his first essays did not engage directly with the journal's

---

[27] [Charles Granville], 'Notes', *The Future* 1.12 (October 1917): 337–40 (p. 340); [Axel Gerfalk], 'Notes of the Month', 2.4 (March 1918): 80–6 (p. 83), [Axel Gerfalk], 'Notes of the Month', 2.5 (April 1918): 110–14 (p. 114).

[28] A. E. Styler, 'A Reply to my Critics', *The Future* 2.5 (April 1918): 138–9 (emphases Styler's).

arguments, there were from the beginning points of similarity. Most obviously, Pound's literary criticism was determinedly international: his first contribution was about Japanese poetry, his second about T. S. Eliot and Dorothy Richardson, but also Fritz Vanderpyl and Jean de Bosschère, and even his recovery of English writers he thought neglected, George Crabbe and Walter Savage Landor, situated their reception in an international context. Many of his essays concerned translation, and his praise for a realism of social satire and verbal precision corresponded with Granville's and Gerfalk's aims for *The Future*. As Granville had pledged the journal to 'the diagnosis of the ills of our present social life' that would discard prejudices and present truth 'naked to our view', as Gerfalk inveighed against dissimulation and called for sincerity, so Pound praised 'the value of words that conform precisely with fact, of free speech without evasions and circumlocutions'.[29]

Over the course of his contributions to *The Future* Pound developed an argument that bridged the social concerns of the journal with the literary experiments of his poem. He attributed the degeneration of poetic language to Romantic and Victorian poets—Wordsworth's 'desert of bleatings', 'muzzy Tennyson'.[30] But he traced their individual faults to a national cause: provincialism and xenophobia after the Napoleonic wars: 'If one sought, not perhaps to exonerate, but to explain the Victorian era, one might find some contributory cause in Napoleon', he wrote in October 1918. 'That is to say, the Napoleonic wars had made Europe unpleasant, England was sensibly glad to be insular. Geography leaked over into mentality.' When it should have been learning from eighteenth-century French culture, 'England cut off her communications, intellectual communications with the Continent. An era of bigotry supervened'.[31] The reviews consistently deride writers, such as Henry Newbolt, who fail to engage with literature beyond British shores; conversely, those who show themselves aware of non-English literatures are praised, even if, as Pound wrote of Marmaduke Pickthall, they do 'not write very well'.[32] The highest praise is reserved for Wyndham Lewis and, especially, James Joyce. Relating *Tarr* and *A Portrait of the Artist as a Young Man* to the work of Dostoevsky and Flaubert respectively, Pound writes that they are the first novels since Hardy and James to 'have a claim to a place in international literature'; Joyce is 'almost the first English-writing author of our generation to accept cosmopolitanism, to accept, that is, an international standard of criticism'.[33]

Pound's review of *A Portrait of the Artist* is particularly significant in the context of his work on the first cantos during this period. He praises two aspects

---

[29] [Granville], 'Notes', p. 273; [Gerfalk], 'The Moving Spirit', p. 46; Pound, 'The Rev. G. Crabbe, LL.B', p. 110.

[30] Pound, 'Crabbe', p. 110.

[31] Ezra Pound, 'Books Current', *The Future* 2.10 (October 1918): 265–6 (p. 266). The same point is made at the beginning of 'Art and Life: Landor (1775–1864)', p. 10.

[32] Ezra Pound, 'Books Current', *The Future* 2.8 (July 1918): 209–10 (p. 209); Ezra Pound, 'Books Current', The Future 2.11 (November 1918), 286–7 (p. 286).

[33] Ezra Pound, 'Books Current', *The Future* 2.12 (December 1918): 311–12 (pp. 311, 312).

of the novel above all: 'the clear-cut and definite sentences' and, especially, Joyce's 'scope', his 'swift alternation of subjective beauty and external shabbiness, squalor, and sordidness'. In the evidence Pound quotes non-translation figures prominently, acting to emphasize the alternation of registers, and creating a shortcut to the higher register:

> The reach of his writing is precisely from the fried breadcrusts [...], and from the fig-seeds in Cranley's teeth to the casual discussion of Aquinas:
>   "He wrote a hymn for Maundy Thursday. It begins with the words *Pange lingua gloriosi*. They say it is the highest glory of the hymnal. It is an intricate and soothing hymn. I like it; but there is no hymn that can be put beside that mournful and majestic processional song, the Vexilla Regis of Venantius Fortunatus.
>   "Lynch began to sing softly and solemnly in a deep bass voice:
>   'Impleta sunt quae concinit
>   David fideli carmine....'
>   "They turned into Lower Mount Street. A few steps from the corner a fat young man, wearing a silk neck-cloth, &c."

Here the Latin of the hymn 'Vexilla regis prodeunt' contrasts both with the 'casual' nature of Stephen's discussion of the respective merits of the hymns of Thomas Aquinas and Venantius Fortunatus, and with the 'fat young man' revealed by turning into Lower Mount Street. The 'reach' Pound praises in *A Portrait of the Artist* is across classes and professional types: 'the great writers of any period [...] must know the extremes of their time', he writes, 'they must not represent a social status; they cannot be the "Grocer" or the "Dilettante" with the egregious and capital letter nor yet the professor or the professing wearer of Jaeger or professional eater of herbs'.[34] But Pound himself was less interested in the depiction and critique of class than of nationality.

During the period in which he was composing the first cantos, Pound wrote frequently on the role of literature in fostering understanding between nations, and the importance of reading literature in foreign languages. 'Provincialism the Enemy', the four-part series he published in the *New Age* in the summer of 1917, defined provincialism as 'an ignorance of the manners, customs and nature of people living outside one's own village, parish, or nation', and 'a desire to coerce others into uniformity'. In contrast with 'coercive' German *Kultur*, Pound argued that 'England and France are civilisation [...] because they have not given way to the yelp of "nationality"' or race: 'England is so many races, even "Little England," that she has kept some real respect for personality, for the outline of the individual'. He cited the works of the realist novelists, Benito Pérez Galdós, Ivan Turgenev,

---

[34] Ezra Pound, 'Books Current', *The Future* 2.6 (May 1918): 161–3 (p. 161, p.162).

Gustave Flaubert, and above all Henry James, as 'an analysis, a diagnosis of this disease': James, he calls 'the crusader [...] in this internationalism'.[35]

The term Pound uses to describe James's work of 'making America intelligible, of making it possible for individuals to meet across national borders' is 'translation'.[36] Unsurprisingly, then, Pound's essays on literary translation were also concerned more broadly with the representation of cultures to each other. His series 'Elizabethan Classicists', 'Early Translators of Homer', and 'Hellenist Series', all in *The Egoist*, aimed to restore the pleasure of reading classical litera-ture, which Pound felt had been reduced to an 'exercise, a means of teaching the language'. For Pound, the translations have their own worth, but he also values them as 'cribs' that will inspire the reader and enable them to work with the source text: 'It is much better that a man should use a crib and know the content of his authors than that he should be able to recite all the rules in Allen and Greenough's grammar'.[37] They also have the value of highlighting 'untranslatable' qualities in the source text, such as Homer's 'magnificent onomatopœia'.[38] In his essays for the *Little Review*, Pound adopted a more belligerent attitude towards what he saw as the cultural isolation of his American readership: the February 1918 issue was given over to Pound's introduction to recent French poetry, which included copious untranslated quotation. 'The time when the intellectual affairs of America could be conducted on a monolingual basis is over', Pound told his readers: 'We offer no apology for printing most of this number in French. The intellectual life of London is dependent on people who understand this language about as well as their own'.[39]

Translation and non-translation alike are for Pound tools in the battle against provincialism and coercion: reading foreign literature, preferably in the original language, cultivated a mind that could 'readily embrace all sides, all claims for tolerance', to return to Minnie Capstick's terms.[40] Pound's literary values are not those of Sydney Alers Hankey, who deplored the 'foreign constructions' in *The Future*'s prize translations, which marred their 'purity of expression'.[41] As his admiration for Joyce's 'swift alternation' between registers shows, Pound values dif-ference over unity, foreignization over domestication, both aesthetically and ideo-logically. Like the Channel tunnel connecting London and Paris that Pound envisioned in 'Provincialism the Enemy', bringing two languages together should not make them alike, but 'accentuate their difference. Nothing is more valuable than just this amicable accentuation of difference, and of complementary

---

[35] Ezra Pound, 'Provincialism the Enemy, I', *New Age* 21.11 (12 July 1917): 244–5 (p. 244).
[36] Ezra Pound, 'Brief Note', *Little Review* 5.4 (August 1918): 6–9 (p. 7); See Katz, *American Modernism's Expatriate Scene*, p. 64.
[37] Ezra Pound, 'Elizabethan Classicists, III', *Egoist* 4.10 (November 1917): 154–6 (p. 155).
[38] Ezra Pound, 'Early Translators of Homer, 1: Hughes Salel', *Egoist* 5.7 (August 1918): 95–7.
[39] Ezra Pound, 'A Study in French Poets', *Little Review* 4.10 (February 1918): p. 3.
[40] Capstick, 'Affairs of Moment: Education for the Future', p. 344.
[41] Alers Hankey, Letter to the editor, p. 43.

values'.[42] It is with this complex of ideas in mind—internationalism, 'direct reading', and non-translation—that we can now turn to *The Cantos*.

Non-translation in the first cantos

The three sections of cantos Pound published in *The Future* were the third published version of the poem's first three cantos, following earlier versions published in the little magazine *Poetry* (June to August 1917) and the American edition of Pound's eighth collection of poetry, *Lustra* (October 1917). Their role in the development of the poem has been understood, following Bush's analysis, as above all moving the text towards a much more compressed presentation of its material.[43] Reading them in the context of *The Future*'s internationalism and promotion of modern language learning alerts us in addition to the arguments made by their multinational settings and references, and their use of untranslated foreign language material. This is not to say that the canto sections were informed directly by the contents of *The Future*, nor that they are of a piece with *The Future*'s other contributions: on the contrary, they are strikingly distinct from the patriotic and pastoral poetry and the humorous stories that make up the bulk of the literary contributions (a poem by John Rodker is an exception).[44] Pound's cantos extracts are longer, more experimental, more difficult, and more self-consciously literary; their only modernist context is that which Pound provides himself in his essays and book reviews. But they are nevertheless a sustained exploration of many of the same internationalist ideas the journal was promoting, and a serious investigation of their implications for literature.

In the first of the *Future* cantos, titled 'Passages from the Opening Address in a Long Poem', Pound takes himself, or his speaker, to Sirmione on Lake Garda, the home of Catullus. After walking 'the airy street' of the village, he walks 'up and out' to the church of San Pietro in Mavino and then to the shore of the lake. He conjures up the scene with a mixture of close reference, paraphrase, translation and non-translation of his literary heritage:

> As well begin here, here began Catullus:
> "Home to sweet rest, and to the waves deep laughter,"
> The laugh they wake amid the border rushes.
> This is our home, the trees are full of laughter,
> And the storms laugh loud, breaking the riven waves

[42] Ezra Pound, 'Provincialism the Enemy, IV', *New Age* 21.14 (2 August 1917): 308–9 (p. 309).

[43] Bush, *The Genesis of Ezra Pound's 'Cantos'*, p. 190.

[44] John Rodker, 'Spring Suicide', *The Future* 1.5 (March 1917): 116. The other contributor from Pound's circle was Iris Barry, who contributed an interesting but fairly conventional short story: see Iris Barry, 'Exeunt', *The Future* 2.5 (April 1918): 135–7.

On square-shaled rocks, and here the sunlight
Glints on the shaken waters, and the rain
Comes forth with delicate tread, walking from Isola
   Garda,
                    Lo Soleils plovil.
It is the sun rains, and a spatter of fire
Darts from the "Lydian" ripples, *lacus undae,*
And the place is full of spirits, not *lemures,*
Not dark and shadow-wet ghosts, but ancient living,
Wood-white, smooth as the inner-bark, and firm of
   aspect
And all a-gleam with colour?
                    Not a-gleam
But coloured like the lake and olive leaves,
GLAUKOPOS, clothed like the poppies, wearing
   golden greaves.
Light on the air. Are they Etruscan gods?
The air is solid sunlight, *apricus.*
Sun-fed we dwell there (we in England now)
For Sirmio serves my whim, better than Asolo,
Yours and unseen.[45]

The first phrase in another language that the reader encounters is a quotation from a song by the Provençal troubadour, Arnaut Daniel, 'Lo Soleils plovil', which Pound italicizes and sets apart on its own line. It is followed by another untranslated quotation, 'lacus undae', this time from Catullus' Carmen XXXI (whose last lines had already given Pound the pseudo-quotation a few lines above, 'Home to sweet rest, and to the waves deep laughter'), and three isolated untranslated words: 'lemures' (the malevolent ghosts of Roman mythology), 'GLAUKOPOS', a Homeric epithet for Athena, and 'apricus'. But all are in fact translated or glossed by the surrounding text: Pound gives 'the sun rains' for 'Lo Soleils plovil', the 'lacus undae' are grammatically positioned as a synonym for the 'Lydian ripples' (Catullus' phrase was 'Lydiae lacus undae', 'Lydian ripples of the lake'), 'lemures' is translated as 'spirits' or 'ghosts', 'GLAUKOPOS' is glossed as 'coloured like the lake and the olive leaves', and 'apricus' is juxtaposed to 'solid sunlight'.

Nevertheless, to a greater or lesser extent, depending on one's knowledge of Latin, Greek, and Provençal, these words and phrases give an effect of non-translation because Pound does not make clear that they are translated in the poem. In fact, in the *Lustra* and *Future* cantos Pound has deliberately removed

[45] Ezra Pound, 'Passages from the Opening Address in a Long Poem', *The Future* 2.3 (February 1918): 63.

the connections between the foreign words and their translations and sources that existed in earlier versions. In the first version of this canto, published in *Poetry* in June, the central section of this passage had read:

> *Lo soleils plovil,*
> As Arnaut had it in th' inextricable song.
> The very sun rains and a spatter of fire
> Darts from the "Lydian" ripples; "*locus undae*," as Catullus,
> "*Lydiae*,"[46]

It is noticeable that Pound retains the untranslated elements alongside their translation or gloss, even during the process of revision and compression the cantos underwent between their publication in *Poetry* in 1917 and in *The Future* in 1918. They are not made redundant by their translation, they are not deemed a dispensable part of the poetry—as so much else in the cantos was. Indeed, their impact was heightened as the surrounding English-language material was reduced or deleted.

The subject of 'Passages from the Opening Address in a Long Poem' is the poet's place in literary history, or more broadly, Western civilization. 'Ghosts move about me patched with histories', begins the canto, and through quotation and reference the poem incorporates the ghosts of Catullus, Browning, Homer, the nineteenth-century French painter Puvis de Chavannes, and the seventeenth-century Italian poet Pietro Metastasio. In the *Poetry* version of this canto the subject had been addressed through a debate with Browning about *Sordello*, the poem that was Pound's major methodological model at this point. There he had debated how to appropriate *Sordello*'s frame narrative of 'the showman's booth', in which a narrator presented the poem as scenes from a diorama: Pound considers turning the booth 'into the Agora, / Or into the old theatre at Arles', either of which would enable him to 'set the lot, my visions, to confounding / The wits that have survived your damn'd *Sordello*'.[47] But the debate with Browning that opened the first canto, though preserved in the second published version, the first *Lustra* canto, was removed from the *Future* canto. Brief references to *Sordello* remained, but its role as a methodological model could no longer be detected: as Bush remarks, the reader of the *Future* cantos 'was left in as much darkness about the relevance of *Sordello* as the reader of *A Draft of XVI Cantos*', the 1925 text that generally corresponds to the cantos of later editions.[48]

The removal of the debate with Browning means that the first canto is no longer about Pound's engagement with Browning as he searches for a method.

---

[46] Ezra Pound, 'Three Cantos, I', *Poetry* 10.3 (June 1917): 113–21 (p. 116). I presume that 'locus' for 'lacus' was a printer's error.

[47] Pound, 'Three Cantos, I', pp. 117–18.

[48] Bush, *The Genesis of Ezra Pound's 'Cantos'*, pp. 190–1.

Instead it begins with an assertion of the method he has chosen, 'Ghosts move about me patched with histories'.[49] In the second *Future* canto Pound made the same change: he removed the last remnants of the opening frame that engaged with another methodological model, Dante's *Commedia* ('Leave Casella' in the second *Poetry* canto and 'O "Virgilio mio"' in the second *Lustra* canto), and made the method his own by starting with what had been the second line in the first two versions, 'Send out your thought upon the Mantuan palace'.[50] The palace, like the ghosts, is characterized by the fragmentary, the partial—'pigment flakes from the stone [...]/ Silk tatters still in the frame'—and this focus on the scraps and fragments that have come down to twentieth-century experience dominates the canto. 'Where do we come upon the ancient people?' he asks, and answers:

> "All that I know is that a certain star"—
> All that I know of one, Joios, Tolosan,
> Is that in middle May, going along
> A scarce discerned path, turning aside
> In "level poplar lands," he found a flower, and
>   wept;
> "Y a la primera flor," he wrote,
> "Qu'ieu trobei, tornei em plor."
> One stave of it, I've lost the copy I had of it in Paris,
> [...]
> Arnaut's a score of songs, a wry sestina;

This shift in the canto's focus from the search for a method to the collection of scraps of culture gives the text a high tolerance for untranslated words and phrases, which emphasize the distinction between Pound's imported material and his own English text. As in the first canto, Pound here provides a version of the foreign material he quotes, though not a full translation, and in the rest of the canto other quotations are left untranslated: 'Rêveuse pour que je plonge', from Mallarmé, the Provençal phrase '*bos trobaire*'.[51]

The third *Future* canto consisted almost solely of Pound's translation of the *nekyia* section of the *Odyssey* through a sixteenth-century Latin translation he had picked up at a bookstall in Paris. In the first version of the third canto, the *nekyia* section, in which Odysseus calls up ghosts for guidance, had appeared as simply one more model for the poem's travel across time and space, like Browning's diorama, Dante's visit to the underworld, and the trance visions of the seventeenth-century Rosicrucian astrologer and alchemist, John Heydon, with which Pound

---

[49] Pound, 'Passages from the Opening Address in a Long Poem', p. 63.
[50] Ezra Pound, 'Three Cantos, II', *Poetry* 10.4 (July 1917): 180–8 (p. 180); Ezra Pound 'Three Cantos of a Poem of Some Length', in *Lustra* (New York: n. pub, 1916), pp. 179–202 (p. 188).
[51] Ezra Pound, 'Images from the Second Canto of a Long Poem', *The Future* 2.4 (March 1918): 96.

began the canto. But for the *Future* canto, Pound cut the first three pages—all the lines about Heydon—to leave the *nekyia* translation almost in the form in which it would appear from 1925 as the Canto I we know today. He did, however, carry over three introductory lines from the *Poetry* and *Lustra* versions:

> I've strained my ear for -*ensa*, -*ombra*, and -*ensa*,
> Have cracked my wit on delicate canzoni,
> > Here's but rough meaning:
> "And then went down to the ship, set keel to breakers […]

In introducing his translation, Pound 'gently complains about the hard work of translating, whether from Latin or Provençal', in Daniel Albright's words.[52] This brief introduction would be deleted by 1925, Pound presumably having decided that his point about translation was made anyway by the end of the canto, where his own 'rough' translation is contrasted with the 'florid mellow phrase' of Georgius Dartona Cretensis' ('the Cretan's') Latin translation of the Homeric Hymns, which had been bound together with the translation of the *Odyssey* by Andreas Divus that Pound had bought. The quotation mixes translation with non-translation:

> The thin clear Tuscan stuff
> > Gives way before the florid mellow phrase;
> Take we the goddess, Venerandam
> Auream coronam habentem, pulchram....
> Cypri munimenta sortita est, maritime,
> Light on the foam, breathed on by Zephyrs
> And air-tending Hours, mirthful, orichalci, with
> > golden
> Girdles and breast bands, though with dark eyelids,
> Bearing the golden bough of Argicida.[53]

Given the prominence that translation and non-translation had now been given in the poem, it is not surprising that in the period of revision that followed the *Future* cantos, Pound moved his translation of the *nekyia* section of the Odyssey, together with most of this non-translated ending, from the third canto to its resting place at the poem's beginning. In doing so, and in deleting all but the briefest references to his other methodological models, Pound made the history of language use his privileged method of his poem's time and space travel.

---

[52] Daniel Albright, *Putting Modernism Together: Literature, Music, and Painting, 1872–1927* (Baltimore, MD: Johns Hopkins University Press, 2015), p. 258.
[53] Ezra Pound, 'An Interpolation taken from Third Canto of a Long Poem', *The Future* 2.5 (April 1918): 121.

Pound's use of the *nekyia* section places his work in a long literary history: he famously wrote to W. H. D. Rouse—a pioneer teacher of the direct method, incidentally—that 'The Nekuia shouts aloud that it is *older* than the rest'.[54] He emphasized the layering of that history not only through drawing attention to the meditations of other languages in the conclusion to the canto, but also—in the *Future* version only—adding a footnote: 'The above Passages from the Odyssey, done into an approximation of the metre of the Anglo-Saxon "Sea-farer"'.[55] But of course these decisions also place *The Cantos* in a large literary geography, characterized above all by diversity of speech, of languages. It is the poem's translation, non-translation and geographical reach that makes most sense of *The Future* context: to comment on his difficulties as a translator, as Pound does at the beginning of the third canto, is to take part in the journal's debates about the priorities of translation. To walk through Sirmione hearing the Provençal of Arnaut Daniel and the Latin of Catullus is to show one's access to knowledge 'as a great whole', as Capstick envisaged, 'appreciating not only [one's] own country but all countries'.[56] It is a poem that makes conspicuous display of its internationalism.

'Actual speaking'

In the following years, as Pound prepared his poem for its first book publication, *A Draft of XVI Cantos* (1925), non-translation would continue to play an important role, along with its close relatives translation and quotation. It would continue to be used to expand the historical and geographical range of the poem, and to provide a shortcut to a higher register, especially in its use of Greek and Latin. But even during these few years, the use of non-translation changes. In the Malatesta cantos (Cantos VIII–XI), written in 1922 and 1923, and first published in *The Criterion* in July 1923, the amount of non-translated material increases substantially. Unlike the *Future* cantos, the Malatesta cantos draw most of this material from a related group of sources—from a coherent body of research—and while the Italian and Latin in comparison to Pound's English still contribute to the sense of range Pound had admired in *A Portrait of the Artist*, another use for non-translation now comes to the fore. In *The Cantos* as a whole the most important work non-translated elements do is to connote authenticity: they suggest the presentation of source material rather than authorial paraphrase, they demonstrate

---

[54] Ezra Pound, letter to W. H. D. Rouse, 23 May 1935, in *The Letters of Ezra Pound: 1907–1941*, ed. D.D. Paige (London: Faber and Faber, 1951), p. 363. On Rouse, see Christopher Stray, *The Living Word: W. H. D. Rouse and the Crisis of Classics in Edwardian England* (Bristol: Bristol Classical Press, 1992).

[55] Pound, 'An Interpolation taken from Third Canto of a Long Poem', p. 121.

[56] Alers Hankey, Letter to the editor, pp. 43–4; Styler, 'A Reply to my Critics', pp. 138–9; Constance Mitcalfe, Letter to the editor, *The Future* 2.5 (April 1918): 140; Sigrid Ettlinger, Letter to the editor, *The Future* 2.6 (May 1918): 171; Capstick, 'Affairs of Moment: Education for the Future', p. 343.

Pound's high valuation of—to take one often non-translated ideogram—'chi'ng ming', in Pound's transliteration, 'right name'.[57] In the letters to Sigismondo Malatesta quoted in Canto IX, the argument between Federigo d'Urbino and Sigismondo in Canto X, and the legal indictment of Sigismondo in the same canto, non-translated Latin and Italian words and phrases are used to denote authentic and individual voices.[58]

Pound had written about the difficulty in translating voice in his 'Early Translators of Homer' series in August 1918. There, he had remarked that 'of Homer two qualities remain untranslated', the 'untranslatable' onomatopœia and 'secondly the authentic cadence of speech; the absolute conviction that the words used, let us say by Achilles to the "dog-faced" chicken-hearted Agamemnon, are in the actual swing of words spoken'. Though he insisted that 'this quality of actual speaking is *not* untranslatable', the essay argued that few of Homer's translators had achieved it: of Pope's translation of book 3 of *The Iliad*, Pound wrote, 'What we definitely can *not* hear is the voice of the old men speaking'.[59] In *The Cantos*, Pound frequently translates quotations of speech, but it also becomes a category of material Pound chooses for non-translation, gaining for the poem a range of distinctive voices that are not his own.

Though this use of non-translation to distinguish between the poem's personae is distinct from its use to create an internationalist and pedagogical text, there is nevertheless a connection with the internationalist debates taking place in *The Future*. I have written elsewhere of the important change Pound's conception of art undergoes in this period, from conceiving of the artwork as a thing-in-itself to valuing it primarily as a record of the artist's thought, a shift marked in *The Cantos* by Pound's collection of 'factive personalities', beginning with Malatesta.[60] The change was informed by several factors, but Pound's interest in post-war schemes to foster collaboration between Europe's intellectuals is particularly relevant. The shift of his attention from product to producer was clearly underway in 1917, when Pound praised England's relative lack of nationalism and its 'real respect for personality, for the outline of the individual' in 'Provincialism the Enemy', but his interest in specific proposals increased towards the end of 1919.[61] In October he wrote about the Fédération Internationale des Arts, des Lettres et des Sciences founded in Paris by Banville d'Hostel, in December he responded with enthusi-asm to a proposal for a 'League of Ideas' from Harry Turner, a St Louis magazine

---

[57] Ezra Pound, *The Cantos*, 4th edn (London: Faber and Faber, 1987), pp. 252, 333, 382, 400; Ezra Pound, *Guide to Kulchur* (London: Faber and Faber, 1938), p. 16. See the second chapter of Mary Paterson Cheadle, *Ezra Pound's Confucian Translations* (Ann Arbor: University of Michigan Press, 1997).

[58] Pound, *The Cantos*, pp. 37–40, 43, 44.

[59] Pound, 'Early Translators of Homer, 1: Hughes Salel', p. 96.

[60] See my *Ezra Pound and the Visual Culture of Modernism* (Cambridge: Cambridge University Press, 2007), pp. 154–62; Pound, *Guide to Kulchur*, p. 194.

[61] Pound, 'Provincialism the Enemy, I', p. 245.

editor, and in January 1920 he made a proposal of his own. Instead of the League of Nations, which he thought too bound by the nationalist concerns of its constituents, he proposed a 'league of peoples' instead of nations, a large, democratically-elected 'International Chamber', which would meet 'not less than six months per year', and would have 'no power of force but only persuasion'. It should be 'a force of international understanding, a moral force constituted in recognition of the futility of violent means'.[62]

The Cantos was conceived in this milieu, and Pound's use of non-translation, important through the whole life of the poem, cannot be divorced from this context. It has a striking aesthetic effect, but to read it only as aesthetic effect is to misunderstand its role. Furthermore, it is to abdicate responsibility for studying and understanding the arguments made through the poem's diverse materials. In 1934, Pound wrote to Sarah Perkins Cope:

> Skip anything you don't understand and go on till you pick it up again. All tosh about *foreign languages* making it difficult. The quotes are all either explained at once by repeat or they are definitely *of* the things indicated. If reader don't know what an elefant is, then the word IS obscure.
>
> I admit there are a couple of Greek quotes, one along in 39 that can't be understood without Greek, but *if* I can drive the reader to learning at least that much Greek, she or he will indubitably be filled with a durable gratitude. And if not, what harm? I can't conceal the fact that the Greek language existed.[63]

The liberating ambition of *The Cantos* is that all world culture, all 'civilization', to use Pound's preferred word during this period, is available to write with, to think with.[64] As in *The Future*, knowledge of national languages in *The Cantos* is valued as enabling insight into the psychology of peoples and people, as extending understanding beyond national perspectives, and contributing, Pound hoped, to international peace.

---

[62] Ezra Pound, '"Esope," France and the Trade Union', *New Age* 25.26 (23 October 1919): 423–4; Ezra Pound, 'Ezra Pound on the League of Ideas', *Much Ado* 10.2 (1919): 16–17; Ezra Pound, 'The Revolt of Intelligence, V', *New Age* 26.10 (8 January 1920): 153–4 (p. 153).

[63] Ezra Pound, letter to Sarah Perkins Cope, 15 January 1934, in *The Letters of Ezra Pound: 1907–1941*, pp. 250–1.

[64] Pound, 'The Revolt of Intelligence, V', p. 153.

6

'I like the Spanish title': William Carlos Williams's *Al Que Quiere!*

Peter Robinson

What's in a title?[1] On 21 February 1917 William Carlos Williams wrote to Marianne Moore of a book that was to have been called *Pagan Promises*, but now had a new and non-translated title, *A Book of Poems/Al Que Quiere!* 'I like the Spanish title', he remarked, 'just as I like a Chinese image cut out of stone. It is decorative and has a certain integral charm.' He did, however, add that 'such a title is not democratic—does not truly represent the contents of the book.'[2] As a consequence, he would add a subtitle: 'or / *The Pleasures of Democracy*'. This composite he also likes, but the publisher doesn't—and the latter got his way. The notes to the first volume of Williams's *Collected Poems* state that the 'book was published as simply *Al Que Quiere!*'[3] This, though, is not quite correct, for above the exclamatory Spanish phrase regularly cited as the book's title there appears on both the buff-coloured dust jacket and the title page: *A Book of Poems/Al Que Quiere!* Is it then the sub-title in Spanish that is not democratic, unlike the book's contents? Or is it the implication of the phrase in light of the super-title (*A Book of Poems*) that introduces it? Or is it something more elusive than both, or either, of these possibilities?

Williams translated the title for Moore as, 'To him who wants it', suggesting that the two parts surviving on the title page of the book published by Edmund Brown at the Four Seasons Press, Boston, in December 1917 are to mean it will 'fit audience find, though few'.[4] In *I Wanted to Write a Poem*, Williams explained, 'I have always associated it with a figure on a soccer field: to him who wants the ball to be passed to him. Moreover I associate it with a particular boy', one whose

---

[1] See, for instance, Hugh Haughton, 'How fit a title...' in *Geoffrey Hill: Essays on his Work*, ed. Peter Robinson (Milton Keynes: Open University Press, 1985), pp. 129–48.

[2] William Carlos Williams, *Collected Poems, Vol. 1: 1909–1939*, ed. A. Walton Litz and Christopher MacGowan (New York: New Directions, 1986), p. 480. *Life* magazine had described the poetry magazine *Others* as revealing 'a democracy of feeling rebelling against an aristocracy of form', cited in Rod Townley, *The Early Poetry of William Carlos Williams* (Ithaca and London: Cornell University Press, 1975), p. 78.

[3] *Collected Poems*, p. 480.

[4] John Milton, *Paradise Lost*, ed. Alistair Fowler, 2nd edn (London: Routledge, 2013): 7, l. 31. For details of the book's editorial genesis, see Townley, *The Early Poetry of William Carlos Williams*, pp. 84–7.

Peter Robinson, '*I like the Spanish title': William Carlos Williams's* Al Que Quiere! In: *Modernism and Non-Translation.* Edited by: Jason Harding and John Nash, Oxford University Press (2019). © the several contributors. DOI: 10.1093/oso/9780198821441.003.0006

'name was Suares, a Spaniard, and as I was half-Spanish, there was a bond.' Williams concludes: 'I was convinced nobody in the world of poetry wanted me but I was there willing to pass the ball if anyone did want it.'[5] The soccer field analogy places the poet both allusively in, and effectively out of, those democratic pleasures such as popular sports, suggesting the loneliness of being on the pitch but ignored by the other players.

There is a trace in the Spanish title of 'To whoever desires'—as if it implied this were a book of poems for the desirous. Such a theme is underlined by a poem with a non-translated Spanish title, a poem called 'Mujer' whose theme it tacitly insinuates:

> Oh, black Persian cat!
> Was not your life
> already cursed with offspring?
> We took you for rest to that old
> Yankee farm,—so lonely
> and with so many field mice
> in the long grass—
> and you return to us
> in this condition—!
> Oh, black Persian cat.

Without the non-translated title, this would seem to be no more than a bagatelle about their domestic cat's feline sexuality and exhausting motherhood. But with the Spanish word for a 'woman' or 'wife' above it, and the specification of the 'Yankee' farm, the Persian cat's getting pregnant again figures an implied miscegenation between the 'foreign' and the 'lonely' local—an implication seemingly arbitrary in its not being a Latino cat, though from a partially Hispanic household. The poem can then be a tacit celebration of the American melting pot in an appropriately oblique form.

The non-translated title strategy and the Persian cat's condition imply a number of complex dangers '*al que quiere*'—implications spelled out in 'Riposte', a poem with a French-derived title and arch apostrophe to its fellow citizens, an address that recurs throughout the book:

> Love is so precious
> my townspeople
> that if I were you I would

---

[5] William Carlos Williams, *I Wanted to Write a Poem: The Autobiography of the Works of a Poet*, ed. Edith Heal (New York: New Directions, 1976), p. 19.

> have it under lock and key—
> like the air or the Atlantic or
> like poetry![6]

Not only is *Al Que Quiere!* a book about the impulse essential to survival, like breathing air, but also a polemic for poetry's being an equally essential and natural impulse. It is as constrainable as the ocean facing the New Jersey shore. The book's appeal, to those who desire, links the embattled obscurity of the writer to the contrasting mores and values of his surroundings, associating the gesture of non-translation with this un-constrainable polemic. The book title's implications don't only touch on the experience of an obscure poet whose work few want to buy, but hint that it is written for those few who live passionately, admit to and accept their sexual and other desires, their loves, for the Spanish verb is used in the expression 'Te quiero'—'I love you'.

§

Titles of works function as promissory or advisory notices for the contents that follow. The New York Public Library copy of *Al Que Quiere!*, digitized by Google, gives the book's language as 'Spanish'.[7] This mishap underlines the standard expectation: that the body of the work will be in the language of its title. It is a liberty claimed by modernist works, and of poetry especially, that they be free of this entailment to a conventional expectation. Yet once the counter-convention was established, it became widespread—as in a book by Ezra Pound called *A Lume Spento* (1908), and one named *Lustra* (1916), and another by T. S. Eliot entitled *Ara Vos Prec* (1920).[8]

But is this is a modernist strategy, or one foreshadowed in poetry of the previous century? Poems such as Swinburne's 'Ave Atque Vale', Browning's 'Cenciaja', Ernest Dowson's 'Non sum qualis eram bonae sub regno Cynarae' or 'Vitae summa brevis spem nos vetat incohare longam' (though some think this an epigraph to 'The days of wine and roses'), or 'Papillons du Pavé' by Vincent O'Sullivan come to mind. Though there are antecedent promptings for such a non-translational florescence in the titles of nineteenth-century works, it is the commonality of the strategy among a loosely associated generation of mainly American poets

---

[6]   *Collected Poems*, pp. 95–6.

[7]   Digitized version of the New York Library copy of *A Book of Poems: Al Que Quiere!* at: https://archive.org/stream/abookpoemsalque00willgoog#page/n6/mode/2up (accessed: 1 January 2017).

[8]   Robert Haas, ed., *American Poetry: The Twentieth Century: Volume One—Henry Adams to Dorothy Parker* (New York: Library of America, 2000) offers such instances as 'Café du Dome' by Elsa von Freytag-Loringhoven, 'Venus Transiens' by Amy Lowell, 'Voyage à l'Infini' by Walter Conrad Arensberg, 'Der Blinde Junge' by Mina Loy, 'En Monocle' by Donald Evans, 'De Aegypto', 'Portrait d'une Femme', 'Les Milwins', and 'Liu Ch'e' by Ezra Pound, 'La Figlia Che Piange' by T. S. Eliot, 'Ars Poetica' by Archibald MacLeish, 'Recuerdo' by Edna St. Vincent Millay, and 'Résumé' by Dorothy Parker.

that forms the context for *Al Que Quiere!* Nor when in a language other than the work below is a title's promissory and advisory role abolished, but adjusted to include the implications in multi-lingual disruption. Then should there be a relation between the style of poems with non-translated titles and the mode of those same poems? In all cases, the language difference, and the historical relationship between languages, is crucial in shaping the implications prompted. It will make a difference to the cultural claim, status, and orientation offered whether the titles are in, for instance, Latin, Greek, Medieval French, Spanish, German, or Italian. These strategies and observations upon them are dependent upon an assumption about the language capacities of the then contemporary poetry readers. I take it that, at the time of publication, the limited availability of these first editions of not-well-known poets placed the works ambiguously in relation to a range of specialist-like readers—one stretching from Williams' university friend Pound, with his emergent, amateur, poly-lingual stretch, to a few bilingual readers (such as those in Williams's own family), and the more numerous single-language speakers with their smatterings of words from other, usually historically contiguous, tongues.

In *How To Do Things With Words*, J. L. Austin makes a passing reference to the role of titles as also doing things. In what were lecture notes, he gestures towards ideas to pursue about how titles and sub-titles are ways of conceding or concluding—suggesting that titles, whether overtly like Williams's, or implicitly, will manifest reader address and attempt to establish a communicative relationship:

> thus we may use the particle 'still' with the force of 'I insist that'; we may use 'therefore' with the force of 'I conclude that'; we use 'although' with the force of 'I concede that'. Note also the uses of 'whereas' and 'hereby' and 'moreover'. A very similar purpose is served by the use of titles such as Manifesto, Act, Proclamation, or the sub-heading 'A Novel...'.[9]

Al Que Quiere! has, as noted, the similarly functioning *A Book of Poems*. Titles also entitle, self-granting by claiming permission to act within the covers of the book in a certain fashion, and with that authorial permission come sets of expectations to be met or evaded. The permission in a title is then a form of promissory negotiation with a reader's needs, needs which Williams's title pointedly, though obliquely, evokes.

Titles in languages other than the work itself may be felt to threaten or puzzle, to offer an initial resistance, acting as a commissionaire at a hotel entrance, or

---

[9] J. L. Austin, *How To Do Things With Words*, 2nd edn, ed. J. O. Urmson and Marina Sbisà (Oxford: Oxford University Press, 1976), p. 75. For discussion of what might be involved in the entitling of art works, see my *Poetry, Poets, Readers: Making Things Happen* (Oxford: Oxford University Press, 2002), p. 150ff.

bouncer outside a nightclub, implying that only appropriately skilled readers need attempt to enter, or that those without the appropriate skills do so at their own risk. Rob Townley observes that the 'untranslated Spanish title, and the epigraph, also in Spanish' are 'further indications of Williams' disregard for the common reader', adding that in 'this snobbery he is ironically like Ezra Pound, whose posturings as an aloof and scholarly genius Williams could never stomach.' Yet this is immediately qualified by noting that although 'Williams insisted that his third book be as "secret" as the two which preceded it, drawing, for instance, on the complex of associations connected with his Spanish heritage, *Al Que Quiere!* is his most outward-directed book to date.'[10] Townley's comments cover the range of ambivalences that such a titular strategy might evoke, and ask whether it is linguistic snobbery to remind readers in a multi-lingual culture that there are others whose native languages may be other than the dominant one.

The complexities of modernist reader-relation strategies are further indicated by Townley's characterization of Pound's project. However motivated by a sense that readers will react badly, or have already ignored the poet, *Al Que Quiere!* might turn the tables by announcing exclusivity. Titles warn us regarding what we are about to read, what they expect us to bring to that reading, what they might be saying about the writer, and what expecting, more generally, about the cultural context for their composition and experience. Williams, we are told, 'knew well the prevailing American attitude towards "furriners" and immigrant people with even slightly dark skin like himself, whether from Spain or Latin America.'[11] Pound challenged his friend along these lines, writing the month before the book appeared on 10 November 1917: 'And America. What the hell do you a bloomin foreigner know about the place.' He means a characteristic critique of his homeland, and is saving Williams from being a pure product: 'You thank your bloomin gawd you've got enough spanish blood to muddy up your mind.'[12] The editor of their correspondence observes: 'Pound defends cosmopolitanism and argues that Williams' mixed ancestry compromises his nationalistic aesthetics', adding that the 'quotations show how early and how firmly racialist assumptions were established in Pound's thinking.'[13] Williams's *In the American Grain* (1925) makes a point of including the consequences of the Spanish conquest among its historical

---

[10] Townley, *The Early Poetry of William Carlos Williams*, p. 87.

[11] Jonathan Cohen, Introduction to William Carlos Williams, in *By Word of Mouth: Poems from the Spanish 1916–1959*, ed. Cohen (New York: New Directions, 2011), pp. xxiv–xxv.

[12] Hugh Witemeyer, ed., *Pound/Williams: Selected Letters of Ezra Pound and William Carlos Williams* (New York: New Directions, 1996), pp. 30, 31. Pound adds later, 'I was very glad to see your wholly incoherent unamerican poems in the *L.R.*' He is referring to 'Improvisations I–III' in the October 1917 issue of the magazine. Williams would quote from this letter in the 'Prologue' to *Kora in Hell*. See William Carlos Williams, *Imaginations* ed. Webster Schott (New York: New Directions, 1970), p. 11.

[13] Witemeyer, *Pound/Williams*, p. 5. Pound's assumptions had not changed when he published 'Dr Williams' Position' in *The Dial* (1928)—see Ezra Pound, *Literary Essays*, ed. T. S. Eliot (London: Faber & Faber, 1954), pp. 390–1.

studies. Such differences further indicate the range of cultural politics implied within the non-translational strategies of each poet's works.

Pound had written a preface to Williams's second book *The Tempers* (1913), published by Elkin Matthews. In a 10 June 1916 letter to Williams, Pound advised that in '[your] new book I should certainly keep at least part of the Tempers.'[14] *Al Que Quiere!* did not reprint from the earlier collection, and, as if challenging Pound's implications in his missive, Williams did include a poem called 'Foreign'. It addresses similarities and differences between 'Artsybashev' who 'is a Russian' and 'I' who 'am an American', but concludes—

> These are shining topics
> my townspeople but—
> hardly of great moment.[15]

The possessive 'my' form of this vocative tends towards a faintly distancing familiarity, preparing for the dismissal of their need to underline belonging by excluding others, a pattern of behaviour particularly noted between successive waves of immigration, as between Pound's and Williams's family histories. The mode of address, to the inhabitants as a whole, also has a wishful or fictional aspect, as if the vocative (in light of the book's title) is not expecting to reach its fellow citizens' ears, but, rather, to claim, Shelley-like, an unacknowledged role—and to do this by a pretended address to one apparent constituency that is directed, by means of its title, to another, to '*al que quiere*'.

§

Though Edmund Brown didn't like 'or *The Pleasures of Democracy*', he did accept non-translated hypertexts in the form of the Spanish title and epigraph. Such a publishing strategy might call for justification, and in a manner received it with the jacket blurb to the first edition—which embraces its publishing project as contemptuous of popularity, and perhaps undemocratic in its attitude to others *en masse*. Nevertheless, it ends by suggesting that the collection it prefaces is in an American grain of democratic inclusiveness and sexual equality, by claiming affinities with an acknowledged forebear. It begins by offering its own paraphrase translation of the Spanish subtitle:

> To Whom It May Concern! This book is a collection of poems by William Carlos Williams. You, gentle reader, will probably not like it, because it is brutally powerful and scornfully crude. Fortunately, neither the author nor the publisher care much whether you like it or not. The author has done his work, and if

[14] Witemeyer, *Pound/Williams*, p. 28.   [15] *Collected Poems*, pp. 79–80.

you *do* read the book you will agree that he doesn't give a damn for your opinion....And we, the publishers, don't much care whether you buy the book or not. It only costs a dollar, so that we can't make much profit out of it. But we have the satisfaction of offering that which will outweigh, in spite of its eighty small pages, a dozen volumes of pretty lyrics. We have the profound satisfaction of publishing a book in which, we venture to predict, the poets of the future will dig for material as the poets of today dig in Whitman's *Leaves of Grass.*[16]

This sales pitch is calculatedly rebarbative on the tightrope of what may be involved in contributing to American culture in the year of its entry into the Great War—for it is simultaneously proud of its self-reliant autonomy, its lack of dependence upon the opinions of others, and yet, by protesting too much, it appears faintly craven to the very readers it simultaneously courts and spurns. It is similarly concerned about the making of money, which it highlights by dismissing slim volumes of verse on this account, faintly contemptuous of poetry as a means to that end, and proud of its commitment to the higher value of America's literary culture as indicated by association with the work of that democratic symbol: Walt Whitman and his *Leaves of Grass.*[17]

The reference to the great predecessor in the blurb might be thought a tacit justification for the collection's Spanish title too. Whitman is said to have 'looked upon Spain as "maternal"',[18] and though he doesn't make a strategy of non-translated titles, he would allow himself 'Salut aux Monde' and 'Our Old Feuillage', as well as Spanish-sounding words, especially those with a democratic implication, familiar enough among lines from 'The Song of the Open Road', whose final section begins 'Allons!': 'Camerado, I give you my hand! / I give you my love more precious than money, / I give you myself before preaching and law; / will you give me yourself?'[19] Williams's letter to Moore asserted that his book's contents—largely, though not exclusively, in English—are democratic, but his Spanish title is not. Yet it might be advisable to trust the title and not the title-provider, for the Spanish *Al Que Quiere!* challenges the equality within that 1917 American culture of languages and language-speakers. Like its jacket blurb, the bilingual full title, *A Book of Poems: Al Que Quiere!* is provocatively ambivalent about its desire or need for readers, and its bilingualism projects an inner dividedness onto a divisively

[16]   *Collected Poems*, p. 480. Reed Whittemore speculates that the poet himself wrote it, because he paid $50 towards the publication, in *William Carlos Williams: Poet from New Jersey* (Boston: Houghton Mifflin, 1975), p. 109.

[17]   Dorothy Dudley took exception to these misleading, as she saw it, prefatory remarks in her largely positive April 1918 review for *Poetry* (Chicago): 'As preface to these poems the publishers have been, I think, foolish in dealing the "gentle reader," as they are pleased to call him, a kind of blow over the head.' See 'A Small Garden Induced to Grow in Unlikely Circumstances', *Poetry* 12.1 (April 1918): 38–43.

[18]   Julio Marzán, Foreword to William Carlos Williams, in *By Word of Mouth: Poems from the Spanish 1916–1959*, ed. Jonathan Cohen (New York: New Directions, 2011), p. xii.

[19]   Walt Whitman, *Poetry and Prose*, ed. Justin Kaplan (New York: Library of America, 1982), p. 307.

prejudicial dominant culture where there will have been many potential readers who would have been more at home with, and able to construe, the first part of the title than the second.

The contractual implications of such titles recall Geoffrey Hill's opinion, expressed in his *Paris Review* interview, that difficulty is democratic:

> I think art has a right—not an obligation—to be difficult if it wishes. And, since people generally go on from this to talk about elitism versus democracy, I would add that genuinely difficult art is truly democratic. And that tyranny requires simplification. [...] And any complexity of language, any ambiguity, any ambivalence implies intelligence. Maybe an intelligence under threat, maybe an intelligence that is afraid of consequences, but nonetheless an intelligence working in qualifications and revelations...resisting, therefore, tyrannical simplification.[20]

Hill's opinion is less ambivalent and qualified than it might be. The 'democratic' here straddles the assumption of a duty to be open to all and an asserted right to benign-intending exclusivity, whether only initial or stubbornly prolonged. It implies responsibilities to attempt self-improvement and cultural assimilation across class and ethnic divides. In a true democracy all are equal, languages and cultures equally valued, the variety and complexity of the world's cultures migrating into and mingling in a space such as the USA ideally available as an inheritance to all without prejudice. This, though, was never exactly the experience of migrants through Ellis Island, and however much the strategy of *Al Que Quiere!* may aim at a higher inclusiveness that would unify the divided strains of its poet's inheritance, the difficulties of local acceptance and tactical assimilation are also called out by the non-translated in this title.

Deriving from a short story by Rafael Arévalo Martínez called, 'El hombre que parecia un cabalo' (1915), the epigraph to *Al Que Quiere!* is also not-translated in the original publication. It further underlines the title's statement of intent as expressed not so much in what it says, as the fact that it too is in a language other than most of the work which it fronts for. Such epigraphs are inevitably allusive to a cultural hinterland other than that of their books' predominant medium:

> Había sido un arbusto desmedrado que prolonga sus filamentos hasta encontrar el humus necesario en una tierra nueva. Y cómo me nutría! Me nutría con la beatitud con que las hojas trémulas de clorófila se extienden al sol; con la beatitud con que una raíz encuentra un cadáver en descompositión; con la beatitud con que los convalecientes dan sus pasos vacilantes en las mañanas de primavera, bañadas de luz;...[21]

[20] Geoffrey Hill, 'The Art of Poetry LXXX', *Paris Review* 154 (Spring 2000): 277.
[21] *Collected Poems*, p. 481.

That the epigraph needed correcting at a number of points from the one presented in the first edition (it has e.g. 'neuva' for 'nueva') might speak to the precariousness and inner division of the poet's biculturalism. Though he grew up in a Spanish-speaking household, he is reported never to have mastered the language, writing to his wife Floss from Spain in 1910, after an encounter with a ticket collector on a train from Madrid: 'You should have heard me slinging choice Rutherford Spanish at him with that peculiar Hackensack accent which you know so well.'[22]

Williams published a translation of this story called, 'The Man Who Resembled a Horse'—made with the help of his father, William George Williams—in *The Little Review* for December 1918. But before citing that translation, it is worth perhaps pausing to consider the effect of encountering this epigraph in the 1917 publication, especially if you have little or no Spanish. The concept of non-translation is, in any case, and in the case of Williams's first mature book of poems, one dependent on the concept of translation that it exists by negating. The possibility of translating, and the in-this-instance contextual refusal to translate the text in another language, must always be present for 'non-translation' to be a relevant interpretive category. There are innumerable un-translated sentences in the world's libraries that aren't exempla of non-translation, because they do not inhabit a space where their translation might be expected but has been refused, denied, or resisted. The publication of Arévalo Martínez's story in the year following the appearance of *Al Que Quiere!* underlines the resistant, non-translated status of the epigraph—not least since commentators can cite a partially authorial translation for this very text. What's more, the years leading up to its publication saw Williams collaborating with his dying father on the translation of a number of poems by the author of the story, as well as ones by José Santos Chocano, Alfonso Guillén Zelaya, Luis Carlos López, and José Asunción Silva for a 1916 Spanish-American Number of Alfred Kreymborg's magazine *Others*, for which Williams worked as a contributing editor. Thus the non-translation of hypertexts in *Al Que Quiere!* is coextensive with, and contextualized by, the translation in a modernist mode of poems by poets from Guatemala, Peru, Honduras, and Colombia.[23]

Here, then, is the poet's and his father's translation of that epigraph, which he could, after all, have made for the Four Seasons publication:

I had been an adventurous shrub which prolongs its filaments until it finds the necessary humus in new earth. And how I fed! I fed with the joy of tremulous leaves of chlorafile that spread themselves to the sun; with the joy with which a

---

[22] Williams, *By Word of Mouth: Poems from the Spanish 1916–1959*, p. 129, citing a manuscript in the Lilly Library, Indiana University at Bloomington.

[23] For the originals and translations of these poems, and a discussion of their joint authorship (despite attribution only to the poet's father in magazine publication), see Williams, *By Word of Mouth: Poems from the Spanish 1916–1959*, pp. xxvii–xxx and 2–23.

root encounters a decomposing corpse; with the joy with which convalescents take their vacillating steps in the light flooded mornings of spring;...[24]

Taken out of the story's context, this passage can read analogically as figuring the experience that has generated these poems—a cultural soil and inspiration that starts somewhere else and yet pushes out to find appropriately fresh resources and nutrients in a different cultural ground. The non-translated Spanish text bars the way, as it were, to a collection of American poems exemplifying both where the adventurous shrub has come from and where the 'new' is heading, where it has fed so deeply. But this newness is bifurcated too, for it can refer both to the culture of America in which the Spanish strains must sound, and to the sound of a new American poetry coming forth from that fresh ground.

The jacket blurb draws attention to various ways in which these two kinds of newness, for this bicultural poet, are themselves in fierce conflict—and in conflict too within the Spanish-speaking household of his upbringing. In *The Autobiography of William Carlos Williams*, the poet notes:

> Spanish and French were the languages I heard habitually while I was growing up. Mother could talk very little English when I was born, and Pop spoke Spanish better, in fact, than most Spaniards. But Pop spoke English too, and as time went on one of my happiest memories of him was when he would some-times read to us in the evening. Those were the marvelous days![25]

Julio Marzán notes of *Yes, Mrs. Williams: A Personal Record of my Mother* (1959), which celebrates the poet's upbringing in a three-language household, that it is 'also a tacit ars poetica, informing us that underlying his amply articulated tenets on poetry is the principle of translation' and that whether 'making poems of life experiences or marvelling at the semantic possibilities in Elena's mispronunci-ations and malapropisms, he was translating ambient aesthetic essence into artis-tic form.'[26] Such a linguistic background, too, would not be accurately represented by the figure of translation, but of non-translation—for it is a characteristic of such households that what takes place is not explicit translation into a normative or dominant language, but rather implied understandings and uses simultan-eously manifested through answering a question in one language by replying in another, itself also understood. In such bilingual circumstances, though there is communication, it is manifested exactly by means of non-translation.

§

<hr>

[24] Rafael Arévalo Martínez, 'The Man who Resembled a Horse', *The Little Review* 5.8 (Dec 1918): 45.

[25] William Carlos Williams, *The Autobiography of William Carlos Williams* (New York: New Directions, 1967), p. 15.

[26] Marzán, Foreword to William Carlos Williams, *By Word of Mouth*, p. xiii.

As well as offering an un-translated title to the entire book, *Al Que Quiere!* contains eight poems, from among fifty-two, titled in languages other than that of their texts. What does a non-translated title entitle its author to have done in the poem itself? 'Sub Terra', the name of the first work in *Al Que Quiere!*, is in Latin, and, like 'Hic Jacet' in *The Tempers*, concerns prospects for the then contemporary poetry. Williams observed: 'Why did I use the Latin title *Sub Terra* for this poem? I was not pretentious—yes, I guess I was. I thought I was contemptuous of Latin but I suppose I wanted to appear a Latin scholar which I was not.'[27] Interspersed with titles in English, it is followed, pretentiously or not, by 'El Hombre', 'Libertad! Igualidad! Fraternidad!', 'Canthara', 'Mujer', 'Danse Russe', 'Keller Gegen Dom', and 'Divertimiento'—plus the poem already cited, as if to make the point, called 'Foreign'. So the book's second language is distinctly Spanish, but with Latin used twice, French both used and alluded to, and German bringing up the rear. Perhaps the most striking of these non-translated titles is 'Libertad! Igualidad! Fraternidad!' which draws attention to its status as non-translated by being an adaptation into Spanish of that democratically resonant French revolutionary slogan.

The poem it heads up is more than equivocal about its democratically egalitarian impulses when confronted with a poor, grimly unhappy road hog, a person whom the poem again only appears to address in a form of *esprit d'escalier*. 'You sullen pig of a man', it begins, 'you force me into the mud / with your stinking ash-cart!', only immediately to recognize him as 'Brother!' and to add that 'if we were rich / we'd stick our chests out / and hold our heads high!' Though immediately inclined to be at odds with the refuse collector because of his bad road manners, the poet recognizes him as an equal and one of those with whom he should show solidarity. It concludes:

> Well—
> all things turn bitter in the end
> whether you choose the right or
> the left way
>   and—
> dreams are not a bad thing.[28]

Thus the turning to the left or right on the road, having the effect of driving the local doctor into the mud, are transfigured into the political decision to move to the left or the right; and to the equality and fraternity of the encounter is added the liberty to drive as you wish. If these are '*The Pleasures of Democracy*' that Williams had in mind when proposing that alternative title, then they too are not

---

[27] Williams, *I Wanted to Write a Poem*, p. 21.   [28] *Collected Poems*, p. 77.

unequivocally positive ones. The publisher may have rejected it not only to avoid title-page clutter, but to free the book from undirected irony too. 'Libertad! Igualidad! Fraternidad!' defends ironically the right to be dreaming on the job, and dreaming, as the poet is, of a society more motivated by the great aspirations of the French Revolution, ones cast into the light of Anglo and Hispanic relations in North America through that translated and yet non-translated title—in a book published less than two months after the Bolshevik Revolution.

The prevalence of non-translated titles in the poetry of the early and high modernist decades indicates that such strategies were shared by writers with distinguishable aesthetic projects—ones which would exfoliate into different, and often conflicted, political and cultural allegiances. Though not the first poem with a non-translated title, 'El Hombre' is the first with a non-translated Spanish one:

> It's a strange courage
> you give me ancient star:
>
> Shine alone in the sunrise
> towards which you lend no part![29]

Marzán provides a reading of the poem through its allusion to a number of Spanish heritages, noting that it is an 'exercise in baroque wordplay' and 'also autobiographical'. He identifies the 'ancient star' as referring 'to Hélène, "bright light" or "star,"' and associates this *belle Hélène* with the poet's now old mother Elena Hoheb Williams, who would be widowed the year following the publication of *Al Que Quiere!* So it is she, commanded by him to 'Shine alone', who gives the poet a 'strange courage'—where 'strange' may mean not only 'unusual' but also 'foreign'. Marzán notes that this 'title is a tribute to Góngora, whom Williams in an essay called "the man!"'[30] Yet here the man is, presumably, also the poet himself, drawing strength from his Puerto Rican, Spanish- and French-speaking mother, who shines brightly in solitary splendour not contributing, it would appear, to the American sunrise going on around her, and yet giving her son the courage to be a man, an 'hombre' in that very light.

'El Hombre' is the poem upon which Wallace Stevens composed his variations in 'Nuances of a Theme by Williams', about which the poet reports he 'was deeply touched.'[31] These appeared first in the same December 1918 issue of *The Little Review* as the story translated as 'The Man who Resembled a Horse', underneath an epigraph citing the whole of its prompting occasion—that's to say, the four lines of the poem, but, perhaps significantly, not its Spanish title:

---

[29] *Collected Poems*, p. 76.
[30] Marzán, Foreword to William Carlos Williams, *By Word of Mouth*, p. xiv.
[31] Williams, *I Wanted to Write a Poem*, p. 23.

I

Shine alone, shine nakedly, shine like bronze,
that reflects neither my face nor any inner part
of my being, shine like fire, that mirrors nothing.

II

Lend no part to any humanity that suffuses
you in its own light.
Be not chimera of morning,
Half-man, half-star.
Be not an intelligence,
Like a widow's bird
Or an old horse.[32]

The nuances that Stevens evokes in the first stanza draw attention to a distancing and non-identification of the original's speaker with the star, as if he was aware of Williams' equivocations regarding his part-Spanish heritage, and the possibility that the 'strange courage' to stand alone implies a desire to be free of that too. Stevens may have been aware of the original's punning on the poet's mother's name, for in the second part he appears to encourage its poet not to be an 'intelligence', not to be 'like a widow's bird'—a repetitive singer in the cage of a woman such as his mother would soon be, 'or an old horse', one such as the man resembled in the epigraph to *Al Que Quiere!* It is possible, then, that in this poem Stevens is advising Williams to free himself from that 'Half-man, half star' condition, his bicultural inheritance, by associating with his English part. Is this why Stevens doesn't cite the Spanish title to the original? He quotes the four text lines of the poem but doesn't indicate the sort of man it is about is 'El Hombre', a word absorbed into spoken American to mean a particular kind of man.[33]

Among the most celebrated non-translated title poems is 'Danse Russe', alluding to performances of the Russian Ballet that had taken place in New York in 1916:

If I when my wife is sleeping
and the baby and Kathleen

---

[32] Wallace Stevens, *Collected Poetry and Prose*, ed. Frank Kermode (New York: Library of America, 1997), pp. 14–15. Stevens's poem may derive from his comments on *Al Que Quiere!* as 'dissipated and obscured' in a 9 April [1918] letter where he states: 'There are very few men who have anything native in them or for whose work I'd give a Bolshevik ruble...But I think your tantrums not half mad enough.' Cited in 'Prologue' to *Kora in Hell* in *Imaginations*, pp. 15–16.

[33] Stevens's relations with the Hispanic emphasize its exoticism, otherness, tacit threat, and deathliness, as in 'Attempt to Discover Life' from *Transport to Summer* (1947) where at 'San Miguel de los Baños, / The waitress heaped up black Hermosas' and 'a cadaverous person, / Who bowed and, bowing, brought, in her mantilla, / A woman brilliant and pallid-skinned'. The poem concludes with non-translated currency: 'The cadaverous persons were dispelled. / On the table near which they stood / Two coins were lying—dos centavos.' (Stevens, *Collected Poetry and Prose*, pp. 320–1).

are sleeping
and the sun is a flame-white disc
in silken mists
above shining trees,—
if I in my north room
dance naked, grotesquely
before my mirror
waving my shirt round my head
and singing softly to myself:
'I am lonely, lonely.
I was born to be lonely,
I am best so!'
If I admire my arms, my face,
my shoulders, flanks, buttocks
against the yellow drawn shades,—

Who shall say I am not
the happy genius of my household?[34]

The French title serves to justify this report on an unusual piece of behaviour on the part of the good doctor—for he might be associating himself at such an hour, his wife and their live-in help asleep, with the sacrificially chthonic folk rhythms of *The Rite of Spring*, and with the sexually liberated suggestions of the new choreography. The 'yellow drawn shades' of the north room figure like the closed curtains of a theatre or the backdrop to a set—in either case the poem, though evoking in its non-translated title a real performance by the Russian Ballet Company, does not have such a performance's openly displayed relation to an audience. The poet's cavorting is not revealed to 'my townspeople' in the physically enclosed and curtained space of the room, and, as a critic has noted, only notionally revealed to them by its publication.

Barry Ahearn has touched on the important issue of the distribution and readership of the poem in the course of commenting on 'Danse Russe':

Williams so vividly presents the dance that we might conclude that the poem nevertheless amounts to a public revelation of something Williams otherwise keeps deeply hidden—his inner fantasy. But how public a revelation was it? Williams first placed this poem in the December 1916 issue of *Others*. Subsequently it appeared in *Others: An Anthology* (1917) and in *Al Que Quiere!* (1917). None of these volumes had a wide circulation in Rutherford. So far as his

---

[34] *Collected Poems*, pp. 86–7.

neighbors were aware of them, Williams might have concealed 'Danse Russe' at the back of his desk drawer.[35]

Ahearn's book is much concerned with the inner contradictions of Williams's poetry, remembering Jekyll and Hyde as a way of figuring this aspect of the poet's work, and this double aspect of the work's performance can also be felt in noting that the publication constraints which meant the work appeared with small publishers in New York and Boston. It wasn't then readily available to the townspeople of Rutherford, New Jersey. Nevertheless, as we have seen, the poet frequently adopts a seemingly direct address to 'my townspeople'. The poem's concluding question ('Who shall say I am not /the happy genius of my household?') might imply the simple answer that everyone else is asleep and no one can see, so he is democratically free to behave as he likes. Yet his singing, 'I am lonely, lonely. / I was born to be lonely, / I am best so!' also indicates that he is not exactly happy, and his happiness as the 'genius' of his household depends on there being others who know, such as those towards whom his title equivocally reaches.

Williams's question, evoking the possible, though negated, existence of those who might deny him the title 'happy genius of my household', expresses both the admired self-reliance and autonomy that allows him to affirm this without any denial. Yet his chanting upon his own loneliness also evokes the possibility of a more affirming and mutual cultural environment. Even in the absence of the apostrophized object, poets are inclined to respond equivocally, and, by calling upon the absence of something or someone, they make these entities present in imagination, possible to contemplation. The act of imagination may often depend upon this absence, but it also tacitly invites a change of status, wants the thought of their presence, even if it benefits from their absence as facilitating the gesture, the revelation of something only partially revealed. Such equivocations are at the heart of non-translated language use as well.

§

Thus it need come as no surprise that there can be found a conflict between the divisions of a bicultural family, and the claims of a vanguard modernity and modernism, conflicts that are at the heart of two of the most important poems in *Al Que Quiere!*—though ones which do not happen to have non-translated titles. While both of Williams's parents had developed artistic and literary tastes and abilities, neither of them warmed to the *dernier cri* of the little magazine culture to which their son contributed. After his father's death on Christmas Day 1918, the poet had a dream in which 'he only looked up at me over his right shoulder and commented severely, "You know all that poetry you're writing. Well, it's no

[35] Barry Ahearn, *William Carlos Williams and Alterity: The Early Poems* (Cambridge: Cambridge University Press, 1994), p. 31.

good." I was left speechless', he adds, 'and woke trembling.'[36] His mother had studied art in Paris, in the later nineteenth century, and, despite his imitating her still life paintings in 'Metric Figure' from the same collection, her tastes were not her son's.[37]

'Dedication for a Plot of Ground' offers a family portrait of Emily Dickinson Wellcome, his English grandmother on his father's side, in terms that help explain the entire stance of *Al Que Quiere!*—terms that, as might now be expected, are by no means unequivocal. The poem builds to its climactic confrontation with what is, in effect, the reader of the poem, by listing things that his grandmother had to resist so as to bring her family to the Americas and survive:

> against flies, against girls
> that came smelling about, against
> drought, against weeds, storm-tides,
> neighbors, weasels that stole her chickens,
> against the weakness of her own hands
> against the growing strength of
> the boys, against wind, against
> the stones, against trespassers,
> against rents, against her own mind.[38]

Among the 'girls / that came smelling around', perhaps, was the poet's own mother, and the rivalry between the two is attested in his autobiography:

Grandma took me over or tried to. But my mother lost her temper and laid the old gal out with a smack across the puss that my mother joyfully remembered until her death. Her Latin blood got the best of her that day. Nor was she sorry; it did her more good, in fact, than anything that had happened to her since coming to the States from Santo Domingo to be married.[39]

The first sentence suggests that the conflict between Williams's English grandmother and his Puerto Rican mother might have focused around linguistic and ethnic dominance in the household culture, a bi-cultural battle being fought out through the poet and his name. In the admired resistance, there is an undercurrent of criticism—for resisting the independence of the local girls and boys, two of whom would become the poet's parents.

The strength of 'Dedication for a Plot of Ground' lies in its articulation of both admiration and astonishment, for at its heart is a division about the preservation of

---

[36] *The Autobiography of William Carlos Williams*, p. 14.
[37] *I Wanted to Write a Poem*, p. 21.   [38] *Collected Poems*, p. 106.
[39] *The Autobiography of William Carlos Williams*, p. 5.

a self and an English heritage, alongside the ambivalences of assimilation. Yet something of the self-reliance and sexualized disdain for those unfit to enter suggested by his book's Spanish title carries into the conclusion to 'Dedication for a Plot of Ground': 'If you can bring nothing to this place / But your carcass, keep out.'[40] Through the stubborn and determined life of his paternal English grandmother he came to have the complex lineage which helps inspire the volume's strategies as a whole. It was, after all, she who brought the poet's father to Puerto Rico when he was five years old, where he would eventually meet the future writer's local mother.

The other especially significant poem, 'January Morning', is a celebration of an improvisational poetic responsiveness to unexpected phenomena, one that Marianne Moore picked out for admiration in a later review of the poet's work.[41] Section one of the 'Suite', as it is subtitled, explains: 'I have discovered that most of / the beauties of travel are due to / the strange hours we keep to see them', exemplifying this by noting:

> the domes of the Church of
> the Paulist Fathers in Weehawken
> against a smoky dawn—the heart stirred—
> are beautiful as Saint Peters
> approached after years of anticipation.

The suite concludes with a section that again turns to the problem of modern poetry's difficulty and its democratic impulse:

> All this—
>   was for you, old woman.
> I wanted to write a poem
> that you would understand.
> For what good is it to me
> if you can't understand it?
>   But you got to try hard—
> But—
>   Well, you know how
> the young girls run giggling
> on Park Avenue after dark
> when they ought to be home in bed?
> Well,
> that's the way it is with me somehow.[42]

---

[40] *Collected Poems*, p. 106.

[41] 'How many poets, old or new, have written anything like "January Morning" in *Al Que Quiere!* [...]?' Marianne Moore, *The Complete Prose*, ed. Patricia C. Willis (London: Faber and Faber, 1987), p. 59.

[42] *Collected Poems*, pp. 100 and 103–4.

But how does the final remark and the comparison of the poet to those giggling girls out late at night relate to the problem of democracy and comprehension? The poem's conclusion strikes a similar note to that of 'Danse Russe', one in which a *risqué* youthful freedom with sexual overtones is adopted as the equivalent of writing free-verse poetry in the loosely responsive sketch-form of 'January Morning'.

The old woman addressed in its final part, the poet's mother Elena most probably, is being invited to see the point and to become one of those who does 'want' the poems her son has written. And the democracy of his art, as exemplified in this book, is underlined here by the idea of having 'to try hard'. This was what Hill's point amounted to in his *Paris Review* interview, trying hard equated with resisting simplification and tyranny. Yet Williams's poem makes painfully clear ('For what good is it to me / if you can't understand it?') that the terms of a democratic reader-writer contract cannot be dictated by one or other party. The responsibility not to simplify is not only matched by an obligation to reader effort, but by the requirement not to obfuscate. There being entitlements on both sides, there will be duties and responsibilities too.

One of those responsibilities, in a modern multi-cultural democracy, such as the United States in the early decades of the twentieth century, is to accept the benefits and the complexities of living in a world where, less than two years before Williams put together the poems for his third book *Al Que Quiere!*, Ludwig Wittgenstein wrote that the '*limits of my language* mean the limits of my world'.[43] Yet among those complexities is the likelihood that for my world not to be a mere illusion, its language has to recognize the existence of languages spoken within its cultural spaces which appear, to those who do not understand them, beyond it. The language limits that are my world include within them languages I know I don't know. The multilingual texts of modernist poems remind us how important it is for our democracies to recognize and embrace the existence within them of what we do not know, but that we do, at least, know we don't know—and for us to be willing, in that light, 'to try hard'.

---

[43] Ludwig Wittgenstein, *Tractatus Logico-Philosophicus*, trans. D. F. Pears and B. F. McGuinness (London: Routledge and Kegan Paul, 1961), 5.6, and *Notebooks 1914–1916*, 2nd edn, ed. H. H. von Wright and G. E. M. Anscombe (Chicago: University of Chicago Press, 1979), 49e. The original German entry is dated 23 May 1915.

7

'The passionate moment': Untranslated Quotation in Pound and Eliot

Stephen Romer

At the risk of being presumptuous, I should like to begin this chapter by briefly exploring why, in one of my own recent poems—a poem of bereavement for a loved one—I should have used, and felt compelled to use, an untranslated quotation, the subject at present under discussion. The words in Latin, *ad te veniam*, and the triplet,

> *non vos relinquam orphanos*
> *vado et venio ad vos*
> *et gaudebit cor vestrum*

come from the Vulgate, from John 14:18 and 16:22, from what is known as the High Priest's Prayer and for me one of the most moving passages in the Gospel. In the context of a harrowing race to the bedside, I wrote,

> *ad te veniam*
>
> and stumbled from the taxi
> hours later
> but wings grown
> to the blazing vertical city
> up to the encampment
> our curtained tent
> on the summit of K3
> where the air had rarefied
> and they left us alone
> tight screened around

Part of the poem, 'In that High Tent', also contains transcriptions of actual SMS messages received during that day.[1] The untranslated quotation falls like a

---

[1] Stephen Romer, *Set Thy Love in Order: New & Selected Poems* (Manchester: Carcanet, 2017), pp. 23–4.

Stephen Romer, *'The passionate moment': Untranslated Quotation in Pound and Eliot* In: *Modernism and Non-Translation*. Edited by: Jason Harding and John Nash, Oxford University Press (2019). © the several contributors. DOI: 10.1093/oso/9780198821441.003.0007

fragment of otherness—it is allusion in the strongest (and modern) sense—not alluding to something implicitly or covertly or figuratively, but by *direct quotation*, which is what I call strong allusion, or mandatory allusion, in the sense that it cannot be missed. Unignorable allusion, that triggers what Michael Riffaterre has called a 'compulsory reader response'.[2] But the fragment trails behind it a whole congeries of context, and storied associations, it opens within the poem a kind of trapdoor, connecting it to a wider commonality, indeed to the wider community of Christendom as it has been fed by the Latin Vulgate. It seems that 'powerful and concurrent reasons'—the expression Newman used about the process that led to his conversion experience—including the faith of my mother, led also to the inclusion of the Latin quotation. Related also are deep memories of hearing that passage from St John read out at Easter, especially the expression, 'I shall not leave you comfortless', and a more recent, sudden encounter of the Latin in an anthem by William Byrd—*non vos relinquam orphanos*.

There is a 'shock of recognition' of sorts, which comes at a particular vulnerable, receptive time, in Eliot's sense. I am aware that without the example of the Modernists, who have made the embedding of untranslated quotation such a recognizable trademark, a kind of hallmark almost, of the 'brand'—the Latin phrase might not have got in there.

The 'untranslated quotation' falls under the rubric Allusion in *The New Princeton Encyclopedia to Poetry and Poetics* and this might be useful and to the point. Allusion: 'A poet's deliberate incorporation of identifiable elements from other sources, preceding or contemporaneous, textual or extratextual.' And also: 'Allusion assumes, (1) prior achievements or events as sources of value; (2) readers sharing knowledge with the poet; (3) incorporation of sufficiently familiar yet distinctive elements and (4) fusion of the incorporated and incorporating elements.'[3]

Turning now to Eliot's practice, on the subject of the status and nature of the quotation, a first sidelight on the question came to me when I re-read the French translation of *Ash-Wednesday*, by Pierre Leyris. Coming to the passages that Eliot borrows directly from the Hail Mary, it was striking to read them returned to their Latin form in the Roman rite. Hence, we get this:

> Teach us to care and not to care
> Teach us to sit still

> Pray for us sinners now and at the hour of our death
> Pray for us now and at the hour of our death

---

[2] See Michael Riffaterre, 'Compulsory Reader Response: the Intertextual Drive', in *Intertextuality: Theories and Practices*, ed. Michael Worton and Judith Still (Manchester: Manchester University Press, 1990), pp. 56–78.

[3] Alex Preminger and T.V. F. Brogan, eds, *The New Princeton Encyclopedia of Poetry and Poetics* (Princeton: Princeton University Press, 1993), p. 39.

> *Apprenez-nous l'amour et le détachement*
> *Apprenez-nous à rester en repos*
>
> *Ora pro nobis peccatoribus nunc et in hora mortis nostrae*
> *Ora pro nobis nunc et in hora mortis nostrae.*

At the end of Part III we have:

> Lord, I am not worthy
> Lord, I am not worthy
>
> but speak the word only
>
> *Domine non sum dignus*
> *Domine non sum dignus*
>
> *sed tantum dic verbo*[4]

One thought that struck me was, why did Eliot himself, never averse to embedding polyglot phrases in his poems, not use the Latin? He writes, firstly, in the Anglo-Catholic tradition—Geoffrey Hill recently called *Four Quartets* part of the 'Anglican lectionary'—so to revert directly, overtly to the Roman rite would have seemed perhaps inappropriate.[5] Another, equally weighty matter concerns the music and rhythm of the phrases, the sudden obtrusion of the Latin seems to me heavy, after the French, as it would after the English in a poem where the rhythm is almost hypnotic at times, and where incantation is paramount. In fact, in the whole of *Ash-Wednesday*, which is a poem after all freighted with allusion, there is only one phrase which is untranslated, *sovegna vos*, which comes from Dante (*Purgatorio* XXVI) and which sank so deeply into Eliot's imagination, and into his auditory imagination, that it recurs like a struck chord, throughout the *Collected Poems*.

Sovegna vos by the time of *Ash-Wednesday*, one feels has become *talismanic* (it is spoken by Arnaut Daniel in *Purgatory* XXVI, introducing the section in Provençal—'*Ara vos prec...*') and which has come to represent for Eliot a whole personal history of hell and purgation; after all, the verse immediately following—*Poi s'ascose nel foco che gli affina*—is universally known as one of the fragments shored against (our) ruin at the end of *The Waste Land*. The Provençal *Sovegna vos* therefore is no light or trifling or passing allusion; it is laden with contextual significance, reminiscent of the strangely lit, somehow excoriated landscape

---

[4] Pierre Leyris, *T. S. Eliot: Poésie* (Paris: Seuil, 1969), pp. 121–7.
[5] Geoffrey Hill, *Collected Critical Writings*, ed. Kenneth Haynes (Oxford: Oxford University Press, 2009), p. 547.

where the lady Matilda wanders, plucking flowers, in *Purgatorio* XXX in which Dante, now left by Virgil who can no longer follow him, and who tells him he can do as he likes, wanders punch-drunk and wide-eyed with the new freedom. Early drafts of *Ash-Wednesday* had the title *al som de l'escalina*, also from *Purgatory* XXVI, and the passage returns, but this time translated and adapted, in the Dantescan passage of *Litle Gidding*—'from wrong to wrong the exasperated spirit/ proceeds, unless restored by that refining fire/ where you must move in measure, like a dancer...'.[6]

To continue tracing the career of *Sovegna vos* throughout Eliot's poems, we find it again as the epigraph to *Poems* (1920), the volume originally entitled *Ara Vos Prec*, from the beginning of the Arnaut Daniel passage in Canto XXVI. As if we needed clarification on this, recall how Eliot describes the closing Cantos of the *Pugatorio*, in 'Dante' (1929): 'in a way these cantos are of the greatest *personal* intensity in the whole poem... It is in these last cantos of the *Purgatorio*, rather than in the *Paradiso*, that Beatrice appears most clearly'.[7] In fact the whole Arnaut passage provides a scattering of epigraphs or embedded untranslated quotation throughout Eliot's entire *œuvre*. The Ricks/McCue edition, with its exhaustive cross-referenced annotations, effectively performs our work for us, signalling each occurrence, and even each cancelled occurrence.[8] In the case of Eliot, such is the density of the poetry, and the *reflets réciproques* of which it consists, that each occurrence is semantically incremental, and indeed the phrase is 'transformed utterly' in each new context. I can think of no equivalent that is so consistent unless it be the fragment of Cavalcanti (*dove sta memoria*) in Pound, notably in Pisan *Canto* 76 where the phrase appears twice, but also with an incremental weight.

In Canto 19, Eliot had already appeared under the guise of Arnaut Daniel— Pound had grasped the importance of Eliot's own self-identification, and the relevant passage of the *Purgatorio*; I like to place Eliot's Dante essay in parallel, or in creative opposition to Pound's great tract on Cavalcanti, two opposing visions, two 'crisis essays' in a sense—and *Purgatorio* XXVI takes on the existential-ontological urgency for Eliot that Cavalcanti's *Canzone* 'Donna mi priegha' did for Pound, translated by him several times, notably in 1928 and forming the body of Canto 36. The burden of my argument, such as it is, is that Dante's Canto XXXVI of the *Purgatorio*, and the *Donna mi priegha* of Cavalcanti, can be seen to structure the *œuvre* of the two Modernists; in Eliot, certainly, the passage in question, or fragments of it, on the evidence of the drafts, served as scaffolding (in the form of epigraphs or section-titles) for *The Hollow Men* and *Ash-Wednesday*. By retaining the quotation in Arnaut's Provençal or, in the case of Pound, Cavalcanti's

[6] T. S. Eliot, *The Poems of T. S. Eliot*, 2 vols, ed. Christopher Ricks and Jim McCue (London: Faber and Faber, 2015), I, p. 205.

[7] T. S. Eliot, 'Dante', in *Selected Essays*, 3rd edn (London: Faber and Faber, 1951), pp. 237–77 (263–4).

[8] *Poems of T. S. Eliot*, eds Ricks and McCue, I, pp. 464–5.

Italian, the deliberation of both poets is unmistakable, and emphatically bears out *Princeton*'s primary description of Allusion as assuming 'prior achievements or events as sources of value'.

Perhaps by misapplication, by catachresis, an indirection—I can adduce a passage from the Conclusion of *The Use of Poetry and the Use of Criticism*—to show how what I shall call the 'talismanic quotation' (the untranslated variety)—stands in, not exactly as an image, it is a logopoeic, not a phanopoeic device—but as a correlative, subsumed under the 'shock of recognition', and also coming to occupy the *power* of an image:

> Why, for all of us, out of all that we have heard, seen, felt, in a lifetime, do certain images recur, charged with emotion, rather than others? The song of one bird, the leap of one fish, at a particular place and time, the scent of one flower, an old woman on a German mountain path, six ruffians seen through an open window playing cards at night at a small French railway junction where there was a water-mill: such memories may have a symbolic value, but of what we cannot tell, for they have come to represent the depths of feeling into which we cannot peer.[9]

And I associate this passage in turn with Yeats's famous description of Symbolist poetry in his 1900 essay:

> A little lyric evokes an emotion, and this emotion gathers others about it and melts into their being in the making of some great epic; and, at last, needing an always less delicate body, or symbol, as it grows more powerful, it flows out, with all it has gathered, among the blind instincts of daily life, where it moves a power within powers, as one sees ring within ring in the stem of an old tree.[10]

Although it is not primarily what Yeats had in mind, this description seems powerfully evocative of the effect of the recurring untranslated quotation throughout a whole *œuvre*. One cannot overestimate the importance of these phrases as structuring devices that mysteriously confer intellectual and (especially) emotional cohesion and a sense of continuity on a poet's work. But of course, as sceptical readers, as 'co-producers' of the text, to adopt the jargon, we must be convinced, or become convinced, of the intellectual and emotional necessity, or aptness, of their recurrence.

The fact of the quotation embedded, but not translated, has a paradoxical double existence, both as a deeply familiar element to the writer (in the case under discussion) and an element that retains all of its *strangeness* and *otherness*

---

[9] T. S. Eliot, *The Use of Poetry and Use of Criticism* [1933] (London: Faber and Faber, 1964), p. 148.
[10] W. B. Yeats, 'The Symbolism of Poetry', in *Essays and Introductions* (London: Macmillan, 1974), pp. 157–8.

for the reader. Taxonomists of intertextuality have noted: 'Inevitably a fragment and displacement, every quotation distorts and redefines the "primary" utterance by relocating it within another linguistic and cultural context.'[11] The interpolation of the quotation is what Riffaterre terms an *agrammaticalité* and it serves to point up not only the 'need' the reader experiences for the intertext to be identified (thus remedying, or filling the 'gap' created by the grammatical anomaly) but the degree of *literariness* of a given text.[12] The whole edifice of incremental meaning generated by repetition of the kind I have described above, comes crashing down of course if we attend to the decrees issued from the wilder shores of intertextual theory (Barthes, Derrida), i.e. that there is no transcendental signifier, that the only 'authority' behind this language (this quotation) is more language. For Barthes:

> Tout texte est un intertexte; d'autres textes sont présents en lui, à des niveaux variables, sous des formes plus ou moins reconnaissables: les textes de la culture antérieure et ceux de la culture environnante; tout texte est un tissu nouveau de citations révolues.[13]

While this cannot be denied—it is in fact a statement of the obvious—the effect of this formula, presumably, is to abolish the singularity of the untranslated quotation, since it is dissolved away in the unending welter of all the other quotations surrounding it; the effect of the theory is fatally to dilute any special hierarchical status we may wish, or the poets may wish, or may wish to have us, their readers, attach to it. Which only goes to show how inimical is the *intentionality* of an Eliot or a Pound to the 'deconstructive turn'.

Setting this aside, and allowing the poets, if we may, a degree of intentionality, Eliot's phrase, *Sovegna vos*, or the *Dove sta memoria* for Pound have a 'personal saturation value', and they are also rolled in the salt waters of the poets' work; and they gain in meaning, just as Eliot's recurrent moments do (the moment in the hyacinth garden, and the moment in the rose garden, or the moment in the arbour where the rain beat) throughout the œuvre, and expecially as they recur more deliberately in each of the *Four Quartets*. They gain in meaning, but it is not discursive meaning, it is emotional meaning and they come to evoke, precisely, 'the depth of feeling into which we cannot peer.'

Definitions (2) and (3) of 'Allusion' in *Princeton*, namely that allusion assumes 'readers sharing knowledge with the poet' and 'incorporation of sufficiently familiar yet distinctive elements' prompts me to add that there exist differing degrees of reader-response within Riffaterre's umbrella-term of 'compulsory

---

[11] Still and Worton, 'Introduction', *Intertextuality: Theories and Practices*, p. 11.

[12] Riffaterre, 'Compulsory Reader Response', pp. 56–8.

[13] See Barthes's entry on 'Texte, théorie du' in the *Encyclopaedia Universalis*, cited in Sophie Rabau, ed., *L'intertextualité* (Paris: GF Flammarion, 2002), pp. 57–9.

reader-response'. For if we are to explore more diligently the nature of the untranslated quotation in the Modernist poem, we need in the case of Pound and Eliot to turn to their *critical* treatments of these quotations. For it is there we shall find the more 'discursive' ground or seed-bed out of which they snatch, or pick, the flower—or the 'summation'—to place in the body of the poem. In terms of 'compulsory reader-response', we need in fact some guarantee of the 'grounded-ness' of the quotation, for it was the showy use of 'foreign matter' that brought upon Pound and Eliot notably the charge of elitism, and that the poets were engaging in a kind of highbrow *badinage* closed to everyone but the happy few. The kind of thing that Fowler in his *English Usage* deplores as bad manners—this splendid passage is quoted in the Ricks/McCue edition in relation to the the use of 'what *cauchemar!*' in 'Portrait of a Lady': 'To use French words that your reader or hearer does not know or does not fully understand, to pronounce them as if you were one of the select few to whom French is second nature when he is not of those few...is inconsiderate & rude.'[14] And it was in a sense the use (or misuse) of quotation that Pound satirizes at the opening of Canto 8—'These fragments you have shelved (shored)'—and which Eliot had suppressed for publication in the *Criterion*.[15]

The more one looks into this matter, truth be told, the more indispensable the critical prose of the two poets and friends seems to be. If the gist of this essay is devoted really to two untranslated quotations only, and to a few ancillary ones, the reason is also to be found in the prose, for these are the phrases and fragments that recur again and again in critical discussion. As early as 1913, in 'The Serious Artist', we find that Pound has already isolated the phrases illustrative of the best poetry, and attempted to define their nature. Of the five he selects, only one is in English—'The fire stirs about her, when she stirs'—one is in Anglo-Saxon, one in French, and two come from Cavalcanti, the second of which is the opening of the Ballata which begins:

> Perch'io non spero di tornar già mai
> Ballatetta, in Toscana

and which of course, translated, is the opening cadence of *Ash-Wednesday*. Of these phrases Pound remarks: 'These things have in them that passionate simpli-city which is beyond the precisions of the intellect. Truly they are perfect as fine prose is perfect, but they are in some way different from the clear statements of the observer [...] by the verses one is brought upon the passionate moment. This

---

[14] *Poems of T. S. Eliot*, ed. Ricks and McCue, p. 405.

[15] For a discussion of this, and of the changing power-relations between Eliot and Pound at the time, see Lawrence Rainey, 'Pound or Eliot: Whose era?' in *The Cambridge Companion to Modernist Poetry*, ed. Alex Davis and Lee M. Jenkins (Cambridge: Cambridge University Press, 2007), pp. 87–113 (pp. 106–7).

moment has brought with it nothing that violates the prose simplicities. The intellect has not found it but the intellect has been moved.'[16] Both in his prose (*The ABC of Reading* is essentially a series of 'sample' favourite snatches of text) and in his poetic practice, a significant part of Pound's genius resides in his gift for quotation. The status of the 'untranslated quotation' in the *Cantos* is a vast and vexatious and various question, and well beyond the remit of this essay. But from Pound's copious critical writings, the quotation in the original language is unquestionably the material upon which he comes to aesthetic, comparative judgement.

There is a celebrated passage in which Pound recalls the impetus behind the composition of *Hugh Selwyn Mauberley* and of Eliot's *Poems 1920*: 'at a particular date in a particular room, two authors, neither engaged in picking the other's pocket, decided that the dilutation of *vers libre* [...] had gone too far...Remedy prescribed *Emaux et Camées* (or the Bay State Hymn Book).'[17] And in later pronouncements Eliot was to confirm this collaboration: 'these poems were largely influenced by Ezra Pound's suggestion that one should study Théophile Gautier and take a rest from *vers libre* in various quatrains.'[18] But one lacks as far as I know a detailed account of the kind of symbiosis or pooling of sources that has Eliot quoting the fragments of Cavalcanti that Pound uses also, and even interpolates in Pisan Canto 75. I would hazard, though, that Eliot went to school with Pound in the matter of the Provençal poets, of Cavalcanti, and even perhaps of Dante (the epigraph to *Prufrock* was supplied nearer 1915, when he was being actively championed by Pound); but according to Ricks/McCue the original epigraph was our by now familiar passage from *Purgatorio XXVI*:

« *Sovegna vos al temps de mon dolor* »—
Poi s'ascose nel foco che gli affina

while the original manuscript of *Prufrock*, dated 1909–1910/1911 in *Inventions of the March Hare* had no epigraph.[19]

By 1926, when he delivered the Clark Lectures at Cambridge, Eliot was quoting (and misquoting, from memory) widely and copiously, including the passage of Cavalcanti's *Sonetto* VII cherished by Pound. But he manages nevertheless to misquote the variant of the line that Pound preferred, the *Che fa di clarità l'aer tremare* is slightly garbled by Eliot into *Che fe de clarità l'aer tremare*; he then quotes the translation by Rossetti, although Pound had published his own

---

[16] Ezra Pound, *Literary Essays*, ed. T. S. Eliot (London: Faber and Faber, 1954), p. 53.
[17] Ezra Pound, *Polite Essays* (London: Faber and Faber, 1937), p. 14.
[18] *Poems of T. S. Eliot*, ed. Ricks and McCue, p. 458.
[19] *Poems of T. S. Eliot*, ed. Ricks and McCue, p. 376.

translation by 1912.[20] I have entered into these details, if only to show the kind of groundwork, and growing familiarity with the material, that enables Eliot and Pound to 'lift' these quotations and implant, or better, incorporate them into their poems at moments of maximum emotional charge, where the reader must come upon them, as upon 'the passionate moment'. So it is that, in his cage at Pisa, in the great opening Canto of that series, Pound brings to mind twice, and without garbling it, the quotation from Cavalcanti, amid a whirl of humorous memories concerning the '*very* aged Snow', the President of Magdalen, and Mr Joyce in Gibraltar.[21]

The same is true, but more intensely so, of the phrase *Dove sta memoria* from Cavalcanti's *Canzone*, the *Donna mi priegha*, so beloved of Pound that he made several translations, one of which forms the first half of Canto 36. And it is in Canto 76, one of the glories of the Pisan series, that the phrase, by now a talisman for Pound, a collocation of great spritual power, occurs twice. In the opening cadence:

> And the sun high over horizon hidden in cloud bank
> > lit saffron the cloud ridge
> > > dove sta memora

which introduces the mysterious manifestation or *darshan* of the three graces formed by,

> Dirce et Ixotta e che fu chiamata Primavera
> > in the timeless air
> that they suddenly stand in my room here
> between me and the olive tree
>
> > > > > > (Pound, *Cantos,* 472)

Even more momentous is the second appearance of the phrase, a few pages later, following on from Pound's moving admission, or recognition:

> > > > nothing matters but the quality
> of the affection—
> in the end—that has carved the trace in the mind
> dove sta memoria
>
> > > > > (*Cantos,* 477)

---

[20] For discussion of these details, see Eliot's Clark Lectures, collected in *The Varieties of Metaphysical Poetry*, ed. Ronald Schuchard (London: Faber and Faber, 1993), p. 107.

[21] Ezra Pound, *Cantos of Ezra Pound* (New York: New Directions, 1986), pp. 464–8.

which looks forward to the similarly affecting admissions of the very late *Cantos*, the *Drafts and Fragments* written when Pound had entered his great silence, a penitential introspection:

> And I am not a demigod,
> I cannot make it cohere.
> If love be not in the house there is nothing.

(Cantos, 816)

Riffaterre's '*agrammaticalité*' in a text, that flags up an allusion in the Modernist style, is nowhere more visible than in Pound's use of the Chinese ideogram, which, for the reader, urgently requires 'remedy' in the sense that he or she must seek help and a glossary; the Chinese character will send him reaching for Carroll F. Terrell's *Companion to the Cantos*....

There is no question that the exotic presence of the untranslated quotation, its otherness, whether in Provençal, or Italian, or Chinese, makes these texts instantly recognizable as examples of High Modernism, and by now a part of literary history that is definitely over. Postmodern examples follow a different agenda, and eschew the kind of intentionality which seems paramount in, say, the Malatesta Cantos, for which the poet went to the archives and transcribed 'whole slabs of the record' in an effort to get historical details right.[22] This is increasingly the case for Pound, when he became obsessed with economic theory, until it became the central matter of his poem including history.

The co-presence of two or more languages within the body of the Modernist poem has become so familiar, that its *absence*, as in *Four Quartets*, is positively disconcerting. This question of non-translation prompts a suggestion which concerns the growing critical disenchantment in some quarters with late Eliot, especially with *Four Quartets*. This is the poem that was for long regarded as the poet's crowning glory, considered so by the poet himself, and proclaimed as such by critics like Helen Gardner, whose pioneering study *The Composition of 'Four Quartets'* (1978) marked a high water point in its public appreciation.[23] There were, however, always dissentient voices, and powerful ones, like C. H. Sisson, and Donald Davie whose essay 'T. S. Eliot: the End of an Era' (1956) performed a demolition job on 'The Dry Salvages'.[24] Newer to the dissenting ranks is the no less powerful figure of Geoffrey Hill, who in a fascinating review-essay of *The Varieties of Metaphysical Poetry*, widens his brief to declare that 'Eliot's poetry

---

[22] See Pound's description of the '"new" historic sense in our time' in Ezra Pound, *Guide to Kulchur* (New York: New Directions, 1970), p. 30.

[23] Helen Gardner, *The Composition of 'Four Quartets'* (London: Faber and Faber, 1978).

[24] See C. H. Sisson, *English Poetry 1900–1950* (London: Methuen, 1981) and Donald Davie, 'T. S. Eliot: the End of an Era' in *The Poet in the Imaginary Museum*, ed. Barry Alpert (Manchester: Carcanet, 1977), pp. 32–41.

declines over thirty years from pitch into tone'. More specifically, he writes, 'It was the pitch of *Prufrock and Other Observations* that disturbed and alienated readers; it was the tone of *Four Quartets* that assuaged and consoled them'.[25] The 'tone' that both Davie and Hill most object to, would seem to be the preacher-professor's voice in the *Quartets*, as in:

> You are not here to verify,
> Instruct yourself, or inform curiosity
> Or carry report. You are here to kneel
> Where prayer has been valid.

And Davie objects to the rambling passage in 'The Dry Salvages':

> It seems, as one becomes older,
> That the past has another pattern, and ceases to be a mere sequence
> Or even development: the latter a partial fallacy
> Encouraged by superficial notions of evolution...

Davie describes this passage as 'stumbling, trundling rhythms,[...] inarticulate ejaculations of reach-me-down phrases, the debased currency of the study circle'.[26] It seems fairly clear what these critics object to, tonally. But 'pitch' for Hill, is what 'disturbed and alienated' the readers of *Prufrock* and of *Ara Vos Prec*. And I would contend that part of the 'pitch', a quality, or an element, that in music you sing or play is precisely the presence of the untranslated word or phrase that seemed so novel and intimidating to early readers. There are only two interpolations, on my count, of foreign language in *Four Quartets*, the Hegelian term *Erhebung* in part 2 of 'Burnt Norton', and the invocation to the Virgin, 'Figlia del tuo figlio', in part 4 of 'The Dry Salvages'. This notable paucity of 'otherness', of that thrilling *ostranenie* produced by the untranslated fragment, is not something often remarked upon by critics of *Four Quartets*, but it may well indeed contribute to a sense of anti-climax, and—to adopt Hill's terminology—to a descent from pitch into tone, from what is played or sung, into what is heard. By contrast, therefore, the presence of the untranslated quotation, especially in the examples I have examined here, may turn out to constitute the element, or one of the elements, indispensable to the raw voltage delivered by Eliot's early work.[27]

---

[25]   Hill, *Collected Critical Writings*, p. 377.   [26]   Davie, 'T. S. Eliot: the End of an Era', p. 34.
[27]   On the thrill of *ostranenie*, see Peter Nicholls's remarks on the 'heterogeneous materials that have "carved the trace in the mind"' in Pound's *Pisan Cantos*. Nicholls cites Jacques Derrida's comments on the function of memory: 'when we learn something by heart, even as we interiorise the poem, we are 'giving it an "intangible singularity"' as it is assimilated to the inner life of the self [...] at the same time [...] the very act of possession recalls us to the otherness or foreignness of those words that poets find themselves remembering and rewriting, the heart now "traversed", says Derrida, "by the dictated

Hill's implication seems to be that the pitch of, say, *The Waste Land*, is conveyed by the poet's total absorption in what he is performing, whereas the tone of *Four Quartets* comes in part from the poet listening out for (second-guessing) what his performance may sound like to his audience. It is certainly true that Eliot's procedures in general are more deliberated, or at least more openly on record in the latter poem than in any other part of his work. This is partly due to the copious correspondence and drafts that are part of the Hayward Bequest, left to King's and Magdalene Colleges in Cambridge, and used by Helen Gardner in her *Composition of 'Four Quartets'*. At the outset, she makes this point:

> One reason for the abundance of material and information about *Four Quartets* is that Eliot, who was often evasive in comments on his earlier poetry, was never evasive about *Four Quartets*. He was willing to talk about the poem and to give direct answers to questions. In speaking of it he never employed the defensive irony that marks so many of his references to *The Waste Land*. He never suggested that he did not himself know 'what he meant' and that a reader's guess was as good as the author's. If asked to explain a reference he did so. The poet who refused to divulge whether Pipit was 'a little girl, an inamorata, a female relative, or an old nurse' was quite ready to say which shrine 'on the promontory' he had in mind and what places he had thought of as being 'the world's end'.[28]

This 'evolution' in Eliot's approach is of great interest in the present context of Riffaterre's 'compulsory reader-response'. Eliot is so to speak 'policing' the *Quartets* in a way he never did the earlier work, and with hindsight, and noting Eliot's own evident satisfaction with the work, this has not helped the reputation of the poem in later critical appraisals.

All this is startlingly visible in the *Paris Review* interview with Donald Hall, when Eliot blithely (Hill might say 'impercipiently') has this to say, contrasting his early and later style:

> That type of obscurity comes when a poet is still at the stage of learning how to use language. You have to say the thing the difficult way. The only alternative is not saying it at all, at that stage. By the time of *Four Quartets*, I couldn't have written in the style of *The Waste Land*. In *The Waste Land*, I wasn't even bothering whether I understood what I was saying.[29]

---

dictation". We may possess the words of others, then, but the fact of this ownership opens a kind of cleavage in the self, revealing otherness where one might have expected to find the impress of the author's own identity.' Nicholls, 'The Poetics of Modernism', in *The Cambridge Companion to Modernist Poetry*, ed. Alex Davis and Lee M. Jenkins (Cambridge: Cambridge University Press, 2007), pp. 51–2.

[28] Gardner, *The Composition of 'Four Quartets'*, pp. 3–4.
[29] Eliot, quoted in Gardner, p. 4.

That last phrase, uttered by the wise and aged eagle, bemused by his younger self, is the very quick of the matter. '*I wasn't even bothering whether I understood what I was saying*' contains a whole poetics, one more akin to the *avant-garde* and closer to the postmodern taste for indeterminacy. It explains in part the radical and perilous nature of the early masterpiece. Certainly the 'fragmentary, chaotic experience of modern man', given its correlative in the shower of quotations with which *The Waste Land* ends, is quite ungovernable in terms of 'reader-response'—a controlled explosion possibly, but with incalculable fall-out. 'Controlled' in the sense that Eliot is aware of his sources and their respective contexts, but he cannot control in his reader the effect of the chemical reaction between the elements, or the co-production of meaning.

One might finally conjecture that the imagery unimpeded by moral censure or even ecclesiastical *bienséance*, the wilder runs of unconscious fantasia in *The Waste Land* is aided also by the embedding of untranslated quotation which has the effect, at least to fresh readers of the poem, of *ostranenie*, of generally unsettling meaning, whereas quotation in *Four Quartets* is more deliberate and volitional. Quite apart from the salient fact that it is *domesticated*—the quotations from Mallarmé for example are translated and adapted. So one might argue, with Hill, that the quotation also becomes integrated into the 'ruminative, well-modulated voice of a man of letters, a tone which so weakens *Four Quartets*.'[30] Whether or not one concurs with that judgement, the level of control is measurable from Eliot's crisply purposeful notes to John Hayward on the 'Sin is behovely' quotation from Julian of Norwich, in part 3 of *Little Gidding*: 'My purpose was this: there is so much 17th century in the poem that I was afraid of a certain romantic Bonnie Dundee period effect and I wanted to check this and at the same time give greater historical depth to the poem by allusions to the other great period, i.e. the 14th century'.[31] So, the untranslated, or in this last case the linguistically remote quotation can be variously mediated; it can indeed appeal, or make common assumption of 'prior achievements or events as sources of value', as it does in *Four Quartets*; it can aid and abet a certain intentionality, it can add historical context and backing, it can provide a kind of diachronic 'verticality'; but used helter-skelter it can equally create a vertiginous effect of cacophonic synchronicity, and of irremediable *otherness*.

---

[30] Hill, *Collected Critical Writings*, p. 579.
[31] *Poems of T. S. Eliot*, ed. Ricks and McCue, II, p. 1031.

8

'Making Strange': Non-Translation
in *The Waste Land*

Jason Harding

'To attempt to explain to an intelligent person—who knows nothing about
twentieth-century poetry—how *The Waste Land* works,' observed Graham Hough,
who viewed modernist poetry as an alarming foreign invasion, 'is to be overcome
with embarrassment at having to justify principles so affected, so perverse, so
deliberately removed from ordinary modes of rational communication.'[1] *The
Waste Land* demanded new forms of attention. According to Frank Kermode, it
'draws upon a tradition which imposes the necessity of form, though it may have
none that can be apprehended without a disciplined act of faith.'[2] On first hearing
Eliot read the poem aloud in June 1922, Virginia Woolf noted in her diary: 'He
sang it & chanted it rhythmed it. It has great beauty & force of phrase: symmetry; &
tensity. What connects it together, I'm not so sure.'[3] In spite of the obscurity of its
bewildering interplay of voices, the poem communicates sonorously and powerfully through rhythms and patterns. It is also a poem dense with allusions to
world literatures and with what this collection terms 'non-translation' and therefore part of the experience of the poem is the experience of encountering what
looks and sounds strange. In *The Waste Land* linguistic alienation is inseparable
from linguistic fascination.[4]

Contemporary reviewers, lacking a critical lexicon in which to absorb *The
Waste Land*'s modernist innovations, were perplexed and vexed by the poem. In
1923, Sir John Squire, editor of London's leading literary monthly, *The London
Mercury*, complained that what is attempted in *The Waste Land* 'is a faithful
transcript, after Mr. Joyce's obscurer manner, of the poet's wandering thoughts in
a state of erudite depression. A grunt would serve equally well; what is language
but communication, or art but selection and arrangement?'[5] If literature is

---

[1] Graham Hough, *Image and Experience: Studies in a Literary Revolution* (London: Duckworth,
1960), p. 28.
[2] Frank Kermode, 'Modernisms Again', *Encounter* (April 1966): 65–74 (p. 66).
[3] *The Diary of Virginia Woolf, Volume II: 1920–1924*, ed. Anne Olivier Bell (London: Hogarth
Press, 1978), p. 178.
[4] In the first American publication of the poem in the November 1922 issue of the New York
monthly *The Dial*, words and phrases from Romance languages were set in italics.
[5] J. C. Squire, 'Poetry', *London Mercury* 8 (October 1923): 655–6 (p. 656).

Jason Harding, *'Making Strange': Non-Translation in* The Waste Land *In: Modernism and Non-Translation*. Edited by:
Jason Harding and John Nash, Oxford University Press (2019). © the several contributors.
DOI: 10.1093/oso/9780198821441.003.0008

communication, then *The Waste Land* represents a flamboyant act of presentational impoliteness. Although reviewers in the United States were generally more receptive to the poem's avant-garde affront to conventional taste, many of them bridled at the disjunction of different languages. Even Eliot's loyal Harvard contemporary Conrad Aiken, writing in the *New Republic* in 1923, acknowledged that the poem had tested the limits of his patience: 'We could dispense with the French, Italian, Latin and Hindu phrases—they are irritating.'[6]

Over time, as academic explicators and exegetes packaged the difficulties of *The Waste Land* into student-friendly critical guidebooks, Eliot repeatedly distanced himself from biographical or sociological explanations of the poem. In 1931, he responded tartly to the 'nonsense' of I. A. Richards's fashionable interpretation of the poem as representative of post-war crisis and the 'disillusionment of a generation': 'I may have expressed for them their own illusion of being disillusioned, but that did not form part of my intention.'[7] In 1937, Cleanth Brooks's enormously influential reading of *The Waste Land* as a progressive search for faith tracing a schematic Grail quest was met by Eliot's patient (yet, one suspects, patronizing) letter: 'Reading your essay made me feel... that I have been a great deal more ingenious than I had been aware of, because the conscious problems with which one is concerned in the actual writing are more those of a quasi musical nature, in the arrangement of metric and pattern, than those of a conscious exposition of ideas.'[8]

In this chapter, I want to suggest that key conceptual terms drawn from Russian Formalism—focused on the complex, intrinsic dynamics of the language of poetry—can help us to comprehend the function of modernist 'non-translation' as a feature of the radical avant-garde experimentation of *The Waste Land*.[9] It should be recalled that the Russian Formalists developed theoretical concepts and analytical tools to tackle the verbal pyrotechnics of the Russian Futurist poets with an unapologetic preference for what Eliot calls 'the arrangement of metric and pattern' rather than a 'conscious exposition of ideas.'[10] In point of fact, Russian Futurism—notably the urban poetry of Vladimir Mayakovsky and Velimir Khlebnikov—was a striking pioneer in the use of extreme deformations of sound

---

[6]   Conrad Aiken, 'An Anatomy of Melancholy', *New Republic* 33 (7 February 1923): 293–5 (p. 295).

[7]   T. S. Eliot, 'Thoughts After Lambeth' [1931], *Selected Essays*, 3rd edn (London: Faber and Faber, 1951), pp. 363–87 (p. 368).

[8]   T. S. Eliot to Cleanth Brooks, 15 March 1937, quoted in *The Poems of T. S. Eliot: Volume I, Collected and Uncollected Poems*, ed. Christopher Ricks and Jim McCue (Baltimore: Johns Hopkins University Press, 2015), p. 575. In *Revisiting 'The Waste Land'*, Lawrence Rainey claims that Brooks's essay on *The Waste Land* 'profoundly shaped the course of criticism on the poem for the next forty years' (New Haven: Yale University Press, 2005), p. 117.

[9]   In his treatment of Russian Formalism, René Wellek asserts: 'Their theories are transferable and adaptable in other lands and times.' *A History of Modern Criticism: 1750–1950: Volume 7, German, Russian, and Eastern European Criticism, 1900–1950* (New Haven: Yale University Press, 1991), p. 325.

[10]   The first volume of the Russian Formalist OPOJAZ group was devoted to the study of poetic sound over sense. See *Sborniki po teorii poètičeskogo jazyka*, I (Petrograd: Tip. Z. Sokolinskago, 1916).

and syntax in order to represent the transformed world of the modern technological city.[11] According to one contemporary Russian critic of Futurist poetry: 'A number of poetic devices found their application in urbanism.'[12] Viktor Shklovsky's manifesto 'Art as Technique' (1917) explored those frictions of poetic language that 'increase the difficulty and length of perception' anticipating Eliot's essay on 'The Metaphysical Poets' (1921), composed at the same time as *The Waste Land*, in which he says, 'it appears likely that poets in our civilization, as it exists at present, must be *difficult*.'[13] Eliot concludes: 'The poet must become more and more comprehensive, more allusive, more indirect, in order to force, to dislocate if necessary, language into his meaning.'[14]

Russian Formalism conceives of poetry as a highly specialized use of language that is quite distinct from ordinary ('practical', 'referential', 'prosaic') language. Viktor Shklovksy's popular catchword 'defamiliarization' or 'making strange' is too often misunderstood as synonymous with 'shock-tactic'. The effects of 'estrangement' are dependent on the very 'literariness' of a text, in which poetic 'shifts'— for example, deviations of rhythm and metre, morphology and syntax—render form 'perceptible' against a background of literary conventions, generic and stylistic, an insight of clear relevance to the neo-epic ambitions of *The Waste Land* with its moments of lyric and elegy, dramatic monologues and dialogues, and excursions into satire. In Russian Formalism, poetry is a dynamic conflicted system. Several commentators have noted that Yuri Tynyanov's evolutionary theory of literary history—'a process of rewritings and deformations as they arise from the conditions of perception and the dynamics of dominance at each present moment'—bears a strong resemblance to Eliot's dynamic concept of tradition.[15] Furthermore, the 'Impersonal theory of poetry' advanced by Eliot in 'Tradition and the Individual Talent' (1919) is allied with Russian Formalist theories of poetry as a supra-personal mask—part of a concerted assault on Romantic theories of poetry as a vehicle for subjective self-expression or confessional.[16]

---

[11] George Hyde discusses Eliot's *The Waste Land* alongside Mayakovsky's *A Cloud in Trousers* in 'The Poetry of the City', *Modernism*, ed. Malcolm Bradbury and James McFarlane (Harmondsworth: Penguin, 1976), pp. 337–48.

[12] Roman Jakobson, *Novejšaja russkaja poèzija* (Prague: Politika, 1921), p. 16. This statement is quoted in English in Victor Erlich, *Russian Formalism: History, Doctrine* (The Hague: Mouton, 1965), p. 195.

[13] Viktor Shklovsky, 'Art as Technique' in *Russian Formalist Criticism: Four Essays*, trans. and with an introduction by L. T. Lemon and M. J. Reis (Lincoln: University of Nebraska Press, 1965), pp. 3–24 (p. 12).

[14] T. S. Eliot, 'The Metaphysical Poets' [1921], *Selected Essays*, pp. 281–91 (p. 289).

[15] See Aleida Assmann, 'Exorcizing the Demon of Chronology: T. S. Eliot's Reinvention of Tradition' in *T. S. Eliot and the Concept of Tradition*, ed. Giovanni Cianci and Jason Harding (Cambridge: Cambridge University Press, 2007), pp. 13–25 (pp. 21–2).

[16] Erlich opines: 'Clearly, insisted the Russian Formalists, there is no point-to-point correspondence between imaginative literature and personality. The notion of the "naïve psychological realists" that art is an oracular outpouring, a spontaneous eruption of emotions, was sharply challenged in terms which would have pleased T. S. Eliot.' *Russian Formalism: History, Doctrine*, p. 203.

Russian Formalism is eloquent on many of the avant-garde techniques that Eliot deploys in *The Waste Land*: metrical and syntactical wrenching; the unravelling and reweaving of lexical and grammatical patterns; the sonic repetition of syncopated jazz rhythms, of onomatopoeic wordless operatic ululations, birdsong, water-dripping and of thunder;[17] and the sheer heterogeneity of a *heteroglossia* in which translation and non-translation, ventriloquism and mimicry, allusion, parody, and pastiche, function to both estrange and disrupt rational discourse by foregrounding the disorientating organization of this poetic text.[18] In particular, I conceive of 'non-translation' as a Russian Formalist literary 'device' (*priem*) 'making strange' (*ostranenie*) ordinary modes of communication; in Eliot's own words, so reminiscent of Shklovsky's pronouncements, such devices are a linguistic constituent of how poetry 'may help to break up the conventional modes of perception and valuation which are perpetually forming, and make people see the world afresh.'[19]

The formal inventiveness of Futurism described by Russian Formalism as *zaum*—free expressive combinations of sound, emotionally charged, assembled from completely new words, nonsensical neologisms, or new ungrammatical combinations of words, *even from languages unknown to the poet*—speaks to the sense in which the sonorous power of *The Waste Land* inheres in sound (or does not sound, cannot be sounded).[20] One further confluence between *The Waste Land* and Russian Formalism lies in the theorizing of *skaz* oral narration, an interaction of spoken and written forms, as in the London pub scene of 'A Game of Chess', switching between high and low linguistic registers, in which a pastiche of Cockney dialect full of colloquial vulgarity gives way to an elevated Shakespeare allusion to Ophelia's final words before her tragic suicide. In this way, *skaz* virtuosity subverts how a text is 'voiced', destabilizing the authority of canonical tradition through incongruous juxtapositions of modes of telling. Eliot's working title

---

[17] 'O O O O that Shakespeherian Rag'; 'Weialala leia / Wallala leialala'; 'Twit twit twit / Jug jug jug jug jug jug'; 'Co co rico co co rico'; 'Drip drop drip drop drop drop drop'; 'DA...DA...DA', *The Poems of T. S. Eliot: Volume I*, pp. 59, 63, 65, 69–71.

[18] The term 'heteroglossia' (literally 'different-speech'), indicating distinct varieties within a single 'language', was promoted by Mikhail Bakhtin, a theorist deeply influenced by Formalist methodology. Bakhtin examined 'the unfolding of social heteroglossia *surrounding* the object, the Tower-of-Babel mixing of languages that goes on around any object; the dialectics of the object are interwoven with the social dialogue surrounding it. The actively literary linguistic consciousness at all times and everywhere comes upon "languages", and not language.' *The Dialogic Imagination: Four Essays*, trans. Caryl Emerson and Michael Holquist (Austin: University of Texas Press, 1981), pp. 278, 295.

[19] T. S. Eliot, *The Use of Poetry and the Use of Criticism* [1933] (London: Faber and Faber, 1964), p. 155.

[20] Viktor Shklovksy characterized *zaum* as a 'peculiar dance of the speech organs', a trans-rational quest for a pure, unmediated meaning of sound, an expressive musical language that was likened by Boris Eichenbaum to children's babble or religious incantation. On *zaum*, see Peter Steiner, *Russian Formalism: A Metapoetics* (Ithaca: Cornell University Press, 1984), pp. 140–71. Christopher Ricks reflects on the 'relation of the sound of sense to the sense of void' in *The Waste Land*, a poem he reads as 'a congregation of voids' marked by 'the encompassing vacuum of silence or rather silences.' *T. S. Eliot and Prejudice* (London: Faber and Faber, 1988), pp. 174–5.

for *The Waste Land* was borrowed from the extensibility of Dickens's bravura theatrical styles of narration: 'He Do the Police in Different Voices'.[21]

By employing Russian Formalist theories 'laying bare' (*obnazhenie*) the devices of avant-garde poetry to analyse the dynamic function of 'non-translation' in *The Waste Land*, I am not claiming any direct influence on Eliot's practice as a poet and critic. Although Russian Formalism reached its heyday in 1922, by the time Eliot became aware of the work of those critics and theorists in Moscow and Petrograd associated with the movement, these groups were already on the defensive as a result of Marxist critiques and later from Stalinist repression. Eliot read the 1925 English translation of Leon Trotsky's *Literature and Revolution*, which delivers an ideological attack on the Formalist critics Trotsky labels 'fellow-travellers'. Trotsky sneers at 'the superficiality and reactionary character of the Formalist theory of art'.[22] Eliot is astute in judging that *Literature and Revolution* is an 'important document in the history of the political direction of culture' but that it 'does not give the impression that Trotsky was very sensitive to literature.' It appears the diversity and pluralism of the Russian writers surveyed by this study proved a barrier to his understanding. Given Trotsky's Marxist hostility to these schools, it is understandable that Eliot's exasperation should issue in the statement: 'Like all his writings, the book is encumbered with discussion of minor Russian personalities of which the foreigner is ignorant and in which he is not interested.'[23]

Roman Jakobson—one of the 'minor Russian personalities' discussed in Trotsky's book—theorizes compellingly on the linguistic textures of what our collection calls modernist non-translation. Jakobson asserts: 'a phoneme that appears only once, but in a key word, in a pertinent position, against a contrastive background, may acquire a striking significance.'[24] The phonetic quality of non-translation (an unfamiliar noise, as it were) necessarily acquires a striking significance. However, Jakobson countered Franz Saran's contention that a critic 'ought to adopt toward verse the attitude of a foreigner who listens to it without knowing the language in which it is written.' On the contrary, Jakobson argues: 'Not a single person perceives the sound form of poetry in his native tongue, its rhythm in particular, as Saran's foreigner does. Indeed, even this foreigner is fictitious; even his perception would not be purely acoustic. He would merely approach the foreign utterance from the standpoint of his own phonological system, with his own phonological habits. He would, so to speak, transphonologize this dissimilarity

[21] See T. S. Eliot, *The Waste Land: A Facsimile and Transcript of the Original Drafts*, ed. Valerie Eliot (London: Faber and Faber, 1971), p. 5, p. 11.

[22] Leon Trotsky, *Literature and Revolution*, trans. Rose Strunsky (London: George Allen & Unwin, 1925), p. 163.

[23] T. S. Eliot, *Notes towards the Definition of Culture* (London: Faber and Faber, 1962), p. 89.

[24] Roman Jakobson, *Language in Literature*, ed. Krystyna Pomorska and Stephen Rudy (Cambridge, Mass.: Harvard University Press, 1987), p. 88.

[between different] phonological systems.'[25] Eliot, likewise, is wary of the critic's ability to perceive a 'pure' poetry of sound: 'We can be deeply stirred by hearing the recitation of a poem in a language of which we understand no word; but if we are then told that the poem is gibberish and has no meaning, we shall consider that we have been deluded.'[26]

In 'Art as Technique' Shklovsky defines the 'language of poetry' as a 'difficult, roughened, impeded language.' He lists precedents: 'According to Aristotle, poetic language must appear strange and wonderful; and, in fact, it is often actually foreign: the Sumerian used by the Assyrians, the Latin of Europe during the Middle Ages, the Arabisms of the Persians, the Old Bulgarian of Russian literature, or the elevated, almost literary language of folk songs.'[27] Jakobson applies more linguistic precision than Shklovsky's provocative polemics when addressing *The Newest Russian Poetry* (the title of a remarkable pamphlet, drafted in 1919 in those Futurist-inspired years before he left Moscow, as an introduction to a collection of Khlebnikov's poetry).[28] In this essay, Jakobson provides an insight into how avant-garde Russian Futurist poetry is replenished from within by linguistic forms. In poetic language, writes Jakobson: 'the connection between the sound aspect and meaning is tighter, more intimate, and consequently, language becomes more revolutionary.'[29]

George Steiner credits Jakobson's 1923 phonological study of Russian and Czech poetry as 'the first instance of a methodical application of modern semantic (or, as they are more technically called, semasiological) criteria to a comparative analysis of the structure and effects of metrical patterns.'[30] When language is operating at full stretch, as in avant-garde poetry, Jakobson maintains that it is not possible to translate from a language (Russian Formalism's 'comparative-projective' model designates a 'source' and 'target' text) without significant loss: 'in jest, in dreams, in magic, briefly, in what one would call everyday verbal mythology and in poetry above all, the grammatical categories carry a high semantic import. In these conditions, the question of translation becomes much more entangled and controversial.... poetry by definition is untranslatable. Only creative transposition is possible.'[31] Using a foreign language in the modernist procedure

---

[25] The original 1923 passage is translated by Peter Steiner in *Russian Formalism: A Metapoetics*, p. 235.

[26] T. S. Eliot, 'The Music of Poetry', *On Poetry and Poets* (London: Faber and Faber, 1957), pp. 26–38 (p. 30).

[27] Shklovsky, 'Art as Technique' in *Russian Formalist Criticism: Four Essays*, p. 22.

[28] George Steiner remarks: 'Through his knowledge of Slavonic philology, of poetics, and of the new theories of language being developed by Saussure, Jakobson united in his own work the principal energies of the Formalist or linguistic-poetic approach.' *Extraterritorial: Papers on Literature and the Language Revolution* (London: Faber and Faber, 1972), p. 137.

[29] Jakobson, *Novejšaja russkaja poèzija*, quoted in English in *Language, Poetry, and Poetics: The Generation of the 1890s, Jakobson, Trubetzkoy, Majakovskjj*, ed. Krystyna Pomorska, Hugh Mclean, Elzbieta Chodakowska, Brent Vine (Berlin: Mouton de Gruyer, 1987), p. 277.

[30] Steiner, *Extraterritorial*, p. 137.

[31] Roman Jakobson, 'On Linguistic Aspects of Translation', *On Translation*, ed. Reuben Brower (Boston: Harvard University Press, 1959), pp. 232–9 (pp. 236, 238). On Russian Formalist translation theory, see Andrey Fyodorov, *Problema stikhotvornogo perevoda* (Leningrad: Academia, 1927).

of non-translation, a poet is transfigured, obliged to yield not only what he possesses, or what he is noted for in his native literature, but now also what is expected in a new, wider cosmopolitan horizon of expectation. The development of a readership for avant-garde practices in those years leading up to, during, and immediately after the First World War—described and analysed in the introduction to this volume—is a crucial factor in the appearance of non-translation in modernist writing.

Critics have always recognized *The Waste Land* as, albeit in a deeply coded way, an anguished commentary on the fractures of polyglot, post-war Europe; or, as Eliot put it in a 1923 review of Joyce's *Ulysses*, 'the immense panorama of futility and anarchy which is contemporary history.'[32] Prized as a linguist, Eliot's duties at Lloyds Bank involved regularly reading material in several languages in order to compose a digest of 'Foreign Exchanges' tracking fluctuations in foreign currencies (inflation would spiral in Germany, Russia, and across Eastern Europe in the early 1920s).[33] After he had begun drafting *The Waste Land*, Eliot worried about the destruction of Europe: 'The whole of contemporary politics etc. oppresses me with a continuous physical horror like the feeling of growing madness in one's own brain.'[34] Russian Formalism was forged in the turbulence of pre-Revolutionary Russia and extinguished by the post-Revolutionary terror. The nebulous interrelationships of political conflict—stained by disorder and violence—with the self-conscious ruptures of modernist literature are (as I demonstrate below) jammed into the linguistic workings of *The Waste Land*.

Speaking during the Second World War, Eliot claimed, 'It is easier to think in a foreign language than it is to feel in it,' explaining: 'A people may have its language taken away from it, suppressed, and another language compelled upon the schools; but unless you teach that people to *feel* in a new language, you have not eradicated the old one, and it will reappear in poetry, which is the vehicle of feeling.' He continued: 'A thought expressed in a different language may be practically the same thought, but a feeling or emotion expressed in a different language is not the same feeling or emotion. One of the reasons for learning at least one foreign language well is that we acquire a kind of supplementary personality; one of the reasons for not acquiring a new language *instead* of our own is that most of us do not want to become a different person.'[35] The ramifications of this passage for Eliot's own practice of non-translation in *The Waste Land* are resonant yet intriguing: the supplementary character opened (or not) by the decision to embrace

[32] T. S. Eliot, '*Ulysses*, Order, and Myth' [1923] *in Selected Prose of T. S. Eliot*, ed. Frank Kermode (London: Faber and Faber, 1975), pp. 175–8 (p. 177).

[33] At Lloyds Bank, Eliot had been put in charge of dealing 'with all the debts and claims of the bank under the various Peace Treaties' (letter to John Quinn, 9 May 1921) but he shared John Maynard Keynes's dismay at the Versailles Treaty, which he referred to as 'that appalling document' (letter to his mother, 22 February 1920). *The Letters of T. S. Eliot: Volume 1, 1898–1922*, ed. Valerie Eliot and Hugh Haughton (London: Faber and Faber, 2009), pp. 557, 446.

[34] Letter to Richard Aldington, 7 April 1921. *The Letters of T. S. Eliot, Volume 1*, p. 550.

[35] T. S. Eliot, 'The Social Function of Poetry', *On Poetry and Poets*, pp. 15–25 (p. 19).

multilingualism offers one line of enquiry; harder to pin down are the sinuous reflections on thoughts and feelings embedded within and transferred across languages, especially as they affect poetry, the language of feelings. Suffice it to say, for Eliot the decision *not* to translate feelings from several languages but place them within the poetic fabric of another, is an artistic decision of profound consequence.

§

In 'Art as Technique' Shklovksy differentiates habitual 'automatic' perception from the sensation of 'speaking a foreign language for the first time.' It is an example used to illustrate the Russian Formalist theory that, 'art exists that one may recover the sensation of life…the author's purpose is to create the vision which results from that de-automatized perception.'[36] *The Waste Land* is framed by an estranging formalist 'shift' foregrounding in the epigraph to the poem two alien languages: 'macaronic Latin,' according to Hugh Kenner, 'pungently sauced with Greek.'[37] On 12 March 1922, Eliot wrote to inform Ezra Pound that he had substituted for the epigraph taken from Joseph Conrad's *Heart of Darkness*—'The horror! the horror!'—a passage (he misquotes) from chapter 48 of Petronius' *Satyricon*: 'Nam Sibyllam quidem Cumis ego ipse oculis meis vidi in ampulla pendere, et cum illi pueri dicerent: Σίβυλλα τί θέλεις; respondebat illa: ἀπο θανεῖν θέλω.'[38] The conversation in this section of the *Satyricon* has been described as a 'highly artful procedure in perspective, a sort of twofold mirroring' and this scene 'points to more than one way of seeing, and looks at things in more than one way.'[39] It offers a scene within a scene. The inner scene tells the story of the Cumaean Sibyl; the outer scene presents Trimalchio boastfully and bibulously spinning this yarn at his extravagant banquet. In the inner scene, captured in the epigraph, the withered Sibyl desperately unwishes her wish for long life: 'I saw with my own eyes the Sibyl at Cumae hanging in a jar, and when the boys asked her: "Sibyl, what do you want?" she answered "I want to die"' (my translation).

The Waste Land's epigraph draws the reader's attention to ways of seeing: it contains a prophetess famous for her powers of foresight and presents an eyewitness account of her, 'oculis meis vidi'. In sum, it demands to be looked at closely,

---

[36] Shklovsky, 'Art as Technique', pp. 11, 12, 22.

[37] Hugh Kenner, *T. S. Eliot: The Invisible Poet* (London: W. H. Allen, 1960), p. 136.

[38] Eliot owned a 1904 Latin edition of Bücheler's selections from the *Satyricon*. The chosen quotation was corrected before publication. Pound's revisions to the manuscript drafts of *The Waste Land* struck out two-fifths of the poem but left Eliot's incorporated non-translation intact. Pound's 'Hugh Selwyn Mauberley' (1920) contained untranslated quotations from ancient Greek, Latin, French, and Italian.

[39] Erich Auerbach, *Mimesis: The Representation of Reality in Western Literature*, transl. William Trask (Princeton: Princeton University Press, 1953), p. 27; Jennifer Formichelli, 'Scenes and Situations in T. S. Eliot's Epigraphs' (PhD Thesis, Cambridge University, 2003), p. 98. I am indebted to Formichelli's reflections on the epigraph to *The Waste Land*.

to decipher its defamiliarizing formalist device of non-translation. The epigraph is an unsettling mixture of different languages (ancient Greek jostles demotic Latin prose), gesturing towards a mingling of old and young, of rich and poor, of learned and vulgarian—the philistine, *nouveau riche* former slave Trimalchio is hosting at dinner a professor of rhetoric, Agamemnon, and his two impecunious students, Encolpius and Ascyltos. It cages a death-wish within the preservation of life, renewing our perception of death in life. It is an epigraph radically destabilizing ways of seeing, foreshadowing *The Waste Land*'s modernist poetics. Seamus Perry believes that this epigraph 'works as a quick tutorial in the way that the poem is going to work. *The Waste Land* builds up meaning by juxtaposing apparently incongruous and incompatible elements, and inviting or challenging or daring the reader to search out the links that might make sense of it.'[40]

In an interview, Eliot recalled *The Waste Land* as 'a sprawling chaotic poem' and 'structureless': 'I wasn't even bothering whether I understood what I was saying.'[41] Michael Levenson, however, has traced how the beginning of the poem establishes a tension between discontinuity and continuity, skilfully teasing out local networks of syntax and lexis, including words and a sentence in German.[42] The incorporation of 'non-translated' fragments is an integral part of the sometimes unexpectedly abrupt, sometimes freer and yet fugitive movements, part of what Daniel Albright discerns as the hallmark of modernist poetics, oscillating between 'extreme systemlessness and radical resystematisation' in which 'form is at best a provisional resting-place amid a constant shifting.'[43]

> April is the cruellest month, breeding
> Lilacs out of the dead land, mixing
> Memory with desire, stirring
> Dull roots with spring rain.
> Winter kept us warm, covering
> Earth in forgetful snow, feeding
> A little life with dried tubers.
> Summer surprised us, coming over the Starnbergersee
> With a shower of rain; we stopped in the colonnade,
> And went on in the sunlight, into the Hofgarten,
> And drank coffee, and talked for an hour.
> Bin gar keine Russin, stamm' aus Litauen, echt deutsch.

---

[40] Seamus Perry, *The Connell Guide to T. S. Eliot's 'The Waste Land'* (London: Connell, 2014), pp. 25–7.

[41] 'T. S. Eliot' in *Writers at Work: The Paris Review Interviews*, Second Series, ed. George Plimpton (Harmondsworth: Penguin, 1977), pp. 89–110 (p. 105).

[42] See Michael Levenson, *A Genealogy of Modernism: A Study of English Literary Doctrine 1908–1922* (Cambridge: Cambridge University Press, 1984), pp. 168–72.

[43] Daniel Albright, 'Modernist Poetic Form', in *The Cambridge Companion to Twentieth-Century English Poetry*, ed. Neil Corcoran (Cambridge: Cambridge University Press, 2007), pp. 24–41 (p. 40).

> And when we were children, staying at the arch-duke's,
> My cousin's, he took me out on a sled,
> And I was frightened. He said, Marie,
> Marie, hold on tight. And down we went.
> In the mountains, there you feel free.
> I read, much of the night, and go south in the winter.[44]

The Russian Formalist critics examined in detail the 'rhythmical impulse' that plays irregularities of rhythm and metre against deformations of grammar or syntax. For Tynyanov: 'Rhythm is the entire dynamics of the poem comprising the interactions among metre (accentual scheme), linguistic relations (syntax), and sound relations (repetitions).'[45] In the opening of *The Waste Land* the repetitive phrasal syntax of the lines ending with participles (breed*ing*, mix*ing*, stir*ring*, cover*ing*, feed*ing*) cascades over line-ends, propelling an expressive flow and flux toward the sudden interpolation of a line of significantly longer length (a four-teener), an unattributed quotation from an unspecified speaker, introducing a 'foreign' rhythmical impulse. Here a German place-name (Starnbergersee) is reinforced by later talk of Munich's Hofgarten and an archduke from the collapsed Austrian Empire, raising disturbing questions about the relation of the macabre title of this part, 'The Burial of the Dead', to the vitality of civilization in post-war Europe. In the cosmopolitan exchanges of modern city life, peopled with the refugees dispersed by the Versailles Treaty, miscommunication is inevitable: 'Bin gar keine Russin, stamm' aus Litauen, echt deutsch', says a shadowy female presence (the German grammar *keine Russin* indicates the speaker's gender).[46] 'I am not Russian, I come from Lithuania, a real German.' But to translate is to make oneself deaf to what Christopher Ricks calls the 'tonal recesses of foreignness', to the strangeness of the voices of the displaced.[47]

In *Extraterritorial*, George Steiner broods on the linguistically 'unhoused' writer, often an émigré or exile, a cosmopolitan who excels in multilingualism.[48] When Eliot composed *The Waste Land*—parading an acquaintance with French, Italian, German, Latin, Greek, and Sanskrit[49]—he was a 'resident alien' in London

---

[44]   *The Poems of T. S. Eliot: Volume I*, p. 55.

[45]   Yurij Tynyanov, 'ob osnovach kino', *Poètika, istorija literatury, kino* (Moscow: Nauka, 1977), 341. This statement is translated by Peter Steiner in *Russian Formalism: A Metapoetics*, p. 185.

[46]   Levenson comments: 'The line of German aggravates the strain, challenging the fragile continuity that has been established.' *A Genealogy of Modernism*, p. 170.

[47]   Ricks, *T. S. Eliot and Prejudice*, p. 191. Valerie Eliot claimed that the spoken inflections of this line were taken from a real-life meeting with the Countess Marie Larisch. Eliot perhaps impersonates the banality of her conversation by rendering the well-known Bavarian song 'Auf den Bergen wohnt die Freiheit' as 'In the mountains, there you feel free.'

[48]   In *Extraterritorial*, Steiner contemplates 'the idea of a writer linguistically "unhoused", of a poet, novelist, playwright not thoroughly at home in the language of his production, but displaced or hesitant at the frontier', p. 4.

[49]   Iman Javadi offers a sober estimation of what he considers to be Eliot's 'substantial shortcomings in his linguistic competence…which previous scholarship has either ignored or glossed', examining

who had confided to his brother: 'It is damned hard work to live with a foreign nation and cope with them – one is always coming up against differences of feeling that make one feel humiliated and lonely. One remains always a foreigner.'[50] Critics have pondered the differences of feeling, inflected by language, nation and culture, that underlies what Ricks calls 'the complications of foreignness and whether a Lithuanian be Russian or German or even perhaps simply Lithuanian?'[51] Independent Lithuania was only fully liberated as a republic in 1922 after fighting free of a century of Russian domination; a national identity fomented by Germany and German-speaking Lithuanians, although threatened by the 'world revolution' spearheaded by Bolshevik Russia. In his duties at Lloyds Bank, Eliot followed the politico-economic crises engulfing ethnic Germans and Russians in the Baltic states. One wonders if he knew of a report in *The New York Times* claiming: 'The Lithuanian people are of Indo-European origin and speak one of the oldest languages in the world, a language remarkable for its striking resemblance to ancient Sanskrit, Latin, and Greek, as well as its complete divergence from the tongues of the neighboring peoples, the Slavs and Teutons.'[52] Not Russian, to be sure, the Lithuanian people, but in a post-war climate of nascent Baltic nationalisms, hardly *echt deutsch*.[53]

Trotsky scolded Russian Formalism for treating content as a function of form: to do so reduces poetry to mere etymology and syntax. This is to misunderstand the intense soldering of form and content in avant-garde art. For Shklovsky: 'The technique of art is to make objects "unfamiliar", to make forms difficult, to increase the difficulty and length of perception because the process of perception is an aesthetic end in itself and must be prolonged.'[54] Shklovsky believed that stylized parody was a key device by which artistic technique makes form perceptible and in the process renews literature—'taking cognizance of form through violating it' as he puts in his study of Sterne.[55] Eliot, too, was a connoisseur of parody.

his credentials in French, German, and Italian. '"Per te poeta fui": T. S. Eliot's Debt to Dante' (PhD Thesis, Cambridge University, 2007), pp. 36–46. In a 1949 lecture, Eliot informed a German audience: 'it has been a matter of regret to me all my life that I am such a poor linguist as I am' (quoted in Javadi, p. 42). Eliot omitted the umlaut from *Öd und leer das Meer* in the first publication of *The Waste Land* even though, unlike earlier occurrences of non-translation in the poem, Wagner's German line is set apart in italics.

---

[50] Letter to Henry Eliot, 2 July 1919. *The Letters of T. S. Eliot: Volume 1*, p. 370.

[51] Ricks, *T. S. Eliot and Prejudice*, p. 192.

[52] 'Language of Lithuania', *The New York Times* (20 April 1919), p. 10. I am grateful to William Brannian for drawing my attention to this article.

[53] Historian James Joll notes that: 'Latvians, Lithuanians and Esthonians had to be content with the alternative and sometimes even simultaneous suppression of their national identity by Germans and Russians.' *Europe Since 1870: An International History* (Harmondsworth: Penguin, 1976), p. 89.

[54] Shklovsky, 'Art as Technique', p. 12. Cf. Eliot's contention: 'we cannot say at what point "technique" begins or where it ends.' 'Preface to the 1928 Edition,' *The Sacred Wood* (London: Faber and Faber, 1928), p. ix.

[55] Viktor Shklovsky, *O teorii prozy* (Moscow: Federatsiia, 1929), p. 180. Quoted in English in Erlich, *Russian Formalism: History, Doctrine*, p. 193.

During the writing of *The Waste Land*, he praised James Joyce's 'marvellous parody of nearly every style in English prose' in the 'Oxen of the Sun' episode of *Ulysses*, which he read in *The Little Review*.[56] The opening of the 'A Game of Chess' section of *The Waste Land* creates a *tour de force* of parodic styles for serious rather than for purely satiric or comic purposes, modelled principally on Enobarbus's enraptured description of Cleopatra in her barge.

In this passage, the ghost of Shakespearean allusion sets up contrapuntal 'rhythmical impulses'.[57] However, Eliot's highly sophisticated parody enacts formalist 'shifts' by means of deviations of stress, variations of pitch, and of juncture. The effect is to emancipate 'A Game of Chess' from Shakespeare's spellbinding language of love, leaving this portrait of a bourgeois boudoir altogether more bitter and sinister. The purple sails of Cleopatra's barge 'so perfumed that / The winds were love-sick with them' are supplanted by an assortment of 'strange synthetic perfumes, / Unguent, powdered, or liquid' on the dressing-table of Eliot's lady.[58] 'A Game of Chess' is encrusted with a lavish diction, almost grotesque sound-patterns, a rich, sickly, artificial style—Cleopatra's vivifying 'smiling Cupids' metamorphose into 'golden Cupidons' adorning a narcissistic mirror. Style has become a dynamic battleground between the old and new, before this dialectic disconcertingly furnishes a rare Latin noun *laquearia* (the only recorded instance of the word in the *OED*), in Shklovsky's terms, exacerbating the difficulty and duration of perception.[59] Ultimately, opaque non-translation disguises a deeply discomforting reformulation of the poem's most troubling motif: female sexuality and violation.

> The Chair she sat in, like a burnished throne,
> Glowed on the marble, where the glass
> Held up by standards wrought with fruited vines
> From which a golden Cupidon peeped out
> (Another hid his eyes behind his wing)
> Doubled the flames of sevenbranched candelabra
> Reflecting light upon the table as
> The glitter of her jewels rose to meet it,
> From satin cases poured in rich profusion.

[56]   T. S. Eliot to Robert McAlmon, 22 May 1921, *The Letters of T. S. Eliot: Volume 1*, p. 564.

[57]   Seamus Perry points out that in the second line of 'A Game of Chess' Eliot's 'dark metrical wit' trims a foot from Shakespeare's pentameters, *The Connell Guide to T. S. Eliot's 'The Waste Land'*, p. 63. William Empson examines the contortions of 'ambiguity of syntax' in the opening of 'A Game of Chess': 'the verse has no variation of sense throughout these ambiguities, and very little of rhythm', *Seven Types of Ambiguity* (Harmondsworth: Penguin, 1995), p. 101.

[58]   William Shakespeare, *Antony and Cleopatra*, II.ii.200–201. *The Oxford Shakespeare*, gen. eds Stanley Wells and Gary Taylor (Oxford: Clarendon Press, 2005, second edn).

[59]   The rarity of the word does not strictly make it a neologism, even if Eliot uses the Latin noun in the nominative plural (laquearia) when the English syntax of the line requires it to be singular (laqueare).

In vials of ivory and coloured glass
Unstoppered, lurked her strange synthetic perfumes,
Unguent, powdered, or liquid – troubled, confused
And drowned the sense in odours; stirred by the air
That freshened from the window, these ascended
In fattening the prolonged candle-flames,
Flung their smoke into the laquearia,
Stirring the pattern on the coffered ceiling.[60]

In 1923, a Cambridge classicist, F. L. Lucas, objected to Eliot's note to line 92 which refers us to Virgil's use of 'laquearibus' in the description of Dido's banquet: 'What is the use of explaining laquearia by quoting two lines of Latin containing the word, which will convey nothing to those who do not know that language, and nothing new to those who do?'[61] In the text and note, Eliot has doubled-down on non-translation. Laquearia means a panelled or a 'coffered' ceiling but as Gareth Reeves suggests in his study of the 'Virgilian' Eliot: 'For Eliot to gloss the word even as he is using it indicates the powerful hold it must have had on his literary imagination.'[62] The word 'laquearia' draws particular attention to itself—a cryptic meaning—reiterated by the textual gloss, and then its mystery deepened and intensified by Eliot's note opening onto Dido's palace. Deciphering this non-translation uncovers a vertiginous trap door leading to Dido's desertion by Aeneas, her frenzy and suicide, and her underworld snub, shunning the Roman hero for the silent embrace of her first husband—'perhaps the most telling snub in all poetry' declares Eliot with a plain but moving pathos.[63]

The double knot of non-translation facilitates a confrontation with abandonment and the betrayal of love—trauma and guilt haunts the sexual politics of *The Waste Land*. Ernst Robert Curtius's 1927 essay on Eliot, written to accompany his translation of *The Waste Land* (the first in German), representing one of the very few contemporary commentaries on the poem recommended by Eliot, astutely perceived that the 'artistic significance' of Eliot's erudite knowledge of languages, literatures and techniques lay in the way experience was 'enhanced, suffused, illuminated': 'The only reason why Eliot could employ these motifs was that they expressed certain essential elements in his own psychological situation, reinforcing and concealing them at the same time.'[64]

There is something in Eliot's use of *laquearia* that resists translation but, in so doing, carries a freight of deep emotion.

---

[60] *The Poems of T. S. Eliot: Volume I*, p. 58.
[61] F. L. Lucas, 'The Waste Land', *The New Statesman* 22 (3 November 1923): 116–18 (p. 117).
[62] Gareth Reeves, *T. S. Eliot: A Virgilian Poet* (London: Palgrave Macmillan, 1989), p. 44.
[63] T. S. Eliot, 'What is a Classic?', in *On Poetry and Poets*, pp. 53–71 (p. 62).
[64] Ernst Robert Curtius, 'T. S. Eliot', *Essays on European Literature*, trans. Michael Kowal (Princeton: Princeton University Press, 1973), pp. 355–99 (pp. 359, 367).

It should not be thought that throughout *The Waste Land* Eliot consistently substitutes non-translation for translation as a defamiliarizing device. In the notes to 'The Fire Sermon' Eliot quotes in Italian Pia dei Tolomei's words from *Purgatorio*, 'ricorditi di me, che son la Pia; Siena mi fé, disfecemi Maremma', as a commentary on the lines 'Highbury bore me. Richmond and Kew / Undid me.'[65] Dante recounts the story that La Pia was murdered in Maremma on the instructions of her husband. 'Disfecemi' is usually translated as 'unmade' but Eliot decides upon 'undid'.[66] Again, the stylistic disruption of an allusive rhythm is expressive, as Eliot violates the balance of Dante's parallel syntax (it is chiasmus) with abrupt rhythm and abrasive sound patterns. Eliot praised Dante's 'very bare and austere style', but it is no match for the arid stoniness of parts of *The Waste Land*.[67] Most notably, 'Death by Water' is a translation of Eliot's 1917 elegy in French for 'Phlébas, le Phénicien' who, like Phoenician Dido, haunts subterranean regions of the text. This section offers a fascinating test-case for Jakobson's theories of the untranslatability of poetry between discrete phonological systems. Far from a literal translation, the eerie delicacy of 'A current under sea / Picked his bones in whispers' enacts the sea-change of Phlebas in *The Waste Land* from demotic French, 'Un courant de sous-mer l'emporta très loin.'[68] We linger over the arrestingly metaphorical trochee '*Picked* his bones in whispers'; the literalism of 'carried him very far' does not carry us so far.[69]

Eliot completed *The Waste Land* in Lausanne where he was undergoing a rest cure at the sanatorium of the Swiss psychiatrist Dr Roger Vittoz, during a leave of absence following a nervous collapse. 'At least there are people of many nationalities', Eliot wrote to his brother in cosmopolitan, multilingual Switzerland.[70] In Lausanne, Eliot finished an autograph fair copy of his synoptic apocalyptic vision of imperial 'Falling towers / Jerusalem Athens Alexandria / Vienna London.'[71] His pencil draft named the 'Polish plains' invaded by swarming 'hooded hordes', which his later note to this passage—transcribed in German from his copy of Hermann Hesse's *Blick ins Chaos*—confirmed as a nightmare of the Russian Revolution: 'Schon ist halb Europa, schon ist zumindest der halbe Osten Europas

---

[65] *The Poems of T. S. Eliot: Volume I*, pp. 75, 65.

[66] Laurence Binyon's translation of *Purgatorio* (Eliot published two cantos in *The Criterion*) selects 'unmade', *The Divine Comedy* (London: Agenda, 1979), p. 213. Eliot uses 'unmade' when he translates La Pia's lines in his study *Dante* (London: Faber and Faber, 1929), p. 38. In 1930, Eliot informed Binyon that he did not want to give the 'erroneous impression that Dante is translatable', *The Letters of T. S. Eliot: Volume 5, 1930–31*, ed. John Haffenden (London: Faber and Faber, 2014), p. 181.

[67] T. S. Eliot, *To Criticize the Critic and Other Writings* (London: Faber and Faber, 1965), p. 129.

[68] *The Poems of T. S. Eliot: Volume I*, pp. 67, 45.

[69] Multiple meanings are part of the richness of 'Death by Water'—'current' in English may evoke 'currency' (such as the foreign exchanges traced by the London banker); whereas 'courant' in French does not chime with the reference in 'Dans le Restaurant' to the sea-merchant's profit and loss (nor echo the stately assonance of 'Forgot…loss' in 'Death by Water').

[70] Letter to Henry Eliot, 13 December 1921. *The Letters of T. S. Eliot: Volume 1*, p. 614.

[71] *The Waste Land: A Facsimile and Transcript of the Original Drafts*, p. 74; *The Poems of T. S. Eliot: Volume I*, p. 69.

auf dem Wege zum Chaos, fährt betrunken in heiligem Wahn am Abgrund ent-
lang und singt dazu, singt betrunken und hymnisch wie Dmitri Karamasoff sang.
Über diese Lieder lacht der Bürger beleidigt, der Heilige und Seher hört sie mit
Tränen.'[72] The insertion of Hesse's German into *The Waste Land* was recognized
by Ernst Robert Curtius as a stylistic device ('in the manner of Apollinaire')
amenable to philology.[73]

In March 1922, Eliot was moved to write a letter to inform Hesse: 'Je trouve
votre *Blick ins Chaos* d'un sérieux qui n'est pas encore arrivé en Angleterre.'[74]
It appears that Hesse's reflections on Dostoevsky as a sick man and a prophet,
whose novel *The Brothers Karamazov* dramatizes and foretells the downfall of
Europe and the chaos in at least half of present day Europe struck a chord with
Eliot. Hesse's gloomy survey of 'Recent German Poetry' commissioned and
published by Eliot in the first issue of *The Criterion* alongside *The Waste Land*
concluded: 'These poets feel, or seem to feel, that there must first be disintegra-
tion and chaos, the bitter way must first be gone to the end, before new settings,
new forms, and new affinities are created.'[75] This observation bears a striking
relevance to Eliot's poem, especially to the difficult task of interpreting *The Waste
Land*'s fragmented multilingual vision of apocalyptic crisis—a bursting of the
great overripe fruits of European civilization—a glimpse into chaos gesturing
towards (possible) redemption.

The Waste Land closes on 'an extraordinary crescendo of apparently heterogeneous fragments'; a 'final, antic swirl of quotations.'[76] Snatches of Italian, Latin,
French, and Sanskrit reverberate in an angular, discordant heteroglossia:

> London Bridge is falling down falling down falling down
> *Poi s'ascose nel foco che gli affina*
> *Quando fiam ceu chelidon* – O swallow swallow
> *Le Prince d'Aquitaine à la tour abolie*

---

[72] 'Already half of Europe, already at least half of Eastern Europe, is on the way to chaos, drives
drunkenly in holy delusion along the edge of the abyss, singing drunkenly, singing hymns, as Dmitri
Karamazov sang. The offended bourgeois laughs at the songs; the saint and seer hear them with tears'
(my translation). *The Poems of T. S. Eliot: Volume I*, p. 76.

[73] Ernst Robert Curtius writes: 'In the notes appended to *The Waste Land* there occur some phrases
from Hermann Hesse's *Blick ins Chaos*. This medley of languages in the poem is one of the stylistic
devices that can often be found in the literature of late antiquity.... Eliot's poetry is made up of such
polyglot elements; French, Italian, Provençal. Also German.... In order to value Eliot's art properly,
one would have to make a philological study of it.' 'T. S. Eliot and Germany', trans. Richard March,
in *T. S. Eliot: A Symposium*, ed. Richard March and Tambimuttu (London: Poetry London, 1948),
pp. 119–25 (pp. 120, 125).

[74] 'I find in your *A Glimpse into Chaos* a seriousness that has not yet occurred in England.' Letter to
Hermann Hesse, 13 March 1922. *The Letters of T. S. Eliot: Volume 1*, p. 645.

[75] Hermann Hesse, 'Recent German Poetry', *The Criterion* 1.1 (October 1922): 89–93 (p. 90).

[76] Perry, *The Connell Guide to T. S. Eliot's 'The Waste Land'*, p. 12; Lawrence Rainey 'With Automatic
Hand: *The Waste Land*', *The New Cambridge Companion to T. S. Eliot*, ed. Jason Harding (Cambridge:
Cambridge University Press, 2017), pp. 71–88 (p. 84).

> These fragments I have shored against my ruins
> Why then Ile fit you. Hieronymo's mad againe.
> Datta. Dayadhvam. Damyata.
>   Shantih   shantih   shantih[77]

The world-mind able to decipher this toppling tower of Babel discovers meaning in the interpenetration of allusions dredged from Eliot's memory. But there are serious problems in simply 'explicating' *The Waste Land*. Roger Sell has pondered student guides to the poem: 'new readers can be forgiven for thinking that, no matter how difficult Eliot's style may seem at first, it probably just had to be that way, and that it will be all plain sailing once they have learned the ropes.'[78] 'What is that sound?' asks 'What the Thunder said' but to interrogate Eliot's self-conscious 'arrangement of metric and pattern' as if it were a 'conscious exposition of ideas' is to overlook his concern that 'the printers are not allowed to bitch the punctuation and the spacing, as that is very important for the sense' on the aesthetic principle (as Eliot explained) that 'the *declamation*, the system of stresses and pauses [is] exhibited by the punctuation and spacing.'[79]

Russian Formalism foregrounds the importance of sound patterning in poetry. Roman Jakobson's pioneering linguistic analysis of Velimir Khlebnikov's radical Futurist experiments with phonology and morphology conceived of it as ineluctably poetry of defamiliarization and dissociation, of arresting fragmentary ruins rather than of new associative totalities.[80] 'What the Thunder said' lays bare 'These fragments I have shored against my ruins' (the initial draft had read 'spelt into my ruins').[81] Eliot's poetics of fragmentation are consonant with a post-war generation that had seen the world they had known break apart.[82] Michael Levenson, one of the most perceptive readers of *The Waste Land*, is attentive to 'sounds that shatter meaning', concluding: 'The different languages create their own violent dislocation of sound, and the quoted texts impose a variety of rhythms.... These voices meet but never harmonize.'[83] In what follows, my closing comments on non-translation in *The Waste Land* place the emphasis on defamiliarization, discomfort and ruins.[84]

---

[77] *The Poems of T. S. Eliot: Volume I*, p. 71.

[78] Roger Sell, *Mediating Criticism* (Amsterdam: John Benjamins, 2001), p. 478.

[79] Letter to John Quinn, 19 July 1922. *The Letters of T. S. Eliot: Volume 1*, p. 707; 'Preface' to Eliot's translation of St-John Perse's *Anabasis* in *The Complete Prose of T. S. Eliot: The Critical Edition, Volume 4, English Lion, 1930–33*, ed. Jason Harding and Ronald Schuchard (Baltimore: Johns Hopkins University Press, 2015), p. 133.

[80] Jakobson's essay has not been translated into English but appears in German in *Texte der russischen Formalisten*, Band II, ed. Wolf-Dieter Stempel (Munich: Wilhelm Fink, 1972).

[81] *The Poems of T. S. Eliot: Volume I*, pp. 71, 346.

[82] On Eliot and fragmentation, see Assmann, 'Exorcizing the Demon of Chronology', pp. 22–4.

[83] Michael Levenson, 'Form, Voice, and the Avant-Garde', *The Cambridge Companion to 'The Waste Land'*, ed. Gabrielle McIntire (Cambridge: Cambridge University Press, 2015), pp. 87–101 (pp. 99, 100).

[84] Cf. George Steiner's claim: '*The Waste Land, Ulysses*, Pound's *Cantos* are deliberate assemblages, in-gatherings of a cultural past felt to be in danger of dissolution.' *After Babel*, p. 466.

Poi s'ascose nel foco che gli affina ('Then he hid himself in the refining fire'). In this line from *Purgatorio* 26, Dante's Italian supersedes the archaic but euphonious words spoken by the Provençal poet, Arnaut Daniel, in his vernacular tongue. Arnaut is the only person in the *Commedia* who talks at any length in his native foreign language. One Dante scholar has observed: 'It is striking that one can translate his Provençal verses word for word into Italian by changing hardly more than the word-endings.'[85]

Curtius pointed out that Dante precedes Eliot in the technique of non-translation: 'In Dante this technique is given a true poetic value.'[86] Punished among the lustful on the seventh cornice of purgatory, Arnaut's shade, weeping and singing, implores Dante to be mindful of his pain, before willingly plunging back into the purgatorial flames. As Stephen Romer notes in this collection, *Purgatorio* 26 was a talismanic passage for Eliot, marked in his private Temple Classics edition and frequently alluded to in his prose and poetry. If, as Massimo Bacigalupo contends, Arnaut in purgatory 'remained an Eliot persona, perhaps *the* persona', it is a mask for suffering and pain stoked by the fires of love.[87]

Quando fiam ceu chelidon is a mistranscription of a line that appears in the extant manuscripts of an anonymous Latin poem *Pervigilium Veneris* as *quando fiam uti chelidon ut tacere desinam* ('When shall I become like the swallow, so that I cease to be silent?'). Eliot came across this invocation to Venus, welcoming the regenerative powers of spring, in Walter Pater's historical novel *Marius the Epicurean* and in Ezra Pound's study *The Spirit of Romance*. Longing for the renewal of love is shadowed by the reference in this passage from *Pervigilium Veneris* to the story of Procne, who was transformed into a swallow after she had revenged the rape and mutilation of her sister Philomela. Eliot's note to the Latin line directs us to the presence of this myth earlier in the poem: 'Cf. Philomela in Parts II and III.'[88] The romantic lyricism of the line of non-translation voices a desire to sing like a bird but also alludes to the silence of Philomela who had her tongue ripped out.

Le Prince d'Aquitaine à la tour abolie ('the prince of Aquitaine, in his ruined tower') appears in the sonnet entitled, in Spanish, 'El Desdichado' ('The Disinherited' after the dispossessed hero of Walter Scott's novel *Ivanhoe*) by the French poet Gérard de Nerval. The sonnet's speaker tries out a series of unhappy poses, including the fantasy that he is the disinherited heir of the troubadour poets. Eliot encountered Nerval in Arthur Symons's *The Symbolist Movement in Literature*, which recounts Nerval's harrowing struggles with mental illness,

---

[85] Nathaniel B. Smith, 'Arnaut Daniel in the *Purgatorio*: Dante's Ambivalence toward Provençal', *Dante Studies* 98 (1980): 99–109 (p. 106).

[86] Curtius, *T. S. Eliot: A Symposium*, p. 120.

[87] Massimo Bacigalupo, 'Dante', *T. S. Eliot in Context*, ed. Jason Harding (Cambridge: Cambridge University Press, 2011), pp. 180–9 (p. 180).

[88] *The Poems of T. S. Eliot: Volume I*, p. 77.

culminating in his suicide hanging from a lamp-post. Symons remarked of Nerval: 'Every artist lives a double life, in which he is for the most part conscious of the illusions of the imagination.'[89] This dreamer and visionary haunted Eliot's imagination. In 1926, he declared: 'In so baffling a poet as Gérard de Nerval, about whom I have never yet been able to make up my mind, there are passages obviously of the daydream type.'[90] Affectation, insane delusion, suicidal despair resonate in this line of non-translation.

The eruption of the transliterated Sanskrit monosyllable DA, a radical formalist shift, struck contemporary readers of *The Waste Land* as alien and unclear. The rumble of thunder immediately spawns an etymological deconstructive free-play. The poem's interpretations of Datta, Dayadhvam, Damyata as 'Give, sympathize, control'[91]—scrambling their order in the fable of the Thunder as told in the sacred Upanishads—transcend philological exegesis. In truth, the meaning of 'What the Thunder said' illustrates Quine's philosophical doctrine of the radical indeterminacy of translation. Can the menacing *sound* of the thunder really be 'translated' into a set of didactic instructions? The poem's first readers did not think so. Edmund Wilson heard 'dry stoic Sanskrit maxims'; Conrad Aiken 'only a series of agreeable sounds which might as well have been nonsense.'[92] Michael Levenson believes that 'by following the bare sound of "Da" with the stern injunctions of a religious ethic,' Eliot is self-consciously foregrounding 'the radically disruptive aspects of voice in the poem.' He views this as a trademark of the postwar avant-garde: 'What Eliot took from his encounter with Dada was a capacity to listen to noise.'[93]

Eliot's note to the thrice-repeated Sanskrit word 'Shantih'—again transliterated—is subversive: 'Repeated as here, a formal ending to an Upanishad. "The Peace which passeth understanding" is a feeble translation of the content of this word.' In 1932, Eliot revised this gloss. Anglican Eliot, embarrassed by an unbaptised suggestion that St Paul's letter to the Philippians represents a 'feeble translation' of the wisdom of the East, equivocated with this revision: ' "The Peace which passeth understanding" is our equivalent to this word.'[94] But there can be no simple equivalence smoothing over alien linguistic and cultural traditions.[95] According

---

[89] Arthur Symons, *The Symbolist Movement in Literature*, revised and enlarged edition (London: E. P. Dutton, 1919), p. 83.

[90] T. S. Eliot, *The Varieties of Metaphysical Poetry*, ed. Ronald Schuchard (London: Faber and Faber, 1993), p. 153.

[91] See note to line 401, *The Poems of T. S. Eliot: Volume I*, p. 76. Eliot's understanding of this Upanishad was sieved through Paul Deussen's German translation.

[92] Edmund Wilson, 'The Poetry of Drouth', The Dial 73 (December 1922): 611–16 (p. 614); Aiken, 'An Anatomy of Melancholy', p. 294.

[93] Levenson, 'Form, Voice, and the Avant-Garde', p. 99.

[94] *The Poems of T. S. Eliot: Volume I*, p. 77.

[95] Christopher Ricks discovers in these notes 'the poignant admission that even so perfect a phrase as 'The Peace which passeth understanding' can no longer effect within our culture what 'Shantih' can effect within its culture.' *T. S. Eliot and Prejudice*, p. 195.

to Manju Jain, Eliot's studies in Indic philosophy at Harvard have been consistently overestimated. Eastern philosophies, she claims, 'gave him an alternative world view but it did not provide him with a mainstay in his search for a defining belief.'[96] The puzzles of *The Waste Land* cannot be solved by reference to Eastern mysticism. The sound and fury at the end of the poem is scarcely soothed by the appropriation of a Vedic mantra torn from Hindu tradition.[97] In Levenson's words: 'The poem is noisy to its end; murmuring, chanting, reciting, laughing, accusing, praying.'[98] Eliot's decision to remove the final full-stop that appeared in his draft is indicative of the defamiliarizing punctuation and spacing affecting the interrelations of sound and sense in this poem: withdrawal of the closure of punctuation alongside an expansive spacing leaves the religious ritual unresolved, perhaps irresolute; it is in process.[99]

The thunder's avant-garde Da-da prepares for the violation of linguistic and cultural boundaries in the poem's apocalyptic end, miming a breakdown of reason and logic. The fragment from *The Spanish Tragedy* ('Hieronymo's mad againe') invokes the ferocious 'antic disposition' of the play's protagonist. Hieronymo tells the soon to be murdered Balthazar: 'Each one of us must act his part / In unknown languages, / That it may breed the more variety. / As you, my lord, in Latin, I in Greek, / You in Italian, and for because I know / That Bel-imperia hath practised the French, / In courtly French shall all her phrases be.' To which Balthazar sensibly objects: 'But this will be a mere confusion, /And hardly shall we all be understood.'[100] All of the languages suggested by Hieronymo appear in *The Waste Land*; three of them in the dramatic confusion of its ending. In the dramatic confusion at the denouement of *The Spanish Tragedy* Hieronymo bites off his own tongue.

The Waste Land yearns after an 'inviolable voice', perhaps nostalgic for the Edenic time before the Fall of Adamic language into a thousand Babylonish dialects.[101] It is a poem acutely self-conscious about the difficulty of communicating with the other, or, indeed, of even making oneself intelligible at all. Russian Formalism demonstrates how the literary device of non-translation disrupts ordinary

[96] Manju Jain, *T. S. Eliot and American Philosophy: The Harvard Years* (Cambridge: Cambridge University Press, 1992), p. 111. Looking back, Eliot claimed his studies in Indic philosophy had left him 'in a state of enlightened mystification', *After Strange Gods* (London: Faber and Faber, 1934), p. 40.

[97] This is what Cleo McNelly Kearns refers to as 'torn from their matrices in whole systems of thought and culture', later amplifying this remark by acknowledging that for Eliot—a student of F. H. Bradley—'There is always some "irreducible residue," some resistance to translation, some grain of meaning that is lost as we reflect one point of view in another, supposedly broader or more inclusive one.' *T. S. Eliot and Indic Traditions: A Study in Poetry and Belief* (Cambridge: Cambridge University Press, 1987), p. 222.

[98] Levenson, 'Form, Voice, and the Avant-Garde', p. 100.

[99] *The Waste Land: A Facsimile and Transcript of the Original Drafts*, p. 80.

[100] Thomas Kyd, *The Spanish Tragedy*, ed. J. R. Mulryne (London: Ernest Benn, 1970), IV.i.171–80, pp. 109–10.

[101] *The Poems of T. S. Eliot: Volume I*, p. 58. The *OED* defines 'inviolable' as 'Not to be violated; not liable or allowed to suffer violence; to be kept sacredly free from profanation, infraction, or assault'.

language in *The Waste Land*, roughening the linguistic surfaces of the poem. As a consequence, the text is, to adopt Roland Barthes's idiom, 'filled with absences and over-nourishing signs.'[102] Eliot did not absorb the lessons of Formalist theorists but he did pay public homage to the self-consciousness about the language of poetry that Stéphane Mallarmé dedicated his life to and he wrote an admiring introduction to the discursive prose of Mallarmé's disciple, Paul Valéry.[103] Valéry's *The Art of Poetry* helps us to think about how the conscious resistance of words— as, for example, in the instances of non-translation I have examined in *The Waste Land*—is a crucial ingredient in the art of poetry: 'you have surely noticed the curious fact a certain *word*, which is perfectly clear when you hear or use it in *everyday* speech, and which presents no difficulty when caught up in the rapidity of an ordinary sentence, becomes mysteriously cumbersome, often a strange resistance, defeats all efforts at definition.' Thus far, Valéry adds nothing significant to the discoveries of Russian Formalism, but when he trespasses beyond a consideration of style to the frontier of metaphysics, his ruminations on the 'strange resistance' of words take on a luminous brilliance to students of *The Waste Land*; for language handled in this way, 'makes us believe that it has more meanings than uses. It was only a *means*, and it has become an *end*, the object of a terrible philosophical desire. It turns into an enigma, an abyss, a torment of thought.'[104]

---

[102] Roland Barthes, *Writing Degree Zero*, trans. Annette Lavers and Colin Smith (New York: Hill and Wang, 1967), p. 48.

[103] For Eliot's debts to French Symbolism, see Stephen Romer, 'French poetry', *T. S. Eliot in Context*, ed. Harding, pp. 211–20.

[104] Paul Valéry, The Art of Poetry, trans. Denise Folliot with an introduction by T. S. Eliot (New York: Bollingen Foundation, 1958), p. 55.

9

'Subrisio Saltat.': Translating the Acrobat in Rainer Maria Rilke's *Duino Elegies*

Caitríona Ní Dhúill

Acrobatics are at work whenever it is a question of making the impossible look like mere gentle exercise. So it is not enough to walk on the tightrope and execute the *salto mortale* at great height. The acrobat's crucial message to the world lies in the smile with which he bows at the end of his performance.[1]

Rainer Maria Rilke's *Duino Elegies*, completed in 1922, contain very few elements that are not German—occasional French and Italian place names, classical references, the figure of 'Madame Lamort'. Of the untranslated elements in modernist poetry that are the focus of this volume, the *Duino Elegies* offer only scant examples: their idiom, while it has been described as 'cryptic' and 'elevated', is thoroughly German, and almost never involves the juxtaposition of different linguistic codes.[2] Yet through their preoccupation with speaking, naming, the sayable, and the voice, the *Elegies* do circle around intractable problems of language and translatability. At the level of composition they may feature few instances of non-translation, but at the thematic level they persistently engage the question of how experience itself—particularly the experience of loss—may or may not be translated into language and poetic expression.

Examining a rare moment of non-German in the *Duino Elegies*—'Subrisio Saltat.', the smile of the acrobat in the fifth elegy—I propose to trace its passage through the apparatuses of commentary, interpretation, and translation that have grown up around this work. Within the text, the 'foreign body' of 'Subrisio Saltat.' has a clearly imaginable function: it appears as an ornate inscription on an urn.

---

[1] 'Akrobatik ist überall im Spiel, wo es darum geht, das Unmögliche wie eine leichte Übung erscheinen zu lassen. Es genügt also nicht, auf dem Seil zu gehen und in der Höhe den *salto mortale* zu schlagen. Die entscheidende Botschaft des Akrobaten an die Mitwelt liegt in dem Lächeln, mit dem er sich nach dem Auftritt verbeugt'. Peter Sloterdijk, *Du musst dein Leben ändern: Über Anthropotechnik* (Frankfurt am Main: Suhrkamp, 2009), p. 307. The translation is my own.

[2] Karen Leeder, introduction to Rainer Maria Rilke, *Duino Elegies*, trans. Martyn Crucefix (London: Enitharmon, 2006), p. 13; Helen Bridge, 'Duino Elegies: A New Translation with Parallel Text and Commentary (by Martyn Crucefix); Sonnets to Orpheus by (M. D. Herter Norton); Orpheus: A Version of Rilke's Sonette an Orpheus (by Don Paterson),' (review), *Translation and Literature* 16.2 (2007): 258–65 (p. 260).

Caitríona Ní Dhúill, 'Subrisio Saltat.': *Translating the Acrobat in Rainer Maria Rilke's* Duino Elegies In: *Modernism and Non-Translation*. Edited by: Jason Harding and John Nash, Oxford University Press (2019). © the several contributors. DOI: 10.1093/oso/9780198821441.003.0009

This image is immediately preceded by a passage which describes an acrobat performing, heart racing, soles burning, tears shooting into his eyes, but still blindly smiling. The smiling acrobat of the fifth elegy is one of a procession of figures—angels, lovers, dolls, animals—who populate the elegies; he belongs to a troupe of street acrobats, drawn after Pablo Picasso's 1905 painting *Les saltim-banques*. In what follows, I compare several English translations of the *Elegies*, focusing on their handling of the passage in which '*Subrisio saltat.*' occurs, with a view to identifying the different readings and approaches that underlie the various solutions. Alongside the discussion of the English translations, I also refer to the recently published first Irish-language version by Máire Mhac an tSaoi, noting the implications for translation of the wider linguistic gulf between Irish and German.[3] A focused comparative analysis of multiple translations, concentrating on a relatively brief moment of text, opens out on to the possibility that translation is itself a theme of the *Elegies*. Examining the relationship between Rilke's poem and Picasso's painting, I discuss the extent to which the acrobat passages in the fifth elegy constitute a particular kind of translation—not between one language and another, but a translation from the visual to the verbal medium. Within the poem, the acrobat's smile itself furthermore 'translates', in the sense of transforms, experience into form, thereby engaging the crucial question of *Verwandlung*, transformation from visible to invisible and from transient to enduring, that the *Elegies* relentlessly pursue. The discussion is ultimately concerned with the analogies between the difficult task of translating this poetry from one language into another and the difficulties that inhere in the translation of experience into (any) language. These latter difficulties are, of course, among the foremost concerns of the *Duino Elegies*.

Translating poetry: a 'ludicrous enterprise'

In a seminar on translating Rilke held at Oxford in May 2013, the Scottish poet Don Paterson, whose *Orpheus* reworks Rilke's *Sonnets to Orpheus* into English in a way that cannot exactly be called translation, claimed emphatically, 'You can't translate poetry. It's a ludicrous enterprise.'[4] At the same event, Paterson spoke of his experience of 'translating something you don't understand in German into something you don't understand in English.' Paterson's characterization of the endeavour of translation as absurd and doomed to failure, and as taking place at or beyond the limits of comprehension, points to the strain modernist poetry

---

[3] Rainer Maria Rilke, *Marbhnaí Duino*, trans. Máire Mhac an tSaoi (Indreabhán: Leabhar Breac, 2013).

[4] 'Voicing the Singing God', with Martyn Crucefix, Don Paterson, and Patrick McGuinness (seminar, Taylor Institution, University of Oxford, 15 May 2013).

places on the translation process. To think translation in relation to such poetry is to think translation's limits, impossibilities, and failures. Translation generally entails a rendering comprehensible, a carrying over of the source text into the target language (to use the ungainly metaphoric pairing commonly found in translation theory), but the translation of poetry, particularly modernist poetry, calls for a different set of metaphors: here, the 'target' is inevitably missed and the 'source' often substantially re-imagined.[5] Paterson has spoken of the flight or gesture a poem makes in the mind, and of the translation of the poem as an emulation of that gesture.[6] In an afterword to *Orpheus*, his rendition of Rilke's *Sonnets to Orpheus*, entitled 'Fourteen Notes on the Version', Paterson notes the alternative lexis often found in the critical literature on English-language versions of Rilke's works. Resistance to, or suspicion of, the enterprise of translation is frequently expressed through terms such as 'version', 'rendering', 'filtering', 'transmutation', 'transposition' or 'poetic equivalent', all used in preference to the term translation itself.[7] One critic writes—affirmatively—of the 'ongoing transformation of [Rilke's] poetry into ever new incarnations', another—more cautiously—of 'get[ting] it differently wrong'.[8]

Theorists of translation, and of poetry, have long insisted that the translation of a poem is in fact an act of productive reception, one that inevitably complicates the evaluative criteria of adherence, accuracy, or fidelity that are used to judge the success or merits of translations of other text-types.[9] If modernist poetry forces us to confront the limits and losses of translation, it also and by the same token helps us to arrive at a richer sense of what *non*-translation, the negation of translation, might mean. Non-translation and non-translatability may come to be seen not as the breakdown of meaning and communication, but as deliberate aesthetic choices, instances of willed opacity that communicate *about* or *beyond*, rather than through, language. Non-translated elements in modernist poetry draw attention to translation itself as a high-wire balancing act over abysses of nonsense, distortion, and communicative failure. The unassimilated 'foreign body' introduced

---

[5] See Rainer Guldin, *Translation as Metaphor* (London: Routledge, 2016), p. 22. In many publications in translation studies, the 'source / target' pairing is introduced as standard terminology, with no reflection on its status as metaphor and little background information offered as to when it entered circulation. See, for example, Basil Hatim and Jeremy Munday, *Translation: An Advanced Resource Book* (Abingdon: Routledge, 2004), p. xx.

[6] 'Voicing the Singing God', see note 4 this chapter.

[7] Don Paterson, 'Fourteen Notes on the Version', in *Orpheus: A Version of Rilke's 'Die Sonette an Orpheus'* (London: Faber, 2006), pp. 73–84.

[8] Bridge, 'Duino Elegies: A New Translation', p. 259; Charlie Louth, review of Rilke's *Duino Elegies* (translated by Martyn Crucefix) and Don Paterson's *Orpheus: A Version of Rilke's Die Sonette an Orpheus, Modern Poetry in Translation* 3.8 (2007): 134–42 (p. 138).

[9] Walter Benjamin, 'Die Aufgabe des Übersetzers', in *Kleine Prosa, Baudelaire–Übertragungen* in *Gesammelte Schriften*, 14 vols (Frankfurt am Main: Suhrkamp, 1972), IV:1, pp. 9–21; Don Paterson, 'Fourteen Notes on the Version'; Francis R. Jones, 'The Translation of Poetry', in *The Oxford Handbook of Translation Studies*, ed. Kirsten Malmkjaer and Kevin Windle (Oxford: Oxford University Press, 2011), pp. 169–82.

earlier, the untranslated and abbreviated Latin phrase '*Subrisio Saltat.*' that concludes the sixth stanza of Rilke's fifth *Duino Elegy*, is offered here as a test case against which some of these ideas may be explored in more depth. As well as comparing the ways in which different translators have dealt with this moment, I consider the impact of the Latin phrase within the original German text, retrace its itinerary through the critical literature on the *Elegies*, and unpack some of its interpretative possibilities in the context of the fifth elegy and the cycle as a whole.

Unabbreviated, the phrase would read either 'Subrisio saltatoris' or 'saltatorum', depending on whether one reads it as singular, 'smile of the acrobat', or plural, 'smile of the acrobats'.[10] (The context suggests the singular, as we shall see.) These two, more precisely one-and-a-half, words of Latin in an otherwise exclusively German text provide a specific—one might say, overly specific—instance of non-translation in modernist literature. My hope is that sustained attention to the phrase, both in its immediate context and through its reception and translation history, will help to illuminate some broader questions concerning translation and translatability, within and beyond the context of the *Elegies*. The discussion proceeds under the following headings: 1. Why Latin? 2. Prose paraphrase; 3. Ekphrasis as translation; 4. Interpretation as (re-)translation (following Hans-Georg Gadamer).

Why Latin?

The obvious answer to the question 'why Latin?' in this particular case—'*Subrisio Saltat.*'—is that Latin is demanded by the logic of the image. The phrase is in Latin because it designates the contents of an apothecary's jar. While it may seem a leap from acrobat to apothecary (via angel, as we shall see), the image belongs firmly within the *Elegies*' wider thematic complex of healing and consolation in the face of suffering and loss. The metaphor grants the acrobat's smile the qualities of a herbal balm. Following the depiction of the young acrobat smiling through his tears 'spite of all' (as Leishman and Spender have it; 'dennoch'—'nevertheless'—in the original), the lyric voice addresses the angel (already a familiar figure from the earlier elegies) as follows:

> Engel! o nimms, pflücks, das kleinblütige Heilkraut.
> Schaff eine Vase, verwahrs! Stells unter jene, uns *noch* nicht
> offenen Freuden; in lieblicher Urne
> rühms mit blumiger schwungiger Aufschrift: '*Subrisio Saltat*'.[11]

---

[10] My thanks are due to Andrej Petrovic for help on this point.

[11] Rainer Maria Rilke, *Duino Elegies, The German text, with an English translation, introduction, and commentary*, trans. J. B. Leishman and Stephen Spender (London: Hogarth Press, 1939), p. 59; Rainer Maria Rilke, *Duineser Elegien* [1923] (Frankfurt am Main: Insel, 1975), p. 35.

To bring home the difficulty of translation, it is worth comparing several English versions of this passage:

> Angel, oh take it, gather it, that small-flowered heal-wort.
> Find some vase to preserve it! Store it among those pleasures
> not yet open to us; on its lovely urn
> celebrate it in words, with a flourish: *Subrisio Saltat.*[12]

> Angel! o pluck that herb with its small blossoms
> and fetch a vase for it, safeguard it well. Set it
> among those other treasures we must wait for
> and do it honour with a precious jar, and with
> the florid, bold inscription: *Subrisio Saltat.*[13]

> Angel! oh, take it, pluck it, that small-flowered herb of healing!
> Shape a vase to preserve it. Set it among those joys
> not yet open to us: in a graceful urn
> praise it, with florally soaring inscription: '*Subrisio Saltat*.'.[14]

To these versions one could add many others—at least seven English translations or versions of the *Duino Elegies* were published in the first decade of the twenty-first century alone. To ask (as a publisher might) whether or why we need quite so many is to miss the point that to translate a work of modernist poetry is a way of reading it. I return to this idea below via the hermeneutics of Hans-Georg Gadamer, for whom, conversely, reading—and particularly the effortful kind of reading called forth by complex poetic and mythopoietic texts like the *Duino Elegies*—itself involves a process of *re*translation. (The concept of mythopoiesis, central to Gadamer's reading of the *Elegies*, is explored in more detail below.) Gadamer maintains that the *Duino Elegies* project subjective content—what he calls 'the world of the heart'—on to a mythical world in a process he names 'mythopoietic inversion'; the reader's task is to reverse this process through a complementary act of 'hermeneutic inversion' which translates the mythic content back into the subjective reality which gave rise to it, without, however, compromising the level of reflection or reflexivity ('das Reflexionsniveau') achieved and demanded by the text.[15] Thus, in Gadamer's hermeneutic model, a process of translation—albeit not in the interlingual sense that is our first concern here—is fundamental to the encounter between reader and poem. But this is to anticipate.

---

[12] Rainer Maria Rilke, *Duino Elegies*, trans. Susan Ranson, in Rilke, *Selected Poems*, ed. Robert Vilain, trans. Susan Ranson and Marielle Sutherland (Oxford: Oxford University Press, 2011), p. 153.

[13] Rainer Maria Rilke, *Duino Elegies*, trans. Stephen Cohn (Manchester: Carcanet Press, 2012), p. 47.

[14] Leishman and Spender, p. 59.

[15] Hans-Georg Gadamer, 'Mythopoietische Umkehrung in Rilkes Duineser Elegien' [1967], in *Gesammelte Werke*, 10 vols (Tübingen: Mohr, 1993), IX, pp. 289–305 (p. 290–1).

The point of examining multiple English translations side by side is to establish, first of all, what options translators of modernist poetry have when faced with a moment of non-translation.

What becomes of the Latin, and of its context, in the various translations? The 'foreign body' seems at first sight to be a moment when the translator's labour is eased: preservation of the original code-switch merely requires the Latin to stay as it is in the English version, much in the same way as translators of Thomas Mann's *Der Zauberberg* (*The Magic Mountain*) from German to English have the option of simply leaving the passages of French dialogue in French.[16] This is the solution adopted by most, but interestingly not all, translators of the *Duino Elegies*. One of the most recent English versions of the *Duino Elegies*, that of Martyn Crucefix (2006), takes the following approach:

> Angel – oh, pluck it, gather its small-flowering, healing herb.
> Conjure a vase and preserve it. Set it there with the other
> pleasures *not* yet open to us and give it
> a precious jar and praise it
> with a bold and flowing inscription:
> *Acrobat, smile of*[17]

Crucefix domesticates this part of the text, rendering the Latin 'foreign body' less foreign; his solution allows him to dispense with the footnote or gloss that this moment usually requires, but at the price of transforming the apothecary's jar-label into some other genre of microtext—an entry in an index or reference work, perhaps.[18]

'*Subrisio saltat.*' does not stand alone: it is the culminating moment of its stanza, and needs to be read as such. It may be set apart *linguistically* from the text that surrounds it, but in terms of the unfolding of the metaphor, the poetic argument, and the metrical disposition of the poem, it forms an integral part of a continuous whole. Thus, the persuasiveness of the translator's solution depends in each case on the overall approach to this whole, and on the ways in which the relationships between its component parts are handled. With regard to the visible—and perhaps more importantly, audible—differences between the versions by

---

[16] See Thomas Mann, *The Magic Mountain* [1924], trans. H.T. Lowe-Porter [1927] (Harmondsworth: Penguin, 1973), pp. 335–43; compare Thomas Mann, *The Magic Mountain*, trans. John E. Woods [1995] (New York: Alfred A. Knopf, 2005), pp. 396–408, which translates the French dialogue into English (italicized, and leaving only the first French sentence in this long bilingual sequence in italicized French). Reading knowledge of French, assumed in an educated Anglophone readership in 1927, is no longer taken for granted by 1995, and the only residue of the original moment of non-translation is typographical.

[17] Rainer Maria Rilke, *Duino Elegies*, trans. Martyn Crucefix (London: Enitharmon Press, 2006), pp. 45–7.

[18] See Ranson, p. 309; Cohn, p. 94; Leishman and Spender, p. 127; Mhac an tSaoi, p. 131.

Ranson, Leishman and Spender, Cohn, and Crucefix quoted so far, the most striking and problematic is the metrical choice made by Cohn, for iambs over the rolling elegiac dactyls. In the original cycle, Rilke reserves iambs for the fourth and eighth elegies, for reasons and with effects that are significant enough to warrant separate discussion.[19] In terms of how individual elements are rendered, 'das kleinblütige Heilkraut', the key image of the passage and the one which translates, in the sense of transmutes, the fleeting smile into something more substantial and essential, immediately presents the translator with the problem of German's greater capacity for forming original compounds of nouns and adjectives. The solutions considered so far opt for a variety of hyphenated combinations, omissions, and paraphrases: 'that small-flowered heal-wort', 'that herb with its small blossoms', 'that small-flowered herb of healing', 'its small-flowering, healing herb'. With the omission of any reference to healing, Cohn misses the botanical dispensary altogether, while the version that is at first sight perhaps the least promising, Ranson's neologistic 'heal-wort', creates the necessary estrangement while keeping some of the rhythmic tightness. But no solution can compensate for the loss of a feature of the original so subtle that it is almost guaranteed to escape the reader's conscious awareness on a first reading: the metrical similarity of the acrobat's smile and the healing herb, a similarity which seals their metaphorical union.

kleinblütige[s] Heilkraut—*Subrisio Saltat.*

Some discrepancies in punctuation of the Latin phrase can be observed between the various English versions. Leishman and Spender, notwithstanding the risk they take with 'florally soaring inscription' (which for the sake of the dactyl makes an adverb, 'florally', of an adjective, thus distorting the relationship between the components of the line), are the most punctilious here in observing the quotation marks and the two full points, the first marking the abbreviation and the second terminating the sentence and stanza. Attention to this level of detail in the punctuation may seem pedantic, but in fact the first of the full points belongs to the inscription on the apothecary's jar and marks it as such. We know that Rilke tried out a number of variants in earlier drafts before arriving at *Subrisio Saltat.*, including:

Pulv. risus saltimb.
Sorris. Saltimb.[20]

As the label on the apothecary's jar that contains and preserves the healing herb, '*Subrisio Saltat.*' follows the real-life conventions of such labelling in using

[19] See Werner Schröder, *Der Versbau der Duineser Elegien: Versuch einer metrischen Beschreibung* (Stuttgart: Franz Steiner, 1992).

[20] Ulrich Fülleborn and Manfred Engel, eds, *Materialien zu Rainer Maria Rilkes 'Duineser Elegien'* 3 vols (Frankfurt am Main: Suhrkamp, 1982), I, pp. 340–1.

abbreviated Latin. In the final published version, the angel is called upon to pluck the herb, but an earlier draft shows us this metaphor emergent, as 'the small-flowered / quickly fading smile' ('das kleinblüthige / rasch eingehende Lächeln').[21]

The terms of comparison the metaphor mobilizes are fragility, rarity, preciousness, and restorative power. The image of a rare and precious plant anticipates the gentian of the ninth elegy which can also be read as a figure of translation at its limits. 'Gentian' in the ninth elegy is not primarily the signified flower, but the signifier itself, the acquired word with which the wanderer returns from the mountain, a word gained through the transformative encounter with the unknown:

> Bringt doch der Wanderer auch vom Hange des Bergrands
> nicht eine Hand voll Erde ins Tal, die Allen unsägliche, sondern
> ein erworbenes Wort, reines, den gelben und blaun
> Enzian.[22]

> The traveller brings from the mountain slope to the valley
> no handful of earth, which cannot be said to the world, but instead
> a word he has won, a pure word, the yellow and blue
> gentian.[23]

In its journey from the fifth to the ninth elegy, the motif of the small precious flower has evolved. The 'heal-wort' requires angelic intervention for its preservation; by the time the gentian appears in the ninth elegy, the argument of the poetic cycle has arrived at the conclusion that language itself, acts of naming and speaking, are sufficient to give mortals a sense of belonging, continuity, and meaning in a world marked by change and loss. The smile, which in the earlier elegies was grouped with a range of phenomena marked for disappearance, from the steam off a hot dish to a phrase of live music ('O Lächeln, wohin?'/'Where do smiles go?'), is transmuted via the flower metaphor into a preservable essence.[24] Of greater significance than the contents of the jar, however, is the writing on its label: '*Subrisio saltat.*' names and marks the capture and distillation of the fleeting moment. Likewise, what remains of the traveller's experience in the ninth elegy is not a material but a verbal trace; while the clod of earth, being speechless and thus unable to transmit meaning, is best left where it is, the name *Enzian* (gentian) can be carried over—translated—from its original context to the wider world. Yet in another sense *Enzian* remains untranslated and untranslatable: it is both the sign of the transformation which the traveller has undergone through his travels, and

---

[21] Fülleborn and Engel, *Materialien zu Rainer Maria Rilkes 'Duineser Elegien'* I, p. 341.

[22] Rilke, *Duineser Elegien*, p. 56.   [23] Ranson, *Selected Poems*, p. 171.

[24] Rilke, *Duineser Elegien*, p. 16.

the verbal foreign body which he introduces into a context that has no direct knowledge of the object it signifies.

Prose paraphrase

It could be argued that the passage from the fifth elegy under discussion here—with its suffering artiste, fleeting hard-won smile, distillation thereof, all brought together in the metaphor of a healing herb—is grist to the mill of the rather instrumental and non-poetic end of Rilke reception which either co-opts him for a new-age secular spirituality or, in an older tradition, seeks to translate his poetic language back into the wise prose of life lessons concerning forbearance and transience, whether in a theological or post-metaphysical framework. This latter sense of translation—the intralingual, as opposed to interlingual, transposition of the lyrical text into a prose paraphrase—is the chief object of criticism in Hans-Georg Gadamer's essays on the *Duino Elegies*, to which we turn presently.[25] Consider the following:

> So among these jars bearing inscriptions like 'Courage', 'Diligence', 'Triumph', 'Calm', and 'Wisdom', there is a special section in the dispensary of life for remedies which cannot yet be used. Here is the urn with the inscription 'Smile of the Dancer' or 'Dancer's Smile'. Here is kept the 'small-flowered herb of healing', and, as there is no reference here to 'powder', we may assume that it has not been ground in any mill.[26]

The acrobat's ability to smile 'spite of all' threatens to shade over into a sort of Rilkean 'Keep Calm and Carry On', in the supposedly non-ideological but in fact deeply and problematically quiescent kind of reading which, as Christa Bürger argued many decades ago, is precisely the risk which the *Duino Elegies* run due to their distinctive mix of opacity and rhetorical grandeur.[27] Kathleen Komar has traced the explosion in recent decades in popular Rilke reception of the *Little Book of Rilke* variety, pitched at stressed neoliberal subjects who may be in need of something stronger than a small-flowered heal-wort.[28] This is not to

---

[25] See Roman Jakobson, 'On Linguistic Aspects of Translation', in *On Translation*, ed. Reuben Brower (Boston: Harvard University Press, 1959), pp. 232–9 (pp. 233–4), for an explication of the differences between interlingual, intralingual, and intersemiotic translation.

[26] Romano Guardini, *Rilke's 'Duino Elegies': An Interpretation*, trans. K.G. Knight (London: Darwen Finlayson, 1961), pp. 148–9.

[27] Christa Bürger, 'Textanalyse und Ideologiekritik: Rilkes erste Duineser Elegien', in *Rilkes Duineser Elegien*, 3 vols, ed. Ulrich Fülleborn and Manfred Engel (Frankfurt am Main: Suhrkamp, 1980–82), II, pp. 264–78.

[28] Kathleen L. Komar, 'Rethinking Rilke's *Duineser Elegien* at the End of the Millennium', in *A Companion to the Works of Rainer Maria Rilke*, ed. Erica A. Metzger and Michael M. Metzger (Rochester, NY: Camden House, 2001), pp. 188–208.

delegitimize Guardini's on the whole sensitive reading, which, first published in 1941, set an important benchmark in the *Elegies'* reception; his chapter on the second elegy is included in the three-volume Suhrkamp collection of materials edited by Fülleborn and Engel that remains the standard introduction to *Duino* and its reception history.[29] Yet Gadamer, in his unfolding of a hermeneutic practice that would explicate complex poetry while resisting the temptation to translate it into prose, targets Guardini, among others, precisely for their tendency to provide prose paraphrase of the poem's ideas and content.[30]

Intralingual translation or paraphrase is, furthermore, historically determined, marking a specific moment in the poem's reception history. In the early twenty-first century, a quizzical or jaded response to Guardini's 'dispensary of life', and to similar readings of the *Duino Elegies* that seek to wrest a 'philosophy' or wisdom from them, perhaps says more about the distance we have travelled in terms of mentality and world history since the first generation of readers. Guardini's reading belongs to an historical context in which the most urgent question many readers confronted in the *Duino Elegies* was that of the possibility or impossibility of transcendence through immanence following widespread demise of faith in any transcendent beneficent God. The question that dominated much discussion of these and other modernist texts was: what sense can be made of life in the absence of an afterlife? Since then, the 'grim insight' ('grimmige Einsicht') that opens the tenth elegy has shifted in contemporary perception from the problems of individual mortality and transcendental homelessness (although these remain present) to a demise and disorientation of rather larger and more irremediably material dimensions: the collapse at the planetary level of the life-support systems on which humans depend. Charlie Louth has suggested that what resonates most powerfully with Rilke's readers today is a sort of 'ecological anxiety' running through his work.[31] In the Anthropocene age, the balms of the botanical dispensary have a new sort of healing work to do; they are either co-opted for an ethic of mindful self-optimization or enlisted for the task of radical, non-anthropocentric re-orientation of the human project. A prominent but controversial (and not always congenial) reader of Rilke, the contemporary German philosopher Peter Sloterdijk, attempts a tightrope walk between these alternatives, as indicated in the quote with which this essay began. Sloterdijk's elaboration of an ethics of asceticism and intellectual athleticism in an era of ecological crisis and degradation

---

[29] Romano Guardini, 'Rainer Maria Rilkes Zweite Duineser Elegie: Eine Interpretation' [1941], in *Rilkes Duineser Elegien*, ed. Fülleborn and Engel, II, pp. 80–104.

[30] Gadamer, 'Mythopoietische Umkehrung', p. 289.

[31] Louth, review, *Modern Poetry in Translation*, p. 142. Further explorations of (proto-) ecological themes in Rilke's works can be found in Luke Fischer, *The Poet as Phenomenologist: Rilke and the New Poems* (London: Bloomsbury, 2016); Eric Santner, *On Creaturely Life: Rilke, Benjamin, Sebald* (Chicago: Chicago University Press, 2006); and John Llewelyn, *The Middle Voice of Ecological Conscience: A Chiasmic Reading of Responsibility in the Neighborhood of Levinas, Heidegger, and Others* (New York: St Martin's Press, 1991).

is certainly a compelling direction in which to think with the acrobat's smile. What Sloterdijk terms *anthropotechnics*—in a book whose title, *You Must Change Your Life*, is taken from the last line of Rilke's sonnet 'Archaic torso of Apollo'—is an attitude or ethic saturated with Rilkean vocabulary and imagery.[32] The belief that we can expand the range of the possible by striving for the impossible; a commitment to the motivating symbolism of the vertical; the insistence that *habit*, whether unconscious or consciously cultivated, is existentially fundamental; the co-optation of the language and iconography of transcendence for a project realizable within, and committed to, the realm of immanence; all of these themes of Sloterdijk's are prose-philosophical echoes and explorations of figures from Rilke's work, particularly the *Duino Elegies* and the *Sonnets to Orpheus*. A systematic examination of Sloterdijk's Rilke reception lies beyond the scope of the present discussion; it may suffice to recall that Rilke's acrobats introduce imagery that culminates, at the end of the fifth elegy, in the figure of the lovers performing breathtaking feats of the heart to an audience who will finally shower them with the true 'coin of happiness' ('ewig / gültige[] Münzen des Glücks').[33] In a move that recurs throughout the *Duino Elegies*, a banal, somewhat shabby reality—here, that of street performers doing tricks on a threadbare rug under the grey skies of a suburb—is transmuted into a sublime excess of feeling; but the very moment that seems to promise transcendence through its intensity and aliveness remains fully immanent, in the sense of this-worldly, through its inextricability from bodily experience and intersubjective relation. The lovers take up the challenge of the acrobats only to outperform them immeasurably in daring and mastery; the vertiginous figure that Sloterdijk will find so eloquent almost a century after Rilke first composed it, that of ladders that no longer lean on the ground but only on each other, is the striking image with which the fifth elegy ends.[34]

Ekphrasis as translation

The quotation from Guardini introduced earlier, concering 'the urn with the inscription "Smile of the Dancer" or "Dancer's Smile"', calls attention to a disagreement among critics as to the best translation of the Latin phrase.[35] The commentary to Leishman and Spender has 'acrobat's smile', as do many others including Judith Ryan in her book on Rilke; Ranson opts for the plural 'acrobats'; yet Guardini glosses it as 'smile of the dancer'.[36] In either case, it is clear from the

---

[32] Rainer Maria Rilke, 'Archäischer Torso Apollos', in Rilke, *Sämtliche Werke*, 12 vols (Frankfurt am Main: Insel, 1955), I, p. 557.

[33] Rilke, *Duineser Elegien*, p. 36.   [34] Sloterdijk, *Du mußt dein Leben ändern*, pp. 199–202.

[35] Guardini, 'Rainer Maria Rilkes Zweite Duineser Elegie: Eine Interpretation', p. 149.

[36] Judith Ryan, *Rilke, Modernism and Poetic Tradition* (Cambridge: Cambridge University Press, 1999), p. 196.

poetic context whose smile is meant. For while *saltator* is indeed also the Latin for dancer, here in an abbreviated genitive, the elegy itself tells us that these are acrobats rather than dancers, travelling and transient, performing under the open sky to onlookers in suburbia. To the internal textual evidence can be added the external evidence of biographical context and dedication: there is no doubt as to the identity of the painting, Picasso's *Les saltimbanques*, to which the poem is a commentary of sorts. We know that *Les saltimbanques* hung on the wall in the home of the fifth elegy's dedicatee, Hertha Koenig, where Rilke stayed in 1915; we know from letters and other texts, including a prose poem of the same title, that the poet's observation of a troupe of actual acrobats in 1906–7 also informed the creation of the figures we encounter in this elegy.[37]

The relation of poem to painting is an ekphrastic one: it involves the verbal representation of a visual representation, hence a representation at two removes. The Picasso reference has generated quite a few problems and confusions for Rilke's translators. Leishman and Spender's commentary speaks at this point of a 'double meaning which cannot be reproduced in translation':

> A glance at Picasso's picture will reveal that the five standing figures might be contained within a large capital D, of which the man in harlequin's dress formed the upright and the little boy the extreme end of the loop: D for *Dasein*.[38]

But the word 'Dasein' does not in fact appear at this point in the text, or indeed anywhere in the fifth elegy. Leishman and Spender's confusion of 'Dastehn' with 'Dasein' sets off a Heideggerian false alarm among the anglophone critics that continues to sound many decades later: Komar, for example, writes of the picture that the 'group of acrobats is arranged roughly in the shape of a capital letter "D" (to form the beginning of the word "Dastehn" or "existence" in line fourteen of the poem)'.[39] Again, the German word for 'existence' is not 'Dastehn', but 'Dasein'; while Jacob Steiner argues that 'Dastehn' is a *part* of 'Dasein', his interpretation at this point leads away from the text towards a speculative paraphrase and cannot serve as a basis for a translator's decision.[40] The confusion between 'Dastehn' and 'Dasein' aside, the main challenge for the translator at this point in the text is the choice of a word whose initial refers through its shape to the grouping of figures in the painting. The translation must opt for loss or distortion:

> Und kaum dort,
> aufrecht, da und gezeigt: des Dastehns
> großer Anfangsbuchstab...[41]

---

[37] See Jacob Steiner, *Rilkes Duineser Elegien* (Bern: Francke, 1962), pp. 101–27.
[38] Leishman and Spender, p. 126.
[39] Kathleen L. Komar, 'The *Duino Elegies*', in *The Cambridge Companion to Rilke*, ed. Karen Leeder and Robert Vilain (Cambridge: Cambridge University Press, 2010), pp. 80–94 (p. 88).
[40] Steiner, *Rilkes Duineser Elegien*, p. 106.   [41] Rilke, *Duineser Elegien*, p. 33.

Scarce have they landed, and there
revealed is the tall, upright, initial D
of their standing's Duration...

(Ranson, p. 151)

And, barely discernible, yet
there in its place and revealed, stands Destiny's
capital letter:

(Cohn, p. 45)

And hardly there,
upright, shown there: the great initial
letter of Thereness, ----

(Leishman and Spender, p. 55)

These 'solutions' variously illustrate the impossibility of translation. Ranson explains the choice of 'Duration' in her commentary by linking through 'endurance' to 'duration' and suggesting that 'Rilke may be referring to the fleeting yet timeless moment of stillness between tricks', but it is quite a stretch to translate 'Dastehn' with 'endurance', and the emphasis on duration *qua* stillness—which would be appropriate elsewhere in the *Elegies*, for instance where the lovers 'sense pure duration beneath' their embraces in the second elegy, seems at odds with the relentless forward movement that drives the acrobats from one trick to the next in the fifth.[42] Cohn's choice of 'Destiny' (which, uncapitalized, is also Crucefix's choice) involves a word with particular freight in this elegy, which three stanzas later brings us the figure of Madame Lamorte weaving the garishly dyed winter hats of destiny or fate ('die Winterhüte des Schicksals').[43] But again, as a translation of 'Dastehn', it is wide of the mark, even if the matching consonants are phonetically appealing. 'Existence' or 'Being' (the latter is A. S. Kline's choice) could both pass muster as versions of 'Dasein', although Heideggerians tend to avoid them, preferring with good reason to retain the German word even when writing in English.[44] Why? Because of the 'da' of 'Dasein', the quality of 'Thereness' that Leishman and Spender choose to prioritize in their version, even at the high price of having three 'theres' in the space of ten words and eliding the small but crucial difference between 'da' and 'dort' (the latter more demonstrative of a particular location than the former). The misreading is compounded in each of the translations: 'Dastehn' simply means 'standing there', and if we look at Picasso's painting we see that this is exactly what the acrobats are doing. Contrary to Guardini's bald assertion that, while *Les saltimbanques* 'probably underlies the descriptive portions of the [fifth] *Elegy*, [...] a comparison of the two would not help our

[42] Ranson, p. 309.   [43] Crucefix, p. 43; Rilke, *Duineser Elegien*, p. 36.
[44] Rainer Maria Rilke, *The Duino Elegies*, trans. A. S. Kline (2004), online edition, retrieved 27 April 2017, available at https://www.poetryintranslation.com/PITBR/German/Rilke.php

understanding of the poem', in fact the confusion which the translations generate *can* be cleared up by looking at the painting.[45] Picasso's acrobats are standing around, taking a break between performances. The demands of the ekphrasis, which calls for a translation that reproduces the capital D of the painting while simultaneously rendering the verbal noun in some recognizable way, faces the translator with an insoluble problem.

That this ekphrastic challenge might be poetically productive is a possibility realized by Máire Mhac an tSaoi's Irish-language version of 2013. Not content with a single solution to this difficult moment of 'Dastehn', Mhac an tSaoi offers three solutions at once (in the third line of the following quotation):

> Ansúd, cé ar éigean, cítear ina choilgsheasamh
> Cinnlitir mhór na marthana,
> *Delta*, an dair, an dé ...[46]

Delta references the alphabet, with the historical and cultural resonances of ancient Greek and the Bible: the acrobats make no claim to be Alpha or Omega, their condition is one of suspension in the in-between. *An dair*, the oak tree, brings Rilke and Picasso into contact with a symbol that, for Irish, German and other cultures, has familiar connotations of strength and endurance, enhanced in the Celtic context by the druidic association; but this is no mere extraneous addition on Mhac an tSaoi's part. In the Old Irish alphabet, each letter had the name of a different tree of which it was the intial: *an dair* thus enriches the uprightness and *thereness* of 'des Dastehns / großer Anfangsbuchstab' with an arboreal image that already, in the Irish context, stands for the letter D.[47] The third element of Mhac an tSaoi's triad, *an dé*, is the most polysemic; it may denote a breath, glimmer or flame—all of which bear the further connotations of life or life force—while also referring, again, to the letter of the alphabet (*a, bé, cé, dé*).[48] Mhac an tSaoi's multiple solutions remind us of the greater linguistic divide separating source and target languages, while also contrasting a figure of the air with one of the earth, the invisible and moving breath of life with the solid and phallic singularity of *an dair*. (The phallic quality is indisputably present in the original—recall the 'son of a neck and a nun' passage that follows shortly after this one.) Mhac an tSaoi's project is focused as much on expanding the poetic possibilities of the recipient language as on providing a recognizable rendering of the source text; here, her deliberate refusal to choose from among three alternatives has the effect of highlighting, and capitalizing on, the translational difficulty posed by the ekphrastic moment.

---

[45] Guardini, *Rilke's Duino Elegies*, p. 132.   [46] Mhac an tSaoi, *Marbhnaí Duino*, p. 49.
[47] On the use of tree names as letter names in Old Irish, see Damian McManus, 'Irish letter-names and their kennings', *Ériu* 39 (1988): 127–68.
[48] My thanks are due to Gréagóir Ó Dúill for help on this point.

If we accept the idea that ekphrasis is itself a form of translation—the productive reception of an image in words, its interpretative transposition from a visual to a verbal medium—then it seems that this moment in the fifth elegy places particular demands on translators precisely because it involves a double translation, first image to word, then German to target language. Interlingual difference is compounded by intermedial; no wonder, perhaps, that the intralingual efforts of critics and commentators to elucidate this moment in the text are liable to involve or cause confusion.

Interpretation as (re-)translation (following Gadamer)

The usual aim of translation is to render something comprehensible, to carry the source text over into the recipient language. Hans-Georg Gadamer, in one of several essays on Rilke's poetry, writes that the original hermeneutic task is to explain the incomprehensible.[49] In Gadamer's hermeneutic theory, the idea of translation is pivotal. Yet, as noted above, this is not a question of translating the 'message' or 'content' of the poem into non-lyrical language. Rather, translation *as process* is crucial to a hermeneutic model that envisages the interpretation of a poem as the reception and continuation of a movement already begun in the poem itself—recall Paterson's figure, quoted above, of the flight a poem makes in the reader's mind, and of translation as an emulation of that gesture. Gadamer's 1967 essay on the *Duino Elegies* sets out the process of 'mythopoietic inversion' ('mythopoietische Umkehrung') these poems enact: the world of the heart is projected out onto a mythical world, peopled by figures of acrobats, angels, dolls, and other agents (what he calls 'acting beings', 'handelnde Wesen'), and with its own distinctive range of landscapes, from suburbs and city streets through gardens and gorges up to the Mountains of Sorrow in the tenth elegy.[50] The corresponding move on the part of the reader—using Gadamer's terms—is that of hermeneutic inversion: the poetic or mythological statement is translated back into the terms of the reader's own understanding ('zurückübersetzt in die eigenen Begriffe des Verstehens').[51] The methodological difficulty lies in the fact that what is to be translated back—from the lyrical to some other, more prosaic and supposedly comprehensible form—was already something that had itself been translated ('daß das Zurückzuübersetzende selber schon ein Zurückübersetztes war').[52] It is through this process of *re*translation that the text becomes comprehensible and ultimately meaningful to the reader: the goal of the hermeneutic inversion is to

---

[49] Gadamer, 'Mythopoietische Umkehrung', p. 289.
[50] Gadamer, 'Mythopoietische Umkehrung', p. 295.
[51] Gadamer, 'Mythopoietische Umkehrung', p. 304.
[52] Gadamer, 'Mythopoietische Umkehrung', p. 295.

make sense of that which had first seemed strange and opaque, to make it speak ('den Text als sinnvoll und sprechend wiederzugewinnen, der sich als fremd und befremdlich zu verbergen schien').[53]

Yet this act of interpretative retranslation does not mark an end to the process set in train by the poem: the hermeneutic inversion does not simply cancel out or reverse the mythopoietic, bringing us in a circular journey from world to text and back to world again. Rather, it enables a further stage in the relationship between reader and poem to become imaginable and ultimately attainable: that of co-presence, of the reader's coming into fuller presence of the poem (and thus of themselves) in all its (their) strangeness. All interpretation should lead, not to a translation or prose paraphrase, but to 'an activation of the resonant ground from which the poetic melody is able to sing more strongly into our ears'.[54] The ultimate goal of interpretation, Gadamer urges, is to do away with itself ('sich selbst aufheben'): explanatory effort melts away in the face of the clarity of the poem's self-utterance. 'A translation *back* must always be possible,' he writes, 'one which allows that which is present in the poem to become present to us.' [55]

Gadamer's concern is with hermeneutics, the act and art of interpretation. Yet the lexis of translation features prominently in his discussion. This is especially striking given the fact that he nowhere mentions interlingual translation from one language to another in his discussion of Rilke, and also in view of his clearly articulated critical stance concerning the inadequacy of intralingual translation or prose paraphrase as an approach to complex lyrical texts. The back-and-forth movement of transposition, explication, paraphrase, rendering comprehensible, that constitutes the preliminary work of hermeneutic practice is only ever a means to an end—the end of coming into full presence of the poem. Once this end has been achieved, the apparatus and labour of translation can be dispensed with. Here, the hermeneutic process mirrors that of language acquisition: once interlingual proficiency is achieved, the infrastructure and effort required to achieve it become redundant, and the speaker begins to be ever more fully present in the 'target' or acquired language. In this regard, the process of coming into presence— whether of a text or in a language—recalls the hypothetical lovers at the end of the fifth elegy, whose level of attainment or artistry—*Können*—is such that the ladders they ascend no longer rest on the ground. Rilke's acrobat, marked out by the untranslated moment of Latin in the poem, furnishes us with a figure for translation itself—as the leap from source to target that is most effectively executed when it belies the effort it costs.

---

[53] Gadamer, 'Mythopoietische Umkehrung', p. 304.

[54] 'Alle Interpretation kann nur darin münden, daß sie den Resonanzboden in Schwingung versetzt, von dem aus sich die dichterische Melodie uns verstärkt ins Ohr singt', Gadamer, 'Mythopoietische Umkehrung', p. 304.

[55] 'Immer muß es eine Rückübersetzung geben können, die das in den Versen Gegenwärtige uns gegenwärtig sein läßt', Gadamer, 'Mythopoietische Umkehrung', p. 304.

10

'Bloom, nodding, said he perfectly understood': James Joyce and the Meanings of Translation

Scarlett Baron

Modernism's deployment of a kaleidoscopic array of languages ranks among its best-known features—a testament to the polyglot erudition of the period's iconic authors and one of the hallmarks of its embrace of difficulty.[1] If the period deserves, as Stephen Yao suggests in his survey of the many translations undertaken by its canonical writers, to be dubbed 'an age of translations', it is also one in which untranslated fragments assume a marked prominence in literary texts.[2] Referring to snippets of foreign-language text as instances of *non*-translation entails thinking about them in a particular light, not merely as moments of accidental oversight but as the mark of a deliberate withholding—whether on the part of author, narrator, persona, or character.

An example of such considered non-translation is clearly at work when, in the third chapter of Woolf's first novel, *The Voyage Out*, Mr Pepper—a desiccated amateur scholar who is variously likened to 'a vivacious and malicious ape' and 'a fossilized fish in a basin'—impelled by Mrs Dalloway's professed enthusiasm for Sophocles's *Antigone*, launches into a recitation from the play's second chorus.[3] Prompted specifically by Mrs Dalloway's impassioned statement that 'I don't know a word of Greek, but I could listen to it for ever -----', Pepper declaims:

> Πολλὰ τὰ δεινά, κοὐδὲν ἀν-
> θρώπου δεινότερον πέλει.
> τοῦτο καί πολιοῦ πέραν
> πόντου χειμερίῳ νότῳ

---

[1] As T. S. Eliot famously declared in 1921, 'poets in our civilization, as it exists at present, must be *difficult*', in 'The Metaphysical Poets' [1921], *Selected Essays*, 3rd edn (London: Faber and Faber, 1951), pp. 281–91 (p. 289).

[2] Steven G. Yao, *Translation and the Languages of Modernism: Gender, Politics, Language* (New York and Basingstoke: Palgrave Macmillan, 2002), p. 5.

[3] Virginia Woolf, *The Voyage Out*, ed. Lorna Sage (Oxford: Oxford University Press, 2001), pp. 12, 14.

Scarlett Baron, *'Bloom, nodding, said he perfectly understood': James Joyce and the Meanings of Translation* In: *Modernism and Non-Translation.* Edited by: Jason Harding and John Nash, Oxford University Press (2019).
© the several contributors.
DOI: 10.1093/oso/9780198821441.003.0010

$$\chi\omega\rho\epsilon\hat{\iota},\ \pi\epsilon\rho\iota\beta\rho\upsilon\chi\acute{\iota}o\iota\sigma\iota$$
$$\pi\epsilon\rho\hat{\omega}\nu\ \acute{\upsilon}\pi'\ o\check{\iota}\delta\mu\alpha\sigma\iota$$

These are lines which many of Woolf's contemporary readers—as well as many late twentieth- and early twenty-first-century readers—would not have been able to read, their failure replicating the aural bewilderment of Pepper's female audience ('Mrs Dalloway', the laconic narrator observes, 'looked at him with compressed lips.') And as the ostensible purpose of Pepper's oration is to illustrate the beauty of Greek sounds to an assembly of listeners, readers unable to read, let alone pronounce, Ancient Greek, confronted with illegible signs on a silent white page, have cause to feel doubly left out.[4]

As this example shows, couching an enquiry about foreign-language use in terms of 'non-translation' usefully focuses attention on the motives underpinning the strategic showcasing of other languages in modernist texts. But the hyphenated term presents challenges as well as advantages. The most significant of these concerns its reversibility: for what is a translation from one point of view may be a non-translation from another. When Joyce attributes incomprehensible words to Eveline's mother in *Dubliners*—'Derevaun Seraun! Derevaun Seraun!'—or when Woolf, in *Mrs Dalloway*, conveys the sound made by the voice of an old woman begging by Regent's Park Tube Station as,

> ee um fah um so
> foo swee too eem oo

or when, at the end of *The Years*, she conveys the singing of a chorus of children as,

> Etho passo tanno hai
> Fai donk to tu do,
> Mai to, kai to, lai to see
> Toh dom to tuh do –[5]

they are translating sound into combinations of letters, but pointedly *not* translating the words their characters are seeking to voice, refusing to shed light for us on what it is that they are trying to communicate. A similar situation arises in the 'Ithaca' episode of *Ulysses* when Stephen Dedalus and Leopold Bloom are explicitly said to address each other in Greek and Hebrew respectively, only for their words to be rendered on the page using the letters of the Roman (rather than Greek and Hebrew) alphabet. Are such renderings translations (in the sense that they are at least legible to the reader), non-translations (even in Roman

---

[4] Woolf, *Voyage Out*, p. 44.
[5] James Joyce, *Dubliners*, ed. Jeri Johnson (Oxford: Oxford University Press, 2000), p. 28; Virginia Woolf, *Mrs Dalloway*, ed. David Bradshaw (Oxford: Oxford University Press, 2000), pp. 68–9; Virginia Woolf, *The Years*, ed. Hermione Lee (Oxford: Oxford University Press, 1999), p. 408.

type, the words are still 'all Greek' to many readers, semantically speaking), or half-translations? Such cases, and their profusion within certain key modernist texts, suggest that it may be more accurate to think of the difference between translation and non-translation as a spectrum rather than as a dichotomy—a spectrum Joyce's works in particular show him to be intent on exploring.

Stephen Hero

Translation and non-translation play a significant part in all of Joyce's works, both as a means of characterization and as a vector of political and literary positions. Both already feature prominently in what survives of *Stephen Hero*, Joyce's draft for *A Portrait of the Artist as a Young Man*. The highly autobiographical Stephen Daedalus walks the streets of Dublin 'with a deliberate unflagging step piecing together meaningless words and phrases with deliberate unflagging seriousness'.[6] Stephen has, as Joyce did, received an extremely thorough training in Latin and been daily exposed to the rituals and Latin liturgy of the Catholic Church. Latinisms—'patria', 'ex cathedra', 'advocatus diaboli', 'Aula Maxima', 'Alma Mater'— pervade the English he hears around him, blending seamlessly into the fabric of everyday speech (*SH* 77, 103, 116, 171, 193). Stephen's own use of Latin is formal, scholastic, consisting largely of quotations from philosophers in whose authority he trusts and whose language he deploys in the original with scrupulous accuracy: '*Pulcra sunt quae visa placent*', he asserts, quoting Aquinas (*SH* 95). In this, he shows himself to have internalized the prescriptions regarding method and order painstakingly inculcated by his Jesuit education. It is not clear how Stephen himself reconciles his aspirations to be a 'fiery-hearted revolutionary' with a writing style which is 'over affectionate towards the antique and even the obsolete and too easily rhetorical' (*SH* 80 and *SH* 27). We see him adhere rigorously to a traditional, regimented, and hierarchical view of language and of the world it structures. He follows established forms and appears to espouse the values they solder. In this, he is not only obviously related to the Stephen of *A Portrait of the Artist as a Young Man*, who dutifully prefaces his writings with the letters of the Jesuit motto 'A.M.D.G.' ('Ad Majoram Dei Gloriam', or 'To the Greater Glory of God'), only signing off below the letters L.D.S. ('Laus Deo Semper', or 'Praise be to God Forever'), but also reflects Joyce's own student practice, as the printed version of 'Trust Not Appearances', one of his own student essays (written whilst he was a pupil at Belvedere College between 1893 and 1898), clearly testifies.[7]

---

[6] *Stephen Hero*, ed. Theodore Spencer [1944], revd edn, incorporating additional manuscript pages from Yale and Cornell University libraries, ed. John J. Slocum and Herbert Cahoon (New York: New Directions Publishing Corporation, 1963), p. 31. Further references will be given parenthetically in the text as *SH*.

[7] James Joyce, *A Portrait of the Artist as a Young Man* [1916]. The definitive text, corrected from the Dublin holograph by Chester G. Anderson, ed. Richard Ellmann (London: Jonathan Cape, 1968),

As Joyce himself did in 'Trust not Appearances', and as Stephen likewise does in *A Portrait of the Artist as a Young Man*, the protagonist of *Stephen Hero* thinks of language in terms of value, and dogmatically prefers old uses to new ones, convinced that words are devalued by translation from one context to another:

> Stephen laid down his doctrine very positively and insisted on the importance of what he called the literary tradition. 'Words, he said, have a certain value in the literary tradition and a certain value in the market-place – a debased value.'   (*SH* 27)

His sense of the value of words is anchored in his belief in etymology, which offers him a way of finding historical interest in even degraded forms of contemporary parlance:

> He read Skeat's *Etymological Dictionary* by the hour and his mind, which had from the first been only too submissive to the infant sense of wonder, was often hypnotized by the most commonplace conversation.   (*SH* 26)

The scholarly high-seriousness of Stephen's attitude to language is emphasized by his friends' less reverent approach. Cranly, for instance, takes pleasure in the comedy of linguistic hybridity. Where Stephen is bent on linguistic distinctions, Cranly likes to mix things up, bandying about a sort of proto-Wakean jumble of half-translated languages:

> Cranly was speaking (as was his custom when he walked with other gentlemen of leisure) in a language the base of which was Latin and the superstructure of which was composed of Irish, French and German...   (*SH* 106)

Though Stephen takes part in the banter, he does so more reluctantly and laconically than his friend:

> Cranly at last observed Stephen walking at the edge of the path and said:
> – *Ecce orator qui in malo humore est.*
> – *Non sum*, said Stephen.
> – *Credo ut estis*, said Cranly.
> – *Minime.*   (*SH* 106)

p. 72; hereafter referred to parenthetically in the text as *P*. James Joyce, 'Trust Not Appearances', in James Joyce, *Occasional, Critical and Political Writing*, ed. Kevin Barry (Oxford: Oxford University Press, 2000), pp. 3–4 (p. 3). The initials make numerous, characteristically distorted returns in *Finnegans Wake* [1939] (London: Faber and Faber, 1975), hereafter referred to parenthetically in the text as *FW*. For example, framing a radio weather forecast as 'Am. Dg' and 'Ls. De.' (*FW* 324 and *FW* 325), or in intermingled form as '*Ad majorem l.s.d.! Divi gloriam.*' (*FW* 418). Each set of letters in fact receives an entry in Clive Hart's catalogue of recurring Wakean motifs—see *Structure and Motif in 'Finnegans Wake'* (Evanston, IL: Northwestern University Press, 1962), pp. 213, 231.

Stephen's linguistic curiosity is not confined to ancient languages. In the course of the novel, he carries out what his father calls 'wayward researches into strange literature' through 'the medium of hardly procured translations' of Ibsen, 'translations of the Hindu and the Greek or Chinese theatres', and 'translations of Turgenieff's novels and stories' (*SH* 87, 40, 42). Stephen's attitude to this foreign literature is one of ardent admiration: in thrall to Ibsen, he 'suffer[s] the most enduring influence of his life' (*SH* 40). Cranly, by contrast, evinces a derisive self-consciousness about the use of foreign languages: 'He had a defiant manner of using technical and foreign terms as if he wished to suggest that for him they were mere conventions of language' (*SH* 124). To Stephen's acutely sensitive ear, in other words, the effect of this arch delivery is to place such non-translated snippets between aural quotation marks. For all his 'instinctive' affection for Cranly, the habit contributes to Stephen's appraisal of his friend as an 'indiscriminate [...] vessel' (*SH* 124). He, by contrast, wants to come across as a natural polyglot, at ease with his store of authoritative foreign quotations, in effortless command of his precious cultural capital.

A Portrait of the Artist as a Young Man

A Portrait opens with an Ovidian epigraph:

> *Et ignotas animum dimittit in artes.*
> Ovid, *Metamorphoses*, VIII, 188.[8]

Here an instance of paratextual non-translation marks the very threshold of the novel. It is, moreover, an instance of scrupulous quotation (an epigraph, writes Antoine Compagnon, is 'a quotation *par excellence*') ambiguously poised between the author's and the character's point of view.[9] Indeed, given what we again come to know in this book about Stephen's proficiency in Latin and his identification with Daedalus, the 'old artificer' he has chosen to regard as his mythical father, the epigraph could well be his, or at least have been chosen as an act of plausible mimicry of his literary tastes and practices (*P* 257). The hypothesis that the epigraph is provided as a retrospective extension of the book's dominant mode of free indirect discourse is supported by the fact that it evinces the kind of linguistic and literary purism (as an act of meticulous, attributed, non-translated

---

[8] The line singled out in Joyce's epigraph is translated as, 'So then to unimagined arts he set his mind' in A. D. Melville's translation of the *Metamorphoses*, ed. E. J. Kenney (Oxford: Oxford University Press, 1986), p. 177.

[9] Antoine Compagnon, *La Seconde Main: ou Le Travail de la citation* (Paris: Seuil, 1979), p. 337. My translation.

quotation) to which we have seen him to be partial in *Stephen Hero*.[10] If an epigraph is, as Gérard Genette suggests, 'a password of intellectuality', then the inclusion of such a capsular inscription, and *a fortiori* of a line excerpted from Ovid, signals the kind of cultural cachet to which Stephen aspires.[11] And though Hugh Kenner specifically dismisses as a 'persistent and recurrent fallacy' the critical tendency to suppose that 'the *Portrait* and *Ulysses* were written by a Stephen Dedalus', the epigraph itself seems deliberately and ambiguously poised between first- and third-person perspectives.[12]

By cryptically foreshadowing Stephen's surname, the epigraph foregrounds a complex nexus of ideological and political undertones surrounding issues of translation and non-translation. In the section of the *Metamorphoses* to which Joyce refers, we read—if we can read Greek, that is—of the feats of Daedalus, the Latin name given to the Greek Δαίδαλος. The epigraph, at once a non-translation *and* a translation, thus immediately, if subtly, invokes a colonial situation, a cultural appropriation. It enacts the drama of translation as power, as Nietzsche understood it:

> And Roman antiquity itself: how forcibly and at the same time how naively it took hold of everything good and lofty of Greek antiquity, which was more ancient! How they translated things into the Roman present! [...] what was past and alien was an embarrassment for them; and being Romans, they saw it as an incentive for a Roman conquest. Indeed, translation was a form of conquest.[13]

Differing readings of Stephen Dedalus's name as a translation—from the Greek 'Δαίδαλος', or from the Latin 'Daedalus'—bear distinct connotations (pitting art versus military might, or the status of the colonized versus that of the colonizer). 'You have a queer name, Dedalus [...] Your name is like Latin', remarks a fellow pupil of Clongowes in *A Portrait* (P 25). Later on, in Chapter IV, his adolescent friends—having discovered that a Greek language and a Greek culture lie behind the Latin and Roman culture in which they are more thoroughly schooled—tease

[10] Although the epigraph, as an instance of verbatim quotation, is not a straightforward exemplar of idiolect-inflected free indirect discourse, it is from a certain perspective assimilable to Hugh Kenner's 'Uncle Charles Principle', which 'entails writing about someone much as that someone would choose to be written about'. The words are Ovid's, not Stephen's—and clearly cited as such—but the fact of quoting from Ovid can be read as part of the book's dominant mode of narration—that is, as a representation of how Stephen might wish his own biography to be framed, or of how he would envisage embarking on his own autobiography. See Hugh Kenner, *Joyce's Voices* (London: Faber and Faber, 1978), p. 21.

[11] Gérard Genette, *Paratexts: Thresholds of Interpretation* [1987], trans. Jane E. Lewin (Cambridge: Cambridge University Press, 1997), p. 160.

[12] Hugh Kenner, 'The *Portrait* in Perspective', *The Kenyon Review* 10.3 (Summer 1948): 361–81 (p. 370).

[13] Friedrich Nietzsche, 'Translation', in *The Gay Science* [1882], trans. Walter Kaufmann (New York: Vintage, 1974), pp. 136–8; quoted in *The Translation Studies Reader*, 3rd edn, ed. Lawrence Venuti (New York: Routledge, 2012), pp. 67–8.

him with punning Greek declensions of his name: 'Stephanos Dedalos! Bous Stephanoumenos! Bous Stephaneforos!' (*P* 173).

Ulysses: non-translated language

By the time Stephen appears on the first page of *Ulysses*, non-translated snippets of Greek and Latin—including his own name—have acquired more defined political implications. Like the epigraph from Ovid that forms the threshold to *A Portrait*, the Roman, colonial version of Odysseus's name chosen as the title of *Ulysses*—itself a derivation from the Latin 'Ulixes'—evokes the analogous subjugation of Ireland to English rule, a subjection manifest in and partly enforced through language, as Stephen had begun to realize in the final chapter of *A Portrait*. 'The language in which we are speaking', he had reflected in his exchange with the English Dean of Studies, 'is his before it is mine. [...] His language, so familiar and so foreign, will always be for me an acquired speech' (*P* 194). Thus *Ulysses*, like *A Portrait*, begins by invoking and reenacting an act of linguistic and cultural overwriting. This thematic undercurrent is further developed in the book's third sentence, in which Buck Mulligan chants the first words of the Catholic Mass: '*Introibo ad altare Dei*' or 'I will go up to the altar of God' (*U* 1: 5).[14] As Kenner explains, the snippet is a translation as well as a non-translation, being a quotation from St Jerome's Latin version of Hebrew words ascribed to a Psalmist in exile ('Va-a-vo-ah el mizbah elohim').[15]

Ireland's colonized condition is uppermost in Stephen's mind on the morning of 16 June 1904. With bitterness he tells the Englishman Haines that he is 'the servant of two masters', 'the imperial British state [...] and the holy Roman catholic and apostolic church' (*U* 1: 638–44). Stephen's surname, a cause of silent pride and superstitious self-belief in *A Portrait*, is declared preposterous for its antique flavour:

> – The mockery of it! he said gaily. Your absurd name, an ancient Greek! [...]
> – My name is absurd too: Malachi Mulligan, two dactyls. But it has a Hellenic ring, hasn't it?   (*U* 1: 34, 41–2)

Although Mulligan pretends to take the sting out of his derision by deeming his own name absurd as well, Stephen understands the jibe: apart from being

---

[14] James Joyce, *Ulysses* [1922], ed. Hans Walter Gabler with Wolfhard Steppe and Claus Melchior (New York: Random House, 1986). Parenthetical references will be given in the following form: *U* episode number: line number.

[15] Hugh Kenner, *Ulysses*, rev. edn (Baltimore, MD: Johns Hopkins University Press, 1987), pp. 34–5. See also Fritz Senn, *Joyce's Dislocations: Essays on Reading as Translation* (Baltimore and London: Johns Hopkins University Press, 1984), pp. 124–5.

singularly aberrant in turn-of-the-century Dublin, Stephen's Greek-sounding patronym is the more incongruous because he, unlike Mulligan, knows no Greek (*U* 1: 77–81).

Mulligan is based on Oliver Gogarty, an Anglo-Irishman educated at Stonyhurst (a Lancashire public school), Trinity College Dublin, and, for two terms immediately preceding his residency in the Martello Tower, at Oxford University. In the course of the eighteenth and nineteenth centuries Greek overtook Latin to become the language of cultural prestige in England. Gogarty studied it, Mulligan speaks it; Joyce did not study it (and subsequently minded that he had not done so), and Stephen does not speak it.[16] In the light of this biographical context, and in the light of Mulligan's taunt about Stephen's name, almost all of the non-translated snippets in 'Telemachus' become legible as oblique barbs intended to parade Mulligan's knowledge and emphasize Stephen's ignorance.[17] Buck coins Homeric epithets, quotes from Homer and Xenophon in transliterated (but not translated) Greek, and even offers Stephen instruction in the language:

> – God! he said quietly. Isn't the sea what Algy calls it: a great sweet mother? The snotgreen sea. The scrotumtightening sea. *Epi oinopa ponton.* Ah, Dedalus, the Greeks! I must teach you. You must read them in the original. *Thalatta! Thalatta!* She is our great sweet mother. Come and look.   (*U* 1: 77–81)

Furthermore, Mulligan's references to Oxford, Matthew Arnold, and Algernon Swinburne ('Algy' in the quotation above) only emphasize the Englishness of his Hellenism—its association, in this context, with a colonial perspective. And just as these allusions are not innocent, neither are the allusions to Nietzsche ('I'm the *Übermensch*. Toothless Kinch and I, the supermen'; 'He who stealeth from the poor lendeth to the Lord. Thus spake Zarathustra'), the more striking in view of the philosopher's conception (quoted above) of translation as conquest (*U* 1: 708–9, 727–8).

Stephen says comparatively little in this episode, and barely any of his utterances comprise those foreign-language snippets to which, as 'Proteus' will show, he is still partial.[18] He seems to be silenced by Mulligan's cultural capital, and

---

[16] Richard Ellmann, *James Joyce*, rev. edn (Oxford: Oxford University Press, 1982), p. 118; R. J. Schork, *Greek and Hellenic Culture in Joyce* (Gainseville: University Press of Florida, 1998), pp. xiii, 239, 245.

[17] As Kenner has noted, the book's first narratorial voice seems to conspire in Buck's Hellenic role-play: 'Since the Buck is Hellenophile—"Mulligan", as he will soon remark, is a dactyl—the first nine words mimick a Homeric hexameter: 'Stately | plump Buck | Mulligan || came from the | stairhead bearing |'—Kenner, *Ulysses*, p. 34 (in Kenner's book the quoted words bear scansion marks).

[18] Stephen's thoughts in 'Proteus' are awash with foreign linguistic material: '*maestro di color che sanno*' (*U* 3: 6–7), '*Nacheinander*' (13), '*Nebeneinander*' (15), '*lex externa*' (48), '*euthanasia*' (52), '*aria di sortita*' (100), '*Descende, calve, ut ne amplius decalveris*' (113–14), '*C'est le pigeon, Joseph*' (162), '*mou en civet*' (177), *Terribilia meditans* (311), '*Natürlich*' (321), '*frate porcospino*' (385), '*diebus ac noctibus iniurias patiens ingemiscit*' (466), are just a few among many examples.

perhaps also by the realization that his love of Latin—historically and symbolically associated with empire (the Roman Empire) as well as with the Catholic Church—places him in a position of conditioned complicity with his oppressors. As he had already intuited in *A Portrait*, his self-appointed mission 'to forge in the smithy of [his] soul the uncreated conscience of [his] race' requires him to find ways to 'fly by' the 'nets' of 'nationality, language, religion' (*P* 257, 207).

As well as a new language, Stephen had expressed his desire for 'a new personal experience'.[19] What he likely had in mind (as his musings about creation in terms of reproduction and gestation would seem to adumbrate) is a sexual partner. But the person he meets in *Ulysses* is Bloom—Irishman, European, Jew, amateur translator. In explaining the introduction into this novel of the character of Leopold Bloom, Joyce had told his friend Frank Budgen that his presence was required because Stephen 'ha[d] a shape that c[ould]n't be changed'.[20] Yet perhaps Stephen does change a little through his interactions with Bloom, in ways which pertain to language and, specifically, to translation. Stephen is, by inclination, a non-translator; Bloom, in contrast, is by inclination a translator; during their late-night encounter, in friendly compromise, they meet half-way.

Before attending to some of their most telling exchanges, it is worth briefly surveying the linguistic backdrop against which these interactions take place. There is a great deal of non-translation in *Ulysses*. Commentary (especially negative commentary) on this aspect of the text tends to focus on the Stephen-centred episodes: the 'Telemachiad', 'Scylla and Charybdis'—in which we return to the mode of scholarly non-translated quotation showcased in the fifth chapter of *A Portrait*—and the 'Oxen of the Sun' episode—which is full of drunken, boastful, pseudo-intellectual banter. The parading of foreign languages, though potentially alienating to readers of these episodes, is by no means confined to them.

Such instances of non-translation roughly can be parsed into into a few broad categories. First, the book contains many Latin words relating to church services taking place in Dublin at various times on 16 June 1904, starting with Mulligan's Black Mass atop the Martello Tower and including the words Bloom hears in All Hallows Church in 'Lotus-Eaters', those he hears at Paddy Dignam's funeral in 'Hades', and the snippets of liturgical Latin wafted over the seaside breeze from the Star of the Sea Church in 'Nausicaa'.

Second, the book is full of Italian musical terms—whether these be the words of songs (the words of Mozart's *Don Giovanni* and Flotow's *Martha* for example), or words indicating the manner of imagined or actual performances ('*vibrato*', '*piano diminuendo*', '*a tempo, strigendo*', etc.).[21]

---

[19] 'When we come to the phenomena of artistic conception, artistic gestation and artistic reproduction I require a new terminology and a new personal experience.' (*P* 214).

[20] Frank Budgen, *James Joyce and the Making of 'Ulysses'* (London: Grayson and Grayson, 1934), p. 107.

[21] See *U* 4: 314, *U* 4: 327–8, *U* 7: 152, *U* 18: 1507–8; *U* 11: 24, 11: 587, *U* 11: 594–5, *U* 16: 1757; *U* 5: 395; *U* 9: 905; *U* 10: 918. See also *U* 11: 541, *U* 17: 1309.

Third, a number of the book's non-translations reflect political intent. The phenomenon is pronounced in 'Telemachus', as discussed earlier in this chapter, but it is also a feature of the 'Cyclops' episode', in which the Citizen's speech features a number of Gaelic locutions ('*Slan leat*', '*Na bacleis*', '*Rameis*') (*U* 12: 819, 12: 884, 12: 1239). His sidekick Lenehan prefers to interject in French, reflecting outdated political sympathies harking back to a time when Ireland had hoped for liberation from the English by the French: '*Conspuez les anglais! Perfide Albion!*' (*U* 12: 1208–9).[22]

Aside from these categories, the vast majority of the non-translated language in *Ulysses* consists of clichés which bespeak the linguistic aspirations (or, less generously, pretensions) of middle-class Dublin. In 'Aeolus', non-translated snippets of Latin, Greek ('the language of the mind', as MacHugh calls it (*U* 7: 564)), and French swell a tide of journalistic stereotypes, literary flourishes, allusive commonplaces, and conversational *bons mots*: '*Pardon, monsieur*', '*Imperium romanum*', '*Cloacae*', '*Entrez mes enfants!*', '*Domine!*', '*Kyrios!* [...] *Kyrie!* [...] *Kyrie Eleison!*', 'OMNIUM GATHERUM', 'ITALIA, MAGISTRA ARTIUM', '*lex talionis*', '*Fuit Ilium!*'[23] In an episode named after the god of wind, nothing emerges so clearly as the assembled journalists' collective determination to give themselves airs. Indeed, while the purpose subtending the episode's headlines and dialogue is, transparently, to project an aura of intellectuality, the sheer excess of the pervasive group mannerism backfires, conveying a pretentious affectation diametrically opposed to the impression of spontaneous sophistication the characters would wish to convey.

Such linguistic habits are by no means confined to the newsroom. Dublin at large is awash with this kind of cliché. Simon Dedalus, briefly present in the *Freeman's Journal* offices before slipping out for a drink with Ned Lambert, betrays the same Aeolian propensity—seemingly typical of the city's shabby-genteel but educated male middle-class—in describing Buck Mulligan, in Virgilian terms, as his son's '*fidus Achates*' (*U* 6: 49). The phrase is reprised in 'Eumaeus', when Bloom, having supplanted Mulligan at Stephen's side, thinks of himself as 'his *fidus Achates*' (*U* 16: 54–5).[24]

Bloom's partiality for foreign phrases, however, is apparent long before 'Eumaeus'. Earlier episodes show him to be eminently prone to use such clichés to frame picture-postcard views of the world around him. In 'Lotus-Eaters', for example, he looks into the window of the Belfast and Oriental Tea Company and daydreams

---

[22] Even the citizen has abandoned such illusions: 'The French! says the citizen. Set of dancing masters? Do you know what it is? They were never worth a roasted fart to Ireland.' (*U* 12: 1385–6). For more on the history of Franco-Irish relations alluded to in this episode, see Scarlett Baron, '*Strandentwining Cable': Joyce, Flaubert, and Intertextuality* (Oxford: Oxford University Press, 2011), pp. 177–91.

[23] *U* 7: 417, 478, 489, 507, 557, 562–4, 604, 754, 756, 910, 1056.

[24] The assumption here is that the phrase, like the rest of the episode, is an instance of the 'Uncle Charles Principle' (see note 10 of this chapter).

of Ceylon, 'The far east [...] Those Cinghalese lobbing about in the sun in *dolce far niente*'. '*Esprit de corps*', he thinks a little later (in a perhaps unintended pun), remembering how girls help each other protect their bodies from desiring gazes such as his own (*U* 5: 29–32, 135).

Men have a markedly greater propensity for this kind of linguistic bombast, presumably on account of their access to an education which would have been denied many women (Dilly Dedalus, whom Stephen surprises surreptitiously purchasing a French primer, is a case in point).[25] In 'Nausicaa', Gerty MacDowell, though *sans* Latin, has picked up a few specimens from the unwritten dictionary of tasteful foreign phrases. Glamorizing herself, she muses about her own 'innate refinement' and 'languid queenly *hauteur*'; wonders whether Bloom has 'an aquiline nose or a slightly *retroussé*'; and reflects on 'the slight *contretemps*' (the term appears again in the Bloom-inflected narration of 'Eumaeus') occasioned by baby Boardman (*U* 13: 97, 13: 420, 13: 6124, 16: 1880). In the context of the episode's flirtation, Bloom likewise reaches for his French, fantasizing about snapshots of '[l]ingerie' and '*deshabille*' seen at the mutoscope in Capel Street (*U* 13: 796). The connection between Gerty and Bloom is emphasized by their resort, at different points in the same episode, to the very same French word, epitomizing the odd combination of distance and near-immobility which characterizes their sexual encounter: '*Tableau!*' (*U* 13: 486, 815).

In 'Eumaeus', the association between scraps of foreign language and cliché (a reflection of the general tendency of non-translated snippets to congeal into set forms) reaches its high–water mark. Exhausted by his adventures in Nighttown but keen to impress a young companion 'blessed with brains', Bloom's mind (conveyed through free indirect discourse) succeeds only in producing an unwittingly comical unfurling of the English language's tritest foreign imports, a veritable hit parade of turn-of the-century Dublin's linguistic orts and scraps (many of them repeating appearances in earlier episodes):

> *à propos, fidus Achates, En route, re, finis, demimonde, confrères, quondam, qui vive, haud ignarus malorum miseris, succurrere disco, etcetera, rara avis, sangfroid, hoi polloi, apropos, protégé, quandary over voglio, Bella Poetria!, Belladonna Voglio, tête-à-tête, post-mortem child, bona fides, apropos, tapis, venue, coup d'oeil, stiletto, dénouement, where ignorance is bliss, entre nous, alias, soi-disant, minutiae, paterfamilias, instanter, corruptio per se, corruptio per accidens, in toto,*

[25] Dilly has 'Chardenal's French primer' in hand when Stephen meets her in 'Wandering Rocks'—*U* 10: 867–8. The 'Penelope' episode features a smattering of Spanish words, but these come under no suspicion as marks of affectation because they mainly relate to Molly's memories of a childhood spent in Gibraltar: 'carabineros', 'coronado' (a mistaken substitution for 'cornudo', which Molly likely intends), 'criada', 'mi fa pieta Masetto [...] presto non son piu forte', 'posadas' (*U* 18: 756, 1394, 1483, 1507–8, 1595).

confidante sotto voce, sine qua non, alias, de rigueur, au fait, crescendo, finale, liaison, ex quibus, Christus, secundum carnem, pro rata, Ubi patria, Alma Mater, vita bene, soi-disant, entourage, prima donna, embonpoint, distinguée, nisi, aplomb, liaisons, quasi, passim, séance, élite, dolce far niente, in medias res, extempore, conversazioni, genus omne, contretemps.

It is this torrent of non-translation, this outpouring of involuntary malapropisms, that led Pound to praise 'Eumaeus' for 'discharging all the clichés of the English language like an uninterrupted river'.[26] However, Wyndham Lewis—seemingly missing the joke—deplored Bloom and Stephen as 'walking clichés' on whom 'a mass of dead stuff is hung'.[27] But for all its gaucheness, 'Eumaeus' is not an indictment. It is, instead, as Kenner has argued, an endearing tribute to Bloom, who, having been 'snubbed, thwarted, cuckolded, ignored, jeered at, slandered, put upon', finally feels 'like the hero of a novel, which for Joyce in fiction after fiction is the apotheosis to which fictional beings aspire'.[28] It is also, perhaps primarily, a humorous *tour de force*, in which virtually all of the episode's rambunctious energy derives from the spectacle of style so deftly and comprehensively hoist on its own petard.

Ulysses: translation and non-translation

In spite of his role in *Ulysses* as an unintentional vector of cliché, Bloom is at times shown to be attentive to words, alert to their status as snippets of translation or non-translation. One of the first things we see Bloom do, in 'Calypso', is translate:

– Here, she said. What does that mean? [...]

– Metempsychosis, he said, frowning. It's Greek: from the Greek. That means the transmigration of souls.

– O, rocks! she said. Tell us in plain words.   (*U* 4: 337–43)

Bloom has some knowledge of Greek, the educated man's inculcated habit of looking to etymology for meaning, and the ability to articulate a decent definition at a moment's notice. Molly, however wants more: what her husband produces is,

---

[26] Ezra Pound, 'James Joyce et Pécuchet' [1922], in *Pound/Joyce: The Letters of Ezra Pound to James Joyce: with Pound's Essays on James Joyce*, ed. Forrest Read (London: Faber and Faber, 1968), pp. 200–11 (p. 206). My translation.

[27] Wyndham Lewis, *Time and Western Man* [1927], ed. Paul Edwards (Santa Rosa: Black Sparrow Press, 1993), pp. 94, 100.

[28] Kenner, *Joyce's Voices*, p. 95.

in her view, but a half-translation.[29] Bloom elaborates, translating his own some-what erudite formulation ('transmigration') into 'plain words':

> – Some people believe, he said, that we go on living in another body after death, that we lived before. They call it reincarnation. [...]
>
> – Metempsychosis, he said, is what the ancient Greeks called it. They used to believe you could be changed into an animal or a tree, for instance. What they called nymphs, for example.   (*U* 4: 362–3, 375–7)

As Bloom's concatenated explication to Molly shows, knowledge of even one's native language is developed through constant acts of translation (explanatory paraphrase being but the conversion of words into more comprehensible lexical forms). In other words, language acquisition, as this passage reminds us, is itself a process of translation.

In the next episode, 'Lotus-Eaters', Bloom engages in mental translation for his own sake. Having wandered into All Hallows Church, he reflects on the language of the officiating priest. As often, his associative thinking produces ripples of linguistic comedy:

> Latin. The next one. Shut your eyes and open your mouth. What? *Corpus*: body. Corpse. Good idea the Latin. Stupefies them first. [...] Rum idea: eating bits of a corpse. Why the cannibals cotton to it.   (*U* 5: 350)

The passage offers an illustration of the evocative power of non-translated words and phrases—of the way in which locutions imported from other languages, having once 'set' into idiomatic form, become emptied of their semantic meaning, and thus the better suited to fostering a state of passive receptiveness in the listener. Bloom's inquisitive mind makes him immune to such 'stupefaction', free to ponder the effectiveness of Latin as a conduit for 'rum ideas', a means of cloaking in grandeur arguably outlandish religious ideas and practices (in this case, those of communion and transubstantiation, which Bloom metaphorically aligns with cannibalism).

Bloom brings the same confused half-memories to bear on the priest's cassock:

> Letters on his back: I.N.R.I.? No: I.H.S. Molly told me one time I asked her. I have sinned: or no: I have suffered, it is. And the other one? Iron nails ran in
>
> (*U* 5: 372).

---

[29] If Molly is dissatisfied with Bloom's first attempt, he later reflects on his wife's faulty translations of foreign linguistic material. Looking back on the events of his day in 'Ithaca', he muses that 'Unusual polysyllables of foreign origins she interpreted phonetically or by false analogy or by both: metempsychosis (met him pike hoses), alias (a mendacious person mentioned in sacred scripture)' (*U* 17: 685–7).

Beyond showing that translation, in the Blooms' household, goes both ways, and beyond providing some highlycomic moments, Bloom's wild guesses regarding the meaning of the Latin initials ('I.R.N.I.' stands for 'Iesus Nazarenus Rex Iudaeorum', 'I.H.S.' for either 'Jesus Hominum Salvator' or 'In Hoc Signo—Vinces', depending on the authority consulted) illustrate the distorting role of memory in dealing with language that is not immediately understood.[30] Bloom's various approximate or erroneous translations bring into relief snippets of foreign language which have become invisible as non-translated matter, and whose meaning has become effaced through the erosive effect of frequent and largely automatic usage.

In 'Lestrygonians', Bloom tries his hand at some silent musical translation as he walks away from Davy Byrne's. The words his mind focuses on—drawn from Act V, scene 5 of *Don Giovanni*, in which the libertine meets his comeuppance—reflect his preoccupation with Molly's approaching tryst with Blazes Boylan:

> *Don Giovanni, a cenar teco*
> *M'invitasti.*
> [...]
> *– A cenar teco.*

What does that *teco* mean? Tonight perhaps.

> *– Don Giovanni, thou hast me invited*
> *To come to supper tonight,*
> *The rum the rumdum*

(*U* 8: 1040–55).

His attempt, though not resoundingly successful ('teco' means 'you', not 'tonight', and his improvised verse, as he observes, '[d]oesn't go properly'), and seemingly flavoured by the 'rum ideas' he considered in 'Lotus-Eaters' ('The rum the rum-dum'), forms part of his characterization as an inquiring mind, cultured if not erudite, polyglot in aspiration if not in fact (*U* 8: 1056).

If Bloom is often to be seen spontaneously engaging in small acts of translation, there are several moments in *Ulysses*—most notably in 'Circe'—when phrases that have occurred earlier in the book are redeployed in translation, both linguistic and conceptual. When Bloom gives birth to octuplets, for example, the children are named by a process of translation involving the re-use of the two-part structure of 'Chrysostomos', the first word of Stephen's interior monologue in 'Telemachus', and one seemingly suggested by the sight of Mulligan's 'white teeth

---

[30] Don Gifford with Robert J. Seidman, *'Ulysses' Annotated: Notes for James Joyce's 'Ulysses'*, revd and expanded edn (Berkeley; London: University of California Press, 1989), p. 94. The three Latin phrases given here translate into 'Jesus of Nazareth, King of the Jews', 'Jesus the Savior of Man', and 'In this Sign—Thou Shalt Conquer'.

glistening here and there with gold points' (*U* 1: 25–6).[31] While 'chryso' is the Latin transliteration of the Greek for 'gold', denoting both the precious metal and its colour, 'stomos' is derived from from the Greek for 'mouth'. Fourteen episodes later, in what is a prime instance of the 'hallucination' technic used in 'Circe', each of Bloom's children has 'his name printed in legible letters on his shirtfront', and each is based on an analogous combination of a word for a precious metal with a word denoting a body part, gesture, or character trait (nose, finger, hand, smile, self, vivacity, wholeness).[32] The enumeration unfolds in Italian, French, German, and Greek, as well as English: 'Nasodoro, Goldfinger, Chrysostomos, Maindorée, Silversmile, Silberselber, Vifargent, Panargyros' (*U* 15: 1823–8).

When Stephen and Bloom spend some time *tête-à-tête* in 'Eumaeus' and 'Ithaca', translation is repeatedly foregrounded. Stephen sings 'an old German song of Johannes Jeep about the clear sea and the voices of sirens [...] which boggled Bloom a bit', immediately improvising their rendition in English:

> *Von der Sirenen Listigkeit*
> *Tun die Poeten dichten.*

These opening bars he sang and translated *extempore*. Bloom, nodding, said he perfectly understood and begged him to go on by all means which he did.

(U 16: 1812–19)

Does Bloom *really* 'understand perfectly', or has something got lost in translation, as Joyce's use here of the perhaps overly definite adverb comically conspires to suggest? Given what we know of Bloom's affability and his particular keenness to make a good impression on Stephen, it seems quite plausible that his polite over-eagerness might reflect a desire to compensate for his continuing bafflement.

If he does 'understand perfectly', what exactly is it that Bloom understands? It seems reasonable to assume that he hears and grasps the meaning of Stephen's concocted translation (the text of which is withheld from the reader)—in which case, does he also deduce the song's connection to the *Odyssey*?[33] The German words Stephen intones in his 'phenomenally beautiful tenor voice' are based on a Renaissance Latin translation of the *Odyssey* entitled 'Dulcia dum loquitur cogitat insidias' (*U* 16: 1820).[34] What Bloom understands, then, is subject to the

---

[31] For a discussion of 'Chrysostomos' and its relation to issues of (linguistic, cultural, narrative, intertextual) translation in *Ulysses*, see Senn, *Joyce's Dislocutions*, pp. 138–43.

[32] The 'technic' of 'Circe' is named as 'hallucination' in the schema Joyce produced in 1921 to help Stuart Gilbert make sense of *Ulysses*. The slightly different schema Joyce produced for Carlo Linati in 1920 lists the episode's 'technic' as 'vision animated to bursting point'. Both are reproduced in Jeri Johnson's edition of the 1922 *Ulysses* (Oxford: Oxford University Press, 1993), on pages pp. 734–5 and 736–9 respectively.

[33] In Gifford and Seidman's translation, the lines read: 'From the Sirens' craftiness | Poets make poems'. See '*Ulysses' Annotated*, p. 562.

[34] Jeep's song adopts the Latin title as its own. See Gifford with Seidman, '*Ulysses' Annotated*, p. 562.

vicissitudes of more than one translation. Stephen's mistaken delivery of 'the end of the ballad' is itself an instance of the distortions texts undergo as they are brought to life by different people, in different places, and at different times. Jeep's line 'Welches das Schiff in Ungluck bringt' ('Which brings the ship into misfortune') is accidentally altered by Stephen to '*Und alle Schiffe brücken*' ('And all ships are bridged'), a meaningless line which even Bloom, for all his alacrity to please and encourage, might struggle to translate into sense (*U* 16: 1883–4).[35]

Perhaps more important than Jeep's song's history of lost and altered meanings, in terms of the overarching human trajectory of *Ulysses*, is the warmth that Stephen's translation and its reception connote—the promise which the attempt to communicate represents. In 'Ithaca', Stephen and Bloom's possible friendship is said to face the 'four separating forces' of 'Name, age, race, creed' (*U* 17: 402–3). In the course of the discussion that follows this listing, each recites and translates for the other—ancient Irish in Stephen's case, ancient Hebrew in Bloom's:

> By Stephen: suil, suil, suil arun, suil go siocair agus suil go cuin (walk, walk, walk your way, walk in safety, walk with care).
>
> By Bloom: kifeloch, harimon rakatejch m'baad l'zamatejch (thy temple amid thy hair is as a slice of pomegranate).   (*U* 17: 727–30)

Here we, like Molly in 'Calypso', are given a literal translation, but the 'plain words' provided in parentheses do not come close to furnishing enlightenment as regards the meaning of the fragments each man recites. Most readers would probably require further explication in order to make sense of the words. As in the example of Jeep's song, the exchange, by withholding information, highlights the limitations of literal translation, showing how insufficient are word-to-word approximations to the restitution of meaning.

Not content merely to compare the sound of the ancient languages associated with their respective races, the two protagonists proceed to a 'glyphic comparison of the phonic symbols of both languages':

> Stephen wrote the Irish characters for gee, eh, dee, em, simple and modified, and Bloom in turn wrote the Hebrew characters ghimel, aleph, daleth and (in the absence of mem) a substituted qoph, explaining their arithmetical values as ordinal and cardinal numbers, videlicet 3, 1, 4, and 100.   (*U* 17:736–40)

As they trace loops and scriptural arabesques on the sheet before them, the reader is, once again, and quite literally this time, left out of the loop. We see Roman-literal translations of the Irish and Hebrew characters in question but remain

---

[35] Gifford with Seidman, '*Ulysses' Annotated*, p. 562.

none the wiser as to how they look on the page or sound when spoken. Our experience of these signs, in other words, is the obverse of Stephen and Bloom's auditory and visual apprehensions.

Critical commentary regarding this description of Stephen and Bloom's scribblings evinces a degree of perplexity about Joyce's choice of 'glyphic' characters. Tim Conley rightly observes that 'One of the fascinating elements in this scene is the "absence of mem."' He suggests one possible explanation:

> Bloom, who has already shown himself on various occasions to be lax in observing his Judaism, may be making a mistake in his Hebrew alphabet. Bad handwriting might produce ק (usually transcribed in English as qoph) for מ (mem).[36]

Schork, in contrast, hypothesizes that the letters, instead of appearing as the result of a failure of memory, are in fact produced by Bloom in accordance with a mnemotechnic aid for the recall of the first numbers of pi (π), 3.14:

> The parenthetical phrase 'in the absence of mem' serves a twofold function. First, it calls explicit attention to the fact that the final Hebrew letter ('goph') in Bloom's transcription is not a *phonetic* parallel to Stephen's Gaelic character 'em', which might seem to call for a symmetrical response of 'mem' (the 13th letter of the Hebrew alphabet = M). Second, it is a clue to the *source* of Bloom's inscription: the recollection of a childhood prop for his notoriously shaky *memory*.[37]

The equivalence works, claims Schork, because 'qoph', which stands for 100, is to be understood not as representing 'the cardinal number' but rather as 'a reminder that the previous digits are to be marked with a decimal point', as in '3.14'.[38] On this interpretation, the fact that Stephen's characters do not 'translate' into Bloom's is counterbalanced by the introduction of a new kind of translation, of letters into numbers—one to be added to the catalogue of types of translation *Ulysses* explores. Whether many readers are in position to 'perfectly understand' so abstruse a demonstration, however, is open to question.

Bloom and Stephen next go on to search for 'points of contact [...] between these languages and between the peoples who spoke them', including 'diacritic aspirations', 'servile letters' (the adjectives punningly translating into political as well as graphic meanings), 'antiquity', common descent from Noah, literary,

---

[36] Tim Conley, *Joyces Mistakes: Problems of Intention, Irony, and Interpretation* (Toronto and London: University of Toronto Press, 2003), p. 73.

[37] R. J. Schork, 'A Graphic Exercise of Mnemotechnic', *James Joyce Quarterly* 16.3 (Spring 1979): 351–4, (p. 353). See also R. J. Schork, *Latin and Roman Culture in Joyce* (Gainesville: University Press of Florida, 1997), pp. 22, 24, 255n12. The 'goph' featured in Schork's quotation (published in 1979) is accurate to the text of the 1922 *Ulysses*—the Gabler edition (1984) amended 'goph' to 'qoph'.

[38] Schork, 'A Graphic Exercise', p. 352.

historical, and religious convergences, 'dispersal, persecution, survival and revival', hopes of 'restoration' and 'political autonomy' (*U* 17: 745–60). Bloom seemingly celebrates these parallels and intersections by chanting a Hebrew anthem—

> *Kolod balejwaw pnimah*
> *Nefesch, jehudi, homijah.*

—but has to stop after the first two lines '[i]n consequence of defective mnemotechnic'. Instead, Bloom gives Stephen 'a periphrastic version of the general text' (*U* 17: 763–4, 766, 768). We, however, are not party to this—nor are we told whether Stephen 'perfectly understood'.

Finally, the two make a 'common study' and formulate 'mutual reflections' on the subject of the Egyptian, Greek, Roman, Semitic, Celtic alphabets, stenography, and the telegraphic code, and Stephen, an aspiring reader of signatures ('Signatures of all things I am here to read)' whose foreign-sounding surname has been variously pondered, declined, and derided, 'appends his signature in Irish and Roman characters' (*U* 3: 2, *U* 17: 769–75).

What, if anything, can be concluded from the myriad instances of translation and non-translation showcased in *Ulysses*, and from Joyce's placement, at its centre, of Leopold Bloom, a translator by inclination if not in terms of linguistic proficiency? To hazard conclusions on the basis of a partial survey of so vast a range of instances is to risk the kind of egregious simplifications which the very profusion of Joyce's writing seems designed to invalidate. With that caveat acknowledged, one might, for the sake of a synoptic overview, propose two types of inference: pragmatic on the one hand, theoretical on the other. If, as Fritz Senn points out, *Ulysses* shows that we are often at risk of being 'locked into our own little cognitive systems' and that 'in certain constellations' we are all 'aliens and fumbling outsiders', translation and the goodwill it can foster among individuals and nations are all the more important.[39] Stephen and Bloom do seem to be getting somewhere in their relationship when they translate for each other, compare the scripts and sounds of ancient languages, and unearth connections between their linguistic and ethnic identities. On a more abstract, theoretical level, the remarkable linguistic diversity of *Ulysses* illustrates the multiplicity and inextricability of semiotic systems. As Joyce notes in 'Ireland: Island of Saints and Sages', 'What race or language can nowadays claim to be pure?'[40] Even ostensibly non-translated language, like Mulligan's opening chant in 'Telemachus', or Stephen's singing of Jeep, has typically been through countless translations before assuming the form in which we encounter it. Considered closely, the plethora of non-translated

---

[39] Senn, *Joyce's Dislocutions*, pp. 59, 53.
[40] James Joyce, 'Ireland: Island of Saints and Sages' [1907], in *Occasional, Critical, and Political Writing*, p. 118.

phrases in *Ulysses* points to the fact that all non-translation is itself translation, and that no translation is really a full translation. In this intimation, it looks forward to the wildly polyglot, ceaselessly 'transluding' (*FW* 419) world of *Finnegans Wake*—a text in which virtually all words seem to bespeak their status as elements in a translation in progress.

11

'There being more languages to start with than were absolutely necessary': James Joyce's *Ulysses* and English as a World Language

John Nash

Who is the first character to speak in the city of Dublin on the morning of Thursday, 16 June 1904, in *Ulysses*? It is Bloom's un-named cat, a real scene-stealer.[1]

To say that she speaks is, on the whole, reasonable, for one of the purposes served by the cat's appearance in the book at all, let alone with such prominence (even if she never reappears), is to emphasize to readers that they have entered a realm of many tongues, some familiar and some foreign, not all of which they will comprehend. A brief consideration of the scene with the cat illustrates something of the complexity of the matter of translation as it appears in Joyce's work (I will come back to this scene at the end of this chapter). One part of that complexity is the matter of non-translation: those snatches of untranslated languages whose occurrence is a marked feature of Joyce's writing. There are, for sure, questions of cultural domination and appropriation involved in practices of non-translation and there is moreover in Joyce a conceptual or theoretical drive to explore the premises on which the matter rests: what is a language? whose is it? what qualifies as a translation?

The cat makes four sounds, represented as 'Mkgnao!', 'Mrkgnao!', 'Mrkrgnao!' and, once she has her saucer, 'Gurrhr!' interspersed with dialogue spoken by Bloom to form a conversation.[2] There is something wonderful in this representation of the cat 'mewing plaintively and long' (*U* 4:33–4). The first three sounds form a group, preceding the satisfaction of the 'warmbubbled milk' (*U* 4:37), each in turn elongating the previous utterance, represented each time by the addition of the

---

[1] Mulligan's mockery of the mass is the first dialogue in the book, and may or may not temporally precede the cat's, which is also around 8am, but Mulligan is at the Martello Tower in Sandycove, not then part of Dublin city.

[2] James Joyce, *Ulysses* [1922], ed. Hans Walter Gabler with Wolfhard Steppe and Claus Melchior (New York: Random House, 1986), see episode 4, lines 16, 25. Subsequent parenthetical references given as *U* followed by episode number and line number.

John Nash, 'There being more languages to start with than were absolutely necessary': James Joyce's Ulysses *and English as a World Language* In: *Modernism and Non-Translation.* Edited by: Jason Harding and John Nash, Oxford University Press (2019). © the several contributors.
DOI: 10.1093/oso/9780198821441.003.0011

letter 'r'. There is an impressive realism to these combinations of consonants. But the figurative is never far from the literal. Rather like the pussens herself, these words spring off the page to attract our attention with complete certainty of their deserving nature: how else, indeed, should a cat's sound be written? how could it be done better? Despite this apparent striving for every nuance of accuracy, the sounds' very rendition carries a self-consciousness that is disarming. Without diminishing its realism, the prose draws attention to its own invention: is there nothing this narrator cannot do, no voice, no language beyond its reach? The cat's sounds carry an intriguing mix of the authentic and the artificial.

Bloom's conversation with the cat includes of necessity a form of non-translation, a proleptic anticipation of those borrowed fragments of languages that will slip into the text. This dialogue represents a small illustration of two languages—if we can accept for the moment the sounds of the cat as snatches of a language—rubbing against one another in mutual regard, suspicion, and respect. It captures well the sense of comprehension combined with incomprehension which non-translation suggests: at once an accommodating pliancy and a resolute estrangement. In context, the cat's sounds appear to have an obvious meaning; at the same time, has any other cat in literature ever spoken this language?

Non-translation represents an important aspect of *Ulysses* that can easily be overlooked in the celebration of its comedy, its styles, its historical detail and significance. *A Portrait* had registered the 'fret' that Stephen felt when confronted by standard English pronunciation and *Finnegans Wake* would go on to perform its 'most unenglish' unique dissection of the language.[3] In *Ulysses*, the coexistence of languages—that fragmented accommodation of other tongues—can seem less politically charged, more overrun by the overwhelming questions of genre and literary styles. It would be more accurate to say that this topic provides one of the conceptual frameworks of *Ulysses* as a whole: right from its start (or starts)—a parody of the Catholic mass intoned in Latin, and the cat's morning 'mrkrgnao'—*Ulysses* questions the definition of language, of a language, of English language.

English as World Language

In this chapter I want to consider how the practice of non-translation has implications for the development and critical practice of 'world literature'. In particular, non-translation offers a route to re-read two related and important literary-historical models that have been influential in conceptualizing world literature:

---

[3] James Joyce, *A Portrait of the Artist as a Young Man* [1916]. The definitive text, corrected from the Dublin holograph by Chester G. Anderson, ed. Richard Ellmann (London: Jonathan Cape, 1968), p. 194. *Finnegans Wake* [1939] (London: Faber and Faber, 1975), 160:22. Henceforth cited parenthetically as *P* and *FW*.

the idea of a 'minor literature', as elaborated initially by Gilles Deleuze and Félix Guattari in their discussion of Kafka, and taken up for instance by David Lloyd in relation to James Clarence Mangan; and that of a 'dominant language' within a 'world history of literature', as discussed by Pascale Casanova. It is important to do so because, remarkably enough, despite the obvious relevance of non-translation, neither model addresses the phenomenon of plurilingual, macaronic writing. The matter of non-translation offers an illuminating index through which to consider, and revise, these influential literary-historical models. I will also take a brief side-step into the contemporary context of language reform by looking at the Society for Pure English.

Joyce is a fitting example through which to explore some of the implications of non-translation for 'minor literature' and Casanova's notion of a world literary marketplace. In the first place, both these models cite Joyce, albeit briefly, as an exemplary figure. And second, Joyce's work has often been celebrated by special-ists for its invocation of languages. The foremost critic in this respect, Fritz Senn (himself a formidable polyglot), treats the process of reading Joyce as one of con-tinual translation within and between languages, calling into question the notion of 'transluding from the Otherman' (*FW* 419:24–5).[4] As Steven G. Yao observes, 'the conceptual foundation' of Senn's 'highly elastic' model of translation has 'its roots in the Modernist effort to rethink both the grounds and the methods of translation as a literary mode'.[5] Of course, this was a model to which Joyce himself contributed: there is, as so often, a certain circularity in reading Joyce.

In *La république mondiale des lettres/ The World Republic of Letters*, Casanova begins a transnational criticism of the practices whereby literary value is accredited; her approach is necessarily 'distant' notwithstanding occasional 'closer' readings. She argues that cultural prestige is afforded by one's choice of language: 'certain languages...are reputed to be more literary than others'.[6] To write in French in the eighteenth century was to write in the language of literature. At any time, to write in, or from, a language or culture that is removed from the height of the hierarchy is to risk oblivion, even though for many it is a necessity. In Casanova's scenario, the translator—like the critic, the editor and the publisher—plays a crucial role as an advocate and creator of value in the literary marketplace, which makes it odd that Casanova devotes little space to the topic of translation, its history and models.

In a subsequent essay, Casanova starts to address that omission. A 'dominant' language signifies literary and cultural power. The sheer number of language

---

[4] See Fritz Senn, *Joyce's Dislocutions*, ed. John Paul Riquelme (Baltimore: Johns Hopkins University Press, 1984), pp. 1–38.

[5] Steven G. Yao, *Translation and the Languages of Modernism* (New York: Palgrave Macmillan, 2002), p. 194.

[6] Pascale Casanova, *The World Republic of Letters*, trans. M. B. DeBevoise (Cambridge, Mass.: Harvard University Press, 2004) p. 17.

users is not in itself hugely significant; it is the number of polyglots that matters: 'a collective bilingualism or plurilingualism…is an unmistakable sign of domination'. That is, a society in which more than one language flourishes is a dominated one. She adds that 'in symmetrical fashion, monolingualism belongs to speakers using a dominant language'. To use the dominant language is to uphold its prestige (a sort of ideology, or illusion, Casanova says), to gain the benefits it bestows as a '"travel permit"'. English is 'the indisputable dominant language' of today; although Casanova sees the shift to English occurring generally only in the late twentieth century (it happens at different times in different societies).[7] In England in aftermath of the First World War, proponents of 'standard English' regarded the language as 'now incontestably the language of the world' and 'on the way to becoming the universal language' given the extent of the English-speaking empire.[8] Indeed, the Northern Peace Union launched an inquiry into favoured languages for international communication, asking countries where none of English, French or German were spoken, which was the most suitable language for universal use. Of 54 replies, 29 favoured English. The next highest were eight nominations for French and five for Esperanto or Ido.[9]

It would not be easy to designate so precisely when this shift to recognizing English as the dominant language occurred in Ireland but certainly the case of Ireland is an interesting example to consider in the light of Casanova's model. Ireland is cited by Casanova as a 'paradigm' for the relationship between dominant and subordinate literary languages and cultures. Focusing exclusively on the period of the literary and Gaelic revivals, Casanova describes the 'choices' that Joyce, Yeats, Hyde, and others made, since, between them, they account for 'the full range of political and linguistic solutions' devised by writers faced with 'the problem of overturning the dominant order'.[10] Yet for all the variety within 'the Irish case', it surely is significantly different to all others in that Ireland had since 1801

---

[7] Pascale Casanova, 'What Is a Dominant Language? Giacomo Leopardi: Theoretician of Linguistic Inequality', trans. Marlon Jones, *New Literary History* 44.3 (2013): 379–99 (pp. 380–1). According to Casanova, the shift from French to English occurred in France in the 1970s and in Spain in the 1980s. On the notion of contact languages shared by interlocutors, see Phyllis Ghim-Lian Chew, *Emergent Lingua Francas and World Orders* (London: Routledge, 2009). On the historical rise of English as an international language see Dick Leith, *A Social History of English* (London: Routledge, 1997), pp. 180–214. On the spread of English as an ideological tool of western national powers, see Robert Phillipson, *Linguistic Imperialism* (Oxford: Oxford University Press, 1992).

[8] George Sampson, *English for the English: A Chapter on National Education* [1921], (Cambridge: Cambridge University Press, 1970), p. 67. Henry Newbolt, 'The Future of the English Language', *Essays by Divers Hands, being the Transactions of the Royal Society of Literature of the United Kingdom*, ed. Frederick S. Boas (London: Humphrey Milford, 1923), pp. 1–16 (p. 14).

[9] [Henry Newbolt], *The Teaching of English in England* (London: His Majesty's Stationery Office, 1924), pp. 67–8.

[10] Casanova, *World Republic of Letters*, p. 304. Casanova is perhaps guilty here of a universalism for which she criticizes Deleuze and Guattari, reading the case study as emblematic of all others: 'The distinctive quality of the Irish case resides in the fact that over a fairly short period a literary space emerged and a literary heritage was created in an exemplary way.…[I]ts overall structure…can be seen to be almost universal' (pp. 304–5).

been a place both within the United Kingdom (at least in part), and so was previously within the political state that ruled the Empire, and at the same time was very obviously marginal and second-class for all that. In addition, Ireland has been and continues to be a place of several coexisting languages, most notably English and Irish, as well as Ulster Scots and the idiom of Hiberno-English.

Joyce, who had good French and Italian, and better Latin than Irish, was intimately a part of the English language and its 'prestige', while also being politically estranged from it. As Stephen Dedalus remarks of his conversation with the dean of studies, the English of his teacher is 'his before it is mine'. There is here a complex sense of disavowal and ownership of the language which Stephen cannot help possessing, making it both 'so familiar and so foreign'. Of course, Joyce's principal point in this episode, exemplified by Stephen's recognition that 'tundish' (*P* 193) is indeed an English word, is to illustrate Stephen's greater mastery of English than those who would teach him, as well as his instinctive recoil from the sound of his own language in the 'standard' accent of authority. Standard English casts a 'shadow' that makes Stephen 'fret' (*P* 194); but the dean too has been nonplussed by the exchange. In their shared confusion, both pupil and dean of studies are alienated by the translations essential even within their own mother tongue. Being 'so familiar and so foreign', any language exists not just in relation to others but is already a combination of languages and dialects that have contributed towards its codified form. It is precisely this simultaneity of 'familiar' and 'foreign' that underpins this chapter, and indeed structures the idea of 'non-translation'.

That Stephen refers to *acquiring* English—the dean's English is, for Stephen, an 'acquired speech' (*P* 194)—has typically been overlooked in discussions of this scene. The term has overtones of a mercantile transaction. The clear implication is that although Stephen speaks English as his first language, he continues to inhabit it at a cost: this remains a transaction. (The place of English as a widely accepted language of commerce is particularly germane to this discussion, to be addressed later in this chapter.) That term 'acquired' gestures initially to the fact all language is learnt, and implies that one is always learning even a naturalized tongue. Joyce makes this point in numerous ways, from the inventiveness of *Finnegans Wake* to the learned languages of Molly Bloom.[11] The idea that English could be learnt in different forms was clearly embedded in Joyce's upbringing, not only in Dublin. Although Joyce was not an 'actual exile', as Casanova claims, the experience of living in Trieste provided him with encounters with an array of languages on an everyday basis.[12] In giving imaginative shape to the problem of

---

[11] See Elizabeth Kate Switaj, 'The Ambiguous Status of Native Speakers and Language Learners in *Ulysses*', *Journal of Modern Literature* 37.1 (Fall 2013): 143–57.

[12] Casanova, *World Republic of Letters*, p. 206. See John McCourt, *The Years of Bloom: James Joyce in Trieste 1904–1920* (Dublin: The Lilliput Press, 2000), pp. 49–56.

language acquisition, Joyce also drew on his own experiences as a teacher of English in Trieste, as Hugh Kenner and others have argued. Both *A Portrait* and *Ulysses* play out the Berlitz method of total immersion in the target language: readers of *A Portrait* are 'Berlitz pupils, moving alert, inductively, substituting, comprehending'; *Ulysses* is 'a Berlitz classroom between covers: a book from which we are systematically taught the skills we require to read it'.[13] Like Berlitz pupils, and like Stephen, readers too must pay their own price. Stephen's comments provide a fitting supplement to Casanova's emphasis on the relations between languages in their reminder of the hybridity of any language, which one is always learning (and unlearning). His alienation within his primary tongue makes the further additional point that the sorts of wider cultural-historical shifts analysed by Casanova are also felt at the individual level. Joyce's point here is of course the loss of Irish as a widely-spoken language in turn-of-the-century Dublin, a loss which adds momentum to the continuing reinvention of English.

In many ways, the arguments of Casanova complement and support the tenor of Deleuze and Guattari's notion of minor literature, that is, a practice of writing that challenges the presumed normality or supremacy of an established, powerful literary culture. Unlike Casanova's broad-ranging study, the theory of minor literature is spun solely around Kafka (deriving from one diary entry). Crucially, as with Stephen Dedalus's fretting over forms of English, minor literature is concerned with the tensions arising within a language and not with relationships between languages. 'A minor literature doesn't come from a minor language; it is rather that which a minority constructs within a major language'; it is a subversion 'from within.'[14] The characteristics of a minor literature are: a large degree of deterritorialization (as in Kafka's Prague German, or Joyce's Dublin English); that the political is inescapable even at the level of individual psychology; and the community values are paramount, hence the individual writer expresses a community ('*literature is the people's concern*'). It is difficult to see Joyce easily fitting this last characteristic. In minor literature, a form of translation has already occurred since it is a 'minor practice of major language', but to introduce the notion of non-translation into minor literature is to remark on the untranslatable and the irrevocable difference that accommodations typically mask.[15]

Despite the broad similarities between their models, Casanova is critical of Deleuze and Guattari for what she sees as their anachronistic sense of Kafka's politics (attributing to him a broadbrush radicalism rather than focusing on his specific national concerns) and their attempt to universalize on the basis of one

---

[13] Hugh Kenner, *A Colder Eye: The Modern Irish Writers* (New York: Alfred A. Knopf, 1983), pp. 153, 155. See also Roy Gottfried, 'Berlitz School Days', *James Joyce Quarterly* 16.3 (1979): 223–38.

[14] Gilles Deleuze and Félix Guattari, *Toward a Minor Literature*, trans. Dona Polan (Minneapolis: University of Minnesota Press, 1986), pp. 16, 18.

[15] Deleuze and Guattari, *Toward a Minor Literature*, p. 18. Their italics.

example. Further, they also 'diminish the specifically literary character' of Kafka's writing.[16] However, these different literary-historical models—both of which explicitly cite Joyce as an example—share an unacknowledged wider ambition. In the words of Casanova, 'linguistically dominated writers in general' have a tendency to seek in their writing 'escape routes from this domination'.[17] Joyce's escape route was under the cover of artistic autonomy; by sidestepping the Gaelic League's invocation to de-Anglicize Ireland, and revivalist myth-making, Joyce could formulate a prosaic Dublin that still overturned the trajectory of the English novel. Casanova echoes many Joyce critics in saying: 'Joyce dislocated English, the language of colonization, not only by incorporating in it elements of every European language but also by subverting the norms of English propriety.'[18] Even so, one would be reluctant to say that Joyce had been 'linguistically dominated' by English even if his distinctively Hiberno-English edge might itself be symptomatic of a broader political domination.

In his application of the idea of minor literature to Mangan and Ireland, David Lloyd asserts that the 'definitive condition' of minor literature is that it 'remain in an oppositional relationship to the canon and the state from which it has been excluded'.[19] Lloyd's characterization of minor literature in these terms introduces a binary of inclusion/exclusion which seems at odds with the sense of a minor register *within* a dominant language. In his own terms, much of modernism, with its strongly parodic strain, might appear minor and radical. Recognizing that this would be question-begging, Lloyd shuts down this possibility, and distinguishes between writers on the basis of intention. So 'Eliot, Pound and Yeats' are said to 'clearly belong within a major paradigm' but implicitly Joyce retains a healthy radical glow.[20] In this respect it is worth noting what Barry McCrea calls the 'reverse phenomenon' of writers who adopt a minor language although they are not native speakers of it, as in his example of Sean Ó Ríordáin's Irish.[21] The model of minor literature can too easily caricature complex situations.

Indeed, the notions of dominant languages and minor literature are too reliant on dualisms of inside/outside and dominant/dominated. Joyce's reminder that English is both familiar and foreign, especially in his own writing, emphasizes that these terms more accurately describe a spectrum of entangled positions. In what follows, I want to consider Joyce's practice of non-translation, in the light of

---

[16] Casanova, *The World Republic of Letters*, p. 203.

[17] Casanova, 'What Is a Dominant Language?', p. 384.

[18] Casanova, *The World Republic of Letters*, p. 315.

[19] David Lloyd, *Nationalism and Minor Literature: James Clarence Mangan and the Emergence of Irish Cultural Nationalism* (Berkeley: University of California Press, 1987), p. 21.

[20] Lloyd, *Nationalism and Minor Literature*, p. 23. See also Marilyn Reizbaum's argument that Joyce is 'modernist and national(ist) in this minor way' in 'The Minor Work of James Joyce', *James Joyce Quarterly* 30.2 (1993): 177–89 (p. 181).

[21] Barry McCrea, *Languages of the Night: Minor Languages and the Literary Imagination in Twentieth-Century Ireland and Europe* (New Haven: Yale University Press, 2015), p. 17.

these literary-historical models, in order to examine how the example of Joyce brings fresh insight to these wider models.

The Hybridity of English

Discussion of non-translation in *Ulysses* can be anchored to an excerpt from the 'Eumaeus' episode. Having escaped the high of nighttown with the manifest psychological torments of 'Circe', Bloom and Stephen now experience the low of a cabman's shelter:

Adjacent to the men's public urinal they perceived an icecream car round which a group of presumably Italians in heated altercation were getting rid of voluble expressions in their vivacious language in a particularly animated way, there being some little differences between the parties.

--*Puttana madonna, che ci dia i quattrini! Ho ragione? Culo rotto!*

--*Intendiamoci. Mezzo sovrano piu...*

--*Dice lui, pero!*

--*Mezzo.*

--*Farabutto! Mortacci sui!*

--*Ma ascolta! Cinque la testa piu...*

Mr Bloom and Stephen entered the cabman's shelter [....] A few moments later saw our two noctambules safely seated in a discreet corner only to be greeted by stares from the decidedly miscellaneous collection of waifs and strays and other nondescript specimens of the genus *homo* already there engaged in eating and drinking diversified by conversation for whom they seemingly formed an object of marked curiosity.

--Now touching a cup of coffee, Mr Bloom ventured to plausibly suggest to break the ice, it occurs to me you ought to sample something in the shape of solid food, say, a roll of some description.

Accordingly his first act was with characteristic *sangfroid* to order these commodities quietly. The *hoi polloi* of jarvies or stevedores or whatever they were after a cursory examination turned their eyes apparently dissatisfied [....] Mr Bloom, availing himself of the right of free speech, he having just a bowing acquaintance with the language in dispute, though, to be sure, rather in a quandary over *voglio*, remarked to his *protégé* in an audible tone of voice *à propos* of the battle royal in the street which was still raging fast and furious:

--A beautiful language. I mean for singing purposes. Why do you not write your poetry in that language? *Bella Poetria!* It is so melodious and full. *Belladonna. Voglio.*

Stephen, who was trying his dead best to yawn if he could, suffering from lassitude generally, replied:

--To fill the ear of a cow elephant. They were haggling over money.

--Is that so? Mr Bloom asked. Of course, he subjoined pensively, at the inward reflection of there being more languages to start with than were absolutely necessary, it may be only the southern glamour that surrounds it.

The keeper of the shelter in the middle of this *tête-à-tête* put a boiling swimming cup of a choice concoction labelled coffee on the table and a rather antediluvian specimen of a bun, or so it seemed. [....]

--Sounds are impostures, Stephen said after a pause of some little time, like names. Cicero, Podmore. Napoleon, Mr Goodbody. Jesus, Mr Doyle. Shakespeares were as common as Murphies. What's in a name?

--Yes, to be sure, Mr Bloom unaffectedly concurred. Of course. Our name was changed too, he added, pushing the socalled roll across.

The redbearded sailor who had his weather eye on the newcomers boarded Stephen, whom he had singled out for attention in particular, squarely by asking:

--And what might your name be?

Just in the nick of time Mr Bloom touched his companion's boot but Stephen, apparently disregarding the warm pressure from an unexpected quarter, answered:

--Dedalus.   (*U* 16:309–74)

This passage is broadly representative of the wider 'Eumaeus' episode whose narrative mask does not only 'reflect the fatigue of the characters or a narrator' but also a 'public, anonymous' voice revealing that language itself is tired.[22] The episode is written in a stilted English that is continually trying too hard to be accurate, and comically failing in the process, often mixing cliché with untranslated phrases. This excerpt adds to that style some overheard vernacular Italian, within a context of linguistic misunderstanding, cultural stereotypes and discussion of the significance of naming. Each of these aspects of non-translation will be addressed in turn.

The language of this Bloomian narrator includes a tissue of accommodated untranslated phrases. In this passage alone we read: *homo*, *sangfroid*, *hoi polloi*, *voglio*, *protégé*, *à propos*, and *tête-à-tête*. Almost all are terms that have been appropriated within English so that they are now commonplace, although Joyce draws attention to their otherness by italicizing them. As Scarlett Baron's chapter

---

[22] Karen Lawrence, *The Odyssey of Style in 'Ulysses'* (Princeton, NJ: Princeton University Press, 1981), p. 168. Senn cautions against the term 'fatigue' to describe the style of Eumaeus. He associates it with Bloom and says it 'imitates the elusive and frustrating striving of language towards validity'. *Joyce's Dislocutions*, pp. 108, 110.

notes, the 'Eumaeus' episode is littered with them: *En route, re, finis, demimonde, confrères, quondam, qui vive, raconteur, de rigueur, via, au fait, finale, denouement, paterfamilias, entourage.* (Oddly enough, *etcetera* is not one of them.) Joyce's text displays a self-conscious appropriation or incorporation of these Romance languages into Germanic English—these phrases are Latin and French, but many are now, *de facto*, English too. Significantly, all the phrases are italicized in Joyce's text, as is convention to indicate non-English, but in many cases they need not have been italicized, so familiar are they, such as the words *venue* and *liaisons* which also appear in 'Eumaeus' in italics. (The former appears not in italics elsewhere [*U* 13:879, 15:2397]).

This issue of loan words and their italicization was addressed in contemporary debates about the nature and future of the English language. Announcing its existence in October 1919, the Society for Pure English set out 'a few definite proposals' of which one was to denounce 'the large and unnecessary importation of foreign words into the English language'.[23] The S.P.E., as it was known, numbered many important members among the several hundred who subscribed, including its driving force Robert Bridges, the poet laureate, alongside several other prominent writers, along with academics, linguists, lexicographers, and political figures.[24] It was far from being a simply conservative, reactionary organization, as its name may misleadingly imply ('pure' does not mean 'the idea that words of foreign origin are *impurities* in English').[25] It was established in part in opposition to education that propounded a 'uniform and town-bred standard of speech' and instead, it sought, at least in the eyes of Bridges, to 'preserve the living and popular character' of varieties of English in 'homespun' terms as used by regional communities, various trades and workers, soldiers, and other groups.[26] So when it railed against loan words it did so because they were not being assimilated into English, so helping it to thrive and adapt, and instead too often retained their non-English spelling and pronunciation. A strong patriotic theme runs through the initial conceptualization of the S.P.E. which, for all its interest in diversity still sought to entrench 'the national character of our standard speech'.[27] Its objection

---

[23] Society for Pure English, Tract no.1 (Oxford: Oxford University Press, 1919), p. 8. The Society was founded Oxford in 1913 but delayed publication due to the First World War. Active until 1948, producing 66 tracts, it became increasingly preoccupied with points of grammar. The only reference to Joyce in its tracts came in an article on colloquialisms by the poet and academic Lascelles Abercrombie. He says that 'Work in Progress' fails because it does not successfully communicate, but he recognizes Joyce as 'a serious artist...driven by dissatisfaction with both the vocabulary and the structure of English into this disaster'. Lascelles Abercrombie 'Colloquial Language in Literature', S.P.E. Tract 36 (1931), p. 520.

[24] Bridges was an admirer of Joyce, having recently read *A Portrait* and recommended it to Roger Fry. See Catherine Phillips, *Robert Bridges: A Biography* (Oxford: Oxford University Press, 1992), p. 310. Furthermore, as Thomas McGreevy noted, Bridges sent Joyce a signed copy of his unexpectedly successful long poem *Testament of Beauty*. See letters to *The Times* and to Desmond MacCarthy in Thomas McGreevy's papers in Trinity College Dublin, TCD MS 8114/12 and 8114/14.

[25] Society for Pure English, Tract no.1, p. 3.   [26] Society for Pure English, Tract no.1, p. 9.

[27] Society for Pure English, Tract no.1, p. 7.

to loan words was precisely that they were a form of non-translation, inhibiting the development of new, English words. In common with other proponents of English as an academic discipline (Newbolt was an active, not unproblematic member), who objected to the continuing primacy of the Classical languages, the S.P.E. saw the inculcation of loan words as a non-translation that adapted English 'to the habit of classical scholars'.[28]

A particular feature of loan words that the S.P.E. objected to—pertinent to this discussion of 'Eumaeus'—was the commonplace rendition of them in italics. 'A paragraph of serious English prose may be sometimes seen as freely sprinkled with italicized French words as a passage of Cicero is often interlarded with Greek', it complained. 'The mere printing of such words in italics is an active force towards degeneration. The Society hopes to discredit this tendency, and it will endeavour to restore to English its old reactive energy; when a choice is possible we should like to give an English pronunciation and spelling to useful foreign words.'[29] A case in point would be 'entourage', which is one of those italicized words in 'Eumaeus': from 1929 Bridges chaired the BBC Committee on Pronunciation and produced a consultation exercise in the S.P.E. tract series, comparing pronunciation that retained its French origin ('ontooráazh') which he contrasted with the English pronunciation of 'courage'. Such domiciled words should normally also be given a new spelling, he argued.[30]

In adopting the practice of parading foreign words in italics, *Ulysses* points towards a form of non-translation that has become something of a cliché. If these untranslated phrases indicate Bloom's social ambition or pretension, in that they stand for a cultural capital that he strives to acquire, so also the narrative of 'Eumaeus' repeats hackneyed terms from the exhausted languages of European civilization and does so in a manner that is calculated and excessive. The effect is that these terms sit uneasily, signifying both their otherness, their resistance to assimilation, and their accommodation as terms easily understood. The narrative voice carries the tiredness of a now-global world language that recycles phrases as mementoes from the accommodated other. This is quite a different point to that made by Virginia Woolf in her essay 'On Not Knowing French'. There, Woolf suggests that native speakers have been dulled by 'old habits and instincts' so that 'ordinary daily English' is 'as tasteless as water', whereas, she suggests, a snippet of another tongue 'even the French of daily use, has wine in it.'[31] That is not the case in 'Eumaeus', in which the domination of English in part rests on its ability to

---

[28] Society for Pure English, Tract no.1, p. 7. On differences between Newbolt and Bridges, see Phillips, *Robert Bridges*, pp. 279–80.

[29] Society for Pure English, Tract no.1, p. 7.

[30] Society for Pure English, Tract no.32 (1931), p. 375.

[31] Virginia Woolf, 'On Not Knowing French', *The Essays of Virginia Woolf, vol.V 1929–1932*, ed. Stuart N. Clarke (London: Hogarth Press, 2009), pp. 3–9 (pp. 3–4).

render *all* language shop-worn and comically over-zealous. Crucially, 'Eumaeus' presents phrases of italicized non-translation alongside its own worn-out English phrases: *à propos* next to 'battle royal' and *tête-à-tête* next to 'choice concoction' (to cite only from the passage above). If English is dominant here, in Casanova's sense of exerting cultural power, 'Eumaeus' suggests not its vitality but its approaching exhaustion.

To compose in clichés is a daring strategy for any writer, and one which Joyce leavens by making these accommodated phrases draw attention to the history and the connotations in the surrounding English. *Ulysses* suggests the extent to which English *already* comprises terms that have been appropriated, drawing on its origins in the Germanic group of languages as well as its incorporation of elements of Romance languages. It implies, then, some of the ways in which any language already comprises non-translation, after long processes of adoption. The hybridity of English is thus emphasized. *Ulysses* thus gives the lie to the presumption of the S.P.E. that there is something innately English about the concoction of English. Significantly, in stressing the incorporation of the italicized words (by sheer number), the text draws attention to the potential 'otherness' of non-italicized words. There are several that are both familiar and foreign, so that, in the context, they may be said to resonate with invisible italics. The apparent neologism 'noctambules' (not italicized) for nightwalkers is a Latinate compound of *nox* and *ambulare* (the *OED* gives 'noctambulist'). Similarly the more regular word 'antediluvian' combines *ante* (before) and *diluvium* (deluge). Perhaps also 'miscellaneous', and others, start to show their origins and to look less English too. Very soon, then, English seems uncertain. Readers question the borders of English and non-English, whether or not in italics, exposing languages' innate plurality. Joyce nudges his readers to consider non-translation in this manner, which necessarily destabilizes the borders of tongues, remarking their contingency and their historicity.

With reference to the models of minor literature and the 'world republic of letters', these examples suggest that Joyce's practice of non-translation does not so much oppose the authority of English as a dominant language as place that dominance in a particular historical and geopolitical perspective. To claim that this is 'minor' in the sense of opposing a dominant tongue is misleading: if Joyce is here 'finding...his own *patois*', in the words of Deleuze and Guattari, then he does so from a conflicted stance that is not simply oppositional.[32] Of course, the formal arrangement of the novel, its wider over-writing of English, its stylistic variations, all contribute to a parodic rewriting of canonical forms and the creation of an epical-yet-prosaic Catholic Dublin in literary histories of Ireland and Europe. The challenge that this presented to established orders is not to be discounted. At the

---

[32] Deleuze and Guattari, *Toward a Minor Literature*, p. 18.

same time, Joyce's point is not bluntly to oppose English but to play upon its internal fissures in the sort of undermining that can only come from deep attachment.

Following shortly after the 'Oxen of the Sun' episode, which parodied anthologies of the development of English literary prose, only to descend into Babelish confusion, the 'Eumaeus' episode underlines the impression of the impermanence of English as the dominant world language. Joyce seems to have anticipated as much in a very early essay, 'On the Study of Languages', in which he placed language development within the context of the rise and fall of empires. Latin, the language of the 'vastest and greatest [Republic] the world has seen', became known even to 'the stranger-hating Briton'. Like Shakespeare, it is now 'in everyone's mouth' although we don't realize it.[33] Joyce was following a path laid out by British Victorians and their descendants in comparing current English dominance to Latin and Roman: his perspective is different, of course, but the assumption remains of a causal link between the spread of imperial territory, linguistic variation, and eventual imperial collapse.

The simplistic 'rise and fall' narrative of linguistic demise and growth overlooks the extent to which languages coexist even to points of confusion. The historian of language, Louis-Jean Calvet makes the point that Latin 'is *alive* in the sense that it continues in the Romance languages whose speakers must have thought for many years that they still spoke Latin'.[34] The transition of English, in Joyce's hands, accords with the transition of England from the recent height of its imperial power. In the terms of Joyce's early essay, 'the advent of an overcoming power may be attested by the crippled diction, or by the complete disuse of the original language, save in solitary, dear phrases'.[35] His discussion of Latin and Rome was meant to invoke an analogy with English and England, implying that a dominant language, even a powerful 'world language', is historically and politically contingent. Certainly, Joyce was not alone in anticipating the 'crippled diction' of English, or in helping to bring it about. In 1901, George Moore had predicted that in fifty years English would be as corrupt as eighth-century Latin, 'a sort of Volapuk, strictly limited to commercial letters and to journalism'; just as in England several commentators feared that it would be as 'broken to pieces' as Classical Latin.[36] The crippling of empire may be partially anticipated in the 'crippled diction' of English but the two are not to be confused; each in different ways goes on echoing for centuries.

---

[33] James Joyce, 'On the Study of Languages', *Occasional, Critical and Political Writing*, ed. Kevin Barry (Oxford: Oxford University Press, 2000), p. 16.

[34] Louis-Jean Calvet, *Language Wars and Linguistic Politics*, trans. Michel Petheram (Oxford: Oxford University Press, 1998), p. 101.

[35] Joyce, 'On the Study of Languages', in *Occasional, Critical and Political Writing*, p. 15.

[36] George Moore, 'Literature and the Irish Language', cited by Tony Crowley, *Wars of Words: The Politics of Language in Ireland 1537–2004* (Oxford: Oxford University Press, 2005), p. 159. Henry Newbolt, 'The Future of the English Language', p. 4.

Universal Languages

The passage from 'Eumaeus' cited above reiterates a debate that would have been familiar to Stephen and the Revivalist figures he meets and discusses: the appropriate language for literary expression. The Revival had been riven by this topic, with the Abbey Theatre performing some Irish language plays (to Joyce's dismay) and Gaelic Revivalists promoting Irish as a literary language and associating English with commercial transactions and the development of modern industrial society.[37] Hence the irony of Bloom's misunderstanding of the Italian he overhears: what he takes to be a beautiful language, a medium of poetry, is in fact a coarse squabble over money. To Bloom's commercial mind, linguistic difference is an impediment to rational exchange even as he recognizes that different languages may hold different qualities. In the passage, Bloom suggests that Italian should be for opera and poetry. Although Stephen may find it odd to have Italian recommended as the language for his poetry, he would surely have encountered similar claims on behalf of Irish. Of course, Bloom and the Gaelic Leaguers have very different imperatives—the one presuming a canonical language of art, the other seeking to overturn that domination through the formation of a vernacular national literature. Yet they share the widely-held presumption that English is the language of modernization; 'serviceable, labour-saving and practical' in the words of Henry Newbolt, 'the most precise' among 'civilised nations'.[38] This was not only a literary question, nor was the assumption necessarily negative. The same assumption can be seen for instance in Otto Jespersen's *Growth and Structure of the English Language*, which was first published in 1905 and went into nine editions by 1938. Jespersen refers approvingly to the 'business-like, virile qualities' of the language; 'a methodical, energetic, business-like and sober language, that does not care much for finery and elegance'. He concludes, echoing Romantic philology: 'As the language is, so also is the nation'.[39] In fact, Joyce drew on Jespersen's book in writing *Finnegans Wake*.[40] In Casanova's terms it is a part of the ideology of the dominant language to presume that certain forms of transaction must be undertaken in this language. One of the qualities of Joyce's writing, in emphasizing the entanglement of linguistic development, is to challenge that ideology.

Bloom's position in the passage is intriguing because he appears to declare a preference for a universal language. His comment, 'there being more languages

---

[37] See for example D. P. Moran, *The Philosophy of Irish Ireland* [1905], ed. Patrick Maume (Dublin: University College Dublin Press, 2006).

[38] Newbolt, 'The Future of the English Language', p. 7.

[39] Otto Jespersen, *Growth and Structure of the English Language* (Leipzig: B.G. Teubner/Oxford: Basil Blackwell, 1926, 5th edition), pp. 10, 16.

[40] See *The 'Finnegans Wake' Notebooks at Buffalo. Notebook VI.B.6*, eds. Vincent Deane, Daniel Ferrer and Geert Lernout (Turnhout, Belgium: Brepols, 2002) and Erika Rosiers and Wim Van Mierlo, 'Neutral Auxiliaries & Universal Idioms: Otto Jespersen in Work in Progress', in *James Joyce: The Study of Languages*, ed. Dirk Van Hulle (Brussels: Peter Lang, 2002), pp. 55–70.

to start with than were absolutely necessary', suggests his dissatisfaction with linguistic difference, despite the fact that he has at least 'bowing acquaintance' with Italian, ancient Hebrew, and Latin (the latter he associates with popular ignorance [*U* 5:350]). These languages seem to be *accoutrements* for Bloom—which makes them also obstacles to the transparency he apparently desires. Bloom's language is the English of commerce, of advertising (utility and repetition are his keystones). Such obstacles to 'progress' might indeed be overcome in Bloom's liberal-utopian 'Nova Hibernia of the future' (*U* 15:1544–5). In 'Circe' he announces a manifesto that includes 'esperanto the universal language with universal brotherhood....Free money, free rent, free love and a free lay church in a free lay state.' (*U* 15:1691–2). If Bloom is a practical pragmatist by day, he is an idealist by night.

Bloom's apparent support for an artificial, universal language, such as Esperanto, implies that he has joined a bandwagon of supporters for the many such languages that were invented, and often soon ditched, in the late nineteenth and early twentieth century. This at least provides a context in which to understand Bloom's remarks. Calvet has noted the intense activity in constructing so-called universal languages between 1879, the date of the invention of Volapuk, and 1914.[41] These concocted languages, that aimed at a universality in that anyone could easily acquire them, and any language could supposedly be translated into, or from them, nonetheless shared a 'striking Eurocentrism'. Calvet goes on:

> the notion of a 'lingua universalis' appeared at the moment in history when the use of Latin as a lingua franca declined among the elites of Europe. It was then embodied in numerous projects at another historical moment, when French, which had taken the place of Latin, itself began to decline in that function. In both cases, we find the same temptation to resolve the problems of international communication *in vitro*, and in the second case we see a close link between the emergence of the 'Esperanto phenomenon' and of nation-states. The very idea of a universal language appears as a response to the national (and linguistic) division of Europe.[42]

The logic behind the *lingua universalis*, so Calvet implies, was a form of imperialist thinking. Emily Apter takes him to have identified 'the causal connections between the rise of universal language ideology and imperialism'.[43] Calvet also directly suggests a pacifist ideology or 'illusion' behind these languages, as is well-known in the case of Esperanto. Bloom's enthusiasm for Esperanto would tie in with his broadbrush pacifism, and yet at the same time his support for the idea of

[41] Calvet, *Language Wars and Linguistic Politics*, p. 195. Calvet lists 42 new languages formed in these years, a list which he says is 'certainly very incomplete' (p. 195).

[42] Calvet, *Language Wars and Linguistic Politics*, p. 197.

[43] Emily Apter, *The Translation Zone: A New Comparative Literature* (Princeton: Princeton University Press, 2005), p. 137.

a universal language appears to go against the commonplace celebration of him as a pluralist who celebrates difference. Since languages develop to serve the needs of their community, to say 'there being more languages to start with than were absolutely necessary' is akin to saying there is too much social diversity.[44] But is Bloom really of this view? To be clear: the now-orthodox view of Bloom as a humanitarian who seeks to see others' points of view is not erroneous; there remains a lot of evidence to support this picture of Bloom's principles (and there may also be a suggestion that his Jewish background would lead towards support for Esperanto).[45] However, to place Bloom's ambitions in the context of late nineteenth-century hankering after a common tongue, an idea that speaks of a Eurocentric universalism, may enrich descriptions of Bloom's variegated character and help modern readers to see something of his difference. (It also provides a context for thinking through the claims that *Finnegans Wake* seeks to embody a form of universal language.)[46]

Bloom's apparent desire for a limit on the number of languages is akin to a form of 'domestication' which he performs when hearing the Latin mass (*U* 5:349–53) and which he attributes to Molly: 'Unusual polysyllables of foreign origin she interpreted phonetically or by false analogy or by both: metempsychosis (met him pike hoses), alias (a mendacious person mentioned in sacred scripture)' (*U* 17:685–7).[47] However, something slightly different is going on in the long quotation from 'Eumaeus' above. For there, readily domesticating foreign words, Bloom and the narrator dwell on linguistic difference, signalled by forms of uncertainty, and represented on the page in italics. The word *voglio* has left Bloom 'rather in a quandary'.

He worries over the word because he thinks back on his earlier mis-recollection of lines from *Don Giovanni* in the 'Calypso' episode. In the bedroom with Molly that morning, digesting the news that Boylan is coming over—ostensibly to bring the programme for Molly's concert recitals—Bloom's mind turns from the possibility of Molly's affair to the lines from Mozart's opera that she will sing: '*Voglio e non vorrei*. Wonder if she pronounces that right: *voglio*' (*U* 4:327–8). In fact, Bloom has mis-remembered the line from *Don Giovanni* which should be '*vorrei*

[44] See Calvet, *Language Wars and Linguistic Politics*, pp. 3–4.

[45] The founder of Esperanto, L. L. Zamenhof, claimed in 1905: 'No one can feel the need for a humanly neutral and non-national language as strongly as a Jew.' Cited in Calvet, *Language Wars and Linguistic Politics*, p. 198. For a sympathetic account of Esperanto and an argument that the universal brotherhood envisaged by Zamenhof has affinities with *Finnegans Wake*, see Nico Israel, 'Esperantic Modernism: Joyce, Universal Language, and Political Gesture', *Modernism/modernity* 24.1 (2017): 1–21.

[46] 'The incorporation of dozens of languages into the syntax of Joyce's sentences certainly facilitates both a "literal" universality as well as posits a "universal" language for the unconscious mind.' Susan Shaw Sailer, 'Universalizing Languages: *Finnegans Wake* Meets Basic English', *James Joyce Quarterly* 36.4 (1999): pp. 853–68 (p. 862). See also Yao, p. 205.

[47] Rosa Maria Bollettieri Bosinelli, 'Joyce Slipping Across the Borders of English: The Stranger in Language', *James Joyce Quarterly* 38.3–4 (2001): 395–409 (p. 401).

e non vorrei—'I would like to and I wouldn't like to'. Bloom's unwitting substitution of *voglio*—I *want*—might make the phrase less subtle but it does introduce the delicate question of his personal volition.[48] The word *voglio* recurs throughout the day (in four other episodes Bloom ponders it), so that by the end of the day, it does so in a changed context. In the episode in the cabman's shelter, cited above, Bloom's self-doubt is more explicit ('rather in a quandary over *voglio*'), that is, he both wonders how to pronounce *voglio* and acknowledges that his reticence towards Molly has left him with an entrenched uncertainty. Mild 'wonder' over correct pronunciation has become deep-seated 'quandary'. Initially, *voglio* had been associated with *Molly's* (presumed) mispronunciation but just as Bloom's repressed doubts about Boylan's visit found their way into his faulty recollection of the operatic phrase, so too his recurrent doubts about *voglio* signal Bloom's uncertainty over *his* pronunciation by referring to Molly's pronunciation. In each case—Boylan, *voglio*—Bloom's problem is simple: he doesn't know the answer, or at least he can't *say* it.

In this scene, then, we can detect Bloom's sexual anxiety and guilt hidden under a double displacement—both onto the 'beautiful language' of Italian and onto his wife's mispronunciation. Characteristically, Bloom struggles to say what he wants; he cannot with confidence pronounce the word, which in any case he misremembers, signifying his core 'quandary' at the heart of the story. As much as he may appear to regret the range of languages, he also finds linguistic diversity a convenient mask. Sometimes a substitute is useful. As Freud said of the wolf man, 'like so many other people' he 'used his difficulties with a foreign language as a screen for symptomatic acts'.[49] Bloom's trouble with *voglio* leads towards a more general observation that non-translation can provide a convenient 'screen' or mask which paradoxically encourages self-expression and the revelation of otherwise unspoken or unpalatable truths.

As languages are conventions, any specific usage can still be wrong and yet completely functional at the same time. Bloom's Italian is wrong—*Bella Poetria!* should presumably be *Bella Poesia!*—but it is functional. Even so, he still misunderstands the Italian speech community at the start of the passage. Stephen tells Bloom that 'like names', so also 'sounds are impostures'. 'What's in a name?' he asks, alluding to *Romeo and Juliet*. When Juliet asks this question of herself, she answers, 'That which we call a rose / By any other word would smell as sweet'.[50] Juliet's concern, like that of Stephen, is that names do matter, which is why each

---

[48] Don Gifford with Robert J. Seidman, *'Ulysses' Annotated: Notes for James Joyce's 'Ulysses'* (Berkeley: University of California Press, 1989), p. 77.

[49] Sigmund Freud, 'From the History of an Infantile Neurosis' ['The Wolf Man'] in *The Standard Edition of the Works of Sigmund Freud*, ed. James Strachey, vol. XVII, p. 94. Cited in Frank Kermode, *Essays on Fiction, 1971–82* (Routledge & Kegan Paul, 1983), p. 23.

[50] William Shakespeare, *Romeo and Juliet*, II.i.85–6. *The Oxford Shakespeare*, gen. eds Stanley Wells and Gary Taylor (Oxford: Clarendon Press, 2005, second edn).

would deny the paternal line. The apparent realism of Juliet's remark takes us back to Bloom's position: 'there being more languages to start with than were absolutely necessary'. Bloom's name 'was changed too', he acknowledges, from Virag to Bloom, but he would not want to see any reason for that to matter. All that matters, from this perspective, in common with the calls for a universal language, is the pragmatic community of language-users. The obvious casualty of this approach is the historical and etymological sense of languages, their hybridity and intertwining, which much of Joyce's writing seems to want to dwell upon.[51] In '*detaining*' the reader (*P* 192), Joyce's language reveals something of its make-up—a richness with which Bloom would appear to be at odds.[52]

Stephen differs from Bloom, and his statement of his own name, 'Dedalus', which is both singular and mythical, is also a statement of a cultural oddity, a word that really does stand out (unlike all those italicized ones). A most improbable Dublin name, Dedalus is a remnant that asserts its difference. The Greeks had maintained their superiority in part by not permitting other languages to be used; all non-Greek speakers were barbarians, or speakers of nonsense. Joyce reminds his readers here—as he had in *A Portrait*—of the Greek heritage that overshadows his alter-ego. For sure, Joyce uses the name Dedalus in order to echo the myth, yet it also serves as a subtle warning that even the most powerful must be superseded. In adopting the Latin form for the title of his book, *Ulysses*, Joyce implies that the linguistic and imperial domination of the Greeks would have to be followed by their collapse. The name Ulysses weighs unknowingly on Stephen Dedalus.

The representation of different approaches to languages in this scene encapsulates a divergence that is at the heart of the novel. An outsider who seeks accommodation, Bloom expresses a unifying or communitarian impulse in seeking to translate all into a 'lingua universalis'. That this reductive impulse is thwarted by the text is one means by which Joyce signals the uncontrollable force of linguistic diversity. The figure of Dedalus, unlike that of Bloom, remains as an emblem of linguistic difference; his role here looks ahead to his later act of declining asylum at Eccles Street. As part of this linguistic diversity, it is important to recognize that the narrative voice cannot simply be equated with Bloom because, among other things, it captures the Italian that Bloom does not grasp. Joyce's narrative, then, displays this divergence of positions—a pulling in different directions between accommodation and refusal, played out in different languages, which echoes this central drama of the host–guest relationship.

---

[51] See Sylvain Belluc, 'Language and (Re)creation: Joyce and Nineteenth-Century Philology' in *James Joyce in the Nineteenth Century*, ed. John Nash (Cambridge: Cambridge University Press, 2013), pp. 168–82.

[52] Stephen cites John Henry Newman's use of the word to illustrate the difference between common terms in 'the literary tradition' and in 'the tradition of the marketplace' (*P* 192).

Non-Translation

In distinction from the dualism that structures the models of Casanova and Deleuze and Guattari, Joyce's non-translation opens up a plurality and hybridity within language, both foreign and familiar. In this reading, non-translation is always with us as a condition of language, which becomes increasingly visible as the political dominance of English wanes. That Joyce explored these questions in his fiction, sometimes in the most down-to-earth forms, can be seen by returning briefly to Bloom and his cat.

A closer inspection of the conversation between Bloom and the cat suggests that those sounds—Mkgnao, Mrkgnao, Mrkrgnao—are not in fact the cat's language at all, but a sort of appropriation, and something like a 'domination' in the terms of Casanova. Yet this still is not quite right: the cat's sounds have been co-opted by the narrative but they remain resolutely un-English; there is an alien otherness to her voice that the narrator's grasp fails to master by simple virtue of the fact that these are not recognizable or repeatable words or sounds. For sure, the ambitious English of the unnamed narrator, or 'arranger', a lurking voice that is distinct from Bloom himself, has taken this opportunity to stretch its muscles.[53] This arranging narrator appears to relish the challenge of getting the cat just so, not to mention the mischievousness with which it imputes to Molly an unconscious echo of the cat in her own first sound, 'Mn' (*U* 4:57). The cat's sounds have been rendered by a talented mimic into a form that English might make understandable. The cat certainly hasn't been echoed in an empathetic grasp of catspeak by Bloom, who does indeed try his hand at communication in her own language, with predictable results: 'Prr. Scratch my head. Prr', he thinks; and he voices aloud to the cat a single, 'Miaow!' (*U* 4:19–20; 4:462). Bloom's attempt to communicate in the language of the cat is a sadly conventional cliché, hardly alike to the narrator's more literary voicing of the cat. In this short exchange, then, Joyce presents two versions of the cat's language—its accommodation or translation into human convention (Miaow!) and a transcription of it as a non-translation (Mrkrgnao!). Joyce's games in 'Eumaeus', including fragments from languages so that we no longer know where English stops and another starts, suggest that language itself is a sort of jostle between these positions of accommodation and otherness. If we attend to the cat's otherness, so too we may hear some of the voices that a dominant language never fully masters. In hearing these echoes, we are reminded of the importance of non-translation in the republic of letters and minor literature, as kernels of tongues that persist into the present.

Here at the start of Bloom's day is a conversation rather like that towards the end of his day, when he and Stephen Dedalus translate for one another 'fragments

---

[53] On the concept of the arranger, see David Hayman, *'Ulysses': The Mechanics of Meaning* (Madison: University of Wisconsin Press, 1982, new edn).

of verse from the ancient Hebrew and the ancient Irish languages' (*U* 17:724–5). In doing so, each also confronts the inescapable difference between languages. However, this later meeting is portrayed around 'points of contact' between the languages (*U* 17:745). This scene may be 'Joyce's ultimate expression of the importance of translation' but, if so, this 'positive vision' of cultural reciprocity needs further context.[54] For here, these ancient languages—one 'extinct', one 'revived'—are reproduced through theoretical learning 'confined to certain grammatical rules of accidence and syntax' (*U* 17:741–4). The exchange takes place within and is controlled by the master-code of English, which takes its place here as the world language of the twentieth century, adopting the guise of a 'universal language', into which these ancient tongues are decoded, setting the parameters to the exercise. The incident is as much one of non-translation (between ancient Hebrew and ancient Irish) and (their) modern domination by the prestige of the new world language, English. The conversation with the cat, however, is slightly different. As I have suggested, it too is presented within English thanks to the virtuoso performance of the narrative voice, but there is also an unknowable quality of the cat's language that makes it impossible to grasp and to dominate fully. It remains tantalizingly out of reach forever, beyond English, beyond human learning.

To what extent can we with seriousness refer to the cat as having a language? If the discussion has perhaps stretched the point, then that surely is what *Ulysses* invites readers to do, not for the sake of solipsism but to ask the genuinely arresting question: what is a language? The rendition of the cat's sounds is finally best considered as the narrator-arranger's manipulation of English to accommodate a communicative sound that is also alien to it, that has no lexicon, no grammar, no alphabet: an attempted appropriation of that which cannot be translated, a translation of a non-translation.

---

[54] Jesse Schotter, 'Verbivocovisuals: James Joyce and the Problem of Babel', *James Joyce Quarterly* 48.1 (2010): 89–109 (pp. 103, 104).

12

Translating Artaud and
Non-Translation

Alexandra Lukes

In a letter dating from 1947 on the topic of the publication of his unclassifiable text *Artaud le Mômo*, the poet and former Surrealist Antonin Artaud writes the following: 'Et accepterai-je d'être traduit? Je ne sais pas.'[1] Undoubtedly, translation here refers to the work in question and, possibly, his works more broadly; however, given the intimate connection between language and being that permeates his entire production, we are left wondering what exactly Artaud intends as the object of translation and whether or not he is referring to himself. But, what does it mean to translate someone? If translation, as it is conventionally understood, refers to that activity by which meaning is transferred from one language to another, where and how does the self come into it?

These questions become all the more significant when we observe the context in which Artaud raised the issue of translation: the publication of *Artaud le Mômo*. This text inaugurates Artaud's return to society after nine years of internment in various mental asylums, by creating a new man, endowed with a new language. Here we find the figure of the Mômo, an amalgam of child and madman, whose body is turned inside out, liberated from his organs, and whose language is a mixture of French and strange syllables, which are ostensibly as incomprehensible as they are unreadable. Indeed, how are we to read, let alone understand, clusters such as 'orch torpch', 'ta urchpt orchpt' or 'aungbli'?

Artaud's later works are filled with such syllabic groupings, which are presented, for the most part, as separate typographically from the sentences written in recognizable French that surround them. The mysterious syllables pose a challenge not only for reading these texts but also for translating them out of French, because the syllables do not belong to a discernible foreign language. The alternating dynamic between recognizable French forms and unrecognizable groupings of letters endows the works with a disconcerting quality of strangeness, whereby the borders between discrete languages become blurred, the conventional

---

[1] Antonin Artaud, *Œuvres*, ed. Evelyne Grossman (Paris: Gallimard, 2004), p. 1147, hereafter referred to parenthetically in the text as *Œuvres*.

Alexandra Lukes, *Translating Artaud and Non-Translation* In: *Modernism and Non-Translation*. Edited by: Jason Harding and John Nash, Oxford University Press (2019). © the several contributors.
DOI: 10.1093/oso/9780198821441.003.0012

understanding of what constitutes a language (and, indeed, a text) is challenged, and the very notion of translatability is called into question.

Translations of these texts typically retain the original's separation between French and syllabic groupings, leaving the latter untranslated and mostly untouched in the foreign-language versions.[2] Indeed, given that the syllables do not correspond to any known language nor do they seem to be created according to any ostensible rules or follow any regular patterns, translators are faced with a baffling challenge. Should they be guided by the clusters' sounds in order to recreate equivalent sonorous effects in the target language, or might they instead attempt to identify in the clusters potentially hidden meanings and reproduce those?

The question of how to translate Artaud's syllables is further complicated by Artaud's description of them as 'emotive', 'invented', and 'faecal' in nature, a characterization that ties them respectively to Artaud's affect, intellect, and body.[3] If we frame this description within a consideration of the close connection that Artaud draws between his work and his life—'Je ne conçois pas d'œuvre comme détachée de la vie' (Œuvres 105)—we are compelled to experience the syllables as the written counterparts to Artaud's vocal eruptions. Doing so involves understanding the complex relationship between language and body that the syllables enact; this, in turn, requires examining the conditions that fostered their appearance, namely, Artaud's experience of internment and the treatments he received (art therapy and electroshocks), all of which radically altered his language, body, and identity, as well as the relationship between them. Furthermore, given that the syllables emerge, in part, from Artaud's own practice of translation, as an unconventional means to reconnect with his body and name, the issue of the syllables' translatability raises fundamental questions about how language relates to identity, which complicate the idea of what it means to translate Artaud.

While the syllables are inevitably the most striking feature of these texts, their significance for addressing problems of translation posed by Artaud does not lie only in their ostensible untranslatability; rather, their importance resides in the tension they create between readability and unreadability, translation and

---

[2] For instance, both Weaver's and Eshleman and Bador's English versions reproduce the originals untouched, while Irwin's Spanish translation makes minor vocalic changes, adding accents to aid pronunciation. See Artaud, *Antonin Artaud, Selected Writings*, ed. Susan Sontag, trans. Helen Weaver (Berkeley and Los Angeles: University of California Press, 1976); Artaud, *Watchfiends and Rack Screams*, ed. and trans. Clayton Eshleman with Bernard Bador (Boston: Exact Change, 1995); Artaud, *Artaud el Momo*, trans. Sara Irwin (Buenos Aires: Need, 1998).

[3] Artaud talks about 'crottes glossolaliantes' (*Œuvres complètes*, 26 vols [Paris : Gallimard, 1956–1994], vol. XVI, p. 32), 'syllabes que j'invente' (quoted in Paule Thévenin, *Antonin Artaud, ce désespéré qui vous parle* [Paris: Seuil, 1993], p. 125), and 'syllabes émotives' (*Œuvres complètes*, XVIII, p. 261). Following Artaud's use of the term 'glossolaliantes', the syllables are typically studied as instances of glossolalia, a phenomenon tied to the triadic tradition of religious mysticism (in the Pentecostal tradition of 'speaking in tongues'), linguistic disorders (such as aphasic pathologies), and poetic experimentation (in line with avant-garde Dada or Surrealist aesthetic practices). This characterization encourages a crossover between critical and clinical discourses, and it accounts for both Artaud's poetic innovations and his post-electroshock babble.

non-translation, by being in constant dialogue with the surrounding French language. As such, they must be contextualized, with regards both to the texts in which they appear and to Artaud's broader poetic programme to renew language and mankind, a programme that relies as much on grammatically correct French as it does on the invented syllables that attempt to undermine it.

Looking at Artaud's later texts, then, in the light of his comment on translation, not only clarifies the role of the syllables within Artaud's poetics, but, by revealing a tension between translation and non-translation, it also deepens our understanding of what translation might be. Asking what it means to translate Artaud uncovers the significance of the physical dimension that is involved in the process of translation and the role of the non-verbal (or pre-verbal), while testing the limits of what we take to constitute identity, language, and understanding. The focus of this chapter will be on two of Artaud's later texts, which pose most compelling problems of readability and translation: the aforementioned *Artaud le Mômo* and the radio play *Pour en finir avec le jugement de Dieu*.

The asylum of Rodez: translation therapy and electroshock treatment

The mysterious syllables made their first appearance in Artaud's writing during his nine years of internment, and in particular at the asylum of Rodez, where Artaud was under the care of the friend and psychiatrist of the Surrealists, doctor Gaston Ferdière, from 1943 to 1946. Here, Artaud underwent a two-fold therapy programme, which conjoined art-therapy (with a strong focus on translation) and electroshock treatment.

As part of his art-therapy, Artaud was encouraged to translate a series of short texts from English: three texts by Lewis Carroll, a poem by Robert Southwell, and a poem by Edgar Allan Poe.[4] Translation was chosen as a therapeutic activity to return Artaud to writing and to a sense of self: he was believed to have lost his identity along with the ability to write, during a breakdown he suffered in 1937 in Ireland, which had led to his internment and to the adoption of a series of alternate names (among which, Antonin Nalpas, J.-C., François Salpan, dieu Le Néant, Arland Antoneo, Antoneo Arlanapulos). To the extent that translation constitutes a mediating activity that brings into a familiar space words that belong to a foreign language and author, it potentially allows for a rediscovery of one's own language and self. Such a conception of translation rejects the idea of a transparent or passive translator by emphasizing instead the physical dimension of the activity itself.[5]

---

[4] For an in-depth analysis of Artaud's translations see Anne Tomiche, *'L'intraduisible dont je suis fait': Artaud et les avant-gardes occidentales* (Paris: Le Manuscrit, 2012), pp. 41–189.

[5] Gaston Ferdière underscores the importance of the physical dimension of Artaud's therapy: *'La main d'Artaud a dû réapprendre à écrire'* (p. 30, italics in the original). See Ferdière, 'J'ai soigné Antonin Artaud', *La Tour de feu* 136 (1977): 24–33.

In the process, not only did Artaud recover his name, and even claimed for himself authorship of the texts he was translating, but he also invented a new way of using language, the novelty of which consisted of introducing enigmatic syllables within the very fabric of French.[6] While obscure symbols appeared sporadically in his earlier writings, his experimentation with the syllabic clusters became systematic when he began translating and reflecting on translation. More precisely, the syllables emerged, in part, as translations of the nonsense-words found in Carroll's poem 'Jabberwocky', and Artaud conceived of them as belonging to a universal language that everyone could read, despite not speaking it. Artaud claimed to have written an entire book, under the title *Letura d'Eprahi Falli Tetar Fendi Photia o Fotre Indi*, 'dans une langue qui n'était pas le français, mais que tout le monde pouvait lire, à quelque nationalité qu'il appartînt' (*Œuvres* 1015).

This language, which derives from translation, but which is itself untranslatable because, Artaud believed, it does not need to be translated in order to be read, is made up of breath-words.[7] Broadly speaking, these words can be defined in two opposing ways. On the one hand, they appear as strings of vocalic syllables that reproduce the internal rhythm of the speaker's breath flow—'ratara ratara ratara / atara tatara rana' (*Œuvres* 1015); on the other, they present themselves as consonantal blocks that intentionally obstruct such breath flow by impeding vocalization—'brimbulkdriquant', 'rangmbde', 'rouarghambde' (*Œuvres* 922).

Both forms underscore a similar conception of translation: as a deeply physical and intimate activity, that calls into play the breath of the body, either by enhancing the breath's natural rhythms or by consciously interrupting them. Translation, for Artaud, is a living activity that draws him, as a translator, back into his breathing body; and it does so by temporarily suspending his ability to use language in its conventional forms. The space opened up for Artaud by translation is thus complex: it is both a verbal and a non-verbal place, where vocalic incantations coexist with consonant clusters; here, the breath flow of the body is compromised by the impending risk of its interruption, and the voice is under the constant threat of being silenced.

The second aspect of Ferdière's therapy programme, electroshock treatment, offers a similar experience of interruption, or suspension, of both linguistic practices and physical awareness. Electroshocks function by inducing a temporary coma in patients, in order to 'reset' their brain patterns and personalities. Artaud refers to the coma as Bardo, the transitional state between death and rebirth in Tibetan Buddhism, of which he identifies three effects: physically, the electric currents cause bone damage and leave the patients with a skewed perception of their bodies; psychologically, the coma erases entire chunks of the patient's

---

[6] Artaud went as far as accusing Carroll, anachronistically, of plagiarizing him (*Œuvres* 1015).

[7] Artaud coins the expression 'mot à soufflets' (*Œuvres* 922) in relation to Carroll's portmanteau words, but the connotation of breath-word can be extended to refer to his own invented syllables (see Gilles Deleuze's term 'mots-souffles' in *Logique du sens* [Paris: Minuit, 1969], p. 108, and Tomiche's analysis of the image of the bellows, *'L'intraduisible dont je suis fait'*, pp. 96–105).

memory, either temporarily or permanently; and linguistically, patients suffer aphasic regression, producing gibberish or infantile babble.[8] These descriptions unequivocally depict an experience of loss of integrity, in which the self is separated from itself and from language. This is because the coma into which the patient falls ruptures the individual's sense of self; and if the patient is lucky enough to return from that state, which is not guaranteed, he is aware of forever having lost large parts of himself.[9]

Despite his widespread and vehement denunciation of the treatment, Artaud ascribes to the shocks the benefit of having returned him to his name and to self-mastery. In a letter to Ferdière, he writes, 'j'ai subi ces derniers temps une secousse terrible mais *salutaire*; et maintenant qu'elle est passée je me sens retrouver la maîtrise de moi [...] Je m'appelle Antonin Artaud' (italics in the original).[10] Such a statement of health should, however, be taken with caution: we must not forget that Artaud was repeatedly pleading with his doctors to stop administering electroshocks and, therefore, the 'recovery' of his name might be a gesture to appease his doctors' conception of what constitutes health.

Whether or not this is the case (and we shall return to this question), Artaud's comment introduces complexity to the experience of electroshock treatment, one that mirrors the complexity that characterizes the space of translation. Just as, in that space, the breath of life is menaced by its extinction because of the co-presence of magical syllables and consonant clusters, so is the state produced by electroshocks defined by a tension between the threat of total dissolution and absolute recovery (however we understand the term recovery in this context). Both translation and electroshock treatment produce what we might call a state of suspension: the translator, in moving between source and target language, must temporarily enter into a limbo space in which both languages coexist but neither is dominant; in the coma induced by electroshocks, the patient is held in balance between life and death, before being brought back to his senses (in both senses of the term).

Both experiences shed light on that moment in which the relationship between self and language is undefined, that moment before language emerges as the primary tool for expressing the self and where the awareness of one's physicality takes precedence over language in the process of understanding. In a different context, we might say that such an experience resembles the infant's tentative first contact with words, which, in moving him into the symbolic order, constitutes both a gain and a loss: it opens up the possibility of thought and communication, at the expense, perhaps, of bodily and sensory communion.

---

[8] For a detailed analysis of the physical, psychological, and linguistic effects of electroshock treatment, see Florence de Mèredieu, *Sur l'électrochoc: le cas Antonin Artaud* (Paris: Blusson, 1996), pp. 133–48, 181–203.

[9] 'Qui a passé par l'électro-choc du Bardo, et le Bardo de l'électro-choc, ne remonte plus jamais de ses ténèbres, et la vie a baissé d'un cran' (Artaud, *Œuvres* 1139).

[10] Artaud, *Nouveaux écrits de Rodez* (Paris: Gallimard, 1997), p. 59.

Having lived through these states of suspension, Artaud begins to formulate ways of retrieving something of the experience from before the rupture induced by language-acquisition. The linguistic idiosyncrasies that he develops could be understood as attempts to recover a pre-verbal sense of self in a verbal world, with a concomitant change in bodily perception. And because such attempts are made after language has been acquired, the form that this language takes is an amalgam of French and invented syllables, both translatable and not translated. Such a language not only redefines the way in which the self can be expressed in language, but it also sheds light on what is at stake in asking what it means to translate someone.

Recovering a pre-verbal self in a verbal world: *Artaud le Mômo*

Significantly, it is through the figure of a child-cum-madman that Artaud recounts his return to consciousness and language in *Artaud le Mômo*; and he does so in a language that moves between melodious babble, articulate French, and unpronounceable guttural sounds.

This dynamic is most obvious in the first of the five texts that the work comprises, 'Le retour d'Artaud, le Mômo'. The most striking characteristic of this text is the way in which sound interacts with content and how both are offset by the syllabic blocks that interrupt them. The poem begins with a strong insistence on the /u/ sound, which punctuates most of the lines: 'onoure', 'ou-ou', 'anavou' (*Œuvres* 1123), 'mou', 'fou', 'genoux', 'trou', 'partout' (*Œuvres* 1124), 'fout', 'itou', 'roues', 'tout', 'où' (*Œuvres* 1125). As the text progresses, this closed and sombre sound gives way to the more open sound /e/: 'enterré', 'cheminée', 'tué', 'encadrer', 'nez', 'renifler', 'serré', 'miserere', 'années', 'inné', 'né' (*Œuvres* 1128). The movement from closed to open sounds has the physical effect of lowering the position of the tongue and bringing it forward, while opening the lips. The opening and outward movement mirrors the content of the poem, which evokes the death of old Artaud—'Le vieil Artaud / est enterré' (*Œuvres* 1128)—and the birth of a new one, 'le Mômo'.

Conversely, the syllabic clusters move in the opposite direction, from fluid vocalization to consonantal blockage. The opening strings of syllables are rhythmical and melodious:

> o dedi
> a dada orzoura
> o dou zoura
> a dada skizi

> o kaya
> o kaya pontoura
> o ponoura
> a pena
> poni

(*Œuvres* 1123, bold in the original)

The second block is similarly readable, albeit dominated by guttural sounds:

> ge re ghi
> regheghi
> geghena
> e reghena
> a gegha
> riri

(*Œuvres* 1126, bold in the original)

But the final section comprises clusters that pose a significant challenge to readability:

> menendi anenbi
> embenda
> tarch inemptle
> o marchti rombi
> tarch paiolt
> a tinemptle
> orch pendui
> o patendi
> a merchit
> orch torpch
> ta urchpt orchpt
> ta tro taurch
> campli
> ko ti aunch
> a ti aunch
> aungbli

(*Œuvres* 1128–9, bold in the original)

This constitutes a movement towards unreadability; or, more precisely, these clusters are unreadable for French speakers because they do not correspond to the phonological rules of French.

In showing the limitations of French phonology, the syllables reveal the existence of a pre-verbal space in which all possible sounds coexist, the space in which infants experiment with a multiplicity of sounds before settling on those of the mother tongue. In such a way then, these clusters might be retroactively broadening the spectrum of sound possibilities; and perhaps, the progressive silencing of our voice that occurs in the last block, in revealing to us how limited we are in the sounds we can produce as adults, encourages us to question such limitation.

The content of Artaud's text confirms these hypotheses. The entire poem circles around the problem of definition and delimitation: Artaud alerts us to our persistent drive to divide the world into categories and to make judgements about those divisions. Writing of himself, 'Il est ce trou sans cadre / que la vie voulut encadrer' (*Œuvres* 1128), he evokes his lifelong battle against all forms of judgement, especially those that establish the categories of madness and sanity and lead to incarceration. But, to what extent is it possible to resist definition and remain in an in-between state of suspension? Furthermore, is such a position at all desirable?[11]

Artaud offers a consideration of these questions in the following section of the poem, which comes immediately after the second block of syllables:

> Entre le cu et la chemise,
> entre le foutre et l'infra-mise,
> entre le membre et le faux bond,
> entre la membrane et la lame,
> entre la latte et le plafond,
> entre le sperme et l'explosion,
> tre l'arête et tre le limon,
>
> entre le cu et la main mise
>   de tous
> sur la trappe à haute pression
> d'un râle d'éjaculation
> n'est pas un point
> ni une pierre
>
> éclatée morte au pied d'un bond
>
> ni le membre coupé d'une âme
> (l'âme n'est plus qu'un vieux dicton)

---

[11] Artaud associates his illness with a state of suspension: 'Il y a donc un quelque chose qui détruit ma pensée; un quelque chose qui ne m'empêche pas d'être ce que je pourrais être, mais qui me laisse, si je puis dire, en suspens' (*Œuvres* 73).

> mais l'atterrante suspension
> d'un souffle d'aliénation

> (*Œuvres* 1126)

These lines distill the essence of the tension we have been examining between limbo and recovery, here described as a movement of suspension and fall. The repetition of the term 'entre' and the reference to a 'suspension d'un souffle' illustrate the state of limbo; in coming out of that state, we are brought down to earth, while still suspended (in the oxymoronic figure of the 'atterrante suspension') by a breath that is both alienating and coming from a place of alienation. Indeed, the infusion of breath that is necessary to give life to the syllables, by returning us to our bodies, alienates us from language—or, from a conception of language that separates it from the body that speaks it. As a result, we come to question the very judgement that defines what constitutes 'alienation' and what does not, in order, ultimately, to reach a state in which we can be done with judgement.

At this point, Artaud embraces the term 'aliéné'. Emerging out of the electro-shock-induced coma, he must choose between two impossible alternatives: 'il fallut choisir entre renoncer à être homme ou devenir un aliéné évident' (*Œuvres* 1140). Artaud does not offer an answer to this alternative, but rather, concludes with an open-ended question followed by syllabic clusters:

> Mais quelle garantie les aliénés évidents de ce monde ont-ils d'être soignés par d'authentiques vivants?
>
> **farfadi**
> **ta azor**
> **tau ela**
> **auela**
> **a**
> **tara**
> **ila**   (*Œuvres* 1140, bold in the original)

Leaving the question open, and ending with these open-sounding syllables, is intended not only to redefine the process of judging between man and madman but also to undermine our attachment to the meanings of such words—or, more precisely, 'mettre en retrait les paroles verbales auxquelles une valeur spéciale a voulu être attribuée' (*Œuvres* 1140). The sidelining of words to which Artaud refers here is achieved by maintaining a tension between words and breath-syllables, between translation and non-translation, in order to suspend our ability to judge. And because translation is, essentially, an activity based on judgement—to the extent that translating involves a meticulous process of choosing between different possibilities, casting aside infinite variants—understanding how Artaud proposes to be done with judgement brings us closer to understanding what it might mean to translate Artaud.

To be done with judgement: from syllables to screams

Artaud addresses the problem of judgement in his last work, the radio play *Pour en finir avec le jugement de Dieu*, by showing what happens when breath-words break into screams.[12] The play consists of five texts, read by four people—Artaud, Maria Casarès, Roger Blin, and Paule Thévenin; each text is followed by sound effects, consisting of xylophonic sounds, drums, and screams. This structure establishes a shift between voices and sounds, similar to the dialogue between correct French and invented syllables that we saw in 'Le retour d'Artaud, le Mômo'. Yet, in the play, the alternating structure takes on a particular form: the texts, which are written in the first person singular and which ostensibly express Artaud's 'je', are spoken by a variety of voices (men and women), whereas the screams belong only to Artaud. This feature is significant: while the 'je' is an empty linguistic cypher that can be inhabited by anyone, the scream of the body can be vocalized only by Artaud. Moreover, the only syllabic clusters that appear in the play are read by Roger Blin. If we thought that the syllables were the mark of Artaud's 'emotive' presence, we realize that they can be embodied by whom-ever breathes them into life.

This difference is fundamental: the syllables maintain the possibility of dia-logue because they are inserted within a readable text that makes room for the breath rhythms of the body; conversely, the screams destroy such a possibility because they shock us entirely out of language. Indeed, the scream is the mani-festation of the body in its rawest form, and the effect that it has on the listener is equally physical: hearing someone else's scream produces an animalistic, instinct-ual reaction, which lays bare the limitations of verbal response.

In finding ourselves in this position, we come close to experiencing the painful return to language that Artaud relives through translation and electroshock treat-ment. As such, the radio play produces a 'shock in reverse' in its listeners because it places them in the position of having to re-emerge into language, without knowing what form such a re-emergence can take or whether it is even possible. Consequently, the very possibility of communication is called into question—or, at least, a form of communication that is based on conventional linguistic practices.

---

[12] On the topic of judgement, language, and the body, see Gilles Deleuze, 'Pour en finir avec le jugement' in *Critique et clinique* (Paris: Minuit, 1993), pp. 158–69. The importance of the scream for Artaud is already visible in his first publication, *Correspondance avec Jacques Rivière*, which includes a poem entitled 'Cri' (*Œuvres* 74).

Artaud's comment on translation reveals the significance of this very issue. And it does so in its formulation: in asking not if he can be translated but if he will 'accept' to be translated, Artaud foregrounds the structure of exchange in language (and in translation) by placing himself in the position of recipient (if we take the term 'accept' to imply receiving or taking from another).[13] Yet, Artaud casts doubt on the functioning of that very structure in his answer: 'Je ne sais pas' (*Œuvres* 1147). Such a non-answer is but another way of placing himself, and us as readers and translators, in a state of suspension, between affirmation and negation. Here, we are brought to question the relationship between language, self, and others as interlocutors. But, most significantly, in interrupting our reliance on verbal communication, Artaud's comment turns our attention to the physical dimension inherent in communication, thereby leading us to view the body differently.

In disrupting linguistic practices, Artaud also changes the way in which the body is perceived. If his treatment of language is guided by the need to recover non-verbal modes of communication in a verbal world, his description of the body displays a similar need to recover a non-mediated connection with his self—and through that, with the outside world—which depends primarily on physical movement and breath rhythms. *Pour en finir avec le jugement de Dieu* proposes such a change, subjecting the body to an anatomical reworking, in the image of 'un corps sans organes' (*Œuvres* 1654).[14]

Man's new body

The process of anatomical transformation begins in the text read by Paule Thévenin, entitled 'La question se pose de...', where the body's physicality is set against the idealization of language. The text is structured as a series of questions (about the universe, consciousness, infinity, nothingness) to which the answer is provided in the form of the refrain, 'Nous ne le savons pas'. Our condition of not-knowing, once again foregrounded, is related to the fact that our questions are composed of strings of words, and, as Artaud explains, words are invented for the purpose of defining and delimiting things—'c'étaient des mots / inventés pour définir des choses' (*Œuvres* 1649). As such, knowledge is impossible, because it fails to take into account that element that escapes linguistic definition—the body

---

[13] Despite a marked tendency towards linguistic self-enclosure, the desire for exchange informs Artaud's entire production, from his first publication, an epistolary dialogue, to his post-Rodez language, which resists locking itself into its own idiolect by tenaciously holding onto French—'Il faut vaincre le français sans le quitter' (*Œuvres complètes*, XXII 13).

[14] It is significant that the change in perception of the body is brought about by the radio, an art form that entails both bodily disappearance and bodily transformation. See Allen S. Weiss, 'Radio Icons, Short Circuits, Deep Schisms', *TDR* 40.3 (Autumn 1996): 9–15 (p. 12).

and, with it, physical pain. The body's painful presence supplants the idea and the words that attempt to define it, through its explosive affirmation:

> C'est qu'on me pressait
> jusqu'à mon corps
> et jusqu'au corps
>
> **et c'est alors**
> **que j'ai tout fait éclater**
> **parce qu'à mon corps**
> **on ne touche jamais.**
>
> (*Œuvres* 1652, bold in the original)

This destructive gesture corresponds to the Mômo's resistance to all forms of delimitation and definition, which, as we have seen, constitutes the impulse behind Artaud's linguistic innovations. But, as in that context such fragmentation was counterbalanced by the impulse to recover a perceived lost whole, here, Artaud's rejection of the imposition of bodily limits takes the form of a proposal to remake man's anatomy.

This proposal appears in the last section of the radio play, which is structured as a dialogue between two voices: one that asks Artaud what the purpose of the broadcast is, and whose line of inquiry is punctuated by accusations of madness—'Vous délirez, monsieur Artaud. Vous êtes fou' (*Œuvres* 1653)—and another that explains the benefits of the work while refuting those accusations word for word—'Je ne délire pas. Je ne suis pas fou' (*Œuvres* 1653). In negotiating his way within such a dialogic structure, which imposes and refutes definitions of madness, Artaud explains that remaking man's anatomy is the only way to be done with judgement:

En le faisant passer une fois de plus mais la dernière sur la table d'autopsie pour lui refaire son anatomie.

Je dis, pour lui refaire son anatomie.

L'homme est malade parce qu'il est mal construit.

Il faut se décider à le mettre à nu pour lui gratter cet animalcule qui le démange mortellement,

> dieu,
>
> et avec dieu
>
> ses organes.

Car liez-moi si vous le voulez,

mais il n'y a rien de plus inutile qu'un organe.

Lorsque vous lui aurez fait un corps sans organes,

alors vous l'aurez délivré de tous ses automatismes et rendu à sa véritable liberté.

Alors vous lui réapprendrez à danser à l'envers

comme dans le délire des bals musette

et cet envers sera son véritable endroit.   (*Œuvres* 1654)

These lines reveal the extent to which the image of the 'body without organs' is complementary to the reworking of language we have been examining. The makeover that Artaud calls for is inherently tied up with language and with the body that speaks it, in two ways. Firstly, the insertion of 'Je dis' in the iteration of the expression 'pour lui refaire son anatomie' suggests that the process of physical recreation occurs in language or as the result of speaking: as Artaud is working on his language, renewing the forms that such a language can take, the body's anatomy is being equally reworked and renewed.[15] Secondly, this renewed anatomy emerges through a dialogue of voices that are discussing the validity of definitions of terms such as madness and delirium; and, in such a form, it is presented as the only tool that can destroy the system of judgement that allows for those very discussions to take place.

If we take a step further in drawing a parallel between the renewal of language and the restructuring of the body we could suggest the following. According to Artaud, language is ailing because it is a faulty construction, as it relies on the articulations of grammar and the system of judgement that defines the meanings of words and cuts up the world according to those meanings. Similarly, the body is ailing because it is badly constructed, as it depends on the articulation of organs, which are self-sufficient entities, governed by automatic reflexes and equally determined by structures of judgement in the form of filter mechanisms.[16] Artaud's attack on organs mirrors his practice of destabilizing words: removing organs is the counterpart to the insertion of breath-syllables.[17] And, if the integrity of French is undermined while being simultaneously maintained, the functioning of the body is similarly retained: through the movement of dance.

---

[15] The possibility of anatomical renewal is complicated by the presence of the autopsy table, because the purpose of an autopsy is to discover the cause of death, not to propose a new body. However, Artaud notes that this process occurs 'une fois de plus', suggesting that death and anatomical rebirth are not incompatible with one another. This might refer to the artificial death induced by electroshock treatment, from which the patient emerges physically and psychologically altered.

[16] Artaud's evocative image becomes richer when we consider the different uses of the term 'organs': they are 'tools' (from the Greek *organon*), self-contained parts of the organism that have a specific vital function; the term also refers to a musical instrument with pipes sounded by compressed air and it can also be used to refer to a person's voice. This complexity shows that the 'body without organs' is used suggestively to think through concepts of identity, selfhood, and language rather than being tied exclusively to experiences of bodily dissolution induced by electroshock treatment or characteristic of certain forms of mental illness.

[17] On the relationship between the disarticulation of language and the organ-less body, see Gilles Deleuze, 'Du schizophrène et de la petite fille' in *Logique du sens*, pp. 101–14, subsequently developed in his famous recuperation of Artaud's image of the 'body without organs'.

Dance, movement, and translation

Dance conjoins physical movement, breath flow, and rhythm; and because it replaces words with gesture and movement, it provides the ideal place for recovering a mode of communication that precedes the acquisition of verbal language.

Yet, Artaud's point is more complex. Firstly, he notes that we are learning to dance *again*, thereby suggesting that we are recovering the knowledge of something we once had, but which has been lost. Secondly, we are relearning a very particular kind of dance, namely, dancing the wrong way round ('à l'envers'). Returning to this knowledge allows us to find our rightful place, which is also described as the right way up ('l'endroit'). The image Artaud uses here hinges on the double meaning of the term 'endroit', which means both 'the right side' and 'place': dancing the wrong way round allows us to find the right place and, in the process, the wrong way round becomes the right way up.[18]

Here we come to the crux of the argument: dancing the wrong way round is the way of suspending judgement; this is because it becomes impossible to distinguish between the two positions, as what is wrong has taken the place of what is right, in putting man in his rightful place. Thus we can no longer judge what is right and what is wrong because these words cease to have the distinct meanings that we attribute to them. Just as the ties of grammar are being undone by breath-syllables, the knots of automatism that are responsible for tying down the body are being undone by the delirium of dance movements. Playing with the terms 'lier' and 'délire', Artaud reveals the therapeutic function of dance: between the 'délire' of dance, that undoes ties by moving off the right path (from its etymology *de-* 'away' + *lira* 'ridge'), and the accusation of madness ('fou à lier'), that leads to being physically tied up, words are emptied of the meanings that we ascribe to them; and dancing becomes the instrument through which we can be done with judgement.[19]

In the postscript added to the published version of the radio play Artaud elaborates on the importance of dance, underscoring its therapeutic role in relation to man's inability to comprehend:

> Le théâtre et la danse du chant,
> sont le théâtre des révoltes furieuses
> de la misère du corps humain

---

[18] Compare the following two renditions into English: 'Then you will teach him again to dance wrong side out / as in the frenzy of dance halls / and this wrong side out will be his real place' (Artaud, *Antonin Artaud: Selected Writings*, trans. Weaver, ed. Sontag, p. 571); 'Then you will teach him again to dance inside out / as in the delirium of dance halls / and that inside out will be his true side out' (Artaud, *Watchfiends and Rack Screams*, trans. Eshleman, p. 307).

[19] We must note that Artaud retains the vocabulary of judgement in explaining this process: the expression 'se décider à' indicates that remaking man's anatomy is the result of a decision, which is a judgement. However, because the language in the play is punctuated by screams, and because screams undermine our ability to think and express ourselves in language, our ability to make judgements is also being undone.

devant les problèmes qu'il ne pénètre pas
ou dont le caractère passif,

> spécieux,
> ergotique,
> impénétrable,
> inévident
> l'excède.

Alors il danse
par blocs de
KHA, KHA

(Œuvres 1662)

Dance, along with theatre and song, are conjoined responses to the intractability of unresolvable problems. But the dance that is being called for is not based on fluid movement; rather, it is described through the staccato movement of the repetition of the syllable 'KHA', which produces a rapid expulsion and inhalation of breath.[20]

In qualifying as 'KHA, KHA' the steps according to which dance occurs, Artaud suggests two things. Firstly, he reverses the assumption that dance is an activity associated with the realm of the ideal because he relates dance to faecality, as is evident in the homonym 'caca'. In this way, dance operates the same kind of displacement of words and their meanings that Artaud achieves with the insertion of breath-syllables into French. This leads to the second point: Artaud's spelling of 'KHA' consists of adding an 'h' (or, a breath) to the term Ka, which refers to the Egyptian conception of the soul. Ka is the immortal spirit that lives on after the death of the body, of which it constitutes the double. By referring to this concept, Artaud associates dance with cycles of life and death, and with notions of afterlife and survival. In this respect, dance provides another perspective on those in-between states that Artaud experiences through translation and electroshock treatment, both of which negotiate complex relationships to death and survival.

Artaud's insistence on the importance of movement and dance for his modifications of both language and body has significant implications for his understanding of translation because, at its core, translation is an act of movement, by which something is carried over from one language to another. The interrupted movement of dance, as proposed by Artaud, ties man to the basest of his bodily functions (via the reference to 'caca'); yet, it also positions man in his rightful

---

[20] The syllable makes its first appearance, in relation to bodily breath, in Artaud's text 'Un athlétisme affectif' in *Le Théâtre et son double (Œuvres* 585). Artaud's work on theatre is essential for contextualizing the invented syllables within the broader context of his poetic programme, but an in-depth analysis of *Le Théâtre et son double* lies outside the scope of this chapter.

place ('son véritable endroit'). As such, it affects language and thought automatisms, in order, ultimately, to undo the very structures by which judgements can be made. Translation, then, as a movement between languages that depends upon judgements in order to produce the translated work, becomes an impossible task; but because translation opens up a space, both verbal and non-verbal, where Artaud can reconnect with his breathing body, it becomes a necessary practice for recovering a lost sense of wholeness. We are thus faced with a tension between the impossibility to translate and the need for translation.

Translation and non-translation

Perhaps one way of thinking about this tension is by looking more carefully at the context in which Artaud's comment on translation appears. This is a letter to the artist Hans Hartung, on the topic of illustrating *Artaud le Mômo*. Artaud was addressing the publisher's request that the work be illustrated, and refused that anybody other than himself illustrate his works:

> Je ne peux souffrir qu'on *illustre* mes oeuvres,
>
> qu'un autre que moi les raconte. Et accepterai-je d'être traduit?
>
> Je ne sais pas.
>
> Et puis Mr. Archtung, je *dessine*.
>
> Je veux dire que je ne dessine pas mais qu'à côté de ce que j'écris, je fais des figures qui ne sont pas des mots mais des barres non des ombres.
>
> Ce que je fais est trop près de moi, trop intime.
>
> Je n'accepterai pas que quelqu'un chie avec moi quand je chie, se lave la queue dans le même bidet que moi.—
>
> Ainsi en est-il de mes écrits.
>
> Ils ne quitteront plus mon for intérieur et un autre que moi ne peut intervenir dans leur manifestation.   (*Œuvres* 1147, italics in the original)

Artaud depicts, here, a very intimate setting, where drawing is inseparable from writing, and both are located deep within Artaud's innermost being.[21] Significantly, the notebooks Artaud used during his internment display an intensely material

---

[21] Artaud explains the importance of drawing in his later works, writing in 1947 that 'depuis un certain jour d'octobre 1939 je n'ai jamais plus écrit sans non plus dessiner' and describing his drawings as 'des gestes, un verbe, une grammaire, une arithmétique, une Kabbale entière' (*Œuvres* 1513). For Ferdière, drawing is as important as writing in Artaud's therapy: '*La main d'Artaud a dû réapprendre à écrire* [...] *La main d'Artaud a dû réapprendre à dessiner*' ('J'ai soigné Antonin Artaud', pp. 30–1, italics in the original).

approach to writing: handwritten words are obscured by scribbles and drawings, cigarette burns and marks on the page, all of which testify to the physical presence of their creator (but which are typically whitewashed from the published versions). It is understandable, therefore, that Artaud would reject an external illustrator for his works, as he considers them to be, to a certain extent, already illustrated.

Conversely, Artaud leaves open the possibility of being translated. There is something about translation that Artaud allows. Perhaps its nature as movement, but a movement that does not bring the original work into the target language and, thereby, away from Artaud's 'for intérieur'; nor one that invites the translator into that intimate place, which, as he states, cannot be shared with anyone else. Rather, translation opens up a space between the 'for intérieur', where his writings are located, and the 'manifestation' of that internal space, through which judgement is suspended.

Such a conception of translation is atypical, because it precludes not only the production of a translated work but also the notion of an original text to be translated, thus implying a refusal on Artaud's part even to publish. Yet, we must not forget that Artaud not only accepts to be published but also actively pursues publication—from his first attempts to interest Jacques Rivière in his poetry for the *Nouvelle revue française* to the numerous letters he sent from Rodez inquiring about the status of his publications.

This tension, between the desire to publish and the refusal to externalize his works, reveals a concern with writing and identity that situates Artaud's reflection on translation within a broader context. In the aforementioned letter to Ferdière, the 'salutary' shock that returns him to his name and to self-mastery is inseparable from his works: 'Je m'appelle Antonin Artaud [...] et c'est sous le nom d'Antonin Artaud que j'ai signé tous mes livres', a statement immediately followed by the list of all his published works, complete with publication details.[22] Here, health is associated with a name, attached to a publication. Yet, Artaud's formulation is significant: in the speech act of 'calling' himself Antonin Artaud and signing his books 'under that name', he is pointing towards a separation between work and being that, as we have seen, runs counter to his entire project.

We cannot, therefore, take Artaud's statement of health at face value: while Artaud's recovery of his name might be hailed by his doctors (and by himself, writing to his doctors) as a triumph, the solidification that such a recovery implies, via its association with the published work, creates a rupture in the being that produces it and is experienced as a loss of self.[23] Artaud's admission of

---

[22] Artaud, *Nouveaux écrits de Rodez*, p. 59–60.

[23] Artaud notes that the work, when separated from the body that produces it, amounts to nothing more than excremental waste: 'Ce que vous avez pris pour mes œuvres n'était que les déchets de moi-même, ces raclures de l'âme que l'homme normal n'accueille pas' (*Œuvres* 163). On the connection between work and excrement, see Jacques Derrida, 'La parole soufflée', in *L'écriture et la différence* (Paris: Seuil, 1967), pp. 253–92 (pp. 270–3).

recovery suggests that identity, by fixing a name and producing works attached to that name, is in itself a form of sickness rather than a symbol of man's health, because it separates the work from the living being that gives life to it; and, in so doing, it reduces that living being to an inert name on a page.[24]

Here we understand the full significance of Artaud's renewed language and reconstructed body. Artaud's breath-words and organ-less body function through disarticulation in order to break down our attachment to structures of meaning and categories of thought, both of which separate the world into distinct parts and subject those parts to the stultifying power of judgement. This practice of disarticulation undermines a conception of health that is founded upon the creation of stable identities and that relies on individual names. In so doing, Artaud's programme to be done with judgement is profoundly vital and life-affirming: in its insistence on breath, movement, and dance, it releases the cry of life in its purest form, unfettered by verbal language and the strictures of thought.

Translation, for Artaud, participates in this vitality. Because of its nature as movement, translation opens up the possibility of displacement of both language and identity: it offers an alternate language for the original to move into and it blurs individual authorship by positioning the name of the translator alongside that of the author. In asking whether he will accept to be translated, but not rejecting that possibility, Artaud is revealing and retaining the relational dynamic inherent in translation: a movement that is between self and other, between language and body, both verbal and non-verbal.

Significantly, this movement must be maintained. This requires that the task of translation not be accomplished, because its completion would imply the production of the translated text, in the target language, separate from the 'for intérieur' where lies the original, which cannot be plied away from Artaud's living body. Such a conception of translation is inherently founded upon a practice of non-translation because Artaud does not allow for his writing to leave his 'for intérieur'. This explains why translators typically do not translate Artaud's syllables: not translating the syllables opens up a space for the true work of translating Artaud to begin, in the form of a movement, both verbal and non-verbal, of connection with bodily breath.

Reflecting on translation reveals the stakes of Artaud's endeavour—his battle against all forms of judgement, through the bodily movement of dance, which returns man to a pre-verbal self in a verbal world and liberates him from automatisms. At the same time, however, Artaud's project redefines how we think about

---

[24] This not only explains Artaud's tendency to reject his name and replace it with others (from his first publication—'Je ne tiens pas à signer les lettres de mon nom' [*Œuvres* 79]—to the flurry of pseudonyms he adopts during the years of his interment), but it also sheds light on the practice of deconstructing his name into its component letters and syllables, at play in many of his syllabic sequences ('ratara' 'atara' 'tatara' [*Œuvres* 1015], 'Les ton aum auda / et non au tou ada / ro et non or' [*Œuvres complètes*, XVIII 261], 'les syllabes de ce vocable: / 'AR-TAU' [*Œuvres* 1420]). In this context, it is also worth noting that Antonin was itself a variant on Artaud's given name, Antoine.

translation itself: it renders us aware of the translative process and of the impossibility of its accomplishment, steering us away from a narrow focus on the product, the translated works, which would be as negligible as Artaud claims the originals to be.[25]

This, in turn, reveals the significance of talking about translating Artaud rather than talking about translating Artaud's works. Translating Artaud cannot be understood as an encounter with the words on the page, which, as we have seen, constitute only one aspect of his physical production. Rather, translating Artaud is a bodily movement that takes us, as readers, but also as viewers, listeners, and breathing beings, into an ever-evolving encounter with another voice and presence, in the process of which we are constantly being moved. For, in translating, we are always, to some extent, translating someone.

---

[25] This conception of translation, in foregrounding the distinction between the process of translating and the product of translation, is akin to Benjamin's characterization of translation as a 'mode' and to his notion of 'translatability', which is independent of whether individual texts are translated or not. In our reading, Artaud takes one step further: translatability can be thought of as relating to the author, independently of whether the original texts are published or not—for, as he notes, 'Si je suis poète ou acteur ce n'est pas pour écrire ou déclamer des poésies, mais pour les vivre' (Œuvres 1019). The problem remains, however, that we encounter Artaud via his published texts and we produce translations of those texts, which, in turn, constitute published works. Despite this reality, the significance of Artaud's reflection on translation is essential not only for getting to the heart of Artaud's project, but also for thinking more deeply about the theoretical stakes of translatability. See Walter Benjamin, 'The Task of the Translator' in Illuminations, ed. Hannah Arendt, trans. Harry Zohn (London: Jonathan Cape, 1970), p. 70.

Bibliography

Abercrombie, Lascelles. 'Colloquial Language in Literature'. Society for Pure English, Tract 36 (Oxford: Oxford University Press, 1931).

Ahearn, Barry. *William Carlos Williams and Alterity: The Early Poems* (Cambridge: Cambridge University Press, 1994).

Aiken, Conrad. 'An Anatomy of Melancholy'. *New Republic* 33 (7 February 1923): 293–5.

Albright, Daniel. 'Modernist Poetic Form'. In *The Cambridge Companion to Twentieth-Century English Poetry*, edited by Neil Corcoran (Cambridge: Cambridge University Press, 2007), pp. 24–41.

Albright, Daniel. *Putting Modernism Together: Literature, Music, and Painting, 1872–1927* (Baltimore, MD: Johns Hopkins University Press, 2015).

Aldington, Richard. 'The Poems of Anyte of Tegea'. *Egoist* II.9 (September 1915): 139–40.

Ames, Keri Elizabeth. 'Joyce's Aesthetic of the Double Negative and His Encounters with Homer's *Odyssey*'. In *Beckett, Joyce and the Art of the Negative*, edited by Colleen Jaurretche (Amsterdam and New York: Rodopi, 2005), pp. 15–48.

Apter, Emily. *The Translation Zone: A New Comparative Literature* (Princeton: Princeton University Press, 2005).

Apter, Emily. *Against World Literature* (London: Verso, 2013).

Arkins, Brian. 'Greek and Roman Themes'. In *James Joyce in Context*, edited by John McCourt (Cambridge: Cambridge University Press, 2010), pp. 239–49.

Armstrong, Rupert H. *A Compulsion for Antiquity: Freud and the Ancient World* (Ithaca, NY: Cornell University Press, 2005).

Arrowsmith, Rupert. *Modernism and the Museum* (Oxford: Oxford University Press, 2011).

Artaud, Antonin. *Œuvres complètes*, 26 vols (Paris: Gallimard, 1956–1994).

Artaud, Antonin. *Antonin Artaud: Selected Writings*, edited by Susan Sontag, translated by Helen Weaver (Berkeley and Los Angeles: University of California Press, 1976).

Artaud, Antonin. *Watchfiends and Rack Screams*, edited and translated by Clayton Eshleman with Bernard Bador (Boston: Exact Change, 1995).

Artaud, Antonin. *Nouveaux écrits de Rodez* (Paris: Gallimard, 1997).

Artaud, Antonin. *Artaud el Momo*, translated by Sara Irwin (Buenos Aires: Need, 1998).

Artaud, Antonin. *Œuvres*, edited by Evelyne Grossman (Paris: Gallimard, 2004).

Assmann, Aleida. 'Exorcizing the Demon of Chronology: T. S. Eliot's Reinvention of Tradition'. In *T. S. Eliot and the Concept of Tradition*, edited by Giovanni Cianci and Jason Harding (Cambridge: Cambridge University Press, 2007), pp. 13–25.

Athenaeus, *The Learned Banqueters*, translated by S. Douglas Olson, Loeb Classical Library, Volume V (Cambridge, MA: Harvard University Press, 2009), pp. 276–7.

Auerbach, Erich. *Mimesis: The Representation of Reality in Western Literature*, translated by William Trask (Princeton: Princeton University Press, 1953).

Austin, J. L. *How To Do Things With Words*, edited by J. O. Urmson and Marina Sbisà (Oxford: Oxford University Press, 1976).

Bacigalupo, Massimo. 'Dante'. In *T. S. Eliot in Context*, edited by Jason Harding (Cambridge: Cambridge University Press, 2011), pp. 180–9.

Bakhtin, Mikhail. *The Dialogic Imagination: Four Essays*, translated by Caryl Emerson and Michael Holquist (Austin: University of Texas Press, 1981).

Baron, Scarlett. *'Strandentwining Cable': Joyce, Flaubert, and Intertextuality* (Oxford: Oxford University Press, 2011).

Barry, Iris. 'Exeunt'. *The Future* 2.5 (April 1918): 135–7.

Barthes, Roland. *Writing Degree Zero*, translated by Annette Lavers and Colin Smith (New York: Hill and Wang, 1967).

Beasley, Rebecca. *Ezra Pound and the Visual Culture of Modernism* (Cambridge: Cambridge University Press, 2007).

Beasley, Rebecca. *T. S. Eliot, T. E. Hulme, Ezra Pound: Theorists of Modernist Poetry* (London: Routledge, 2007).

Belluc, Sylvain. 'Language and (Re)creation: Joyce and Nineteenth-Century Philology'. In *James Joyce in the Nineteenth Century*, edited by John Nash (Cambridge: Cambridge University Press, 2013), pp. 168–82.

Benjamin, Walter. 'The Task of the Translator'. In *Illuminations*, edited by Hannah Arendt, translated by Harry Zohn (London: Jonathan Cape, 1970), pp. 69–82.

Benjamin, Walter. 'Die Aufgabe des Übersetzers'. In *Kleine Prosa, Baudelaire-Übertragungen* in *Gesammelte Schriften*, 14 vols (Frankfurt am Main: Suhrkamp, 1972), IV:I, pp. 9–21.

Bing, Peter. *The Scroll and the Marble: Studies in Reading and Reception in Hellenistic Poetry* (Ann Arbor: University of Michigan Press, 2009).

Bollettieri Bosinelli, Rosa Maria. 'Joyce Slipping Across the Borders of English: The Stranger in Language'. *James Joyce Quarterly* 38.3–4 (2001): 395–409.

Bowman, Alan K. et al., eds, *Oxyrhynchus: A City and its Texts* (London: Egyptian Exploration Society, 2007).

Bridge, Helen. 'Duino Elegies: A New Translation with Parallel Text and Commentary (by Martyn Crucefix); Sonnets to Orpheus by (M. D. Herter Norton); Orpheus: A Version of Rilke's Sonette an Orpheus (by Don Paterson)', (review). *Translation and Literature* 16.2 (2007): 258–65.

Brotchie, Alastair, ed. *A True History of the College of 'Pataphysics*, translated by Paul Edwards (London: Atlas, 1995).

Brotchie, Alastair. *Alfred Jarry: A Pataphysical Life* (London: Massachusetts Institute of Technology Press, 2011).

Budelmann, Felix. ed. *The Cambridge Companion to Greek Lyric* (Cambridge: Cambridge University Press, 2009).

Budgen, Frank. *James Joyce and the Making of 'Ulysses'* (London: Grayson and Grayson, 1934).

Bürger, Christa. 'Textanalyse und Ideologiekritik: Rilkes erste Duineser Elegien'. In *Rilkes Duineser Elegien*, 3 vols, edited by Ulrich Fülleborn and Manfred Engel (Frankfurt am Main: Suhrkamp, 1980–82), II, pp. 264–78.

Burnet, John. *Early Greek Philosophy*, 2nd edition (London: Adam and Charles Black, 1908).

Bush, Ronald. *The Genesis of Ezra Pound's 'Cantos'* (Princeton, NJ: Princeton University Press, 1976).

Butler, Christopher. *Early Modernism: Literature, Music and Painting in Europe, 1900–1916* (Oxford: Oxford University Press, 1994).

Butler, Nicholas Murray. *The International Mind: An Argument for the Judicial Settlement of International Disputes* (New York: Scribner's, 1912).

Calvet, Louis-Jean. *Language Wars and Linguistic Politics*, translated by Michel Petheram (Oxford: Oxford University Press, 1998).

Campbell, David. *Greek Lyric* (Cambridge, MA: Harvard University Press, 1990).

Capstick, Minnie. 'Affairs of Moment: Education for the Future'. *The Future* 1.12 (October 1917): 343–4.

Carson, Anne. *If not, winter: Fragments of Sappho* (Croydon: Virago, 2002).

Casanova, Pascale. *The World Republic of Letters*, translated by M. B. DeBevoise (Cambridge, MA: Harvard University Press, 2004).

Casanova, Pascale. 'What Is a Dominant Language? Giacomo Leopardi: Theoretician of Linguistic Inequality', translated by Marlon Jones. *New Literary History* 44.3 (2013): 379–99.

Cavafy, C. P. *C. P. Cavafy: The Collected Poems*, translated by Evangelos Sachperoglou, edited by Anthony Hirst and Peter Mackridge (Oxford: Oxford University Press, 2007).

Charpentier, Henry. 'De Stéphane Mallarmé'. *Nouvelle revue française* 158 (November 1926): 537–45.

Cheadle, Mary Paterson. *Ezra Pound's Confucian Translations* (Ann Arbor: University of Michigan Press, 1997).

Chisholm, A. R. 'Mallarmé: "Ses purs ongles…"'. *French Studies* 6.3 (1952): 230–4.

Chisholm, A. R. 'Mallarmé and the Riddle of the Ptyx'. *AUMLA: Journal of the Australasian Universities Language and Literature Association* 40 (1973): 246–8.

Claudel, Paul. 'La Catastrophe d'Igitur'. *Nouvelle revue française* 158 (November 1926), 531–6.

Cohn, Robert Greer. *Towards the Poems of Mallarmé* (Berkeley: University of California Press, 1965).

Collinge, N. E. 'Gongyla and Mr. Pound'. *Notes and Queries* 203 (June 1958), 265–6.

Compagnon, Antoine. *La Seconde Main: ou Le Travail de la citation* (Paris: Seuil, 1979).

Conley, Tim. *Joyces Mistakes: Problems of Intention, Irony, and Interpretation* (Toronto and London: University of Toronto Press, 2003).

Cope, Jackson I. 'From Egyptian Rubbish-Heaps to "Finnegans Wake"'. *James Joyce Quarterly* 3.3 (1966): 166–70.

Crowley, Tony. *Standard English and the Politics of Language* (London: Palgrave Macmillan, 2003).

Crowley, Tony. *Wars of Words: The Politics of Language in Ireland 1537–2004* (Oxford: Oxford University Press, 2005).

Curtius, Ernst Robert. 'T. S. Eliot and Germany', translated by Richard March. In *T. S. Eliot: A Symposium*, edited by Richard March and Tambimuttu (London: Poetry London, 1948), pp. 119–25.

Curtius, Ernst Robert. 'T. S. Eliot'. In *Essays on European Literature*, translated by Michael Kowal (Princeton: Princeton University Press, 1973), pp. 355–99.

Cuvigny, Hélène. 'The Finds of Papyri: The Archaeology of Papyrology'. In *The Oxford Handbook of Papyrology*, edited by Roger S. Bagnall (Oxford: Oxford University Press, 2009), pp. 30–58.

Dante Alighieri, *The Divine Comedy*, translated by Laurence Binyon (London: Agenda, 1979).

Daumal, René. *Pataphysical Essays*, translated by Thomas Vosteen (Cambridge, MA: Wakefield, 2012).

Daumal, René and Julien Torma. *Pataphysical Letters*, translated by Dennis Duncan and Terry Hale (London: Atlas, 2012).

Davie, Donald. 'T. S. Eliot: The End of an Era'. In *The Poet in the Imaginary Museum*, edited by Barry Alpert (Manchester: Carcanet, 1977), pp. 32–41.

Deleuze, Gilles. *Logique du sens* (Paris: Minuit, 1969).

Deleuze, Gilles. *Critique et clinique* (Paris: Minuit, 1993).

Deleuze, Gilles and Félix Guattari. *Toward a Minor Literature*, translated by Dona Polan (Minneapolis: University of Minnesota Press, 1986).

Delgano, Emily. *Virginia Woolf and the Migrations of Language* (Cambridge: Cambridge University Press, 2011).

Derrida, Jacques. *L'écriture et la différence* (Paris: Seuil, 1967).

Derrida, Jacques. 'Des Tours de Babel'. In *Difference in Translation*, edited and translated by Joseph F. Graham (Ithaca, NY: Cornell University Press, 1985), pp. 165–207.

Derrida, Jacques. 'Mallarmé', translated by Christine Roulston. In *Acts of Literature*, edited by Derek Attridge (London: Routledge, 1992), pp. 110–26.

Diels, Hermann. *Die Fragmente der Vorsokratiker* (Berlin: Weidmannsche Buchhandlung, 1903).

Doolittle, Hilda [H. D.] 'The Wise Sappho'. In *Notes on Thought and Vision & The Wise Sappho* (San Francisco: City Lights, 1982), p. 69.

Dowling, Linda. *Language and Decadence in the Victorian Fin de Siècle* (Princeton: Princeton University Press, 1986).

Dudley, Dorothy. 'A Small Garden Induced to Grow in Unlikely Circumstances'. *Poetry* 12.1 (April 1918): 38–43.

Edmonds, J. M. 'More Fragments of Sappho'. *The Classical Review* 23.5 (1909): 156–8.

Edwards, Paul. 'Faustroll: Portrait of the Author as a Pataphysician'. In Alfred Jarry, *Three Early Novels*, translated and introduced by Alastair Brotchie, Paul Edwards, Alexis Lykiard, and Simon Watson Taylor (London: Atlas, 2006), pp. 119–26.

Eliot, T. S. 'Preface to the 1928 Edition,' *The Sacred Wood* (London: Faber and Faber, 1928).

Eliot, T. S. *Dante* (London: Faber and Faber, 1929).

Eliot, T. S. *After Strange Gods* (London: Faber and Faber, 1934).

Eliot, T. S. 'The Metaphysical Poets' [1921]. In *Selected* Essays, 3rd edition (London: Faber and Faber, 1951), pp. 281–91.

Eliot, T. S. 'Thoughts After Lambeth' [1931]. In *Selected Essays*, 3rd edition (London: Faber and Faber, 1951), pp. 363–87.

Eliot, T. S. 'The Music of Poetry'. In *On Poetry and Poets* (London: Faber and Faber, 1957), pp. 26–38.

Eliot, T. S. 'The Social Function of Poetry'. In *On Poetry and Poets* (London: Faber and Faber, 1957), pp. 15–25.

Eliot, T. S. 'What is a Classic?'. In *On Poetry and Poets* (London: Faber and Faber, 1957), pp. 53–71.

Eliot, T. S. *Notes towards the Definition of Culture* (London: Faber and Faber, 1962).

Eliot, T. S. *Collected Poems, 1909–1962* (London: Faber and Faber, 1963).

Eliot, T. S. *The Use of Poetry and Use of Criticism* [1933] (London: Faber and Faber, 1964).

Eliot, T. S. *To Criticize the Critic and Other Writings* (London: Faber and Faber, 1965).

Eliot, T. S. *The Waste Land: A Facsimile and Transcript of the Original Drafts*, edited by Valerie Eliot (London: Faber and Faber, 1971).

Eliot, T. S. '*Ulysses*, Order, and Myth' [1923]. In *Selected Prose of T. S. Eliot*, edited by Frank Kermode (London: Faber and Faber, 1975), pp. 175–8.

Eliot, T. S. *The Varieties of Metaphysical Poetry: the Clark Lectures at Trinity College, Cambridge, 1926, and the Turnbull Lectures at the Johns Hopkins University, 1933*, edited by Ronald Schuchard (London: Faber and Faber, 1993).

Eliot, T. S. *The Letters of T. S. Eliot: Volume 1, 1898–1922*, edited by Valerie Eliot and Hugh Haughton (London: Faber and Faber, 2009).

Eliot, T. S. *The Letters of T. S. Eliot: Volume 5, 1930–31*, edited by John Haffenden (London: Faber and Faber, 2014).

Eliot, T. S. *The Poems of T. S. Eliot*, 2 vols, edited by Christopher Ricks and Jim McCue (London: Faber and Faber/Baltimore: John Hopkins University Press, 2015).

Eliot, T. S. 'Preface to *Anabasis*'. In *The Complete Prose of T. S. Eliot: The Critical Edition, Volume 4, English Lion, 1930–33*, edited by Jason Harding and Ronald Schuchard (Baltimore: Johns Hopkins University Press, 2015), pp. 132–7.

Ellmann, Richard. *James Joyce*, rev. edn (Oxford: Oxford University Press, 1982).

Empson, William. *Seven Types of Ambiguity* (Harmondsworth: Penguin, 1995).

Erlich, Victor. *Russian Formalism: History, Doctrine* (The Hague: Mouton, 1965).

Ettlinger, Sigrid. Letter to the editor. *The Future* 2.6 (May 1918): 171.

Fang, Achilles. 'A Note on Pound's "Papyrus"'. *Modern Language Notes* 67.3 (March 1952): 188–90.

Ferdière, Gaston. 'J'ai soigné Antonin Artaud'. *La Tour de feu* 136 (1977): 24–33.

Fischer, Luke. *The Poet as Phenomenologist: Rilke and the New Poems* (London: Bloomsbury, 2016).

Flack, Leah Culligan. *Modernism and Homer: The Odysseys of H. D., James Joyce, Osip Mandelstam, and Ezra Pound* (Cambridge: Cambridge University Press, 2015).

Forbes, Nevill. *Word-for-Word Russian Story-Book* (Oxford: Basil Blackwell, 1916).

Formichelli, Jennifer. 'Scenes and Situations in T. S. Eliot's Epigraphs' (PhD Thesis, Cambridge University, 2003).

Forster, E. M. *Pharaohs and Pharillon* (London: Hogarth Press, 1923).

Fowler, Rowena. 'On Not Knowing Greek: The Classics and the Woman of Letters'. *Classical Journal* 78 (1983): 337–49.

Fowler, Rowena. 'Moments and Metamorphoses: Virginia Woolf's Greece'. *Comparative Literature* 51.3 (Summer 1999): 217–42.

Fowler, Rowena. 'Virginia Woolf: Lexicographer'. *English Language Notes* 39 (2002): 54–70.

Fülleborn, Ulrich and Manfred Engel, eds. *Materialien zu Rainer Maria Rilkes 'Duineser Elegien'*, 3 vols (Frankfurt am Main: Suhrkamp, 1982).

Fyodorov, Andrey. *Problema stikhotvornogo perevoda* (Leningrad: Academia, 1927).

Gadamer, Hans-Georg. 'Mythopoietische Umkehrung in Rilkes Duineser Elegien' [1967], in *Gesammelte Werke*, 10 vols (Tübingen: Mohr, 1993), ix, pp. 289–305.

Gallup, Donald. *Ezra Pound: A Bibliography* (Charlottesville: University Press of Virginia, 1983).

Gange, David. *Dialogues with the Dead: Egyptology in British Culture and Religion, 1822–1922* (Oxford: Oxford University Press, 2013).

Gardner, Helen. *The Composition of 'Four Quartets'* (London: Faber & Faber, 1978).

Genette, Gérard. *Paratexts: Thresholds of Interpretation* [1987], translated by Jane E. Lewin (Cambridge: Cambridge University Press, 1997).

Gere, Cathy. *Knossos and the Prophets of Modernism* (Chicago and London: University of Chicago Press, 2009).

[Gerfalk, Axel]. 'Important Notice'. *The Future* 2.2 (January 1918): 29.

[Gerfalk, Axel]. 'The Moving Spirit'. *The Future* 2.3 (February 1918): 46–7.

[Gerfalk, Axel]. 'Notes of the Month', *The Future* 2.4 (March 1918): 80–6.

[Gerfalk, Axel]. 'Notes of the Month', *The Future* 2.5 (April 1918): 110–14.

Ghil, Réné. *Les Dates et les oeuvres: Symbolisme et poésie scientifique* (Paris: Crès, 1923).

Ghim-Lian Chew, Phyllis. *Emergent Lingua Francas and World Orders* (London: Routledge, 2009).

Gifford, Don with Robert J. Seidman. *'Ulysses' Annotated: Notes for James Joyce's 'Ulysses'* (Berkeley and London: University of California Press, 1989).

Gikandi, Simon. *Writing in Limbo: Modernism and Caribbean Literature* (New York: Cornell University Press, 1992).

Glasheen, Adaline. *Third Census of 'Finnegans Wake': An Index of Characters and their Roles* (Berkeley and Los Angeles: University of California Press, 1977).

Gottfried, Roy. 'Berlitz School Days'. *James Joyce Quarterly* 16.3 (1979): 223–38.

[Granville, Charles]. 'Reviews of Books: Modern Languages'. *The Future* 1.2 (December 1916): 64.

[Granville, Charles]. 'Important Announcement: Competitions'. *The Future* 1.3 (January 1917): 79.

[Granville, Charles]. 'Notes'. *The Future* 1.10 (August 1917): 273–6.

[Granville, Charles]. 'Notes'. *The Future* 1.12 (October 1917): 337–40.

[Granville, Charles]. 'Competitions: Our Awards'. *The Future* 2.2 (January 1918): 38.

Graves, Robert. *The Crowning Privilege* (London: Cassell, 1955).

Gregory, Eileen. *H. D. and Hellenism: Classic Lines* (Cambridge: Cambridge University Press, 1997).

Grenfell, B. P. 'Oxyrhynchus and its Papyri'. *Archaeological Report (Egypt Explorations Fund)* (1896–7): 1–12.

Griffiths, G. Rhys. Letter to the editor. *The Future* 2.3 (February 1918): 76.

Guardini, Romano. *Rilke's 'Duino Elegies': An Interpretation*, translated by K. G. Knight (London: Darwen Finlayson, 1961).

Guardini, Romano. 'Rainer Maria Rilkes Zweite Duineser Elegie: Eine Interpretation' [1941]. In *Rilkes Duineser Elegien*, 3 vols, edited by Ulrich Fülleborn and Manfred Engel (Frankfurt am Main: Suhrkamp, 1980–82), ii, pp. 80–104.

Guldin, Rainer. *Translation as Metaphor* (London: Routledge, 2016).

Haas, Albert. 'Souvenirs de la vie littéraire à Paris'. *Les Soirées de Paris* 24 (May 1914): 251–74.

Haas, Robert, ed. *American Poetry: The Twentieth Century: Volume One—Henry Adams to Dorothy Parker* (New York: Library of America, 2000).

Hankey, S. Alers. Letter to the editor. *The Future* 2.2 (January 1918): 43–4.

Hardy, Thomas. *The Variorum Edition of the Complete Poems of Thomas Hardy*, edited by James Gibson (London: Macmillan: 1979).

Hart, Clive. *Structure and Motif in 'Finnegans Wake'* (Evanston, IL: Northwestern University Press, 1962).

Hatim, Basil and Jeremy Munday. *Translation: An Advanced Resource Book* (Abingdon: Routledge, 2004).

Haughton, Hugh. 'How fit a title…'. In *Geoffrey Hill: Essays on his Work*, edited by Peter Robinson (Milton Keynes: Open University Press, 1985), pp. 129–48.

Hawkins, Eric W. *Modern Languages in the Curriculum* (Cambridge: Cambridge University Press, 1987).

Hayman, David. *'Ulysses': The Mechanics of Meaning*, new edition (Madison: University of Wisconsin Press, 1982).

Heidegger, Martin. *Basic Concepts*, translated by Gary E. Aylesworth (Bloomington: Indiana University Press, 1998).

Hesse, Hermann. 'Recent German Poetry'. *The Criterion* 1.1 (October 1922): 89–93.

Hill, Geoffrey. 'The Art of Poetry LXXX'. *The Paris Review* 154 (Spring 2000): 277.

Hill, Geoffrey. *Collected Critical Writings*, edited by Kenneth Haynes (Oxford: Oxford University Press, 2009).

Horne, Philip, ed. *Henry James: A Life in Letters* (London: Penguin Books, 1999).

Hough, Graham. *Image and Experience: Studies in a Literary Revolution* (London: Duckworth, 1960).

Huang, Yunte. *Transpacific Displacement: Ethnography, Translation, and Intertextual Travel in Twentieth Century American Literature* (Berkeley and Los Angeles: University of California Press, 2002).

Hyde, G. M. 'The Poetry of the City'. In *Modernism*, edited by Malcolm Bradbury and James McFarlane (Harmondsworth: Penguin, 1976), pp. 337–48.

Ioannidou, Ioanna and Leo Knuth. 'Greek in "The Mookse and the Gripes"'. *A Wake Newslitter* 8 (1971): 83–8.

Ioannidou, Ioanna and Leo Knuth. 'Greek in "Burrus and Caseous"', *A Wake Newslitter* 10 (1973): 12–16.

Israel, Nico. 'Esperantic Modernism: Joyce, Universal Language, and Political Gesture'. *Modernism/modernity* 24.1 (2017): 1–21.

Jain, Manju. *T. S. Eliot and American Philosophy: The Harvard Years* (Cambridge: Cambridge University Press, 1992).

Jakobson, Roman. *Novejšaja russkaja poèzija* (Prague: Politika, 1921).

Jakobson, Roman. 'On Linguistic Aspects of Translation'. In *On Translation*, edited by Reuben Brower (Boston: Harvard University Press, 1959), pp. 232–9.

Jakobson, Roman. *Language in Literature*, edited by Krystyna Pomorska and Stephen Rudy (Cambridge, MA: Harvard University Press, 1987).

James, Henry. *The Bostonians* (London: Macmillan, 1886).

James, Henry. *The Letters of Henry James*, 2 vols, edited by Percy Lubbock (London: Macmillan, 1920).

James, Henry. *The Complete Notebooks of Henry James*, edited by Leon Edel and Lyall H. Powers (New York and Oxford: Oxford University Press, 1987).

Jarry, Alfred. *Gestes et opinions du docteur Faustroll, pataphysicien*. In *Oeuvres complètes*, 8 vols (Monte Carlo: Éditions du Livre, 1948), I, pp. 195–320.

Jarry, Alfred. *Exploits and Opinions of Doctor Faustroll, Pataphysician: A Neo-Scientific Novel*, translated by Simon Watson Taylor. In *Three Early Novels*, translated and introduced by Alastair Brotchie, Paul Edwards, Alexis Lykiard and Simon Watson Taylor (London: Atlas, 2006), pp. 117–218.

Javadi, Iman. '"Per te poeta fui": T. S. Eliot's Debt to Dante' (PhD Thesis, Cambridge University, 2007).

Jespersen, Otto. *Growth and Structure of the English Language*, 5th edition (Leipzig: B.G. Teubner/Oxford: Basil Blackwell, 1926).

[Jolas, Eugene]. 'Proclamation: The Revolution of the Word'. *transition* 16–17 (June 1929): 13.

[Jolas, Eugene]. 'Glossary'. *transition* 22 (February 1933): 177–9.

Joll, James. *Europe Since 1870: An International History* (Harmondsworth: Penguin, 1976).

Jones, Francis R. 'The Translation of Poetry'. In *The Oxford Handbook of Translation Studies*, edited by Kirsten Malmkjaer and Kevin Windle (Oxford: Oxford University Press, 2011), pp. 169–82.

Joyce, James. *Finnegans Wake* [1939] (London: Faber and Faber, 1975).

Joyce, James. *Stephen Hero*, edited by Theodore Spencer, John J. Slocum and Herbert Cahoon (New York: New Directions Publishing Corporation, 1963).

Joyce, James. *A Portrait of the Artist as a Young Man* [1916]. The definitive text, corrected from the Dublin holograph by Chester G. Anderson and edited by Richard Ellmann (London: Jonathan Cape, 1968).

Joyce, James. *Ulysses* [1922], edited by Hans Walter Gabler with Wolfhard Steppe and Claus Melchior (New York: Random House, 1986).

Joyce, James. *Ulysses* [1922], edited by Jeri Johnson (Oxford: Oxford University Press, 1993).

Joyce, James. *Dubliners* [1914], edited by Jeri Johnson (Oxford: Oxford University Press, 2000).

Joyce, James. *Occasional, Critical and Political Writing*, edited by Kevin Barry (Oxford: Oxford University Press, 2000).

Joyce, James. *The 'Finnegans Wake' Notebooks at Buffalo. Notebook VI.B.6*, edited by Vincent Deane, Daniel Ferrer and Geert Lernout (Turnhout, Belgium: Brepols, 2002).

Jusdanis, Gregory. 'Farewell to the Classical: Excavations and Modernism'. *Modernism/modernity* 11.1 (January 2004): 37–53.

Kahane, Ahuvia. 'Blood for the Ghosts? Homer, Ezra Pound, and Julius Afranius'. *New Literary History* 30.4 (1999): 815–36.

Karlin, Daniel. *Proust's English* (Oxford: Oxford University Press, 2005).

Katz, Daniel. *American Modernism's Expatriate Scene: The Labour of Translation* (Edinburgh: Edinburgh University Press, 2007).

Kearns, Cleo McNelly. *T. S. Eliot and Indic Traditions: A Study in Poetry and Belief* (Cambridge: Cambridge University Press, 1987).

Kenner, Hugh. 'The *Portrait* in Perspective'. *The Kenyon Review* 10.3 (Summer 1948): 361–81.

Kenner, Hugh. *T. S. Eliot: The Invisible Poet* (London: W. H. Allen, 1960).

Kenner, Hugh. *The Pound Era* (Berkeley and Los Angeles: University of California, 1973).

Kenner, Hugh. *Joyce's Voices* (London: Faber and Faber, 1978).

Kenner, Hugh. *A Colder Eye: The Modern Irish Writers* (New York: Alfred A. Knopf, 1983).

Kenner, Hugh. *Ulysses* (Baltimore, MD: Johns Hopkins University Press, 1987).

Kermode, Frank. 'Modernisms Again', *Encounter* (April 1966): 65–74.

Kermode, Frank. *Essays on Fiction, 1971–82* (Routledge & Kegan Paul, 1983).

King, Julia and Laila Miletic-Vejzovic. *The Library of Leonard and Virginia Woolf: A Short-title Catalogue* (Washington: Washington State University Press, 2003).

Komar, Kathleen L. 'Rethinking Rilke's *Duineser Elegien* at the End of the Millennium'. In *A Companion to the Works of Rainer Maria Rilke*, edited by Erica A. Metzger and Michael M. Metzger (Rochester, NY: Camden House, 2001), pp. 188–208.

Komar, Kathleen L. 'The *Duino Elegies*'. In *The Cambridge Companion to Rilke*, edited by Karen Leeder and Robert Vilain (Cambridge: Cambridge University Press, 2010), pp. 80–94.

Koulouris, Theodore. *Hellenism and Loss in the Work of Virginia Woolf* (London and New York: Routledge, 2010).

Kromer, Gretchen. 'The Redoubtable PTYX'. *Modern Language Notes* 86.4 (1971): 563–72.

Kyd, Thomas. *The Spanish Tragedy*, edited by J. R. Mulryne (London: Ernest Benn, 1970).

'Language of Lithuania', *The New York Times* (20 April 1919), p. 10.

'L'Apostrophe de Pataphysique'. *Subsidia Pataphysica* 0 (1965): 84.

Lawrence, Karen. *The Odyssey of Style in 'Ulysses'* (Princeton, NJ: Princeton University Press, 1981).

Lecercle, Jean-Jacques. *The Violence of Language* (London: Routledge, 1990).

Leeder, Karen. Introduction to Rainer Maria Rilke, *Duino Elegies*, translated by Martyn Crucefix (London: Enitharmon, 2006).

Leith, Dick. *A Social History of English* (London: Routledge, 1997).

Levenson, Michael. *A Genealogy of Modernism: A Study of English Literary Doctrine 1908–1922* (Cambridge: Cambridge University Press, 1984).

Levenson, Michael. 'Form, Voice, and the Avant-Garde'. In *The Cambridge Companion to 'The Waste Land'*, edited by Gabrielle McIntire (Cambridge: Cambridge University Press, 2015), pp. 87–101.

Lewis, Wyndham. *Time and Western Man* [1927], edited by Paul Edwards (Santa Rosa: Black Sparrow Press, 1993).

Leyris, Pierre. *T. S. Eliot: Poésie* (Paris: Seuil, 1969).

Liddell, Henry George and Robert Scott. *A Greek-English Lexicon based on the German work of Francis Passow* (Oxford: Oxford University Press, 1843).

Liddell, Henry George and Robert Scott. *A Lexicon: Abridged from Liddell and Scott's Greek-English Lexicon* (New York: Harper, 1880).

Liebregts, Peter. *Ezra Pound and Neoplatonism* (Madison, NJ: Farleigh Dickinson University Press, 2004).

Llewelyn, John. *The Middle Voice of Ecological Conscience: A Chiasmic Reading of Responsibility in the Neighborhood of Levinas, Heidegger, and Others* (New York: St Martin's Press, 1991).

Lloyd, David. *Nationalism and Minor Literature: James Clarence Mangan and the Emergence of Irish Cultural Nationalism* (Berkeley: University of California Press, 1987).

Lobel, Edgar. Σαπφοῦς μέλη: *The Fragments of the Lyrical Poems of Sappho* (Oxford: Clarendon Press, 1925).

Lorimer, Norma. *The Wife out of Egypt* (New York: Brentano's, 1913).

Louth, Charlie. 'Review of Rilke's *Duino Elegies* (translated by Martyn Crucefix) and Don Paterson's *Orpheus: A Version of Rilke's Die Sonette an Orpheus*'. *Modern Poetry in Translation* 3.8 (2007): 134–42.

Lucas, F. L. 'The Waste Land'. *The New Statesman* 22 (3 November 1923): 116–18.

Mallarmé, Stéphane. *Divagations* (Paris: Bibliothèque-Charpentier, 1897).

Mallarmé, Stéphane. *Poésies*, 8th edition (Paris: Nouvelle Revue française, 1914).

Mallarmé, Stéphane. *Oeuvres complètes*, edited by Henri Mondor and G. Jean-Aubry (Paris: Gallimard, 1945).

Mallarmé, Stéphane. *Vingt poèmes de Stéphane Mallarmé*, edited by Emilie Noulet (Paris: Minard, 1967).

Mallarmé, Stéphane. *Oeuvres complètes*, 2 vols, edited by Bertrand Marchal, 2nd edition (Paris: Gallimard, 1998).

Mann, Thomas. *The Magic Mountain* [1924], translated by H.T. Lowe-Porter [1927] (Harmondsworth: Penguin, 1973).

Mann, Thomas. *The Magic Mountain*, translated by John E. Woods [1995] (New York: Alfred A. Knopf, 2005).

Mao, Douglas. *Solid Objects: Modernism and the Test of Production* (Princeton, NJ: Princeton University Press, 1998).

Marinetti, Filippo. 'Destruction of Syntax—Wireless Imagination—Words-in-Freedom (May 1913)'. In *Modernism: An Anthology*, edited by Lawrence Rainey (Oxford: Blackwell, 2005), pp. 27–34.

Martínez, Rafael Arévalo. 'The Man who Resembled a Horse'. *The Little Review* 5.8 (Dec 1918): 45.

Martino, Pierre. *Parnasse et Symbolisme (1850–1900)* (Paris: Armand Colin, 1925).

Marzán, Julio. Foreword to William Carlos Williams, in *By Word of Mouth: Poems from the Spanish 1916–1959*, edited by Jonathan Cohen (New York: New Directions, 2011).

Mauron, Charles. *Mallarmé l'obscur* (Paris: Denoël, 1941).

McCourt, John. *The Years of Bloom: James Joyce in Trieste 1904–1920* (Dublin: The Lilliput Press, 2000), pp. 49–56.

McCrea, Barry. *Languages of the Night: Minor Languages and the Literary Imagination in Twentieth-Century Ireland and Europe* (New Haven: Yale University Press, 2015).

McGreevy, Thomas. Papers in Trinity College Dublin, TCD MS 8114/12, TCD MS 8114/14.

McManus, Damian. 'Irish letter-names and their kennings'. *Ériu* 39 (1988): 127–68.

de Mèredieu, Florence. *Sur l'électrochoc: le cas Antonin Artaud* (Paris: Blusson, 1996).

Miller, Joshua L. *Accented America: The Cultural Politics of Multilingual Modernism* (Oxford: Oxford University Press, 2011).

Miller, Paul Allen. 'Black and White Myths: Etymology and Dialectics in Mallarmé's "Sonnet en yx"'. *Texas Studies in Literature and Language* 36.2 (1994): 184–211.

Milton, John. *Paradise Lost*, edited by Alastair Fowler, 2nd edition (London: Routledge, 2013).

Mitcalfe, Constance. Letter to the editor, *The Future* 2.5 (April 1918): 140.

Montserrat, Dominic. 'News Reports: The Excavations and their Journalistic Coverage'. In *Oxyrhynchus: A City and its Texts*, edited by Alan K. Bowman et al. (London: Egyptian Exploration Society, 2007): pp. 28–39.

Moore, H. E. *Modernism in Language Teaching* (Cambridge: Heffer, 1925).

Moore, Marianne. *The Complete Prose*, edited by Patricia C. Willis (London: Faber & Faber, 1987).

Moran, D. P. *The Philosophy of Irish Ireland* [1905], edited by Patrick Maume (Dublin: University College Dublin Press, 2006).

Moulton, James Hope. *From the Rubbish-heaps of Egypt: Five Popular Lectures on the New Testament* (London: Kelly, 1916).

Nagy, Gregory. 'Poetics of Fragmentation in the Athyr Poem of C. P. Cavafy'. In *Imagination and Logos: Essays on C. P. Cavafy*, edited by Panagiotis Roilos (Cambridge, MA: Harvard University Press, 2010), pp. 265–72.

Newbolt, Henry. 'The Future of the English Language'. In *Essays by Divers Hands, being the Transactions of the Royal Society of Literature of the United Kingdom*, edited by Frederick S. Boas (London: Humphrey Milford, 1923), pp. 1–16.

[Newbolt, Henry]. *The Teaching of English in England* (London: His Majesty's Stationery Office, 1924).

Nicholls, Peter. 'The Poetics of Modernism'. In *The Cambridge Companion to Modernist Poetry*, edited by Alex Davis and Lee M. Jenkins (Cambridge: Cambridge University Press, 2007), pp. 51–67.

Nicolas, Henri. *Mallarmé et le Symbolisme* (Paris: Larousse, 1965).

Nietzsche, Friedrich. 'Translation'. In *The Gay Science* [1882], translated by Walter Kaufmann (New York: Vintage, 1974), pp. 136–8.

North, Michael. *The Dialect of Modernism: Race, Language and Twentieth-Century Literature* (New York: Oxford University Press, 1994).

Noulet, Emilie. *L'Oeuvre poétique de Stéphane Mallarmé* (Paris: Droz, 1940).

O Hehir, Brendan and John Dillon. *A Classical Lexicon for 'Finnegans Wake'* (Berkeley: University of California Press, 1977).

Obbink, Dirk. 'Vanishing Conjecture: Lost Books and their recovery from Aristotle to Eco'. In *Culture in Pieces: Essays on Ancient Texts in Honour of Peter Parsons*, edited by Dirk Obbink and Richard Rutherford (Oxford: Oxford University Press, 2011), pp. 20–49.

Ogden, C. K. 'James Joyce's Anna Livia Plurabelle in Basic English'. *Transition* 21 (1932): 259–62.

Ogden, C. K. 'The Magic of Words'. *Psyche* 14 (1934): 9–88.

Ogden, C. K. 'Word Magic'. *Psyche* 18 (1938): 19–95.

Ogden, C. K. and I. A. Richards. *The Meaning of Meaning: A Study of the Influence of Language upon Thought and of the Science of Symbolism*, 2nd edition (London: Kegan Paul, 1927).

Ovid. *Metamorphoses*, edited by E. J. Kenney, translated by A. D. Melville (Oxford: Oxford University Press, 1986).

Pankhurst, E. Sylvia. *Delphos: The Future of International Language* (London: Kegan Paul, Trench, Trübner, 1927).

Parsons, Peter. *City of the Sharp-Nosed Fish: Greek Papyri Beneath the Egyptian Sand Reveal a Long-Lost World* (London: Phoenix, 2007).

Paterson, Don. *Orpheus: A Version of Rilke's 'Die Sonette an Orpheus'* (London: Faber, 2006).

Pearson, Roger. *Unfolding Mallarmé: The Development of a Poetic Art* (Oxford: Clarendon Press, 1996).

Pelling, Christopher. 'Fun with Fragments: Athenaeus and the Historians'. In *Athenaeus and his World*, edited by David Braund and John Wilkins (Exeter: University of Exeter Press, 2000), pp. 171–90.

Perloff, Marjorie. *The Poetics of Indeterminacy: Rimbaud to Cage* (Princeton, NJ: Princeton University Press, 1981).

Perry, Seamus. *The Connell Guide to T. S. Eliot's 'The Waste Land'* (London: Connell, 2014).

Phillips, Catherine. *Robert Bridges: A Biography* (Oxford: Oxford University Press, 1992).

Phillipson, Robert. *Linguistic Imperialism* (Oxford: Oxford University Press, 1992).

Plimpton, George. 'T. S. Eliot'. In *Writers at Work: The Paris Review Interviews*, Second Series, edited by George Plimpton (Harmondsworth: Penguin, 1977), pp. 89–110.

Pomorska, Krystyna, Hugh Mclean, Elzbieta Chodakowska, and Brent Vine, *Language, Poetry, and Poetics: The Generation of the 1890s, Jakobson, Trubetzkoy, Majakovskjj* (Berlin: Mouton de Gruyer, 1987).

Pound, Ezra. 'In the World of Letters'. *The Future* 1.2 (December 1916): 55–6.

Pound, Ezra. *Lustra* (London: E. Matthews, 1916).

Pound, Ezra. 'Sword-Dance and Spear-Dance: Texts of the Poems used with Michio Itow's Dances'. *The Future* 1.2 (December 1916): 54–5.

Pound, Ezra. 'Three Cantos of a Poem of Some Length'. In *Lustra* (New York: n. pub, 1916), pp. 179–202.

Pound, Ezra. 'Art and Life: Beddoes (and Chronology)'. *The Future* 1.11 (September 1917): 318–20.

Pound, Ezra. 'Art and Life: Landor (1775–1864)'. *The Future* 2.1 (November 1917): 10–12.

Pound, Ezra. 'Elizabethan Classicists, III'. *Egoist* 4.10 (November 1917): 154–6.

Pound, Ezra. 'Provincialism the Enemy, I'. *New Age* 21.11 (12 July 1917): 244–5.

Pound, Ezra. 'Provincialism the Enemy, IV'. *New Age* 21.14 (2 August 1917): 308–9.

Pound, Ezra. 'The Rev. G. Crabbe, LL.B.'. *The Future* 1.4 (February 1917): 110–11.

Pound, Ezra. 'Three Cantos, I'. *Poetry* 10.3 (June 1917): 113–21.

Pound, Ezra. 'Three Cantos, II'. *Poetry* 10.4 (July 1917): 180–8.

Pound, Ezra. 'Books Current'. *The Future* 2.6 (May 1918): 161–3.

Pound, Ezra. 'Books Current'. *The Future*, 2.8 (July 1918): 209–10.

Pound, Ezra. 'Books Current', *The Future* 2.10 (October 1918): 265–6.

Pound, Ezra. 'Books Current'. *The Future* 2.11 (November 1918): 286–7.

Pound, Ezra. 'Books Current'. *The Future* 2.12 (December 1918): 311–12.

Pound, Ezra. 'Brief Note'. *The Little Review* 5.4 (August 1918): 6–9.

Pound, Ezra. 'Early Translators of Homer, 1: Hughes Salel'. *Egoist* 5.7 (August 1918): 95–7.

Pound, Ezra. 'Images from the Second Canto of a Long Poem'. *The Future* 2.4 (March 1918): 96.

Pound, Ezra. 'An Interpolation taken from Third Canto of a Long Poem'. *The Future* 2.5 (April 1918): 121.

Pound, Ezra. 'Passages from the Opening Address in a Long Poem'. *The Future* 2.3 (February 1918): 63.

Pound, Ezra. 'A Study in French Poets'. *The Little Review* 4.10 (February 1918): 3.

Pound, Ezra. '"Esope," France and the Trade Union'. *New Age* 25.26 (23 October 1919): 423–4.

Pound, Ezra. 'Ezra Pound on the League of Ideas'. *Much Ado* 10.2 (1919): 16–17.

Pound, Ezra. 'The Revolt of Intelligence, V'. *New Age* 26.10 (8 January 1920): 153–4.

Pound, Ezra. *Polite Essays* (London: Faber and Faber, 1937).

Pound, Ezra. *Guide to Kulchur* (London: Faber & Faber, 1938; and New York: New Directions, 1970).

Pound, Ezra. *The Letters of Ezra Pound, 1907–1941*, edited by D. D. Paige (London: Faber and Faber, 1951).

Pound, Ezra. *Literary Essays*, edited by T. S. Eliot (London: Faber and Faber, 1954).

Pound, Ezra. *Collected Shorter Poems*, 2nd edition (London: Faber and Faber, 1968).

Pound, Ezra. *Pound/Joyce: The Letters of Ezra Pound to James Joyce, with Pound's Essays on James Joyce*, edited by Forrest Read (London: Faber and Faber, 1968).

Pound, Ezra. *Cantos of Ezra Pound* (New York: New Directions, 1986).

Pound, Ezra. *The Cantos*, 4th edition (London: Faber and Faber, 1987).

Preminger, Alex and T.V.F. Brogan, eds. *The New Princeton Encyclopedia of Poetry and Poetics* (Princeton, NJ: Princeton University Press, 1993).

Quine, W. V. O. *Word and Object* [1960], new edition (Cambridge, MA: Massachusetts Institute of Technology Press, 2013).

Quintus Septimius Florentis Christianus [Florent Chrétien]. *Epigrammata ex libris Graecae Anthologiae* (Paris: Robertus Stephanus, 1608).

Rabau, Sophie, ed. *L'intertextualité* (Paris: Flammarion, 2002).

Rainey, Lawrence. *Revisiting 'The Waste Land'* (New Haven: Yale University Press, 2005).

Rainey, Lawrence. 'Pound or Eliot : Whose Era?'. In *The Cambridge Companion to Modernist Poetry*, edited by Alex Davis and Lee M. Jenkins (Cambridge: Cambridge University Press, 2007), pp. 87–113.

Rainey, Lawrence. 'With Automatic Hand: *The Waste Land*'. In *The New Cambridge Companion to T. S. Eliot*, edited by Jason Harding (Cambridge: Cambridge University Press, 2017), pp. 71–88.

Reeve, Henry. 'The Literature and Language of the Age'. *Edinburgh Review* 169 (April 1889), 328–50.

Reeves, Gareth. *T. S. Eliot: A Virgilian Poet* (London: Palgrave Macmillan, 1989).

Reizbaum, Marilyn. 'The Minor Work of James Joyce'. *James Joyce Quarterly* 30.2 (1993): 177–89.

Richards, I. A. 'Mr. Eliot's Poems'. *New Statesman* (20 February 1926): 584–5.

Richards, I. A. *Mencius on the Mind: Experiments in Multiple Definition* (London: Kegan Paul, 1932).

Ricks, Christopher. *T. S. Eliot and Prejudice* (London: Faber and Faber, 1988).

Ricks, David. '"A faint sweetness in the never-ending afternoon"? Reflections on Cavafy and the Greek Epigram', *Κάμπος: Cambridge Papers in Modern Greek* 15 (2007): 149–69.

Riffaterre, Michael. *The Semiotics of Poetry* (London: Indiana University Press, 1978).

Riffaterre, Michael. 'Compulsory Reader Response: the Intertextual Drive'. In *Intertextuality: Theories and Practices*, edited by Michael Worton and Judith Still (Manchester: Manchester University Press, 1990), pp. 56–78.

Riikonen, H. K. 'Ezra Pound and the Greek Anthology'. *Quaderni di Palazzo Serra* 15 (2008): 181–94.

Rilke, Rainer Maria, *Duino Elegies, The German text, with an English translation, introduction, and commentary*, translated by J. B. Leishman and Stephen Spender (London: Hogarth Press, 1939).

Rilke, Rainer Maria. 'Archaïscher Torso Apollos'. In Rilke, *Sämtliche Werke*, 12 vols (Frankfurt am Main: Insel, 1955), I, p. 557.

Rilke, Rainer Maria. *Duineser Elegien* [1923] (Frankfurt am Main: Insel, 1975).

Rilke, Rainer Maria. *The Duino Elegies*, translated by A. S. Kline (2004), online edition, retrieved 27 April 2017, available at https://www.poetryintranslation.com/PITBR/German/Rilke.php

Rilke, Rainer Maria. *Duino Elegies*, translated by Martyn Crucefix (London: Enitharmon Press, 2006).

Rilke, Rainer Maria. *Selected Poems*, edited by Robert Vilain, translated by Susan Ranson and Marielle Sutherland (Oxford: Oxford University Press, 2011).

Rilke, Rainer Maria. *Duino Elegies*, translated by Stephen Cohn (Manchester: Carcanet Press, 2012).

Rilke, Rainer Maria. *Marbhnaí Duino*, translated by Máire Mhac an tSaoi (Indreabhán: Leabhar Breac, 2013).

Robinson, Peter. *Poetry, Poets, Readers: Making Things Happen* (Oxford: Oxford University Press, 2002).

Rodker, John. 'Spring Suicide'. *The Future* 1.5 (March 1917): 116.

Romer, Stephen. 'French poetry'. In *T. S. Eliot in Context*, edited by Jason Harding (Cambridge: Cambridge University Press, 2011), pp. 211–20.

Romer, Stephen. *Set Thy Love in Order: New & Selected Poems* (Manchester: Carcanet, 2017).

Rood, Tim. *The Sea! The Sea!: The Shout of the Ten Thousand in the Modern Imagination* (London: Duckworth, 2004).

Rosenthal, Richard S. *Rosenthal's Common-Sense Method of Practical Linguistry: The Spanish Language* (New York: International College of Languages, 1917).

Rosiers, Erika and Wim Van Mierlo. 'Neutral Auxiliaries & Universal Idioms: Otto Jespersen in Work in Progress'. In *James Joyce: The Study of Languages*, edited by Dirk Van Hulle (Brussels: Peter Lang, 2002), pp. 55–70.

Ruthven, K. K. *A Guide to Ezra Pound's Personae (1926)* (Berkeley and Los Angeles: University of California Press, 1969).

Rutter, Mabel S. Letter to the editor. *The Future* 1.11 (September 1917): 334.

Ryan, Judith. *Rilke, Modernism and Poetic Tradition* (Cambridge: Cambridge University Press, 1999).

Sampson, George. *English for the English: A Chapter on National Education* [1921], new edition (Cambridge: Cambridge University Press, 1970).

Sandomir, Irénée-Louis. 'Exégèse du mot *ptyx*'. *Opus Pataphysicum* 86 (1959): 91–5.

Sandomir, Irénée-Louis. 'Exegesis of the Word *Ptyx*', translated by Dennis Duncan. *Journal of the London Institute of 'Pataphysics* 4 (2011): 13–16.

Santner, Eric. *On Creaturely Life: Rilke, Benjamin, Sebald* (Chicago: Chicago University Press, 2006).

Schlegel, Friedrich. *Philosophical Fragments* [1798], translated by Peter Firchow (Minneapolis: University of Minnesota Press, 1991).

Schork, R. J. 'A Graphic Exercise of Mnemotechnic'. *James Joyce Quarterly* 16.3 (Spring, 1979): 351–4.

Schork, R. J. *Latin and Roman Culture in Joyce* (Gainesville: University Press of Florida, 1997).

Schork, R. J. *Greek and Hellenic Culture in Joyce* (Gainesville: University Press of Florida, 1998).

Schotter, Jesse. 'Verbivocovisuals: James Joyce and the Problem of Babel'. *James Joyce Quarterly* 48.1 (2010): 89–109.

Schröder, Werner. *Der Versbau der Duineser Elegien: Versuch einer metrischen Beschreibung* (Stuttgart: Steiner, 1992).

Schubart, Wilhelm. 'Neue Bruchstücke der Sappho und des Alkaios'. *Sitzungsberichte der Königlich Preussischen Akademie der Wissenschaften* (Berlin, 1902), pp. 195–206.

Schubart, W. and U. von Willamowitz-Moellendorff, eds. *Lyrische und dramatische Fragmente, Berliner Klassikertexte, V* (Berlin: Weidmannsche Buchhandlung 1907).

Schweighäuser, Johann. *Athenaei Naucratitae Deipnosophistarum libri quindecim* (Societas Bipontinae, 1804).

Seelbach, Wilhelm. 'Ezra Pound und Sappho fr. 95 L.–P. ' *Antike und Abendland* 16.1 (1970): 83–4.

Sell, Roger. *Mediating Criticism* (Amsterdam: John Benjamins, 2001).

Senn, Fritz. *Joyce's Dislocutions: Essays on Reading as Translation*, edited by John Paul Riquelme (Baltimore, MD: Johns Hopkins University Press, 1984).

Shakespeare, William. *The Oxford Shakespeare: The Complete Works*, gen. eds Stanley Wells and Gary Taylor, 2nd edition (Oxford: Clarendon Press, 2005).

Shaw Sailer, Susan. 'Universalizing Languages: *Finnegans Wake* Meets Basic English'. *James Joyce Quarterly* 36.4 (1999): 853–68.

Sheppard, Richard. 'The Crisis of Language'. In *Modernism*, edited by Malcolm Bradbury and James McFarlane (London: Penguin, 1976): pp. 323–36.

Sheppard, Richard. 'Modernism, Language and Experimental Poetry: On Leaping over Bannisters and Learning How to Fly'. *Modern Language Review* 92.1 (1997): 98–123.

Sherry, Vincent. *The Great War and the Language of Modernism* (Oxford: Oxford University Press, 2003).

Shklovsky, Viktor. 'Art as Technique'. In *Russian Formalist Criticism: Four Essays*, translated with an introduction by Lee T. Lemon and Marion J. Reis (Lincoln: University of Nebraska Press, 1965), pp. 3–24.

Sisson, C. H. *English Poetry 1900–1950* (London: Methuen, 1981).

Sloterdijk, Peter. *Du mußt dein Leben ändern: Über Anthropotechnik* (Frankfurt am Main: Suhrkamp, 2009).

Smith, Nathaniel B. 'Arnaut Daniel in the *Purgatorio*: Dante's Ambivalence toward Provençal'. *Dante Studies* 98 (1980): 99–109.

Society for Pure English, Tract no. 1 (Oxford: Oxford University Press, 1919).

Society for Pure English, Tract no. 32 (Oxford: Oxford University Press, 1931).

Society for Pure English, Tract no. 6 (Oxford: Oxford University Press, 1933).

Squire, J. C. 'Poetry'. *London Mercury* 8 (October 1923): 655–6.

Steiner, George. *Extraterritorial: Papers on Literature and the Language Revolution* (London: Faber and Faber, 1972).

Steiner, George. *After Babel: Aspects of Language and Translation*, 2nd edition (Oxford: Oxford University Press, 1992).

Steiner, Jacob. *Rilkes Duineser Elegien* (Bern: Francke, 1962).

Steiner, Peter. *Russian Formalism: A Metapoetics* (Ithaca: Cornell University Press, 1984).

Stevens, Wallace. *Collected Poetry and Prose*, edited by Frank Kermode (New York: Library of America, 1997).

Stray, Christopher. *The Living Word: W. H. D. Rouse and the Crisis of Classics in Edwardian England* (Bristol: Bristol Classical Press, 1992).

Stray, Christopher, ed., *Classical Dictionaries: Past, Present and Future* (London: Duckworth, 2010).

Styler, A. E. 'Our Prize Essay: Which Language Should be Adopted for International Intercourse, and Why?' *The Future* 2.2 (January 1918): 37.

Styler, A. E. 'A Reply to my Critics'. *The Future* 2.5 (April 1918): 138–9.

Switaj, Elizabeth Kate. 'The Ambiguous Status of Native Speakers and Language Learners in *Ulysses*'. *Journal of Modern Literature* 37.1 (Fall 2013): 143–57.

Symons, Arthur. *The Symbolist Movement in Literature* [1899], revised and enlarged edition (London: E. P. Dutton, 1919).

Taylor-Batty, Juliette. *Multilingualism in Modernist Fiction* (London: Palgrave Macmillan, 2013).

Terrell, Carroll F. *A Companion to the Cantos of Ezra Pound* (Berkeley and Los Angeles: University of California Press, 1993).

Thévenin, Paule. *Antonin Artaud, ce désespéré qui vous parle* (Paris: Seuil, 1993).

Tiffany, Daniel. *Radio Corpse: Imagism and the Cryptaesthetic of Ezra Pound* (Cambridge, MA: Harvard University Press, 1998).

Tomiche, Anne. *'L'intraduisible dont je suis fait': Artaud et les avant-gardes occidentales* (Paris: Le Manuscrit, 2012).

Townley, Rod. *The Early Poetry of William Carlos Williams* (Ithaca, NY and London: Cornell University Press, 1975).

Trotsky, Leon. *Literature and Revolution*, translated by Rose Strunsky (London: George Allen & Unwin, 1925).

Turner, Sir Eric. 'The Graeco-Roman Branch'. In *Excavating in Egypt: The Egypt Exploration Society, 1882–1982*, edited by T. G. H. James (London: British Museum Publications, 1983), pp. 161–78.

Uzanne, Octave. 'Choses et personnes qui passent: heure d'automne'. Echo de Paris (5 October 1905): 1.

Valéry, Paul. *The Art of Poetry*, translated by Denise Folliot with an introduction by T. S. Eliot (New York: Bollingen Foundation, 1958).

Venuti, Lawrence. *The Translator's Invisibility: A History of Translation* (London: Routledge, 1995).

Venuti, Lawrence. *The Scandals of Translation: Towards an Ethics of Difference* (London: Routledge, 1998).

Venuti, Lawrence. *The Translation Studies Reader*, 3rd edition (London and New York: Routledge, 2012).

Wais, Kurt. *Mallarmé: Ein Dichter des Jahrhundert-Endes* (Munich: Beck, 1938).

Weiss, Allen S. 'Radio Icons, Short Circuits, Deep Schisms'. *TDR* 40.3 (Autumn 1996): 9–15.

Wellek, René. *A History of Modern Criticism: 1750–1950: Volume 7, German, Russian, and Eastern European Criticism, 1900–1950* (New Haven: Yale University Press, 1991).

Wharton, H. T. *Sappho: Memoir, Text and Selected Renderings with a Literal Translation* (London: John Lane, 1885).

Whitman, Walt. *Poetry and Prose*, edited by Justin Kaplan (New York: Library of America, 1982).

Whittemore, Reed. *William Carlos Williams: Poet from New Jersey* (Boston: Houghton Mifflin, 1975).

Whorf, Benjamin Lee. *Language, Thought, and Reality: Selected Writings of Benjamin Lee Whorf*, edited by John B. Carroll, Stephen C. Levinson and Penny Lee, 2nd edition (Cambridge, MA: Massachusetts Institute of Technology Press, 2012).

Williams, Marion. Letter to the editor. *The Future* 1.8 (August 1917): 303–4.

Williams, William Carlos. *The Autobiography of William Carlos Williams* (New York: New Directions, 1967).

Williams, William Carlos. *Imaginations*, edited by Webster Schott (New York: New Directions, 1970).

Williams, William Carlos. *I Wanted to Write a Poem: The Autobiography of the Works of a Poet*, edited by Edith Heal (New York: New Directions, 1976).

Williams, William Carlos. *Collected Poems, Vol. 1: 1909–1939*, edited by A. Walton Litz and Christopher MacGowan (New York: New Directions, 1986).

Williams, William Carlos. *By Word of Mouth: Poems from the Spanish 1916–1959*, edited by Jonathan Cohen (New York: New Directions, 2011).

Wilson, Edmund. 'The Poetry of Drouth'. *The Dial* 73 (December 1922): 611–16.

Witemeyer, Hugh, ed. *Pound/Williams: Selected Letters of Ezra Pound and William Carlos Williams* (New York: New Directions, 1996).

Wittgenstein, Ludwig. *Tractatus Logico-Philosophicus*, translated by D. F. Pears and B. F. McGuinness (London: Routledge and Kegan Paul, 1961).

Wittgenstein, Ludwig. *Philosophical Investigations*, translated by G. E. M. Anscombe (Oxford: Blackwell, 1967).

Wittgenstein, Ludwig. *Notebooks 1914–1916*, edited by H. H. von Wright and G. E. M. Anscombe (Chicago: University of Chicago Press, 1979).

Woolf, Virginia. *Between the Acts* (London: Hogarth Press, 1941).

Woolf, Virginia. *The Diary of Virginia Woolf, Volume II: 1920–1924*, edited by Anne Olivier Bell (London: Hogarth Press, 1978).

Woolf, Virginia. *Jacob's Room* [1922] (London: Hogarth Press, 1980).

Woolf, Virginia. 'On Not Knowing Greek'. In *The Common Reader, First Series* (London: Hogarth, 1984), pp. 23–38.

Woolf, Virginia. 'The Perfect Language'. In *The Essays of Virginia Woolf, Volume II: 1912–1918*, edited by Andrew McNeillie (New York: Harcourt Brace Jovanovich, 1987), pp. 114–19.

Woolf, Virginia. *Night and Day* [1919], Definitive Collected Edition (London: Hogarth Press, 1990).

Woolf, Virginia. *The Years* [1937], edited by Hermione Lee (Oxford: Oxford University Press, 1999).

Woolf, Virginia. *Mrs Dalloway* [1925], edited by David Bradshaw (Oxford: Oxford University Press, 2000).

Woolf, Virginia. *The Voyage Out* [1915], edited by Lorna Sage (Oxford: Oxford University Press, 2001).

Woolf, Virginia. *Moments of Being*, edited by Jeanne Schulkind (London: Pimlico, 2002).

Woolf, Virginia. 'On Not Knowing French'. In *The Essays of Virginia Woolf, Vol. 5: 1929–1932*, edited by Stuart N. Clarke (London: Hogarth Press, 2009), pp. 3–9.

Worton, Michael and Judith Still, eds. *Intertextuality: Theories and Practices* (Manchester: Manchester University Press, 1990).

de Wyzewa, Téodor. 'M. Stéphane Mallarmé'. *Le Figaro* (8 December 1892), p. 1.

Yao, Steven G. *Translation and the Languages of Modernism: Gender, Politics, Language* (New York and Basingstoke: Palgrave Macmillan, 2002).

Yao, Steven G. 'Translation'. In *Ezra Pound in Context*, edited by Ira B. Nadel (Cambridge: Cambridge University Press, 2010), pp. 33–42.

Yeats, W. B. *Essays and Introductions* (London: Macmillan, 1961).

Index

For the benefit of digital users, indexed terms that span two pages (e.g., 52–53) may, on occasion, appear on only one of those pages.